RASHI'S TORAH
COMMENTARY

RASHI'S TORAH COMMENTARY

Religious, Philosophical, Ethical, and Educational Insights

PINCHAS DORON

JASON ARONSON INC.
Northvale, New Jersey
Jerusalem

This book was set in 10 pt. New Baskerville by Pageworks of Old Saybrook, CT and printed and bound by Book-mart Press, Inc. of North Bergen, NJ.

10 9 8 7 6 5 4 3 2 1

Library of Congress Cataloging-in-Publication Data

Doron, Pinchas.
    Rashi's torah commentary / by Pinchas Doron.
      p. cm.
    Includes an English translation of selections from Perush Rashi al ha–Torah.
    Includes bibliographical references.
    ISBN 0–7657–6095–9
    1. Rashi, 1040–1105. Perush Rashi 'al ha–Torah. 2. Bible. O.T. Pentateuch—Commentaries. I. Rashi, 1040–1105. Perush Rashi 'al ha–Torah. English. Selections. II. Title.
    BS1225.S6D6713 2000
    222'.1077—dc21
                                       99–17463
                                              CIP

Printed in the United States of America on acid-free paper. For information and catalog write to Jason Aronson Inc., 230 Livingston Street, Northvale, NJ 07647–1726, or visit our website: www.aronson.com.

Dedication

This volume is dedicated to the memory of my beloved son, Binyamin, whose untimely passing was a great shock to the entire family. May he be a *Meylitz Yosher* (a good advocate) for all of us.

Contents

Approbations   ix

Preface   xvii

Introduction   xxiii

1 GENESIS   1

B'reishit   3

Noach   23

Lech Lecha   29

Vayeira   35

Chayey Sarah   43

Toldot   45

Vayetze   47

Vayishlach   49

Vayeyshev   51

Mikeyts   53

Vayigash   55

Vayechi   57

2 EXODUS   63

Shemot   65

Vaeira   69

Bo   71

Beshalach   75

Yitro   79

Mishpatim   85

Terumah   89

Tetzaveh   91

Ki Tisa   95

Vayakhel   101

Pekudei   103

3 LEVITICUS   109

Vayikra   111

Tzav   115

Shemini   117

Tazria   121

Metzora   123

Acharei Mot   125

Kedoshim   127

Emor   135

Behar   139

Bechukotai   145

4 NUMBERS   157

Bamidbar   159

Naso   163

Behaalotcha   171

Shelach 185

Korach 195

Chukat 197

Balak 207

Pinchas 223

Matot 231

Mas'ei 235

5 DEUTERONOMY 237

Devarim 239

Vaetchanan 245

Ekev 257

R'ei 265

Shoftim 273

Ki Teitsei 279

Ki Tavo 287

Nitzavim 291

Vayeilech 295

Ha'azinu 297

Vezot Hab-rachah 301

Subject Index 314

Index of Biblical Verses 327

Approbations

Approbation—Translation

Rabbi David Cohen

With the help of Heaven.

Honorable, well-known, and praiseworthy Rabbi Pinchas Doron, Shlita, greetings and blessings and all best wishes always.

He sent me his book in English explaining obscure passages in Rashi on the Torah, requesting words of blessing from me. Surely, he already made his name with his works in Hebrew. Now, besides the pearls of wisdom found in his books, his outstanding personality, in desiring to benefit the general public with his wonderful works, is very noticeable. I therefore say to him: May his hands be strengthened for the sake of Torah and Tradition and may he deserve to continue in his holy work with even more power and strength than hitherto.

I bless him with all my heart and soul, and seek his welfare and the welfare of his Torah.

David Cohen

Rabbi, Beit Hamidrash Gevul Ya'aveytz
4th of Adar, 758 (March 2, 1998).

Approbation—Translation

Rabbi Moses Feinstein   Moshe Feinstein
455 F.D.R. Drive   Dean of Yeshiva Tiferet Yerushalim
New York, N.Y. 10002

Behold, Mr. Pinchas Doron, who is an esteemed person and is engaged in disseminating Torah, is preparing for print two important books for the public: the first "Interpretation of Difficult Passages in Rashi" is designated for people with a Torah background—to deepen and broaden their understanding and knowledge of the holy words of Rashi on the Torah—especially in the most obscure passages. Important Torah-scholars have testified that the author's interpretations are very felicitous. The second work in English—the spoken language of America—is named *A Practical Guide to the Talmud.* It will serve well the scores of thousands of Yeshiva students, especially adults who have come to Torah and Judaism at a later age, and they thirst to delve into the "Sea of the Talmud," but find it hard because of the specialized language and subject matter of the Gemara. The author elucidates with great clarity hundreds of expressions, concepts and terms found in the Talmud. Also, dozens of topics according to the Principles of Talmudic Hermeneutics and other matters necessary for the understanding of a page of Gemara—and all in the English vernacular.

I therefore endorse his efforts as a good deed, and everyone who is capable should support him in publishing the above two works. I confer my blessing to everyone who assists the author in the above matter, he shall be blessed from Heaven with all good things. I add a special blessing to the author that he should merit to write more books and works for the promulgation of the Torah and its honor.

I hereby affix my signature on this day, the 13th of Adar I, 744.

Moshe Feinstein

Approbation—Translation

Rabbi S. Kamenetsky

With the help of Heaven in the year 5758 of the Jewish Calendar.

In honor of the revered Rabbi Yehoshua Pinchas Doron Shlita.

In the way of Peace and Blessings.

I was happy to see the results of his labors in explaining Rashi on the Chumash in the spoken language (English) to explain and elucidate the holy words of the Teacher of Entire Israel, *ztz"l* (= of blessed memory), and as the Ramban stated that over one drop of ink of Rashi one has to purify himself for seven days (to be able to explain it). Already over 200 supercommentaries to his holy words were written.

Now, he (P. Doron) already published "bright sparks" and many benefit from him and he does not really need my approbation, since the great (scholars) of this generation already approve of his holy work. I come merely to add my blessing that his thoughts may find wide acceptance and that the multitude should benefit from this. May he merit to complete his work.

May the Almighty console him for the past (= loss of his child) and may he have lots of *nachas* from his family.

With a profound blessing

Shmuel Kamenetsky

Approbation—Translation

Rabbi Yaakov Perlow
1569 47th Street
Brooklyn, N.Y. 11219

Wednesday, 17th of Adar I, 749 (1989)

Books of commentary upon Rashi's Commentary on the Torah are very numerous, and the more one delves into the words of the holy commentator par excellence of the Torah, to elucidate the profound meanings of his Torah interpretations, the more one finds in them. I saw the book *Interpretations of Difficult Passages in Rashi, Part I,* written by the esteemed rabbinic scholar R. Pinchas Doron, may he live, with the Approbation of our Master the Gaon Rabbi Moshe Feinstein, *ztz"l,* of the year 744 (1984) and behold it is an important and venerable contribution adding understanding and elucidation in many places in Rashi's comment for those who delve into them scrupulously. Now he is continuing with volume 2, of which I saw parts of Sefer Vayikra (Leviticus). His work in this volume is the same as in the first volume. I therefore come in these lines to strengthen his hands; Hashem should be with him that he may see the completion of his work, and that his work should be widely accepted in Israel for the benefit of the multitudes.

One who writes and signs in honor of the Torah and its students.

Yaakov Perlow

Approbation—Translation

Rav Simon Schwab
736 West 186th Street
New York, N.Y. 10033

The honorable author R. Pinchas Doron Shlita is a rare person and (Torah) scholar who expended great labors to interpret difficult passages in Rashi's commentary on the Chumash. He showed me examples of his supercommentary. He also has an approbation from the great Gaon, the Teacher of Israel, Rabbi Moshe Feinstein, *ztz"l*. Now "who can come after the King." Hence he surely does not need my approbation. I only come to strengthen his hands to publish his book for the benefit of those who learn Chumash with the commentary of the holy Rashi, that they should be scrupulous with every single of his words, so as to understand his profound meanings—for all Rashi's words are "holy of holies" above.

I hereby affix my signature on the 20th of Shvat, 5749 (1989).

Shimon Schwab

Preface

The volume presented herewith is intended to elucidate difficult passages in Rashi on the Torah and, at the same time, bring to the fore the profound religious, philosophical, ethical, and educational ideas inherent in them, but only alluded to by Rashi in very few and sometimes obscure terms. I deal here only with such of Rashi's comments that *I* found difficult and challenging, and which contain such profound ideas. I literally "struggled" with these "Rashi's" to find answers and solutions to the numerous questions and problems they presented to me. It is quite possible that other students of Rashi will find questions and problems in his commentary in places that I did *not* find problematic. On the other hand, there are probably students who find no difficulty at all in the verses that presented a problem to me in Rashi's comments to them.

In the course of searching for solutions and answers to the problems and questions I had in Rashi's comments, I studied many of the major commentaries on Rashi, such as, the greatest among them, R. Elijah Mizrachi, of the greatest Torah scholars of the fifteenth and sixteenth centuries—known by his acronym Ha-RAM, i.e., "The Rabbi Elijah Mizrachi." After him in importance are such giants in the interpretation of Rashi as: the famous *Taz* (= Turei Zahav on Shulchan Aruch) in his supercommentary on Rashi entitled *Divrei David*; the Maharal of Prague in his work on Rashi, *Gur Aryeh*, and his older brother R. Chaim in his book *Be'er Mayim Chaim*; R. Mordechai Yafeh in his work *Levush Ha-Orah*; *Nachlat Yaakov* by R. Jacob son of Aaron; *Sefer Hazikaron* by R. Abraham Bakrat Halevi of the Spanish exile; *Amar Ne'ke* by R. Ovadiah of Bartenura; *Maskil LeDavid* by R. David Pardo. Also the following works on Rashi: *Be'er Yitzchak* by R. Isaac Horowitz; *Devek Tov* by R. Shimon Osenburg Halevi; *Siftei Chachamim* by R. Shabtai Bass; *Havanat Hamikra* by R. Zev Wolf Heidenheim; *Zechor le-Avraham* by R. Abraham Berliner. In our own time, probably the most insightful commentator on Rashi was the late Grand Rabbi of Lubavitch, Rabbi Menachem Mendel Schneersohn o.b.m. in his *Be'urim le-Ferush Rashi al ha-Torah*, which are a collection of his many hundreds of most insightful discourses in the now legendary "Farbrengens"—"gatherings." His enormous fluency in all Rabbinic literature and sharp insights are nothing less than astounding!

From all of the above and other commentators on the Torah such as: the Ramban, Rashbam (Rashi's oldest grandson), Seforno, "Chizkuni" by R. Chizkiah ben Manoach, and others I culled whatever could serve as answers to my numerous questions and problems. The statements of the above commentators on Rashi and others I cited by name and almost always verbatim—if they related directly to the questions and problems I raised. If their comments related only indirectly to my questions, I cited them in the footnotes.

However, the early authorities were exceedingly learned and wise (reflected in the Hebrew simile: "Their heart (= mind) was wide open, like the doorway to the Sanctuary"). Therefore, in numerous places in Rashi's commentary where I encountered difficulties, they did not, and did not address my questions at all. In our day and age, however, understanding is greatly diminished, and many matters that were quite clear to those spiritual giants, have become difficult and at times even obscure to us. It is therefore not surprising at all that in numerous passages in Rashi where I experienced difficulties, I did not find in the supercommentaries on Rashi—even among the greatest of them—anything "to quench my thirst," and provide a satisfactory answer to my many questions. I was therefore obliged, after great effort, to provide my original answers.

With Hashem's help I was able to find in almost all cases interpretations and answers that satisfied me—and I hope and pray that my readers will find them satisfactory.

Besides answers to questions and solutions to problems I had, I interpreted many of Rashi's comments and developed the important ideas and profound moral lessons inherent in Rashi's terse comments, that appear at first glance to be almost simplistic.

The order of the commentary is as follows: Each verse interpreted begins with the "caption words" (*dibur hamatchil*) in Rashi that require interpretation. In the commentary itself, marked by the abridgement "Comment." (= commentary), I begin with the questions to be asked on Rashi's comment. After these comes the commentary, which serves as an answer or answers to the questions that were asked. In those cases where I had no questions on Rashi's comment, the Commentary serves as a searching analysis of the various profound ideas inherent in Rashi's comments, but only alluded to briefly.

References to hundreds of verses in the Bible are given in parentheses, as a rule after citing the verse itself or part thereof. References to Rabbinic literature [Babylonian and Jerusalem Talmud (Yerushalmi)], Midrashic literature and commentaries (and even to supercommentaries on Rashi, if not related directly to the questions at hand) are usually given in footnotes—each *Parasha* with its own enumeration of footnotes. In places where the comments of one of the great supercommentaries on Rashi (such as *Mizrachi, Gur Aryeh, Divrei David, Maskil Le-David,* etc.) are an important part of the commentary, his comments are cited in his name in the text, not in the footnotes.

I sincerely hope that I contributed somewhat to the understanding of the holy, profound words of the Teacher of Israel (a fond interpretation of the Hebrew acronym Raban Shel Israel = Rashi) to whom my family dates back.

Our Sages state: "The envy of writers increases wisdom" (cf. *Bava Batra* 21a; 22a). Therefore I most earnestly ask of the readers of this volume that should they find anything in the following pages that they do not agree with, or God forbid—mistakes, that they should inform me of the same together with their reasons for their objections—so that I may be able to correct what requires correction in a future edition of the work.

Introduction: Rashi's Methodology in his Torah Commentary

Numerous articles and books were written throughout the generations attempting to delineate Rashi's methodology in his commentary on the Torah.[1] Also the greatest among Rashi's commentators dealt with this matter.[2] Of the greatest contributions to this field of study is that of the late Grand Rabbi of Lubavitch, Rabbi Menachem Mendel Scheersohn o.b.m., who for some thirty years—from 1965 until 1995—devoted hundreds of

---

[1]See for example the extensive studies of A. M. Lifschutz: "Rashi" (Hebrew); Yeshayahu Wolfsberg: "Mishkalo ha-Machshavti shel Perush Rashi al ha-Torah" (The conceptual significance of Rashi's Commentary on the Torah"); Dr. A. Ovadiah: "Rashi's commentary on the Torah and his commentators" (Hebrew)—the above and others appear in: *Sefer Rashi*, edited by Rabbi J. L. Maimon, Mosad Harav Kook, Jerusalem, 1956. See also the extensive study by E. Z. Melamaed, "Perush Rashi Lamikra," in his monumental work: *Mefarshei ha-Mikra Darcheihem ve-Shi-toteihem*, Magnes Press, Jerusalem, 1978, pp. 353–446. Cf. also the studies on Rashi in the anthologies: *Rashi*, edited by Dr. Simon Federbusch, World Jewish Congress, 1958; *Rashi Anniversary Volume*, American Academy for Jewish Research, 1941; M. Lieber, *Rashi*, Jewish Publication Society, Philadelphia, 1906, reprinted Hermon Press, New York, 1970; S. Kamin: *Rashi: Peshuto shel Mikra Umidrasho shel Mikra*, Magnes Press, Hebrew University, Jerusalem, 1986; E. Shereshevsky: Rashi: The Man and his Times; Jason Aronson, Northvale, N.J. 1996.

[2]See for example the introduction of R. David Pardo to his important supercommentary on Rashi, *Maskil le-David*; likewise R. Abraham Bakrat Halevi's work *Sefer Hazikaron*—Introduction to the 1978 edition; also the greatest of Rashi's commentators, R. Elijah Mizrachi deals with this question—as already pointed out in the introduction to *Maskil le-David*; see also the chapter "Klal Gadol al Be'ur Rashi" at the beginning of *Devek Tov* by R. Shimon Ausenburg Halevi, reprinted by *Bet Hasefer*, 1974. Likewise the great commentators Taz in his work *Divrei David* and R. Isaac Horowitz in his *Be'er Yitzchak* (in numerous places) (see the introduction by Rabbi J. Kuperman) deal with Rashi's methodology.

discourses in his famous "farbrengens"—"gatherings" to expounding passages in Rashi. In these discourses he also dealt with Rashi's methodology
in his Torah commentary. Based on these discourses five volumes of *Be'urim
le-Ferush Rashi al ha-Torah* were published in a number of editions, the latest
by Kehat, Brooklyn, N.Y., 1993 and *K'lalei Rashi* (Rules in Rashi) by R.T.
Blau, Ozar Hachasidim, Brooklyn, N.Y., 1980.

Were we to attempt to review, albeit briefly, all that was said and written
regarding Rashi's methodology in his Biblical commentaries, we would not
do justice to the task. In the framework of a brief introduction to a volume
that does not deal primarily with Rashi's methodology, but rather with the
elucidation of some difficult and obscure passages in his commentary,
suffice it to delineate some general principles that touch on Rashi's methodology that will make it easier for the intelligent reader to understand
Rashi's method in his Torah commentary. For lack of space, we can cite
only one or two examples that illustrate the principle in question.

1) As is well known, Rashi strove to give the "plain sense" of the verse.
He himself announces this intention several times in his commentary, e.g.,
Gen. 3:8: "They heard," etc.—There are many *Agadic* (homiletical)
Midrashim and our Rabbis arranged them in proper order in Gen. *Rabbah*
and in other (collections of) Midrashim, but I come only to give the plain
sense of the verse, and such homiletical interpretations (*Agadah*) as clarify
the text of Scripture in its proper sequence.[3] We see from this statement
that Rashi set for himself two goals: one to explain the "plain sense" of the
verse; second, to cite the Midrash on the condition that "it clarifies the text
of Scripture," namely: it is *close* to plain sense, although it is *not* the simplest
meaning. It is worth paying attention to the verse in Proverbs that Rashi
cites to describe the kind of homiletical interpretation (*Agadah*) he is
prepared to cite in his commentary, namely: it must "clarify the text of
Scripture in its proper sequence." In his commentary on Proverbs 25:11
he explains the phrase *al ofanav* "by the words"—*al kano*. The Heb. *kan*
means "basis," i.e., Rashi cites only such midrashim as have a basis in
clarifying the text, though they are *not* the primary meaning of the word
or verse they relate to. By this definition any Midrash that does *not* correspond to or clarify "the Biblical text"—the words of the verse—in any way,
has no place in Rashi's commentary.

Rashi repeats this goal in Exod. 6:3 stating: ".... But our rabbis explained it in reference to the above. ... However the Midrash is *not* commensurate with the text ... therefore I say let the verse be explained accord-

---

[3]Cf. Proverbs 25:11 where Rashi explains *davar davur al ofanav* "According to its
fundamental meaning." Ibn Ezra explains: "In its proper aspect, without seeking
esoteric meanings."

ing to "plain sense" in the proper sequence, and the Midrash may be applied (additionally)....[4]

2) The above rule about interpreting *only* the plain sense of the verse and citing only such midrashim as clarify the text notwithstanding, Rashi regarded numerous midrashim as the plain sense. The reason is because in those verses Scripture *alludes* to the Rabbinic exegesis either by an unusual word order, or by superfluous words, or yet by a *special* word, phenomena that we would not expect in the "plain sense." All these are allusions that the Torah *intends* these particular verses to be exegeted in accordance with the rabbinic Midrash. If this is the intention of the Torah, then the Midrash in these instances is *the true* plain sense![5]

3) At times Rashi will cite homiletical midrashim that are not the plain sense, if they answer a question the student may have. Thereby they fall into the category of "an *Agadah* that clarifies the text of Scripture in its proper sequence."[6]

4) Generally, when Rashi writes both the plain sense and the Midrash, he cites the plain sense first and then the Midrash. However, in relatively few cases Rashi cites first the Midrash and after it the plain sense. This is his method in verses where the Midrash expresses a profound religious, philosophical, moral, or educational idea that Rashi wishes to highlight. Example: Gen. 1:4: "God saw that the light was good"—Here, too, we need the statement of the *Agadah*: He saw that the wicked do not deserve to use it (the primeval light) and he set it aside for the righteous in the Future World. But according to plain sense explain it as follows...." Here Rashi teaches us the principle: "The reward for keeping *mitzvot* (commandments) is not in this world."[7]

Another example: Gen. 1:1 "In the beginning God created"—This verse *must* be exegeted the way our Rabbis do: For the sake of the Torah, which is called *reishit*—"the beginning" of "His way" (Prov. 8:22), and for the sake of Israel who are called: "the beginning" or "choice":—*reishit* of

---

[4]See also Rashi on Gen. 3:23–24; Exod. 33:13. This is also Rashi's method in interpreting the Prophets and Writings, cf., e.g., Isaiah 26:11; Jeremiah 33:25; Psalms 68:34; 78:63.

[5]See our Heb. commentary: *Be'ur Setumot Be-Rashi*, Part II (Levit.) on: Levit. 6:10, 6:13, 8:34, 14:8, 15:11, 19:14, 21:9, 22:24, 22:28, 24:3, 24:20, 25:8, 25:24. At times the allusion in the verse is by use of a non-grammatical form, e.g.: Numbers 7:1,12:1.

[6]Cf, e.g., our Heb. commentary *Be'ur Setumot Berashi*, Part III on: Numbers 22:26, 32, 23:21, and cf. Rashi on Gen. 3:8, 23–24, 6:3, etc.

[7]*Kiddushin* 39b.

His crop (Jer. 2:3). But if you wish to explain it according to its "plain sense" then explain it thus ...."

In the above Rashi wished to underscore the virtues of the Torah and the Jewish People, both of which are of supreme importance to the world, and therefore the world was created in their merit.[8] So important is this idea, that Rashi precedes the Midrash to the plain sense, and returns to this idea many times in *Parshat Bereishit*, as explained fully in our comments to verses touching upon this idea.

5) At times Rashi alludes to a Midrash (from the Talmud or from the midrashic collections on the Torah)—a *halachic* (i.e., "legalistic") Midrash, or *Agadic* (i.e., "homiletical") Midrash, without quoting it. He does not quote the Midrash because it does not "clarify the words of the text," i.e., it is not close to plain sense, but he alludes to it because it is interesting and important for several reasons: At times the Midrash alluded to contains an important ethical or educational moral, or a religious idea—for whose sake Rashi sees fit to draw the student's attention to the Midrash that learns that particular moral or idea from that verse—even though this derivation is not the "plain sense." For example, Gen. 3:24: " 'The revolving sword' which has a blade to threaten him that he should not enter the Garden again." The Aramaic translation of *lahat* is *shnan*—"a blade." ... "And there are *Agadic midrashim*, but I come only to give the plain sense."

Now in Gen. *Rabbah* Chap. 21:9 this entire verse is exegeted in various ways, e.g.: "The flame" (*lahat*)—corresponding to: "His attendants are flaming fire" (Psalms 104:4);[9] *hamithapechet*—"the revolving, turning"—they (the angels) are ever-turning, sometimes they are men (Gen. 18:2), sometimes women (Zachariah 5:9), sometimes spirits (Psalms 104:4). Another explanation: *mikodem*—lit. "at the east" means: before (*mikodem*), i.e., Gehenna was created before the Garden of Eden .... 'The flame' corresponds to: "The day" (i.e., "sun") "that is coming to burn them" (Malachi 3:19, i.e.,

---

[8]Rashi emphasizes the virtues of the Torah also in his comment on Psalms 105:8, "He remembered His covenant forever, the Word He commanded for a thousand generations"—"The Torah which G-d commanded to proclaim to the world after a thousand generations, but seeing that the world could not exist without Torah, He removed (from being created—born) 974 of these generations (and gave the Torah after *only* twenty-six generations after creation). One can *also* explain according to plain sense ... Similarly in Proverbs 15:30 Rashi writes: 'Enlightened eyes' means "In the Torah"; 'will gladden the heart'—i.e., "If people ask him anything (in Torah) and he knows the answer. But according to plain sense, understand it literally."

[9]Namely, the word *lahat* means "angels" and does not refer to the adjoining word *cherev*—(sword).

Gehenna burns man); 'that revolves'—that revolves around man and burns him from head to foot and from foot to head (i.e., the fire of Gehenna). Adam said: "Who will save my children from this burning fire?" R. Huna in the name of R. Aba said: 'Sword' refers to circumcision, as it says: "Make for yourself flint knives" (lit. swords—*charvot*) "and circumcise the Israelites a second time" (Joshua 5:2). The Rabbis say: 'sword' refers to Torah, as it says: "and a double-edged sword is in their hand" (and the verse begins with: "The lofty *praises of God* are in their throats," i.e., Torah—Psalms 149:6)."

We suggest that Rashi hinted: "And there are *Agadic midrashim*" so that the student should study them and realize the great virtues of circumcision and the study of Torah, which have the power to save one from the fire of Gehenna. However, since these *midrashim* do *not* "clarify the text of the verse," Rashi does not quote them verbatim.[10]

6) Unlike in his commentary on the Talmud, where he cites *halachic* Midrashim (i.e., Mechilta, Sifra, Sifrei) and the Tosefta verbatim, in his Torah commentary he often cites Midrashim and Talmudic statements with significant changes from the sources: at times he deletes, and sometimes adds, explanatory remarks to the sources he quotes. All this is done with the view of making the source more intelligible to the student and adjusting it, as far as possible, with the "plain sense" that Rashi comes to explain.[11] Sometimes Rashi combines two Tanaitic sources into one, because he believes there is no controversy between them.[12] Whenever Rashi deletes or adds to his source (Sifrei, Talmud, etc.), one has to examine the reason for these changes.[13] At times Rashi adds words to the Midrash to explain it.[14]

The following is an example of a combination of a number of sources into one unit; Gen. 15:5: "He took him outside ..." Rashi: But according to the Midrash God told him: Go out of your astrological predictions that you saw in the planets that you will not have a son. "Abram" will not have a son, but "Abraham" will have one; "Sarai" will not give birth, but "Sarah"

---

[10]Cf. also Gen. 4:8, 27:41; Exod. 13:17, 35:3; Levit. 3:17,7:6; Numbers 5:10, etc. One must ponder each such Midrash alluded to by Rashi, in order to discover which idea (moral, educational, religious, *halachic*) Rashi meant to emphasize. Cf. *Eruvin* 19b to the effect that Abraham saves from the fire of Gehenna those who fulfill his covenant—circumcision.

[11]Cf. *Klalei Rashi*, Chap. 8: "Citation of Sources and Names, and changes from the Source," pp. 61–65.

[12]Cf. e.g., our commentary to Numbers 36:11; Deut. 11:13, 34:5.

[13]See, e.g., Numbers 12:23, 13:5, and our commentary thereto.

[14]See our comments to Deut. 14:21–22.

will. Another explanation: He took him out of the atmosphere of the world and raised him above the stars, this is the meaning of "gazing"—*habatah* from above downward.

This comment is a combination of three rabbinic sources:

a) Gen. *Rabbah* 44:10: "(Abram said) the star urges me and says: Abram will not beget, God told him: It is as you say; Abram and Sarai will not beget, but Abraham and Sarah will beget children."

b) Gen. *Rabbah* 44:12: "God raised him above the dome of the sky." This is what he meant by: "Look down toward heaven—the word *habeit*— "gaze" means only: from above downward."

c) *Shabbat* 151a: "Abram said to Him: Master of the world, I gaze into my astrology, and I am not destined to beget a son. He said to him: "Go out of your astrological predictions, for Israel has no planet (that governs it)."[15]

Another example briefly: Deut. 16:19: "You shall show no partiality." Rashi: "Even during the depositions of testimony, it is a warning to the judge that he should not be "soft" on one and "hard" on the other plaintiff (up to here from *Ketubot* 46a); one standing, the other sitting (from *Shevuot* 30a); for when the plaintiff sees that the judge honors the other one, he will forget his arguments (lit. "his arguments will become blocked"—from *Shevout* 30b).

7) When Rashi offers two or more explanations of one expression, it means that each explanation answers a certain question that the other explanations do not answer—together they remove all difficulties in the verse, or at least most of them. All the explanations offered are usually commensurate with the plain sense of the verse. The *first* explanation Rashi gives is the one closest to plain sense, but does not suffice by itself.[16] Likewise, when Rashi mentions the names of Rabbinic authorities (from the Midrash or Talmud) whose opinions he cites, it means that he sees the opinion of the first Rabbi he cites as the closest to the plain sense.[17]

Example: Gen. 7:11: "In the second month—Rabbi Eliezer says that is

---

[15]Meaning: The Jewish People's fate is not determined by the stars and planets, like that of other nations. Rather G-d alone determines their destiny. Although there was no Jewish People yet at that time (and Abraham had the status of a non-Jew or: "son of Noah"), but the reference is to Abraham's children, who would be the progenitors of the Jewish People, the Gemara uses this phrase ("Israel has no planet"), which was stated about the Jewish People. It is also possible that the Rabbis considered Abraham as a Jew, since he fulfilled the entire Torah even before it was given.

[16]See, e.g., our comments on Numbers 22:30.

[17]*Klalei Rashi*, p. 43. Cf. our commentary on Gen. 27:1 s.v. *vatich'henah*.

Marcheshvan; Rabbi Joshua says that is Iyyar." In *Rosh Hashanah* 11b where this controversy is mentioned, the Talmud cites first the opinion of R. Joshua. Rashi changed the order because he sees the opinion of R. Eliezer as closer to plain sense. In the course of *Parshat Noah* Rashi follows R. Eliezer's opinion and makes all calculations in reference to the Flood according to his opinion.[18]

8) Rashi does not usually give the names of the Rabbis in the Talmud or Midrash whose opinions he cites. Even where he cites a controversy, he usually states the varying opinions without mentioning names, but in a general way, such as: "Some of our Rabbis say ... and others say," or: "Our Rabbis differ in this matter, some say ... and some say ...."[19]

9) When Rashi mentions the name of a Sage who made a statement (a Tanna or Amora) it relates to the "plain sense" of the verse. Each time a name is mentioned there is a special reason for it, which one must ponder. After delving into the matter it appears that the Sage's statement is congruent with his consistent approach in others of his statements. It therefore behooves him especially to have made the particular statement.[20]

10) Rashi's approach to Targum Onkelos:
The Aramaic translations, especially Targum Onkelos to the Torah and Targum Jonathan to the Prophets, were sanctified by the Jewish People at all times, because they were used in the synagogues as accompaniments to the reading of the Torah and for the Haftorah. Therefore Rashi refers to Onkelos as an aid to his commentary to the Torah and to Jonathan in his commentary to the Prophets.
   a) A very common term in Rashi is *k'targumo*—"as the Targum has it," which means that Rashi agrees with Targum Onkelos, whether it is the "plain sense" of the verse or not. In most cases he merely states *k'targumo*, but does *not* actually quote the Targum. But sometimes he writes *k'targumo* or, *v'targumo* and proceeds to quote the Targum itself. Why does he not rely on the student to look up the Targum himself, as he does in most cases? There are a number of reasons for this:
      1. In Hebrew words with more than one meaning, the Targum

---

[18]Cf. Rashi Gen. 7:12, 8:3–5,14. In 8:13 he mentions R. Joshua but states R. Eliezer's opinion *first.*
[19]Cf. e.g., Gen. 6:9, 9:22, 17:19, 22:1; Exod. 13:11, 24:16, 25:25, 29, 29:42, 21:23; Levit. 21:9, 27:28; Numbers 6:9; Deut. 15:14, 19:5.
[20]See *Klalei Rashi*, pp. 62–63; cf. our commentary to Deut. 11:22–24, 12:23, 13:5. Cf. the Lubavitcher Rebbe's explanations at great length in his work *Be'urim le-Ferush Rashi al Ha-Torah* on Gen. 37:35 (pp. 249–252); 2:2 (pp. 18–22); 44:43 (pp. 275–277); 42:4 (pp. 287–289), etc., ed. Otzar Hachasidim, Brooklyn, N.Y. 1993.

determines which is the meaning intended in any given verse, e.g.: Levit. 23:16 *haShabbat hashvi'it*—"the seventh Sabbath"—"As the Targum renders *shvu'ata shvi'ata*—"the seventh week." Here Rashi quotes the Targum to prevent an error: The Hebrew Shabbat has two meanings: a) the Sabbath day (seventh day), b) the entire week is called Shabbat. If we translate in this verse *haShabbat*—"the Sabbath Day" (seventh day of the week), it would coincide with the opinion of the Saducees who took the phrase *mimochorat haShabbat*—"on the morrow of the Sabbath" to mean on Sunday. According to them, therefore, the Festival Shavuot always falls on a Sunday—which is contrary to the *halachah* (rabbinic law)! Whereas the Rabbis render the phrase *mimochorat haShabbat*—"on the morrow of the first day of Passover," start counting the Omer and on the fiftieth day (whichever day of the week it happens to be) celebrate Shavuot!

2. Rashi also quotes the Targum if two versions exist in Onkelos; or if there are two Aramaic expressions for a certain Hebrew word; or to negate Targum Jonathan, who renders differently.[21]

3. In rare words in the Torah (or Prophets) Rashi quotes the Targum in order to explain the Hebrew expression, e.g., Exod. 12:4: *tachosu—titmanun* "You will count yourselves." The word *titmanun* is more easily understood, because the word *minyan* is common in rabbinic parlance: *nimnin 'al ha-Pesach*—"one counts oneself in on the Passover sacrifice."

4. At times Rashi quotes the Targum because the verse is elliptic and the Targum completes the missing word, e.g., Gen 41:56. *et kol asher bahem*—"as the Targum renders" *di b'hon 'ibura*—"in which there was grain"; Numbers 2:20 *alav* (upon) *ketargumo—udismichin 'alohi*—"those next to him (not upon him")"; Deut. 32:5 *shicheyt lo*—(lit. "they corrupted him"), as the Targum renders: *chavilon l'hon la lay*—They corrupted themselves, not Him."

b) Sometimes Rashi writes only: *k'targumo peirusho*—"the meaning is as the Targum renders," e.g., Gen. 4:7 *halo im teitiv s'eyt—k'targumo peirusho* or: *peshuto k'targumo*—"the plain sense is as the Targum" renders, e.g., Gen. 46:30—*amutah hapa'am*—"this time I shall die"—*peshuto k'targumo*. In such cases Rashi means that one *must* explain the verse as the Targum renders it—even if this is not the plain sense of the words.

c) Just as Targum Onkelos obviates anthropomorphic and anthropopathic expressions in the Torah, namely: He changes

[21]Cf. *Klalei Rashi*, pp. 74, 114–15.

any biblical expression relating to God that expresses any actions or emotions that normally describe human behavior or reactions, such as: physical movement, emotions such as: anger, sorrow, joy, etc.—so does Rashi obviate anthropomorphisms, explaining the physical expressions in a manner commensurate with God's honor, e.g., Gen. 6:6: "the Lord *regretted* ... and His heart was *saddened*," which Onkelos renders: "The Lord changed His *Word* that He made man on earth, and He said by His Word to break their harshness by His Will." Similarly Rashi writes: "Man became an object of sadness to the heart of the Omnipresent (meaning:), it occurred to God to sadden him (man), *and this is Onkelos' rendition.*" Rashi identifies with Onkelos' opinion and therefore cites him first.

Further examples are: Exod. 33:22 *vesakoti kapi*—"I shall shield you with My Hand" ... the Targum renders *ve'again bemeimri*—"I shall protect you with My Word." This is a euphemism in honor of the One above, "for He does not need to actually *shield* him with a hand." Also in Exod. 19:4: "... *va'esa etchem*—"I carried you," Rashi: "But Onkelos renders *va'esa* ("I carried") like *va'asi'a*—"I made you journey"; he corrected the expression in honor of God." Also in Deut. 32:40: *ki esa el shamayim yadi*—"When I raise My Hand toward Heaven," Rashi: "I always make the place of My *Shechinah* reside in Heaven, as the Targum renders." The intent of the Targum and Rashi is to obviate any physical understanding of the word *My hand*, because it is not "honorable towards the One above."[22]

Indeed Onkelos is *very* consistent in obviating *every* expression describing God that smacks of anthropomorphism, and changes it to one that is more "honorable to the One Above."[23] However, Rashi does not follow Onkelos in *every* place. For example regarding the Tower of Babel in Gen. 11:5: "The Lord *went down* to see, etc." where Onkelos renders: "God *revealed*

---

[22]Cf. also Rashi on Exod. 19:18: "The furnace (*hakivshan*)—of limestone." I might think that it (the smoke) was *only* that of a furnace and no more? It therefore states: "Burning in fire to the heart of Heaven" (Deut. 4:11). Why then does it say: "furnace"? To enable the ear to hear what it is capable of hearing—*he gives people a symbol recognizable to them*; Similarly; "He roars like a lion" (Hosea 11:10)—who gave strength to the lion, but (only) G-d? Yet the verse compared Him to a lion? However, *we compare Him to His creatures*, in order to enable the ear to hear what it is capable of hearing." Comp. Rashi on Levit. 17:10 and our commentary thereto: Deut. 29:19; Numbers 23:21; Isaiah 63:1.

[23]Maimonides in *The Guide to the Perplexed* Part I, Chap. 27 highly praises Onkelos

Himself to punish the builders of the city, etc." Rashi explains:
"He did not need this (to *go down*), but it comes to teach the
judges that they should not convict the plaintiff until they see
and understand." This does not mean, God forbid, that Rashi
accepts the expression "He *went down*" literally. He is merely
using this expression to teach the judges a moral lesson, i.e.,
"A judge has only what he *sees*"[24] to go by. Judges must examine
the case very carefully, not judge hastily by hearsay—"Be deliberate in judgment."[25]

Similarly, in the verse: "Let us *go down*" (Gen. 11:7) Onkelos
renders: "Let us *reveal* Ourselves, etc." However Rashi explains:
"He consulted His Court due to His exceeding humility." Rashi
means to teach us the importance of humility; the Almighty
acts humbly to serve as an example for us to follow: "Just as
he is humble, you too should be humble."[26] Thus we see that
educational considerations override even the principle of
obviating anthropomorphic expressions in relation to God.

d) Sometimes Rashi disagrees with Targum Onkelos and
marks that by the introductory remark: "But Onkelos translates," e.g., Gen. 43:3 "Do not see my face unless your brother
is with you"—"Do not see me without your brother (being)
with you. But Onkelos rendered: Only *when* your brother is
with you—he interpreted the matter according to the context,
but was not particular to translate in accordance with the
wording of the text." Similarly in Gen. 25:3: *"Ashurim u-
Letushim*—"These are names of heads of nations." But as for
the rendition of Onkelos,[27] I cannot fit it into the wording of
the text." Sometimes Rashi writes "But Onkelos rendered"
when he means that it is not the plain sense of the verse, but

---

for this tendency, saying: "Onkelos the proselyte was a complete master of the
Hebrew and Aramaic languages. He made it his goal to remove anthropomorphisms. Any description in Scripture that brings one to think of G-d in physical
terms, he interprets it as is appropriate to the context .... This is a wonderful thing,
indicating the degree of perfection of this Master (Onkelos) and the excellence
of his commentary and understanding of matters as they are" (not as they appear
to be in physical expressions pertaining to G-d).

[24]*Bava Batra* 131a.

[25]*Avot* 1:1.

[26]Cf. Rashi Deut. 11:22: "To walk in all His ways—He is merciful, you too be
merciful; He acts with lovingkindness, you too act with lovingkindness" (Sifrei).
Comp. Rashi Gen. 1:26: "Let us make man."

[27]"The children of Dan became camps, regions, and islands."

is still worthy of citing because it is not far from the plain sense.[28]

e) When Rashi writes: "But Onkelos who rendered ..." it means that his translation is not the "plain sense," but a midrashic interpretation. However it is a very interesting explanation and is plausible, therefore Rashi explains Onkelos and shows how he arrived at his rendition. For example in Exod. 22:2: "He shall surely pay—but Onkelos who translated: 'If the eyes of the witnesses fell upon it (saw it) adopted a different method ..., i.e., it is not the simple meaning.'[29]

f) At times Rashi discusses the Targum not to understand the Hebrew word in the verse, but to clarify the Targum itself and his way of understanding the verse, e.g., Exod. 33:9: "He spoke with Moses ...." Its Targum is u-mitmalel im Mosheh, lit. "He spoke to Himself with Moses," which is in honor of the Shechinah, as in: "He heard the Voice speak (to Himself) to him"—Numbers 7:89.[30]

g) Sometimes Rashi determines the correct reading in the Targum, e.g., Gen. 43:2: "When they finished kad sheytziu—when they finished." But one who translates kad sefiku—"when they were sated" is in error. Similarly in Deut. 24:5: vesimach means: "He should make his wife happy," and the Targum is: veyachadi yat ittei—"He should make his wife happy" (causative), but he who translates veyechedi im ittei—"He should be happy with his wife" is in error, for this is not the translation of vesimach (causative) but of vesamach."[31]

---

[28]See our commentary to Deut. 17:18: Be'ur Setumot Be-Rashi, Part IV, pp. 181–182 and note 68.

[29]Comp. Rashi to Exod. 23:2: "You should not follow the many for evil" where Rashi explains Onkelos' rendition, then remarks: "But I say, to explain it in proper sequence according to plain sense it must be explained thus ...." This proves that the Targum is not the plain sense.

[30]See also Rashi on Exod. 16:14 ("and kagir—"like chalk," which Onkelos translates is an addition ..."); Deut. 5:18; and comp. Rashi on Gen. 43:15–16 where he clarifies Onkelos' method. See, however, Klalei Rashi, p. 74, that in the Lubavitcher Rebbe's view: "It is not Rashi's way to explain Targum Onkelos."

[31]See also Rashi on Gen.15:11 s.v. " al hapegarim." Cf. however Klalei Rashi, p. 73, parag. 7: "Rashi does not generally determine the correct reading in Targum Onkelos." We agree that "generally" Rashi does not determine the correct reading in Targum Onkelos. However, in order to prevent an error in the understanding of the Targum or the verse, he does determine the correct reading "occasionally."

11) An elliptic verse:

In regard to numerous verses Rashi says: "It is a short (elliptic) verse" and he proceeds to complete the missing word or phrase in the verse. Example: Gen. 41:13: "He returned to his post;" Rashi: "*Pharaoh*, who was mentioned above, as stated: 'Pharao was angry at his servants'; hence this is a short verse; it did not specify who returned, because there is no need to specify who returned? Whoever had the authority to return, that is Pharao. This is the manner of all short (elliptic) verses: regarding one upon whom it is incumbent to do (anything) they are vague."

Here is an example of the entire phrase that is missing in the verse and Rashi fills it in. Exod. 22:22: "If you do cause him pain ... Rashi: "This is a short verse, it cut off and did not specify what his punishment will be, like: "Therefore anyone who kills Cain" (Gen. 4:15)—it cut off and didn't specify his punishment (see Rashi there). Here too, "If you do cause him pain"—it is a cut-off expression, namely: *In the end you will get your punishment.* Why? "For if he cries out to Me, etc."[32]

12) Metathesis in verses:

In a number of places Rashi remarks that it is necessary to change the place of a word in a verse in order to understand its plain sense. He uses the term that the Rabbis already used, i.e., *mikra mesoras* (lit. "a castrated verse") "a metathesis in the verses." Example, Gen. 2:19: "and whatever the man called a living creature, etc."—Rashi: "Transpose it and explain thus: "Any living creature that the man called a *name*, is its name forever." (Rashi added the word "name.")

Another example: Numbers 22:33: "I would have killed you too"— Rashi: "This is a transposed verse, it is like: 'I would have even killed you,' namely: 'Not only would I have caused your delay, but even killing you.' "[33]

13) There is no chronological order in the Torah:

Already the talmudic Sages took note of the fact that a number of sections in the Torah (and a number of prophecies) are written not in the order they were stated or occurred. Rather, things that were earlier in time,

---

[32]See further examples of "elliptic verses": Gen. 13:6, 29:2, 39:4; Numbers 24:12 (where Rashi adds: "The Targum explains the elliptic statement of the Hebrew text"); 33:54.

[33]Cf. also Rashi on Gen. 40:5: lit. "They dreamed a dream both of them," Rashi: "Both of them dreamed a dream. This is the plain sense"; 41:57, lit. "All the land came to Egypt to buy, to Joseph"—Rashi: "All the land came to Egypt to Joseph, to buy." In these two verses Rashi changes the order of the words without even remarking that they are transposed verses" (= *mikra mesoras*). Cf. also Exod. 16:20; Levit. 1:15; Numbers 19:7; Deut. 4:38.

come later in the text, and vice versa.[34] Rashi points out in a number of places that the rabbis already said that such-and-such *Parashah* or verse are written out of order, e.g.: Levit. 14:44; 16:23.

Besides the places already noted by the Rabbis, Rashi adds many other examples of the rule, lit. "There is no earlier or later in the Torah," of which we shall cite several cases:

1) Gen. 6:3: "His days shall be (one hundred and twenty years)"; Rashi: "Up to 120 years shall I delay my anger against them, and if they do not repent, I will bring the Flood upon them. If you ask: From the time Japhet was born until the Flood only one hundred years passed?[35] There is no earlier or later in the Torah," for the decree was already made twenty years before Noah had children—and so we find in Seder Olam.[36]

2) Gen. 35:29: "And Isaac expired," Rashi: "There is no earlier or later in the Torah," for the sale of Joseph preceded Isaac's death by twelve years, since when Jacob was born Isaac was sixty years old ... and Isaac died in Jacob's 120th year. If you subtract sixty from 180, 120 will remain. Joseph was sold when he was seventeen, and that year was the 108th year of Jacob ..."[37]

3) Exod. 31:18: "He gave to Moses, etc." Rashi: "There is no earlier or later in the Torah," for the episode of the golden calf preceded the command to construct the Tabernacle by many days, since on the seventeenth of Tammuz the Tablets were broken, and on Yom Kippur the Holy One, blessed be He, became appeased toward Israel (i.e., forgave them), and the next day they began to bring contributions for the Tabernacle, and it was erected on the first of Nisan."

4) Levit. 8:2: "Take Aaron," Rashi: "This *Parashah* was stated seven days *before* the erection of the Tabernacle,[38] for there is no earlier or later in the Torah."

---

[34]Cf. *Pesachim* 6b; *Bava Kama* 85a; *Menachot* 55b; *Nidah* 33a; *Yerushalmi: Shekalim* Chap. 6, *halacha* 1; *Sota*, Chap. 5:3; *Tanchuma Terumah* 8; *Mechilta Beshalach* 15:9; *Yalkut* Jeremiah 264.

[35]"Only one hundred years passed," since Noah was 500 years when he begat his oldest son Japhet (Gen. 5:32), and he was 600 when the Flood began (7:5); hence Japhet was 100 years old.

[36]*Seder Olam*, a chronological Midrash attributed to the Tanna Rabbi Yossie of the second century C.E. Cf. *Seder Olam*, Chap 28.

[37]And Isaac lived for another twelve years—which was the 120th year of Jacob, when Isaac died.

[38]"Seven days *before* the erection of the Tabernacle," which took place on the first of Nisan and on the twenty-third of Adar the eight days of "initiation" (*miluim*) began.

5) Numbers 9:1: "In the first month," Rashi: "The *Parashah* at the beginning of the Book (Numbers 1:1) was not said until the month of Iyyar (the second month). You thus learn that there is no earlier or later in the Torah."[39]

It would seem that related to the rule "there is no earlier or later in the Torah" is another rule, viz. lit. "We exegete juxtapositions,"[40] i.e., since there is no chronological order in the Torah, we must ponder why the Torah juxtaposed one *Parashah* to the other *not* in the order of events? Even Rabbi Judah who does not exegete juxtapositions in most of the Torah,[41] yet in Deuteronomy he too derives from juxtapositions.[42] Since the Torah is *not* a mere history book, there is no supreme importance to the *order* of events, which preceded the other. Of greater significance is the conceptual and/or the *halachic* (legal) connection between the events or commandments. Indeed, whenever the Rabbis "exegete juxtapositions" we derive from such exegesis an important idea or principle in Jewish law or life in general.

Furthermore, the controversy between Rabbi Judah and Rabbi Shimon if we ought to "seek reasons for the commandments"[43] or not, is similar to the controversy whether "we exegete juxtapositions or not." It is interesting that Rabbi Judah who does *not* exegete juxtapositions, also holds that we ought *not* to look for reasons for the commandments. It appears the above three rules are interrelated conceptually.

14) Interpreting a verse according to the context: Besides explaining the meaning of words in the verse, and explaining the content and meaning of the entire verse, Rashi also explains the entire context of several verses—in such places where it is possible to err. In such cases he says that: "the verse refers to" (... *hamikra musav*) or: "is connected to the previous verse" (*mechubar lamikra shelma'alah haymenu*) or: is connected to the verse after it (*nimshach lamikra shelacharav*), and similar designations.[44]

Example: Deut. 11:7: "For it is your own eyes that see ...," Rashi: "It refers to the verse *above* (verse 2!): 'For it is not with your children who did not see, etc., but with you, that "your own eyes, etc."'"

---

[39]Cf. also Gen. 1:1, 18:3; Exod. 4:20, 18:13; etc.

[40]*Berachot* 10a.

[41]*Berachot* 21b; *Pesachim* 28b; *Yevamot* 4a, 67b.

[42]The reason is that Deuteronomy, whilst its sanctity is not less than that of the other Books of the Torah, is the words of Moses, who is reviewing all that was said previously (in Exod.-Numbers)—and surely it is *not* a mere review. Therefore the combinations and juxtapositions of Moses have much to teach us (*Shitah Mekubetzet*).

[43]Cf. *Bava Metzia* 115a.

[44]Exod. 25:40; Levit. 11:34; Deut. 4:44.

Sometimes Rashi separates two adjoining verses and even between two parts of the same verse, which ostensibly are part of the same sentence! For example: Gen. 2:24: "Therefore a man should leave," Rashi: "the Divine Spirit (i.e., God) says so, in order to forbid "sexual aberrations" (i.e., adultery, incest, bestiality, homosexuality) to the "Sons of Noah" (i.e., all nations of the world)." Meaning: verse 24 is *not* a continuation of Adam's statement in verse 23: "This time it is a bone from my bones, etc." Rather it is the statement of the Torah.

Here is an example of the separation of one verse, assigning it to *two* speakers; Gen. 37:20: "We shall see what will become of his dreams," Rashi: "Rabbi Isaac said: This verse begs to be exegeted homiletically—the Divine Spirit says so; they are saying: 'Let us kill him,' but the verse concludes: 'But we shall see what will become of his dreams,' i.e., We will see whose words will come to pass, yours or Mine! (God's) It is impossible that they should have said: 'We shall see what will become of his dreams,' for as soon as they kill him, his dreams will surely come to naught!'"[45]

15) The technical arrangement of Rashi's commentary: Generally Rashi copies the verse as a "caption" *dibur hamatchil*—*only* the words he is about to explain and no more. When he quotes from the verse a few words and adds *vego*—"etc." it means that his comment relates to the entire verse or to half of it—and sometimes to the entire topic or *parashah*.[46] Usually Rashi explains under each "caption" only *one* aspect of the word or phrase. Hence, if he wants to explain *two* different aspects regarding the word or phrase he cites from the verse, he quotes the same word or phrase again as a "caption" before explaining the second aspect.

Examples; Gen. 1:26: "Let us make man," Rashi: "We learn from here the humility of the Holy One, blessed be He, since man is in the image of the angels and they will be envious of him, therefore He consulted them (Let us ...)." Afterward Rashi quotes again in a "caption" "Let us make man"—even though they (angels) did not help Him in his creation (of man) and there is room for atheists to argue (that God is *not* the sole Creator, as he needed the aid of the Angels—"Let us make ...") nevertheless the verse did not hold back (from using the plural: Let us) in order to teach good manners (that the great—God in this case—should consult with the small in human relations, as God consulted the angels, although He had no need to do so).

It is Rashi's way to interpolate his own words of explanation into the

---

[45]See further telling examples in: Gen. 17:9; Exod. 23:21, 25:9; Deut 3:2, 10:8; 12:8, 32:35; Judges 5:31.

[46]See *Klalei Rashi*, pp. 50–51, numbers 1–6.

words of the verse, so that the verse and the words of Rashi become *one* sentence—without regard to the period which the *printers* (not Rashi himself) placed between the words of the verse and Rashi's words. Hence, at times, the sentence begins with words from the verse (the "caption": *dibur hamatchil*), on which Rashi comments, and continues with Rashi's words. It, therefore, looks, at first glance, as if Rashi's words begin in the *middle* of a sentence. However, when read *together* with the "caption," then Rashi's words are a direct continuation of the words in the verse. This characteristic adds special charm to his commentary, for it unites with the verse into one unit. It is very important to pay attention to this fact, because alertness to this propensity of Rashi will make it easier for the student to understand many of his comments, that would otherwise be difficult to comprehend.

Sometimes Rashi adds in the middle of the verse one or two words of his own as an explanation. Here are several examples: Gen. 12:16: "He treated [Pharao] Abram well for her sake"; Gen. 14:20: "He [Abraham] gave him tithes from everything [he had]"; Gen. 32:19: "To your servant, to Jacob [am I, i.e., do I belong]"; Exod. 22:6: "If the thief is found he shall pay [the thief] double [to the owner]."[47]

16) Rashi always bears in mind that which he *already* explained before. Therefore when he comes to explain his comments, we must take into consideration this tendency.[48]

17) In his commentary on Leviticus Rashi relies almost entirely on the Gemara or on the Midrash on Leviticus *Sifra* (*or Torat Kahanim*).[49] Nevertheless, he often makes significant changes in citing both. One must ponder the reasons for these changes. One must also consider why he prefers occasionally the version of the Gemara even though he usually follows the *Sifra* in Leviticus? In our commentary to Leviticus we consider these questions.

18) Rashi is inclined to follow Rabbi Akiva's opinion, even in places where it disagrees with the accepted ruling.[50] Moreover, In Rashi's view the Ruling: "The law is like Rabbi Akiva against any (rabbinic) colleague" is valid not only in *legal* matters, but also in the interpretation of a biblical verse not relating to law.[51]

---

[47]Cf. also Gen. 31:20; Exod. 5:20; Numbers 16:5; etc.
[48]See our Heb. commentary *Be'ur Setumot Be-Rashi*, Part II, pp. 24–26.
[49]See ibid., p. 60, note 27. Mostly his comments are based on *Sifra*, although with important changes.
[50]Cf. e.g., ibid., p. 91, note 50.
[51]Cf. *Be'ur Setumot Be-Rashi*, Part IV, p. 148 on Duet. 14:6; Part I, pp. 55–56 on Exod. 12:16.

19) Rashi explains an expression or a word the first time that it appears in the Torah.[52]

20) When giving the "plain sense" of the verse, Rashi considers whichever explanation is closest to plain sense, even if it is opposed to the accepted legal ruling.[53]

21) In rare cases the reading of *our* printed editions of Rashi is preferable to that of the first printed edition of 1474–75.[54]

22) Rashi explains *only* the words he excerpted from the verse as a "caption" (*dibur hamatchil*), no more.[55]

23) Rashi does *not* normally explain the motives for commandments.[56]

24) Rashi does not explain the reason for the juxtaposition of two portions in the Torah,[57] unless there is a question or problem.[58]

25) Rashi does not usually explain "plene" (full) and "lene" (missing) spellings in the Biblical text.[59]

26) Rashi does not give references to Biblical verses without any commentary.[60]

27) Rashi does not give the names of chapters in Tractates in the Talmud. Where he does, one must ponder the reason for the exception.[61]

---

[52]Cf. *Be'ur Setumot Be-Rashi*, Part II, pp. 32, 171 on Levit. 7:26, 25:4; and Part III, pp. 71–72, 167–168 on Numbers 8:11, 18:1.
[53]Cf. our Heb. commentary on Exod. 12:16; Levit. 18:7, 19:32, 20:14, 21; 25:41, 27:8.
[54]Cf. our Heb. commentary on Levit. 22:8, *Be'ur Setumot Be-Rashi*, Part II, p. 145; Part IV, Deut. 7:13—p.73, n. 20; 13:7—p. 140; 14:3—p. 146.
[55]Cf. our Heb. commentary on Numbers 2:2, 3:15, 19:9; *Be'ur Setumot Be-Rashi*, Part III, pp. 7–9; 13–15; 175–76.
[56]Cf. ibid. Numbers 3:46—pp. 22–23.
[57]Cf. our commentary to Numbers 6:2, 8:2, 20:1, 28:2 (Hebrew).
[58]Cf. our Heb. commentary on Deut. 14:21–22, pp. 153–54.
[59]Cf. our Heb. commentary on Numbers 6:23, pp. 49–51.
[60]Cf. our commentary on Numbers 20:1, pp. 185–87.
[61]Cf. our commentary on Numbers 21:35, pp. 208–10.

28) Rashi quotes *Agadic* (homilectical) Midrashim that are not close to the "plain sense" if they display the love of Israel or contain lofty ethical ideas.[62]

29) At times Rashi cites Rabbinic statements that are *not* based on a verse, but regarding which the Rabbis had oral tradition; e.g., that Moses killed Og the King of Bashan[63]; that Midian and Moav "always hated each other."[64]

30) Rashi is very careful not to disagree with the Talmudic Rabbis even in matters *not* related to legal rulings (*halachah*); this is in opposition to Ibn Ezra.[65]

31) Rashi's remark: "The Midrash *in Agadah*" (*u-Midrasho be'agadah*), in opposition to the usual designation "And its Midrash is" (*u-Midrasho*), comes to point out that the Midrash Rashi cites is from the *Agadah* in the *Talmud*, rather than from Midrash Rabbah or other midrashic collections."[66]

32) A "verbal analogy" (*g'zeirah shavah*) is not the "plain sense" of the verse, even though one does not arrive at such a verbal analogy by one's own reasoning without an oral tradition from one's teachers as to the existence (from Sinai) of such an analogy in the particular words.[67] However, *occasionally* such a verbal analogy reveals the true meaning and intent of the verse. In these verses it *is* the plain sense of the verse.[68]

33) When Rashi says: "And *I* say, etc." (*ve'omer ani* etc.), he is pointing out that from here on is *his own* interpretation, in distinction to the previous comments that are based on the statements of the Rabbis or Targum Onkelos.[69]

34) Sometimes the necessity for a certain interpretation is determined by Rashi's love for the Jewish People and his sensitivity to its honor.[70]

---

[62]E.g., "From the work ("Yesod") of Rabbi Moses the Preacher, cf. our comments on Numbers 19:22, pp. 181–84.

[63]Cf. our commentary on Numbers 21:35. pp. 208–10.

[64]Cf. our commentary on Numbers 22:4, pp. 211–13.

[65]Cf. our commentary on Numbers 26:24, pp. 265–67.

[66]Cf. our commentary on Numbers 28:15, 29:35, pp. 281–82, 286–87.

[67]Cf. our commentary on Numbers 22:30, pp. 223–25.

[68]Cf. our commentary on Deut. 19:17, pp. 192–94.

[69]Cf. our commentary on Numbers 23:22, pp. 235–37.

[70]Cf. our commentary on Deut. 4:28, 10:15, 20:3—pp. 40–41, 93-94, 197–98.

35) At times the consolation of the Jewish People is a sufficient cause for a certain explanation.[71]

36) Sometimes Rashi abridges a Rabbinic statement and cites only a summary thereof.[72]

37) The designation of "Midrash *Agadah*" defines it as being *far* from "plain sense"—as opposed to a regular "Midrash." However, it *is interesting* on account of the moral contained therein.[73]

38) Rashi does not cite *all* the opinions mentioned in the Midrashim on a given verse, only those that are close to the "plain sense" of the verse.[74]

39) At times one may arrive at the correct reading in Rashi by studying carefully the Midrash on which his comment is based—as opposed to our printed version.[75]

40) The reading of the First Printing of Rashi (1474-75) at times answers questions that arise from our printed editions.[76]

41) Sometimes Rashi cites a Midrash unknown to us.[77]

42) When Rashi states that a certain inference is "implied" (*mashma*) by the verse, it is the "plain sense" of the verse, not a Midrash.[78]

43) As the "Teacher of the Generations" Rashi sees it as his duty to prevent errors by the common folk. He therefore explains according to the *halachic* rulings transmitted by the rabbis, even if that goes against the rendition of Targum Onkelos, whom he often follows.[79]

44) Rashi does not cite homiletical interpretations that are far removed from plain sense, unless they remove some difficulty.[80]

---

[71]Cf. our commentary on Deut. 2:15, pp. 22–23.
[72]Cf. our commentary on Deut. 7:11, 12:25—pp. 69–70, 129.
[73]Cf. our commentary on Deut. 8:1, pp. 80–81 and note 68.
[74]Cf. our commentary on Deut. 11:15—pp. 102–3.
[75]Cf. our commentary on Deut. 11:19-21, pp. 106–7.
[76]Cf. our commentary on Deut. 11:28—pp. 109–10.
[77]Cf. our commentary on Deut. 12:5—pp. 114–15.
[78]Cf. our commentary on Deut. 14:6—pp. 148.
[79]Cf. our commentary on Deut. 14:21—p. 152; 22:10—pp. 218–19.
[80]Cf. our commentary on Deut. 15:8—p. 157 and note 261.

45) Rashi alludes to rabbinic interpretations *without* explaining them if they are not the accepted ruling (*halachah*) or if they are too complicated.[81]

46) Because of Rashi's high regard for the honor of God and Israel, he sometimes adds statements *in their honor* that are not absolutely necessary for a simple explanation of the verse he is interpreting.[82]

47) In his commentary Rashi shows consideration even for the understanding of the young child who is in the category of "At the age of *five* to begin studying Bible.[83]

48) Rashi cites only *midrashim* that are close to "plain sense" of the verse—whether they are in accordance with the accepted rulings (*halachah* or not—even of an individual opinion against the majority).[84]

49) When Rashi writes" "I do not know, etc." it means that he was aware of various explanations, but could not decide which of them is the best.[85]

In the above forty-nine points we have touched only upon the major and mostly-known principles of Rashi's methodology in his Torah commentary. It is obvious to any serious student of Rashi that there is room to enlarge upon many other aspects characteristic to "The Teacher of Israel," which Rashi was lovingly dubbed, based on the Hebrew acronym of his name: Rashi = *R*aban *Sh*el *I*srael,[86] such as: Rashi the grammarian[87]; Rashi doubts—the places where Rashi writes "I do not know *aini yode'a*; *lo yadati*, etc."—if he does *not* know, why mention the fact, rather than keeping silent?[88]; foreign words (*belashon am zar* = *b'la'az*) (in the language of another nation) in Rashi[89]; linguistic coinage of Rashi, etc. Even of the

---

[81]Cf. our commentary on Deut. 16:2—pp. 162–63.

[82]Cf. our commentary on Deut. 16:3—pp. 164–65; 28:54—pp. 271–72.

[83]Mishna *Avot* 5:22. Cf. our commentary on Deut. 20:11, pp. 201–02; 22:1—214–15.

[84]Cf. our commentary on Deut. 21:22—pp. 212–13 and note 49 there.

[85]Cf. our commentary on Deut. 33:24—pp. 355–56.

[86]See *Sefer Rashi*, p. 6; *Klalei Rashi*, p. 5 end.

[87]See E. Z. Melamed: *Mefarshei Hamikra Darcheihem ve-Shitoteihem*, pp. 398–414.

[88]Ibid., pp. 422–24. With some of these cases of "I do not know," etc., we have dealt in our Hebrew commentary to these places. Here is a list of places in the Torah (only) where Rashi states: I do not know, etc.": Gen. 28:5, 35:13, 43:11; Exod. 22:28, 24:13, 25:21, 28:4; Levit.: 10:20, 13:4, 19:20, 27:3; Numbers: 21:11, 26:13, 26:16; Deut.: 33:24.

[89]E. Z. Melamed, op. cit., pp. 442–43.

"Rules in Rashi" we have mentioned only a small part.[90] As stated, however, we attempted to touch only upon what appear to us as major points. "The rest, go and study."[91]

---

[90]In the book *Klalei Rashi* Rabbi Tovia Blau collected 212 Rules in Rashi—the numerical value of the Hebrew word rabbi = *Grand Rabbi*! (alluding to the late Lubavitcher Rebbe o.b.m. from whose writings Rabbi Blau culled these rules).
[91]Hillel's response to the would-be proselyte, *Shabbat* 31a.

Genesis

B'reishit

1:1 *B'reishit*—"When God was first creating . . ."

RASHI: Rabbi Isaac said: "The Torah should have really begun with the verse: "This month shall be to you [the beginning of months...]" (Exodus 12:1) because this is the first commandment that Israel was commanded (as a nation). Why, then, does it begin with: "When God was first creating (heaven and earth)? Because of [the idea expressed in the verse]: "The power of His deeds He declared to His people to give them the inheritance of nations" (Psalm 111:16). Namely: if the nations complain to Israel: "You are robbers because you took the lands of seven nations (who lived in Canaan when the Israelites arrived from the Egyptian exile) by force," Israel will be able to answer: "The entire land belongs to God. He created it and gave it to whomever He pleased. When He wished, He gave it to them (the seven nations), and when He wished, He took it away from them and gave it to us."[1]

COMMENT: Rashi answers an inherent question: Since the most important part of the Torah is contained in its commandments, instructions (the word "Torah" means "instruction"), why does it not begin with the first commandment given to Israel as a nation (the "instructions regarding Rosh Chodesh and Passover" in Exod. Chap. 12)?

Answer: The Torah begins with an account of the creation to *instruct* us in the most basic religious truth that God is the Creator and Master of the universe. Since He gave the Land of Canaan to the Jewish people, we have a *legal* right to it. This lesson is in keeping with the meaning of "Torah = instruction."

1:1 *B'reishit bara*—"When God was first creating. . . ."

RASHI: This passage requires a homiletical interpretation, as our rabbis explained it: [God created the world] for the sake of the Torah, which is

---

[1]Gen. *Rabbah* Chap. 1; *Yalkut* Exod. 12:2; Tanchuma Buber 11.

called *reishit*—"the beginning," or: "first principle" of his way [Prov. 8:22], and for the sake of Israel who are called: "the beginning," or: "choice"— *reishit* of His crop [Jeremiah 2:3]. However, if you wish to explain the passage according to its "plain sense," then explain it thus: "At the beginning of creation of heaven and earth, when the earth was without form and void...."

COMMENT: Although generally Rashi gives the "plain sense" of the verse,[2] here he cites the homiletical (midrashic) interpretation even before the plain sense, because it teaches a very important philosophical and religious idea, namely: The *purpose* of creation—*why* and for *whom* the world was created is more important that *how* it was created. The Torah is not, primarily, a history book, but rather a book of laws and ethical "instructions." Hence the "why and for whom" of creation are more important than the "how." "Israel-and-the-Torah" are two in one, namely: Israel exemplifies by its way of life the principles of the Torah. The purpose of both Israel and the Torah is to praise the Lord, as the prophet says: "I have created this nation (Israel) for Myself, that they may recount My praise" (Isaiah 43:21).

1:2   *V'ruach E-lohim m'rachefet*—
"and the Spirit of God was hovering."

RASHI: "The Throne of Glory" was standing in the air, hovering above the waters (suspended there) by the breath of God's mouth and by His command—as a dove hovers above its nest.[3]

COMMENT: "The Throne of Glory" symbolizes God as the presiding *Judge* of the world, as a King who sits on the throne of judgment. The "hovering" of the Throne in *mid-air* means that the forces of creation had not yet fully descended, for it was still at the beginning of creation. The Throne of Glory also symbolizes the *spiritual* aspect of creation: although a *physical* world was created, the intention was that it should strive toward spirituality—to the Throne of Glory. Hence the Throne of Glory representing spirituality was *presiding*—"hovering" over the acts of creation. The Torah (= instruction) wishes to teach us this moral lesson from the outset!

---

[2]See his comment on Gen. 3:8.
[3]Gen. *Rabbah* 2; *Chagigah* 15a.

1:4   *Vayar E-lohim et ha'or ki tov vayavdel*—"God saw how good the light was, and He separated the light from the darkness."

RASHI: Here, too, we need a homiletical (midrashic) explanation of the rabbis (*Agadah*): God saw that the light was too good to be used by wicked people, and so He set it apart for the use of the righteous in the World-to-Come (after the coming of the Messiah).[4]

But according to "plain sense," "He separated" should be explained thus...

COMMENT: Here, too, Rashi cites the homiletical interpretation before the plain sense, because it highlights an important religious tenet: "The (major) reward for observing precepts is not in this world" (*Kidushin* 39b). The primeval light was a *spiritual* light, too good for the wicked, and reserved for the righteous in the future world. The "righteous" refers to the Jewish People, which cf. Isaiah 60:21: "Your people are *all* righteous." A "spiritual light" means that it enabled one to comprehend profound truths of the Torah, that are impossible to fathom otherwise. Hence the "first light" was created for the sake of the Torah, just like the entire creation, as mentioned above. That this is the meaning of Rashi's comment is apparent from Rabbi Samuel bar Nachman's statement in Gen. *Rabbah* 3:4[5] and from Rabbi Elazar's statement in *Chagigah* 12a.[6]

1:5   *Yom echad*—"Day one."

RASHI: According to the regular form of expression in this chapter, it should have stated: "The first day," as it states regarding the other days: "second, third, fourth." Why does the verse state: "day one"? Because God was then the Only One in His world—the angels were not created until the second day. Thus it is explained in Gen. *Rabbah* (Chapter 3).

COMMENT: The Hebrew expression "Yom echad" could mean either: "day one," "the first day" (as in Gen. 2:11 *Shem ha'echad Pishon* "The name of the first (river) was Pishon"), or "day *of the* one." But for "the first day" an ordinal, not a cardinal number, would normally be used: *yom rishon*. Rashi cites the Midrash in Gen. *Rabbah* to emphasize an important religious principle, namely: Since the angels are incorporeal, and transcend human experience, one might be misled into believing that they were never cre-

---

[4]*Chagigah* 12a; Gen. *Rabbah* 3:11,12; Exod. Rabbah 18:35.
[5]Cf. the commentary *Etz Yosef* there.
[6].Cf. Maharsha there.

ated, but rather co-existed with God! Hence the Torah uses an irregular expression *yom echad*—here meaning "day of the One," to teach us the important lesson that *everything* in the universe (even the angels) was created. There is neither an eternal matter, as the Greeks believed, nor eternal spirit (like the angels).

1.6   *B'toch hamayim*—"in the middle of the water."

RASHI: In the (exact) center of the water, because there is the (same) distance between the upper waters and the expanse as there is between the expanse and the waters that are on the surface of the earth. From this one may infer that the upper waters are suspended (in space) by the King's (God's) command.[7]

COMMENT: "In the middle of the water" cannot be taken literally; our experience tells us that the "expanse" (heavens) is *not* in the middle of the water. Rashi explains that "in the middle" really means "equidistant"—there is the same distance between the expanse and the "upper waters" as there is between it and the water on earth. Since the "upper waters" are not lying *on* the heavens, they must be suspended in the air by the will of God.

Since water is a physical object, it must be governed by the law of gravity. The "upper waters" are *not* above the gravitational field of the earth, because we know from experience (astronauts) that above the gravitational field there is a relative vacuum, but no water. Therefore, the phrase: "the upper waters are suspended by the King's command" means that God suspended the laws of gravity insofar as the "upper waters" are concerned.

From this we learn that the occurrence of miracles is inherent in the very act of creation: a miracle means that at a given time and place (e.g., the splitting of the Red Sea by Moses), God suspends the laws of nature for the sake of an individual or a nation.[8]

1:11   *Eitz p'ree*—"Fruit tree(s)."

RASHI: That the taste of the tree should be like the taste of the fruit. But the earth did not do so, rather: "The earth brought forth trees which *bear* fruit..." (verse 12)—but not the tree itself was fruit (edible). Therefore, when Adam was cursed for his sin, the earth, too, was remembered on account of its sin, and was cursed.[9]

---

[7]*Chagigah* 10a: Gen. *Rabbah* 4.
[8]Cf. Gen. *Rabbah* 5:4 the statements of R. Yochanan and R. Elazar to that effect.
[9]Gen. *Rabbah* 5.

COMMENT: By stating that the earth "sinned," Rashi means that originally it was in the *nature* of the earth that man should be able to till the ground in such a *way* that the *tree* would have the taste of the fruit. When man was cursed for his sin, the power to till the ground in such a way was taken from him. This is the meaning of: "Cursed be the ground because of *you*" (3:17), namely: man will *not* have the power to work the land according to its original nature (to produce trees that *are* fruit). The statement that "the earth's *sin* was remembered and it was cursed," is only a figure of speech.

The above interpretation expresses the Talmudic dictum: "Whatever the Holy One, blessed be He, created in His world, He did not create even one thing in vain."[10] Since God *can* create trees that not only bear fruit, but are themselves fruit, it would have been a partial waste to create trees that only *bear* fruit. Only through man's sin was the power taken away from him. The earth, as such, is incapable of "sinning" or doing "good"—freedom of will was granted only to man, only in connection with fulfilling or disobeying the dictates of the Torah—which is God's will.

1:14 *V'hayu l'otot*—"And they shall serve as signs."

RASHI: When the luminaries are eclipsed it is a bad sign for the world, for it is said: "Be not afraid of the signs of heaven" (Jeremiah 10:2), (meaning), When you do the will of God, you do *not* have to fear punishment.

COMMENT: Eclipses of the sun and moon are a sign that God's will is *not* being fulfilled on earth.[11] Eclipses of the sun and moon are a bad sign for the other nations of the world, but not necessarily for Israel, because Israel's fate is dependent solely on the keeping of the Torah—which is the embodiment of God's will. This idea echoes the Talmudic saying: "The Jewish People is not governed by the heavenly bodies" (but by God alone).[12]

u'lemo-adim—"and for Festivals."

RASHI: It refers to the future, when Israel would be commanded regarding the Festivals, which are calculated by the birth of the new moon.

COMMENT: Since at the time when the luminaries were fixed in the sky, there were as yet no festivals; what is the meaning of "and for Festivals"?

[10] *Shabbat* 77B; *Bamidbar* Rabbah 18:18; *Zohar* I 23a; III 107a.
[11] Cf. *Sukkah* 29a.; Mechilta, *Bo; Pirke de Rabbi Eliezer*—Chapter 7.
[12] Cf. *Shabbat* 156a; *Nedarim* 32a.

Rashi explains that this statement refers to the future. Here again we have the idea that the world was created for the sake of Israel, since one of the (major) functions of the luminaries is to facilitate the Jewish Festivals!

The Jewish calendar is a lunar one (in which there are approximately 354 days). The dates of the various Festivals mentioned in the Torah (Leviticus Chapter 23) are according to the lunar months. Therefore, the Festivals (Passover, Shavuot, Sukkot, Rosh Hashanah, Yom Kippur) are all dependent on the appearance (the "birth") of the new moon for their calculation.

1:15 *V'hayu li'm'orot*—"And they shall serve as lights."

RASHI: *Also* this is their function—to shine upon the earth.

COMMENT: From the expression: "*Also* this . . ." it would seem that Rashi intimates that "shining upon the earth" is really their *secondary* and less important function. The main functions of the sun and moon are those enumerated in verse 14: to separate day from night; to serve as signs; for Festivals; for days and years. All these are involved directly or indirectly in Israel's fulfillment of the Torah and its commandments. In this light these functions are *more* important than "to shine upon the earth." This ties in well with Rashi's philosophy expressed in his comment on verse 1, namely that the world was created for the sake of the Torah and for the sake of Israel.

1:16 *V'et hakochavim*—"And the stars."

RASHI: Because He diminished the moon, He increased its host (of stars, which help light up the earth at night) in order to appease it.[13]

COMMENT: The difficulty here is: Why is there no separate command for the creation of the stars stating: "Let there be stars, and there were stars"? Are they inferior to the sun and moon in any way, that they do not deserve a special command? According to the Talmudic statement[14] that Rashi cites, the stars are indeed inferior—they are only appendages to the moon—to appease it for having been diminished in size!

This is remarkable, for we know that the stars are far greater in size

---

[13]Gen. *Rabbah* 6.
[14]*Chullin* 60b.

and power than the moon. (And some of them are even bigger than the sun!) One must conclude that in their importance to the *Jewish People* (for whose sake the entire world was created, Rashi on verse 1), the sun and moon are of greater value, since they determine the Jewish calendar and Festivals (especially the moon), which the stars do not!

1:25   *Vaya'as*—"He made."

RASHI: He perfected them with their full will and in their full *size* (height).[15]

COMMENT: In *Chullin* 60a Rashi explains that the talmudic expression *b'tzivyonam* means: "*in the image that they (the animals and beasts) themselves chose.*" This means that if they had been asked *before* creation if they wished to be created in *this* image, each one of them would have agreed.

By the phrase: "in their full height/size" Rashi means that the animals and beasts were created in their *adult* size, not as infants as they are born now. All this points to a perfect creation!

The above interpretation negates the theory of evolution. For if the animals and beasts were perfected during their creation in their *present* forms, then there was no gradual evolution of the species over millennia, as that theory holds!

1:26   *V'yirdu bid'gat hayam*—
"They should rule the fish of the sea."

RASHI: The Hebrew expression: *V'yirdu*—"they should rule" may imply "ruling" as well as "going down." Hence: if man is worthy, he will "rule" over the beasts and animals; if he is not worthy, he will descend even *lower* than they are, and the beasts will rule over him.[16]

COMMENT: Man's status vis-à-vis the animal world depends upon his conduct alone. Man was put in this world to observe the moral dictates of the Torah. If he does so, he will rule the animal kingdom; if not, he will be ruled by it—since he will not deserve any special, privileged status, and physically most beasts are stronger than man!

---

[15] *Chullin* 60a.
[16] Gen. *Rabbah* 8.

1:29-30 *Lachem yi'hyeh l'ochla ul'chol chayat ha'aretz*—
"They shall be yours for food, and for all the land animals."

RASHI: God made all the animals and beasts equal to humans with regard to food, and He did *not* permit Adam and his wife to kill a creature (in order) to eat meat. Rather all together (humans and animals) were to eat every green plant. But when the (period of) the sons of Noah came, He permitted them to eat meat, as stated: *"Every* creeping thing *that lives* shall be yours to eat, *just like* the green grasses"—which I permitted to the first man, so "I give you *all* these" (Gen. 9:3).[17]

COMMENT: The original intention of the Torah was that man be a vegetarian or even a vegan. The permission to eat flesh is a concession to man's desires and weaknesses. Therefore, in the future world, when man will have the power to overcome his desires and weaknesses, he will *not* eat flesh.[18] However, once the eating of flesh *was* permitted, it became part of the Torah, and therefore figures prominently in the laws of sacrifices and Festivals.[19] After the Flood, the Torah considered it beneficial for the new (weakened) constitution of the human body to eat flesh![20]

1:31 *Yom hashishi*—"The sixth day."

RASHI: The Torah added the letter *hey* (h) to the word *shishi*—"sixth" at the end of the work(s) of creation to indicate that God made a condition with them (the works of creation, that they continue to exist only) on the condition that Israel would accept the five books of the Torah (the numerical value of the letter h is 5).[21]

COMMENT: The statement that all the works of creation were made to depend for their continued existence upon Israel's acceptance of the Torah, is in line with Rashi's philosophy that the entire world was created for the sake of Israel and the Torah—as already expressed above in verse 1.

---

[17]Cf. *Sanhedrin* 59b; Tanchuma *Bereshit* 1.

[18]Cf. Rabenu Bachya here, and compare Isaiah 65:25.

[19]Hence the talmudic statement in Pesachim 109A: "There is no joy but in the meat of peace-offerings."

[20]Comp. Seforno Gen. 8:22.

[21]Tanchuma *Bereshit* 1; *Shabbat* 88a.

2:2   *Va'ychal E-lohim bayom hash'vi'i—*
"And on the seventh day God finished."

RASHI: Another explanation: What was the world still missing? Rest! (When) *Shabbat* came—rest came: (only then) was the work (of creation) finished and completed.[22]

COMMENT: According to this explanation, the meaning of *bayom hash'vi'i* is: "By means of the seventh day (God finished His work)." God's work was not completed because *rest* was still lacking. But with the rest of the seventh day His work was completed. According to this explanation the Sabbath is an *integral* part of creation, as rest is a necessity for all created things, especially humans.

Some say that if rest had not been created, the Jews would have no time to study Torah during the week, and the world could not exist without Torah (as Rashi pointed out above in 1:1). Therefore God created the Sabbath, when it is forbidden to work and Jews have time to study Torah. Hence *because* of rest the heavens and earth exist.[23]

2:3   *Va'y'varech, va'y'kadesh—*"He blessed and He declared holy."

RASHI: He blessed it (the seventh day) through the manna, that on all (other) days of the week one Omer for each of them (the Israelites) would fall, but on the sixth day a double portion fell. He also declared it holy through the manna, that it should not fall *at all* on the Sabbath.[24] This verse is written with reference to the future.

COMMENT: The idea of "blessing"—*b'rachah* in Hebrew expresses *material increase*, as in Numbers 6:24: "He will *bless* you," where Rashi comments: "that your property should increase." "Here, too, God blessed..." must refer to some material increase, namely: an increase in the amount of manna on Friday, because of the Sabbath. Conversely, the idea of "holiness"— *k'dushah* in Hebrew, is a negative one and implies *refraining* from some forbidden action. Here, God declared the Sabbath *holy* in that the manna *refrained* from falling on the Sabbath.

The fact that Rashi explains the blessing and holiness of the seventh day *only* in reference to a relatively short period in the history of the Jews,

---

[22]Gen. *Rabbah* 10.
[23]Cf. *Siftei Chachamim.*
[24]Gen. *Rabbah* II. *Pesikta Rabbati* 23.

although the verse is couched in *universal* terms—"because on it He ceased from *all* His work"—is consistent with Rashi's general approach that the world was created for the sake of the Torah and Israel (above 1:1).

2:5   *Ki lo himtir*—"Because He had not caused it to rain."

RASHI: And why did He not make it rain? Because: "There was no man to till the soil"—and there was no one to recognize the goodness of rain. When Adam came (was created) and realized that rain was necessary for the world, he prayed for it and it fell, and trees and herbs grew.[25]

COMMENT: The Torah teaches us here two very important concepts:

1)   Trees, plants, etc., exist only for the benefit of man: for his food, shelter, making utensils, etc., Therefore, as long as there was no man it was not necessary for God to make it rain so that the trees and plants could grow—without man to use them, they need not grow!

2)   God waited until man *prayed* for rain to teach us the importance of gratitude, and that man is dependent on God for his sustenance and well-being. This is the very essence of prayer—the realization that man is dependent on God for *everything* and must show gratitude for His bounty. This is the meaning of the talmudic statement: "The Holy One, blessed be He, desires the prayers of the pious,"[26] because the righteous, through their prayers, express and teach these very concepts to ordinary people.

2:7   *Afar min ha'adamah*—"From the dust of the earth."

RASHI: Another explanation: He took his dust from the place about which it is said: "An altar of earth shall you make for Me" (Exodus 20:24) (namely: From the place where the Temple and altar would stand in the future, as if to say): "Would that (this holy earth) may be an atonement for him, so that he may be able to endure."[27]

COMMENT: According to this explanation, God had in mind already at the time of creation of man, the Jewish People and the Torah; for it is the

[25] *Chullin* 60b.
[26] *Yevamot* 64a.
[27] Gen. *Rabbah* 14; Jerusalem Talmud *Nazir*, Chapter 7, Section 2.

Jewish People who were commanded in the Torah: "An altar of earth shall you make for Me" (Exodus 20:24). Thus, we may say that not only the world at large, but *man* specifically was created for the sake of the Jewish People.

2:18   *Eizer k'negdo*—"A helper, as opposed to him."

RASHI: If he is worthy [she will be] a helper; if he is not worthy [she will be] against him, to fight him.[28]

COMMENT: The Sages meant by this homiletical interpretation to express the idea of woman's equality to man. For woman to be man's helper, the man must *deserve* this privilege, because she is not an *inferior* being, merely to be *used* by man. She, being equal to man, is capable of rising up against him—should he not deserve her help!

2:21   *Mi'tzalotav*—"Of his sides."

RASHI: [The Hebrew word *mi'tzalotav* means] "Of his sides," as in: "and for the (second) side of the tabernacle" (Exodus 26:20). Hence the rabbis said: "Two faces (sides) were created."[29]

COMMENT: According to this explanation Adam and Eve were Siamese twins that were cut apart.[30] The conception of Adam and Eve as Siamese twins underscores again the basic equality of men and women, since Siamese twins are equal literally in *everything*.

3:5   *Ki yodei'a*—"Because He knows."

RASHI: Every craftsman dislikes his fellow craftsmen (since they are his competitors). God ate of the tree (of Knowledge) and created the world.[31]

---

[28] *Yevamot* 63a; *Pirke de Rabbi Eliezer* 12; Gen. *Rabbah* 17.
[29] *Berachot* 61a; *Eruvin* 18a; Gen. *Rabbah* 17.
[30] Cf. Rashi above 1:27.
[31] *Berachot* 32b.

Vi'hyitem kei'lohim—"And you will become like gods."

RASHI: Creators of worlds.[32]

COMMENT: The serpent implied: since God hated the idea of Adam and Eve becoming "craftsmen-creators" like Himself, He forbade them to eat the fruit. Inherent in the serpent's charge: "God ate of the tree and created the world" is the theory, prevalent in ancient Greek philosophy, of eternal matter; the Tree of Knowledge existed even *before* the creation of the world, alongside of God, so to speak. Hence the Tree was the eternal matter from which the rest of the world evolved—and there was *no* "creation out of nothing"—which is a basic tenet of Judaism!

Furthermore, the serpent's statement that God was *afraid* that Adam and Eve would become "creators of worlds," if they ate of the Tree of Knowledge, implies that God is *not* omnipotent and is afraid of rivals! This is sheer blasphemy. By punishing and humiliating the serpent, the Torah shows without entering into any philosophical discussions, how erroneous such ideas are![33]

3:7   *Aley t'einah*—"Fig leaves."

RASHI: That was the tree of which they ate; the very thing that caused their downfall. (The fig tree) also improved their condition (it gave them the material from which to make the loincloths). But the other trees prevented them from taking their leaves.[34]

And why was the tree not identified? Because the Holy One, blessed be He, does not wish to cause pain to any creature, so that people would not put the tree to shame and say: "This is the tree through which the world was punished."[35]

COMMENT: The Torah *hints* at the identity of the tree in order to teach us two important lessons: 1) Natural objects, such as trees, were created for the benefit and pleasure of mankind. But it depends on how man uses them; they can serve him if he uses them wisely, but they can also cause his downfall if he abuses them by improper use (much as the eating of the figs by Adam and Eve). 2) If God never wishes to grieve any creature, even though He is the Creator and Master of them all, and can dispose of them

---

[32]Gen. *Rabbah* 19.
[33]Gen. *Rabbah* 19:1.
[34]*Sanhedrin* 70b; Gen. *Rabbah* 15.
[35]Midrash Rabbi Tanchuma on Gen. 21:1.

at will—all the more so should we humans not cause pain to one another, since all of us were created in His image, and no one can claim superiority over anyone else!

3:14   *Ki asitah zot*—"Because you did this."

RASHI: From here we learn that one should not speak in favor of one who instigates (to idolatry; we do not give him a chance to explain and justify his crime). If God had asked him, "Why did you do this?," he could have answered, "When there is a contradiction between the words of the teacher (= God) and the words of the pupil (= the serpent), whose orders should be obeyed?" ("Obviously God's—the teacher's words should be followed." Therefore, it is not *my* fault that Adam and Eve did not obey You.)[36]

COMMENT: The serpent is considered to have instigated Adam and Eve to idolatry, because he promised them that if they ate from the Tree of Knowledge, "You shall be like gods," which Rashi explained to mean: "Creators of worlds" (verse 5). This indeed is the essence of idolatry—a challenge to God's supreme authority as Creator and Master of the universe. The serpent argued that Adam and Eve, too, could be gods!

3:18   *V'kotz v'dardar tatzmiach lach*— "Thorns and thistles shall it bring forth for you."

RASHI: The earth (shall bring forth thorns and thistles); when you sow it with various types of *seeds* it will grow, instead, thorns and thistles—artichokes and cardoons (= thistle-like plants), which *can* be eaten after (special) preparation (hence they are of some use).[37]

COMMENT: It is inconceivable that the earth shall produce *anything* that is *no use* to anyone because everything that results from God's creation *must* have some purpose. Thorns and thistles sprouting from the earth—which is God's creation—must in some way be able to serve man, for whom the world was created. The curse thus contains a partial blessing. Therefore Rashi adds: (artichokes and cardoons) "which *can* be eaten after...."

---

[36]Cf. *Sanhedrin* 29a.
[37]*Beitza* 34a; Gen. *Rabbah* 20.

3:21   *Kotnot or*—"Garments for the skin."

RASHI: Some *aggadic* (homiletical) interpretations say that they were as smooth as fingernails, *attached to their skin* (not like our clothes, which stand *away* from the skin). Others say that they were made of something that *comes* from the skin, like the wool of hares, which is soft and warm—and of *that* He made garments for them (but not from skins).[38]

COMMENT: Neither of these opinions maintains that the garments were made of the skins. Since God would have had to kill at least one animal in order to obtain skins, Rashi prefers to explain the Hebrew phrase "*kotnot*" or literally: "garments of skin," according to the homiletical explanation of the Midrash, and not according to *plain* sense that the garments were made of skins.

God, the giver of life, does not take life away unnecessarily, neither that of a human, nor that of an animal. Since Adam and Eve were forbidden to eat flesh, they had no use or need for a dead animal. God certainly did not need to kill an animal in order to make garments for Adam and Eve— He had many other materials at His disposal (like the wool of hares, etc.). Hence Rashi prefers to explain that the garments were *not* made of skins.

3:22   *V'ata pen yishlach yado*—
"What if he should stretch out his hand."

RASHI: If he lives forever, he is likely to mislead people into saying: "He, too, is a god (since he lives forever)."

COMMENT: In the above comment Rashi answers the following question: From this verse one gets the impression that it would be *terrible* if man were to eat from the Tree of Life and live forever, and therefore he had to be driven out of the Garden of Eden. Why would it be *terrible* if he *did* live forever?

Rashi answers that not eternal life *itself* is terrible but its possible consequences: People would be misled into believing that Adam was a god, too, since he, like God, would be living forever. Such a theological error could not be allowed to occur. Therefore, God drove him out of the garden, to prevent him from eating of the Tree of Life. The Torah, being the supreme truth, had to *record* the reason why man was driven out of the Garden of Eden. The Torah meaning "instruction" teaches us that man cannot rise above his mortal state to become a "god." This is in sharp

---

[38]Gen. *Rabbah* 20; *Sotah* 14a; *Pirke de Rabbi Eliezer* 14; Tanchuma Buber, *Bereshit* 24.

contrast to some *"men"* in history, e.g. the Pharaohs, Antiochus IV, Epiphanes, who proclaimed themselves to be *gods.* Contrast also the Babylonian Epic of Gilgamesh, wherein the survivor of the Flood, Utnapishtim, joins the pantheon and becomes a god. The Torah spares us from such false beliefs!

4:15   *Vayasem Hashem l'Kayin ot*—
"And the Lord put a mark on Cain."

RASHI: He engraved on Cain's forehead a letter of His (Divine) Name.[39] Other editions of Rashi add the following:

Another explanation of: "Anyone who finds me will kill me" (verse 14) refers to cattle and beasts. As to human beings, there were none yet of whom he should have been afraid—except for his father and mother, and he was not afraid that *they* would kill him. Cain said: "Until now all beasts feared *me*," as is stated: "And the fear of you shall be upon all beasts, etc." (9:2). But *now,* because of this *sin,* the beasts will no longer fear me, and will kill me. Therefore, God immediately "put a mark upon him"; that is, He again made the beasts fear him.

COMMENT: Rashi does not clarify from whose name did God engrave a letter on Cain's forehead—from God's name, or from Cain's name? Neither does Rashi state which letter it was. Targum Jonathan says explicitly that it was a letter from God's name, but does not state which letter. The Maharshal (cited in *Siftei Chachamim*) states that it may have been a letter from Cain's name. It is also possible that it was the letter h (*hey*) from God's name, symbolizing the word "horeyg-kill" from the phrase: "Anyone who kills Cain...."

From the fact that Rashi does not commit himself, but says only: "He engraved on Cain's forehead a letter from *his* name," one could surmise that the letter was one which appears in *both* God's and Cain's names—and that could only be a *yod.* Hence Rashi's statement could be interpreted both ways. We preferred to render: "From His (Divine) Name" for two reasons: 1) A letter from God's Name would signify God's protection of Cain, and presumably the beasts stood in awe of this protection. 2) Targum Jonathan says so explicitly.

Cain's fear that on account of his sin the beasts would no longer fear him, is in line with Rashi's comment on 1:26 that if man is unworthy he will descend even *lower* than the animals, and the beasts will rule over him. Man deserves a privileged status as ruler of the animal kingdom only as

---

[39]Targum Jonathan and *Pirke de Rabbi Eliezer*—Chapter 22.

long as he fulfills his mission of abiding by God's will, as expressed in the Torah. If he fails to do that, this privilege is taken away from him. Being by nature weaker than most beasts, man can be ruled and even killed by them!

4:19 *Va'yikach lo Lemech*—"Lemech took for himself."

RASHI: The Torah did not have to mention all this (about Lemech's wives), except to teach us from the end of the story (of Lemech), that God kept His promise that: "Revenge shall be taken of Cain after seven generations" (4:24). Lemech arose, after he had begotten children and thus had raised the seventh generation (from Cain) and killed Cain. That is what he (meant when he) said: I have killed a man by wounding him" (4:23, namely: I have killed Cain, etc.).

COMMENT: Since Torah is *"instruction, teaching,"* why was it necessary to mention that Lemech took two wives, and to give their names, etc.? According to the pattern of verse 18, it should have stated simply: "And Lemech begot Yuval, etc." What lesson could be learned from the story of Lemech's wives? Rashi answers that for the sake of the *end* of the story, from which we learn an *important lesson,* namely that God kept His promise that revenge would be taken after seven generations, the *entire* story of Lemech and his wives is related.

If God does *not* punish for a sin immediately, it does *not* mean that the sin is "forgotten and forgiven," but that sometimes punishment is deferred—except when a person repents, in which case punishment is rescinded altogether.

4:26 *Az huchal*—"Then it was begun."

RASHI: (The word *huchal*—"it was begun") is an expression of "profaneness" (*chulin*), namely: People began calling the names of men and the names of idols by the name of God, making them into idols, and calling them (men and idols) "gods."[40]

COMMENT: According to Rashi's interpretation, this verse serves as a prelude to the story of the Flood, giving one of the reasons for its occurrence. The genealogy that follows in Chapter 5 is also an introduction to the Flood

---

[40]Targum Jonathan; Gen. *Rabbah* 23.

story in that it shows the origin of the principal character of the Flood account—Noah.

That people should call *themselves* gods and also worship other people and idols could not be tolerated for very long. God and the Torah, being the epitome of truth could not allow such a momentous theological error to endure. Such corrupt beliefs *had* to be eradicated. Hence the Flood had to come, if only because of the propagation of such erroneous beliefs.[41] Surely it was to prevent such misleading beliefs that Adam and Eve were banished from the Garden of Eden, and prevented from eating from the Tree of Life, as Rashi points out in his comment on 3:22!

5:32 *Ben chamesh mei'ot shanah*—"Five hundred years old."

RASHI: Rabbi Judah asked: Why did all the previous generations have children at the age of one hundred, and Noah at 500? Because the Holy One, blessed be He, said: "If Noah's children are wicked, they will perish in the Flood, and it will grieve this righteous man (Noah). But if they are righteous, I shall have to trouble him to build many more arks (to save all the righteous ones). God therefore kept Noah from having children until he was 500 years old, so that Japheth, the oldest one, would not reach the punishable age (100 years) before the Flood." For it is written: "For when a young boy shall die, he will be a hundred years old" (Isaiah 65:20) meaning: In the future world one will be liable for punishment only after the age of 100 years. And so it was before the giving of the Torah.[42]

COMMENT: One ark *was* sufficient because Noah's sons had children only *after* the Flood (cf. 10:1). However, why did "minors," under the age of 100, die in the Flood (except for Noah's family)? One explanation is that it was clear to God that they would have turned out wicked had they survived the Flood. This is also the reason that Er and Onan died (Gen. 38:6–10) for: "spilling the seed on the ground" even though they were below 100 years of age—because God knew that they would continue committing this sin.[43]

This explanation is unacceptable, because we know from the case of Ishmael that God judges a person *only* in light of his present condition—regardless of his future conduct. If at *present* he is worthy of being saved,

---

[41]But there *were* also other causes, which Rashi mentions in his comments on 6:11–13.

[42]Gen. *Rabbah* 26; Tanchuma Buber parag. 39; Shochar Tov on Psalm 1; *Sanhedrin* 91b.

[43]Divrei David.

his life is spared, even if he will be wicked in the future![44] One must therefore conclude that all who perished in the Flood were *already* wicked at that time.

It would seem that the reason that the punishable age, both before the giving of the Torah and in the future world (in Messianic times) was and will be 100 years old, is because of the length of time people lived and will once again live in the future. Since the prophet Isaiah regards a person who will die at the age of 100 as "a boy" (Isaiah 65:20), this is equivalent to a thirteen-year-old boy in the period between the giving of the Torah until the coming of the Messiah. Since people lived, and after the coming of the Messiah will once again live, for *hundreds of years*, they did not and will not fully mature before the age of 100—and therefore cannot be fully responsible and punishable for their deeds. With the shortening of man's life-span to seventy to eighty years (and longer in rare cases), the process of maturation also quickened. Therefore one can hold a thirteen-year-old boy and a twelve-year-old girl responsible for their actions.

6:6   *Va'yinachem Hashem ki asah—*
"And the Lord consoled Himself that He created."

Rashi: It was a consolation to Him that He created him on *earth*, because if man were one of the *heavenly* beings, he would also have caused *them* to rebel (against God).[45]

Comment: The word *ba'aretz*—"on earth" emphasizes that God's "consolation" derived from the fact that He had made man "on earth," not in heaven. Were man one of the heavenly beings, like the angels, he would have caused them to rebel, too. The expression: "if man were one of the *heavenly beings*" is taken to mean if he were only soul, without body, thus similar to the heavenly beings such as angels. Accordingly, sin is not only due to man's body—the soul sins along with the body.[46]

One must assume that the "heavenly bodies" (angels, *seraphim*, etc.), too, have free will, just as man has—otherwise it would be impossible for man to cause them to rebel against God! The most one can say for the "heavenly beings" is that they are *inclined* to be good (i.e., to fulfill the missions they are charged with) rather than evil. This propensity to do good does not, however, put them on a *higher* level than man. On the contrary, if man, who is *naturally* inclined to do evil (see Gen. 8:21), overcomes his

---

[44]Rashi on Gen. 21:17.
[45]Gen. *Rabbah* 27.
[46]Cf. Gur Aryeh.

inclination and does only good, because that is the will of God, then *he* is on a higher level than the angels, who have no great battle with the "evil inclination." This idea is expressed in the Rabbinic statement: "The righteous are greater than the ministering angels."[47]

6:6   *Va'yitatzev*—"And He grieved."

RASHI: *"Man* became an object of grief to the heart (mind) of God": It entered *into* God's mind to grieve (punish) man. This is how Targum Onkelos translates the verse.

Another explanation of the verse is: *va'yinachem*—"He regretted," that is: The thought of God changed from the attribute of Mercy to the attribute of Judgment. He considered what to do with man, whom He had made on earth, etc.

COMMENT: Since Rashi explained that *va'yinachem*, according to the first explanation, means: "He consoled Himself," then the phrase (*va'yitatzev el libo*) cannot mean: "He grieved in his heart (mind)" because "consolation" and "grief" are mutually exclusive. Therefore Rashi says the phrase is elliptical and we have to supply the word *ha'adam*—"the man," namely: Mankind became an object of grief to His heart, because He decided to grieve—punish man for his corruption.

According to the second explanation that *va'yinachem* means: "He regretted," this does *not* mean that God decided that it was a *mistake* to have created man in the *first place*. This is the meaning of *"regret"* in human experience—wishing one never had done a certain deed. This would be incompatible with God's omniscience, it would imply an imperfection in the creation, that God, so to speak, had made a *mistake!*

Therefore, Rashi says that *nichum* means: "reconsidering what to do"— in the *present* situation what should be done? God never *regretted* that He had created man; it was and remained a good deed. However, since He endowed man with freedom of the will, and man used it to disregard God's Will, and became utterly corrupt, *now* God must do with man differently than originally planned. That is the meaning of Rashi's statement: "The thought of God changed from the attribute of Mercy to the attribute of Judgment." When God created man He planned for him only the best (attribute of Mercy), but provided man followed God's dictates. Now that man had become corrupt by completely disregarding God's Will, he must be punished (attribute of Judgment).

---

[47] *Sanhedrin* 93a: Shochar Tov on Psalm 33:18

6:7   *Mei'adam ad b'heimah*—"Men together with beasts."

RASHI: They (the beasts) too corrupted their ways.[48]

Another explanation (for the destruction of the animals) is: Everything was created for man; when man is destroyed what need is there of animals? (*Sanhedrin* 108a).

COMMENT: According to the first explanation, the beasts and birds, etc., also sinned, by mixing with other species. (According to one opinion in *Sanhedrin* 108a, to which Rashi alludes, even men and beasts had sexual relations!) According to this opinion one must say that the beasts, creeping things, and the birds were also charged with preserving the purity of their species. This may be included in God's command at the time of creation of the beasts and creeping things: "Let the earth bring forth living creatures of *every kind*: cattle, creeping things and land-beasts of *every kind*" (Gen 1:24). The emphasis is on the word "kind," the Hebrew of which *l'minah*— means literally—"according to its kind"; that is, each species should preserve its purity and not intermingle with other species.

Similarly, in the case of the birds, it is stated: "The waters brought forth... and all the winged birds of *every kind*" (1:21), where the Hebrew *l'mineihu*—means—"according to *its* kind," with the same intent.

The animals and birds, etc., *must have* been enjoined not to "intermarry," otherwise they could not be punished, for there is a Torah principle stating: "One does not punish unless one forewarns"[49]—which applies to God no less than to man!

According to the second explanation, it is not *necessary* to say that the beasts, birds, etc., "sinned" (although this is *not* ruled out). However, since their whole *raison d'etre* was for the benefit of man, once man was gone, there would be no need for their continued existence. This underscores the centrality of man in the universe. This centrality is emphasized by the Torah itself.[50]

---

[48]They behaved unnaturally, or immorally, having sexual relations with others than their own species. *Sanhedrin* 108a.

[49]*Sanhedrin* 56b; *Sifrei Shoftim* 18:12.

[50]See above 1:28: "Be fruitful and increase; fill the earth and *master* it; and *rule* the fish of the sea, the birds of the sky, and every living thing that creeps on earth."

Noach

6:13 *Ki mal'ah ha'aretz chamas*—
"For the earth is filled with lawlessness."

RASHI: Their fate was sealed on account of robbery.

COMMENT: One may ask: Why was their fate sealed *only* on account of robbery, and not on account of sexual immorality or idolatry, for which one must allow himself to be killed rather than transgress them, and on account of which punishment of an indiscriminate character comes upon the world— killing good and bad alike (Rashi or this verse)?

One can explain this in accordance with the Rabbinic statement: "Great is peace; for even if Jews worship idols, but there is peace between them, the Holy One blessed be He, says: "I cannot, so to speak, subjugate them...." Therefore, as long as they did not rob and steal, and there was peace among them, they were not punished. But when they began robbing and stealing— which is the cause of quarrels and hatred, they were punished for *all* their previous sins as well.[51]

Furthermore, idolatry is a sin between man and God. God can, so to speak, forgo His honor, if the continued existence of the *entire* humanity is at stake! Likewise, sexual misconduct is practiced clandestinely and does not destroy the fabric of society like stealing and robbery, which are done in public and disrupt the peace. Indeed, peace is so great that the six Orders of the Mishna end with the word "peace," and one of God's names is "Peace!"[52]

7:2 *Ha'tehorah*—"The pure (clean) animal."

RASHI: (Those cattle) which will in the *future* be permitted to Israel as clean; we thus learn that Noah studied the Torah.[53]

---

[51]Cf. Torah *Temimah* here.
[52]Cf. *Vayikra* Rabbah 9:9; *Derekh Eretz Zuta* 11.
[53]Gen. *Rabbah* 26.

Shivah shivah—"Seven pairs."

RASHI: In order that he might offer some of them as a sacrifice when leaving the ark.[54]

COMMENT: One may ask: How did Noah study Torah before it was given? It cannot be said that God Himself taught him Torah, since the Torah was meant specifically for the Jewish People, which did not exist yet.

One might say that Noah applied his faculty of reasoning very vigorously, straining himself in an effort to understand the will of God. Thus he succeeded by his own efforts to arrive at the various commandments of the Torah—among them the commandments relating to sacrifices. This is also the meaning of the statement that the Forefathers studied Torah before it was given.[55]

However, why did Noah take *seven* pairs of each clean animal? (To bring sacrifices that many were not needed—two pairs of each would have sufficed!)

The Maharal in his commentary on Rashi, *Gur Aryeh*, explains that they were to correspond to the six seasons: seed time, harvest, cold, heat, summer, winter, and the seventh pair to propagate the species.

One may explain the concept "corresponding" as a thanksgiving for past kindnesses, namely: Noah thanked the Lord for the continuance of the seasons, without which it would be difficult for man to exist and function—which had indeed ceased during the period of the Flood.[56] It was also a prayer for the future, that the seasons should continue to abide, and never cease as they did during the Flood.

8:2   *Vayisachru ma'ynot t'hom*—
"The fountains of the deep were stopped up."

RASHI: When they were opened it was stated that *all* fountains were opened (7:11), whilst here the word "all" is missing: The reason is that those that were essential to the world were left unstopped, such as the hot springs of Tiberias and their like.[57]

COMMENT: It may be asked: If the world needed the hot springs, such as those in Tiberias and their like, why were they not created in the six days

---

[54]Gen. *Rabbah* 26.
[55]*Yoma* 28b.
[56]Cf. Rashi on 8:23.
[57]Gen. *Rabbah* 33; *Sanhedrin* 108a.

of creation? One answer is that before the Flood these hot springs were *not* essential to the world, because people were healthier and stronger. But *after* the Flood, they became weakened.[58]

To the above one may add: Above 7:12: "The *rain* was upon the earth." Rashi comments: "Whereas below (7:17) it states: The *Flood* was, etc.? But the explanation is this: When He poured down the water *at first*, He made it fall with mercy (gently), in order that, if the people would repent, it would be a rain of blessing; but when they did not repent, it became a (destructive) Flood."

Our sages state: "Every single utterance that came forth from the mouth of the Holy One, blessed be He, *for good*, even if it was on *condition*, He did not rescind it."[59] In the case under discussion: *if* they would repent (condition), the water would have become "rain of blessing." Hence, God is obligated to fulfill the statement He uttered "for good." Therefore, *some* of the nether fountains were channeled to serve for the benefit of mankind, such as the hot springs of Tiberias and their like.

8:7 *Ya'tzo vashov*—"To and fro."

RASHI: It flew in circles round and round the Ark and did *not* go on its errand, for it suspected Noah regarding its mate, as we learn in the *Agadah* of Chapter *Chelek.*[60]

COMMENT: In the Talmud[61] it is stated that Noah called the raven "wicked." However, Rashi does *not* cite Noah's answer to the raven's accusation. It seems, therefore, that Rashi did not consider the raven wicked. On the contrary, his loyalty to his mate exhibited an admirable trait in the raven.

In light of the above, Rashi's comment in the following caption is very fitting, thus: *Ad y'voshet hama'yim*—"until the waters were dried up." The plain sense of this phrase is what it plainly implies (until the waters of the Flood were dried up). But the midrashic explanation is: The raven went to and fro in the world, being kept in readiness for another errand during the time when the rain was withheld (and the waters dried up) in the days of Elijah, as it is said, "And the ravens brought him bread and meat (1 Kings 17:6)." Meaning: Since the raven exhibited an admirable trait of loyalty and love for his mate, it merited to be sent on another meritorious errand— to provide bread and meat for Elijah at the time of the drought—which

---

[58]Cf. *Siftei Chachamim.*
[59]*Berachot* 7a.
[60]*Sanhedrin* 108b.
[61]*Sanhedrin* 108b.

is similar to the Flood in that drought causes a destruction of the crops just as the Flood did.

9:5   *Miyad ish achiv*—"Of every man for that of his brother."

RASHI: Who loves him like a brother and slays him accidentally, will "I" require it, unless he goes into exile (to one of the Cities of Refuge) and prays for forgiveness for his sin. For even one who kills by accident needs atonement; therefore if there are no witnesses (to the deed) to make him liable to banishment, and he does not humble himself (does not flee to the Cities of Refuge, nor asks forgiveness), the Holy One, blessed be He, will require it of him, as our rabbis explain the text: "But God causes it to come to his hand" (Exodus 21:13) in Tractate *Makkot*.[62] "The Holy One, blessed be He causes them (the man who killed by accident and did not flee to the Cities of Refuge, and the man who killed with premeditation) to meet at the same inn, etc. (The former is ascending a ladder, falls upon the latter and kills him and has therefore—the accident having been seen by men—to go into exile to the Cities of Refuge.)"

COMMENT: One who kills by accident requires atonement because he did not take sufficient care that his actions should not cause any damage. Had he been righteous, no accident would have occurred on his account, as is stated: "*No* harm befalls the righteous" (Proverbs 12:21). Rashi states: "As our rabbis explain the text... in Tractate *Makkot*," and only hints at their exegesis briefly: "The Holy One ... causes them to meet at the same inn, etc." without citing the *entire* explanation of the rabbis, because it is *not* the *plain sense* of the verse. At most it is only close to "plain sense."

However, this Midrash is very interesting since it teaches a very important lesson, namely: God does not forego sin *entirely*, whether committed premeditatedly or accidentally, even if the punishment is at times delayed.[63]

9:12   *L'dorot olam*—"For generations forever."

RASHI: The word *l'dorot*—"for generations" is written without a *vav*, or "defective, missing"—implying that "for generations" does not include *all* generations. Or, the sign will be necessary for generations that are "defective, missing" in faith, because there will be generations that will need no

---

[62]10b.
[63]Cf. our interpretation above 4:19, and Introduction rule 3.

sign, since they were completely righteous, such as the generation of
Hezekiah, King of Judah, and the generation of Rabbi Shimon ben Yochai.[64]

COMMENT: Rashi's intention is not that only in these two generations there
were completely righteous people. On the contrary, R. Shimon ben Yochai's
generation was not righteous since he himself declared: "I can absolve the
entire world from judgment,"[65] which Rashi explains to mean: "For my
merit, 'I will carry the burden of their sins' and will absolve them from
judgment." Hence, R. Shimon ben Yochai and his son Rabbi Elazar alone
were the righteous ones.

Moreover, the rainbow was not to be seen in R. Joshua ben Levi's
generation either, which means that they, too, were righteous![66] We must
therefore explain that every generation that has completely righteous people,
as in the generations of R. Shimon b. Yochai, Hezekiah, King of Judah (and
R. Joshua b. Levi), the righteous protect their generation, so that they
should not be liable for annihilation by a Flood. That is why they are not
in need of the rainbow sign.

In Gen. *Rabbah* 35:12 we read: "The word *l'dorot* without the letter *vav*
twice, excluding two generations: that of Hezekiah and that of the Men of
the Great Assembly. R. Hezekiah substitutes the generation of R. Shimon
ben Yochai for that of the Men of the Great Assembly." In the entire Bible
the word *dorot*—"generations" is written with either one or two letters *vav*,
except here where it is without any *vav*!

What is the special merit of these generations? The answer is: Regarding the generation of Hezekiah, it is stated in *Sanhedrin* 94b: "They inves-
tigated (the population as to their knowledge of Torah) from Dan to Be'er
Sheba, but did not find a single ignoramus, etc."—hence all studied Torah.

Regarding the generation of the Great Assembly it was said: "... and
they take an oath with sanctions to follow the teaching of God... and to
observe and do all the commandments of the Lord, our Lord, His rules
and laws" (Nehemiah 10:30). Hence they, too, kept the entire Torah and
did not need a sign of the covenant (rainbow). The generation of R.
Shimon ben Yochai was a generation of apostasy and forced conversion,
whose merit is very great, as is evident from Gen. *Rabbah* 34:9. It was
perhaps for this reason that Rashi preferred to cite as an example the
generation of R. Shimon b. Yochai, rather than that of the Great Assembly:
Also Rashi's generation was one of apostasy and forced conversion, due to
the Crusades, just like R. Shimon b. Yochai's generation. Hence, there was
a great affinity between the two periods. Rashi may well have intended to

---

[64]Gen. *Rabbah* 35.
[65]*Sukkah* 45b.
[66]Cf. *Ketubot* 77b.

console and comfort his own generation, and each generation that suffers from gentile persecutions, by showing that their merit is very great!

11:9   *U'misham hefitzam*—"And from there He scattered them."

RASHI: This teaches that they have no portion in the world to come.[67] Which sin was greater: that of the generation of the Flood or that of the generation of the Dispersion? The former did not rebel (lit. "stretch forth their hand") against God; the latter did rebel against God to war against Him (surely, then, the sin of the generation of the Dispersion was greater) and yet the generation of the Flood were drowned and these (of the Dispersion) did *not* perish from the world?! But (the reason is that) the generation of the Flood were robbers and there was strife among them. Therefore they were destroyed. However, the generation of the Dispersion conducted themselves in love and friendship, as is stated: "They were one people and had one language." You may learn from this how hateful (to God) is strife and how great is peace.[68]

COMMENT: Question: Surely the generation of the Flood also rebelled against God since they worshipped idols? Answer: In the generation of the Dispersion (Tower of Babel) the rebellion was a public one, since they came to war against God. There is no greater desecration of God's Name than that! On the other hand, while the generation of the Flood did indeed worship idols, they did not do so publicly, as a show of rebellion. Hence, the desecration of the Name of God was not as great.

Moreover, since the generation of the Flood were quarrelsome people, society cannot endure in a state of strife—therefore they were annihilated. Whereas at the time of the generation of Dispersion, there was peace in the world, and society was not disintegrating. In such a state of affairs, God could, as it were, "forego" His Honor—i.e., idol worship, which is in essence a rebellion against Him—as long as society remains intact. This, therefore, is the power of peace!

---

[67] *Sanhedrin* 107b.
[68] Gen. *Rabbah* 38.

Lech Lecha

12:8   *O'holo*—"His tent."

RASHI: This word is written with a *hey* at the end (suffix), instead of the usual *vav* (oholo), so that it may be read *o'halah*—"her tent," to intimate that first he pitched a tent for his wife and afterward for himself.[69]

COMMENT: Why did Abram have two tents, one for himself and one for his wife? One can readily understand in the case of Leah and Rachel, who were rivals to each other, that for the sake of household peace, and for modesty, it was necessary that each wife should have her own tent—as is evident from Gen. 31:33. But Abram, who in the meantime had only one wife, should not have needed more than one tent? Moreover, what lesson does Rashi teach us with the statement that Abram pitched his wife's tent before his own?

The answer to the above questions is that Rashi (and the verse) comes to teach us several lessons: First, a great measure of modesty prevailed in the relationship between Abram and Sara, and therefore they needed two tents. For there are times when a woman is shy even in the presence of her husband, especially during her menstrual period. Now, since Abram took very seriously his wife's feelings, he pitched two tents—one for himself, the other for Sara.

Second, the verse teaches us the moral expressed by the Psalmist: "Every honorable princess dwelling within" (Psalms 45:14), namely: a Jewish princess stays within and does not roam the streets.

Third, Rashi teaches us that Abram honored his wife more than himself; therefore he pitched her tent before his own. This deed served as an instruction to Abram's descendants, as the Talmud states that a man is obliged to love his wife as much as himself, but honor her even more than himself.[70]

---

[69]Gen. *Rabbah* 39.
[70]See *Yevamot* 62b, end.

13:13   *Ra'im va'chataim*—"Evil and sinful."

RASHI: "Evil"—in their persons (bodies); "and sinful"—with their wealth.[71]

COMMENT: The Talmud *Sanhedrin* 109a states: "Rabbi Judah said: 'evil' means: in their bodies (persons), as is written: 'And how can I do this most wicked thing';[72] 'and sinners' means: with their wealth, as it is written: 'and you shall incur guilt.'"[73] In a *Baraita* we have learnt: "evil—with their wealth," as is written: "and you will be mean to your needy brother and give him nothing." (Deut. 15:9 in context of charity); "and sinners—in their persons" (bodies), as is written: "and I will have sinned to God" (Gen. 39:9 in the matter of Potiphar's wife).

The above controversy is explained as follows: It is agreed by all that the latter half of the verse adds a graver sin. However, R. Judah holds that sinning in monetary matters is graver, because he is thereby evil both to God and to people. Whereas the *Baraita* holds that money one can return to its rightful owner, whereas a sin with one's *body* cannot be rectified— hence it is worse.[74]

Targum Onkelos holds like the *Baraita* that "evil" refers to money and "wicked, sinners" refers to their bodies. Perhaps the converse is true: The *Baraita* holds like Onkelos, who may have preceded this *Baraita* in time.

Rashi, however, cites as "plain sense" the opinion of R. Judah in the Talmud, because he was a later authority in accordance with the rule: "The law is like the later ones" (= the later [or: latest] authorities).[75] We see from this that this rule is applicable not only in matters of law, but even in regard to homiletical exegesis of the text![76]

14:23   *Im michut v'ad s'roch na'al*—
"So much as a thread or a sandal-strap (tie)."

QUESTION: What really is the difference between "a thread" and a "sandal-strap" (tie); surely they serve a similar purpose?

---

[71] *Sanhedrin* 109a; cf. also Onkelos and Gen. *Rabbah* 41.
[72] To lie with Potiphar's wife, Gen. 39:9.
[73] In regard to delaying the payment of a vow, and regarding the withholding of wages from a hireling – which are monetary matters; cf. Deuteronomy 23:22, 24:15.
[74] See *Torah Temimah*.
[75] See: *Talmudic Encyclopedia*, Vol. 9, Colls. 341–45 for the application of this principle and numerous citations.
[76] Our explanation obviates Mizrachi's objection to Rashi. See also *Gur Aryeh*.

ANSWER: "A thread" (*chut*) refers to some head-cover[77]—a kind of turban or "kafia" that the Arabs wear to this day—which is tied with a thread. Accordingly Abram is telling the King of Sodom: "I will not take anything from you—from head to foot."

One may further explain the phrase in light of the well-known talmudic statement that in the merit of Abram's statement: "So much as a thread"— *michut*, the Jewish People received the precept of "fringes—*tzitzit*," which is made of "threads"; and in the merit of "a sandal strap" we received the mitzvah of tefillin (phylacteries, whose straps are akin to sandal-straps or ties).[78] By this exegesis Abram is telling the King of Sodom: "I do not wish to receive *mitzvot*-precepts by means of you: 'I shall not take anything that is yours.'" Rather, everything has to come through my own merit![79]

15:5   *Va'yotzey oto hachutzah*—"He took him outside."

RASHI: The plain sense is that He brought him outside his tent to see the stars. But its Midrashic explanation is: He told him: "Go out (= give up) from your astrological speculations—that you have seen by the planets that you will not raise a son. Abram (your old name) may not have a son, but Abraham will have a son. Sarai will not give birth, but Sarah will give birth. I will give you other names and your destiny (*mazal*—planet—luck) will change."

Another explanation: He took him out of the terrestrial sphere, and raised him above the stars. This is why the verse uses the term *habeit* = "*look down*"—from above downward.

COMMENT: One may ask: How will their destiny change by merely giving them different names; is there, God forbid, magic involved in the change of names? The above can be answered by realizing that assigning a different name really means giving the person a new task, namely: publicizing God's name in *all* the world, not only in Aram. Rashi states explicitly regarding the phrase *av hamon goyim*—"the father of a multitude of nations": that it means, "father to the entire world" (see below 17:5 and Rashi).

Similarly with regard to Sarah, Rashi states: "Sarah in a general sense is her name: she shall be princess over all."[80] Immediately after receiving

---

[77]See Rashi Isaiah 3:18 on *v'ha'shvisim*.

[78]Cf. at length *Chullin* 89a–b.

[79]Although the above interpretation is not, strictly speaking, a commentary on Rashi's comment, it is in the spirit of Rashi's interpretations. Hence, we incorporate it here.

[80]Below 17:15; cf. *Berachot* 13a.

the new name Abraham was commanded regarding circumcision, the meaning of which is that he entered the category of becoming a Jew. We have a rule "Israel has no planet,"[81] namely: The Jewish People is not governed by the planets, but rather God alone determines their destiny. This, therefore, is the meaning of Rashi's statement: "I will give you other names and your destiny will change."

Furthermore, since Abraham and Sarah, so to speak, converted by receiving their new tasks, and with the commandment of circumcision to Abraham, hence: "A gentile who converted is like a newborn baby,"[82] and they are now new people. Therefore their destiny changes.

That giving a new name means appointment to a new task is evident from a number of places, e.g.: "See I have called by name Bezalel son of Uri, etc." (Exodus 31:2, 35:30), at which point he was assigned the task of making the vessels of the Tabernacle. Similarly, "He reckons the number of the stars; to each He gives its name" (Psalms 147:4), meaning: Each star has a specific task in the world (not only that God knows the *number* of all the stars. This would be nothing remarkable; since He created them, obviously, then, He knows their number!).

The task of Abraham and Sarah from now would be to publicize the Name of God in the entire world (not only in Aram). This is also the major task of the Jewish People, as the prophet states: "The people that I formed for Myself, that they might declare My praise" (Isaiah 43:21).

17:1   *Ve'h'yei tamim*—"And be perfect, blameless."

RASHI: Another explanation: At present you lack five organs: two eyes, two ears, and the (sexual) organ. I will add a letter (i.e., the letter *hey*, the numerical value of which is five) to your name (Avram—which equals 243), so that the total of the letters of your name (Avraham) will be 248, as the number of limbs of your body.[83]

COMMENT: The meaning of the phrase: "You lack five organs" is that until now Abram did not have moral control over these five organs. He did not have the power to shut his eyes from seeing evil, or to stop up his ears so as not to listen to gossip, tale-bearing, etc.; he likewise could not control his sexual desire. Now, with the addition of the letter *hey* to his name—which means bestowing moral power—and especially in conjunction with

---

[81] *Shabbat* 156a; *Nedarim* 32a, see Rashi and Maharsha there.
[82] *Yevamot* 22a; *Bechorot* 47a.
[83] *Nedarim* 32b.

the precept of circumcision, which is integrally connected with the name-change—as is apparent from the context—(especially verses 9–10)—he will be in control of these organs, too.

In light of the above, one must understand that circumcision is not only an action affecting the body, but affects also the soul, and gives a Jew the strength to behave morally—specifically with regard to these five organs that are so hard to control. (In a similar vein the Ran writes in *Nedarim* 32b: "The eyes and ears of a person are not in his control, for surely he sees and hears even against his will. But after he (Abraham) was circumcised, God made him King (ruler) even over these—so that he should look at and hear only things that are a mitzvah-commandment, to hear and look.")

17:22   *Mei'al Avraham*—"From (over) Abraham."

RASHI: This is a more fitting expression to use of God and we learn (from it) that the righteous are the Chariot of the Omnipresent God.[84]

COMMENT: God went up *mei'al*—"from above" Abraham suggests that He had previously been "*al*—above" him. It is a more fitting (lit. "clean expression"—*lashon n'kiyah*) expression to say that God (or the angels, cf. Rashi on Gen. 18:2—*nitzavim alav*) was above Abraham than that He was with him or beside him, which may have imparted the impression that God and Abraham are equals—as if one friend is leaving the other. Now that it says *Mei'al Avraham*—"from above Abraham" we get the impression that God governs and leaves at His will. Our Sages learn from *mei'al* and similar expressions such as *v'hinei Hashem nitzav alav*—"Behold, God was standing above him" (28:13), or: *va'ya'al mey'alav E-lohim*—"God went up from above him" (35:13) that there is no intercessor between God and the righteous— that they are the Chariot, the direct bearers of His Glory on earth as are the angels in heaven (cf. Ezekiel Chapter 1).

The import of the idea that "The righteous are the Chariot of the Omnipresent (God)" is as follows: Just as a chariot brings its rider to wherever he wishes to go, so too, the righteous bring God, as it were, to every place in the world. They do so by publicizing God's Name in the world, both by personal example, as well as by instructing the people in the right path. Thus they serve as a "tool, instrument" in the hands of God, much as a chariot serves as an instrument to its rider.[85]

---

[84]Gen. *Rabbah* 47.
[85]Compare *Gur Aryeh.*

Vayeira

18:3   *Va'yomer a-donai im na, etc.*—
"And he said: My Lord, if now, etc."

RASHI: Another explanation is that the word *a'donai* is holy, referring to God: He asked God to wait for him while he ran and invited the travelers. For although this is written after: "and he ran to meet them," yet the conversation took place beforehand....

COMMENT: This explanation is in line with the statement of the Sages: "Welcoming guests (hospitality) is a greater deed than welcoming the Presence of the *Shechinah*."[86]

One must understand this statement to mean that God himself prefers hospitality to the reception of the *Shechinah*; for if He had not preferred it, there would not be a mitzvah in showing hospitality, but rather a sin, God forbid!

But why, indeed is hospitality greater than receiving the *Shechinah*? The answer is that welcoming the Presence of the *Shechinah* is largely in honor of the person to whom the Almighty in His graciousness deigned to appear, since He Himself stands in no need of such a "welcome"—since: "The entire world is full of His glory!" (Isaiah 6:3).

However, by the act of hospitality a number of good qualities are cultivated, such as: lovingkindness, brotherly love, and friendship among people. This is precisely what God wants, as expressed by the prophet: "He has told you, O man, what is good, and what the Lord requires of you: Only to do justice and to love goodness, and to walk modestly with your God" (Micah 6:8).

Now, when it comes to Abraham's hospitality, there is, in addition to all the above, also publicizing the Name of God in the world, as the rabbis said, that after the guests ate and drank, Abraham would tell them: "Bless Him from whose bounty you ate and drank, etc."[87] Whereas in welcoming the Presence of the *Shechinah* all these qualities do not come to light.

---

[86] *Shabbat* 127a; *Shevuot* 35b and see Maharsha.
[87] *Sotah* 10a; Gen. *Rabbah* 49:43.

19:33   *Va'tashkena, etc.*—"They made (their father drink)."

RASHI: They were provided (by Providence) with wine in the cave, for the purpose of bringing forth from them two nations.[88]

COMMENT: Why did God supply them with wine that caused them to sin with their father; isn't He, so to speak, an accomplice to the sin they committed?!

One must, therefore, say that Lot's daughters had good intentions, namely: the perpetuation of the human race. They thought that the entire world was destroyed, as during the Flood, as Rashi pointed out above in 19:31. They felt they were fulfilling a positive commandment, in accordance with the prophetic dictum: "He did not create it (the earth) a waste; but formed it for habitation" (Isaiah 45:18). Since they intended their act to be "for the sake of Heaven," God showed them gratitude by supplying them with wine in the cave, in order to bring forth from them two nations.

Many of the classic supercommentaries on Rashi[89] see the word *hu*—lit. "He" as alluding to God who supplied them with wine. Compare Rashi's comment on: *va'yishkav imah balailah hu.* "And he lay with her that (*hu*) night," where Rashi comments: "with God's help Issachar was born."

The question may be raised: What was the reasoning of Lot's daughters, due to which they allowed themselves to commit incest? Even if their intention was for the perpetuation of the human race, still, it is in the category of "a precept brought about by committing a sin!" (which is not considered a positive commandment).

It would appear that they held that in this case there was only a precept and the prohibition of incest did not apply, because as Rashi points out: "There is no fatherhood to a non-Jew."[90] Hence, although it was a "shameful" act—as Rashi points out—it was not a capital crime. This may be further elucidated by Rashi's comment on: "If a man marries his sister ... it is a disgrace (Heb. *chesed*—lit. "a kindness") (Leviticus 20:17), Rashi: "The Midrashic explanation of the word *chesed*—a kindness is: Should you ask, "Surely Cain married his sister? The Omnipresent God did an act of kindness (by allowing Cain to marry his sister) in order to settle (lit. "build") His world through Cain, as is stated: "The world was created by kindness" (*chesed*—Psalms 89:3)."[91] We see then, that when it comes to settling the

---

[88]Gen. *Rabbah* 51.
[89]E.g.: *Divrei David; B'er Mayim Chaim; Gur Aryeh; Maskil L'David* to our verse.
[90]Gen. 20:12, comp. Ruth Rabbah 2:14.
[91]See *Sanhedrin* 58b and Rashi there.

world, it is a "kindness" to marry one's sister. The same, therefore, applies to lying with one's father—this is the Will of God![92]

20:11 *Rak ein yir'at E-lohim*—"Surely there is no fear of God."

RASHI: When a stranger comes to a city do people ask him whether he would like to eat or drink, or do they ask him about his wife—"Is this your wife?" or "Is this your sister?"

COMMENT: Question: How is their questioning about his wife proof that "there is no fear of God in this place"? Surely such questions are not asked even on account of human morals and modesty. If so, this is a matter of general morals and good manners, and not necessarily a matter of "fear of God"?

Answer: Even if they had established human morals, they could still have transgressed all imaginable sins, if they had no "fear of God"—which is the only factor that restrains human desires. Indeed, we find many examples in the history of mankind where the most enlightened nations, with the most advanced cultures—such as the German Nazis—exhibited the greatest cruelty known in history—divesting themselves completely of the "image of God" within them—only because they had no "fear of God."

This is also the reason that the social commandments, such as regarding sexual aberrations, theft, falsehood, gossip, tale-bearing, and the like, were commanded by the Torah, namely: to endow them with the authority of Divine commandments. Hence their fulfillment is a matter of "fear of God." For actually one might ask: "Surely these precepts—both the positive and the negative social commands—are mandated by human reason. If so, what need was there for the Torah to command them? The answer is that were it not for explicit commandments to fulfill them, people would find all sorts of excuses not to keep them, such as: Commandment X is not appropriate for our (modern) age; or for this or other situatiosn or conditions. Only a Divine mandate lends them authority at all times, in all places, and in all situations and conditions!"

---

[92]Comp. *Zohar* to our verse: "There was Heavenly help in this act; that He prepared King Messiah to issue from this act," i.e., God arranged the act, so that King Messiah should derive from it, namely from Ruth the Moabite, from whom issued David, the King Messiah.

21:1   *Hashem pakad et Sarah*—"The Lord took note of Sarah."

RASHI: The Torah places this section after the preceding one to teach you that whoever prays for mercy on behalf of another, when he himself is also in need of that very thing (for which he prays on the other's behalf), the one who prays will be answered first (by God), for it is said (at the end of last chapter): "And Abraham prayed for Avimelech and his wife, etc." and immediately afterwards it states here: "And the Lord took note of Sarah"— i.e., He had already remembered her before He healed Avimelech.

COMMENT: Rashi at *Bava Kama* 92a states: "Since the verse does not state *vayifkod et Sarah*—'The Lord took note (with a "*vav* conversive," which converts the future *yifkod*—"He shall take note" to the past: He took note *vayifkod*), but rather: *pakad*—a simple past: "He took note." This means God took note (of Sarah) even before Avimelech.

Rashi's remark is based on the following rule in Hebrew syntax: If a verb in the simple past tense (e.g., *pakad,* —*himtir,*—*yada*) comes after a number of verbs, all of which have the "*vav* conversive," that turns the future into past (such as: *vayitpalel,*—*vayirpa,*—*va'ygaresh,* —*va'yeileidu*), in such a case the meaning of the "simple past" verb is "pluperfect," i.e., the action expressed by the "simple past" verb precedes the last action expressed by the "*vav* conversive." Here the meaning is that the action of the verb *pakad*—"He took note" (remembered), which is a "simple past" precedes in time that expressed by *va'yirpa E-lohim et Avimelech,* namely: Sarah was answered regarding pregnancy before Avimelech's wife and his maid-servants.[93]

One may ask: Why, indeed, is the one who prays for another answered first; surely he prayed for another, not for himself? Answer: He needs to be answered first, in order not to transgress the commandment: "Love your neighbor as yourself" (Levit. 19:18). The emphasis is on "as yourself," namely: A person's love for himself comes before his love for another. Only through self-love can one arrive at love for another. If so, as long as he needs the same things for which he prayed on his friend's behalf, his self-love is not complete—and he cannot arrive at love for his neighbor as himself.

It is an accepted principle that God, in a manner of speaking, keeps the Torah, which the rabbis derived from: "He tells His commands to Jacob, His statutes and rules to Israel" (Psalms 147:19): "Whatever He Himself

---

[93]Compare Rashi above 4:1 on *v'ha'adam yada*; 19:24 *himtir al S'dom.*

does, He tells Israel to do and observe."[94] Therefore, wishing to fulfill the mitzvah: "Love your neighbor as yourself," the Lord must, as it were, answer the prayer's needs first—before He answers the needs of the one prayed for—so that he may arrive at the love of his neighbor as himself—he must be complete first, as explained above.

21:12 Sh'ma bekolah—"Listen to her voice."

RASHI: We may infer from this statement that Abraham was inferior to Sarah in respect to prophecy.[95]

COMMENT: Why, indeed, was Abraham inferior to Sarah in regard to prophecy? One cannot assert that Sarah was more pious than Abraham, for we do not find any of the Sages claiming this. Rather, we should explain it thus: Prophecy (or: "the divine spirit"—Ruach ha-Kodesh) is a capacity above intellect, a kind of intuitive feeling of the truth—beyond intellectual grasp—even of an exceedingly wise man like Abraham.

In the realm of grasping the truth beyond or outside of intellectual means, women's power can be greater than that of men, as is commonly asserted that women have a greater measure of intuition than men. Perhaps one should understand in this light the rabbis' statement: "The Almighty gave a greater degree of understanding to woman than to man,"[96] namely: "Woman has more intuition than man, and the same applies to the divine spirit."

22:13 V'hinei ayil—"And behold a ram."

RASHI: It was prepared for that purpose from the six days of Creation.[97]

COMMENT: From the words "and behold a ram" one may infer that there had been no ram there previously, and it appeared suddenly at a place where it would not normally be. Who, then, brought it here? The rabbis explain that it was predestined for that purpose from "the six days of Creation," a phrase used for many things that are of great significance in

---

[94]Shemot Rabbah 30:9. See there the debate between the Sages and a Roman regarding this question; cf. Vaykira Rabbah, which derives this from Levit. 26:3: "If you will follow My laws and observe My commandments."

[95]Shemot Rabbah 1.

[96]Nidah 45b.

[97]Avot 5, 6.

Jewish history, e.g.: the opening of the earth (which swallowed up Korach, Datan, and Aviram—Numbers Chap. 16); the mouth of the donkey (that rebuked Bilam—Numbers 22:28–30); the Manna (that the Israelites ate in the desert); Moses' staff (with which he performed the signs before Pharaoh); the legendary worm (that cut the stones for the construction of the Temple—the shamir); the tablets of the Ten Commandments, and others. Those, too, were created in the "six days of Creation"—on the Eve of Sabbath at twilight[98]—because: "There is nothing new (namely: no new creation) under the sun."

The special significance of this ram in Jewish history is that on every Rosh Hashanah we invoke the memory of the *Akedah*—the binding of Isaac—before the Lord, by blowing the Shofar, which is made of a ram's horn. We pray to the Lord that in the merit of Abraham and Isaac He should forgive our sins, and inscribe us into the Book of Good Life, as stated in the Midrash.[99]

22:13   *B'karnav*—"By its horns."

RASHI: It was running toward Abraham, but Satan caused it to be caught and entangled among the trees.[100]

COMMENT: The ram was running toward Abraham in order to fulfill the task for which it was created. Satan was entangling it among the trees in order to thwart Abraham's purpose, thinking that, perhaps, when Abraham saw that there was no ram—while he had already gone through all the fatherly pain and bound Isaac, perhaps he would offer up Isaac after all—so that all the pain and bother should not be in vain.

Moreover, Satan may have thought that Abraham would not pay attention to the angel's restraining words, for he would think it was the Satan's scheme (not an angel) in order to make him fail the test. Now that Abraham saw the ram, he understood that the angel's words came from God Himself (and were not Satan's scheme).

Furthermore, one might explain that Satan did not wish that in future generations the Children of Israel should use the ram's horn (Shofar) to invoke the merit of *Akedah* each Rosh Hashanah. I daresay that Satan meant it "for the sake of Heaven": so that Jews should not depend upon the merits of Abraham and Isaac at the time of the *Akedah*, but rather repent and

---

[98]Cf. *Pesachim* 54a, and commentaries to the Talmud.
[99]Gen. *Rabbah* 22:13.
[100]*Pirke de Rabbi Eliezer,* Chapter 31.

improve their behavior—so that they may be inscribed in the Book of Good Life in their own merits each year. Our rabbis taught us, on another occasion, that Satan performs his deeds "for the sake of Heaven"[101]—since Satan, too, is an angel and only performs his mission, on which he was sent by God!

---

[101]See *Bava Batra* 16a: Rabbi Levi said: "Satan and Peninah (Elkana's wife, who teased Chanah and brought her to tears"—cf. I Samuel 1:6–7) meant it 'for the sake of Heaven,' etc."

Chayey Sarah

24:42   *Va'avo hayom*—"I came today."

RASHI: Today I started on my journey and today I arrived here. We may infer from this that the earth (road) shrunk for him (i.e., the journey was shortened in a miraculous manner). Rabbi Acha said: "The (ordinary) conversation of the patriarchs' servants is more pleasing to God than (even) the Torah (religious discourse) of their children; for the chapter of Eliezer (the account of his journey) is repeated in the Torah (i.e., written once as a narrative, and repeated as part of the conversation of the patriarch's servant), whereas many basic principles of the Torah are derived only from slight allusions given in the Text."[102]

COMMENT: Why, indeed, is the conversation of the servants of the patriarchs more pleasing to God than the Torah of their children; what is the import of this statement?

It would appear that the reason for this assertion is that from Eliezer's conversation one can learn a number of moral lessons, e.g.: the importance of kindness, for it was due to this trait *alone* that Eliezer was ready to take Rebecca for Isaac. Also, to what extent one must stay far from an intimation of theft, since Abraham's camels "would go out muzzled to avoid robbery" (Rashi above, verse 10). Another lesson: How careful one must be in choosing a wife. Another lesson: that we should thank God for good news (Rashi below, verse 52)—and other good qualities possessed by Rebecca and Eliezer.

Conversely "the Torah of the children" deals largely with practical legal matters, and much less with matters of ethics and good manners—with the exception of a few notable texts, such as: the Tractates *Avot, Derech Eretz,* and the like. From the point of view of moral lessons and manners, one can learn more from the story of Eliezer than from a chapter of equal length in the rest of the Torah.

---

[102]Gen. *Rabbah* 60.

24:67   *Ha'ohelah Sarah imo—*
"Into the tent of his mother Sarah."

RASHI: He brought her into the tent and she became exactly like his mother Sarah—that is to say (the structure of these three words, lit. "into the tent—his mother Sarah," and *not*: "to the tent *of* his mother Sarah" signifies as much as): "and, behold, she *was* Sarah, his mother!" For while Sarah was living, a light (candle) had been burning (in the tent) from one Sabbath Eve to the next Sabbath Eve; there was a blessing in the dough (a miraculous increase), and a cloud was always hanging over the tent (as a Divine protection)—but since her death all these had stopped. However, when Rebecca came they all reappeared.[103]

COMMENT: The three blessings that reappeared with Rebecca's arrival correspond to the three precepts that women are obliged to perform, i.e.: 1) A candle burning from Sabbath Eve to Sabbath Eve corresponds to candle lighting, 2) A blessing in the dough corresponds to the precept of Challah, 3) A cloud hanging over the tent corresponds to the observance of the laws of menstruation (*Nidah*): "tent" alludes to marital relations, as stated at the time of giving the Torah: "Return to your tents," meaning to your wives, but: "You stand here with Me" (Deuteronomy 5:27–28)—from which the rabbis learn that Moses was commanded by God to separate from his wife.[104]

Furthermore, the cloud hanging over the tent symbolizes the presence of the *Shechinah* (Divine Presence) in their house, reminiscent of the rabbis' statement: "Man and wife, if they merit it—the Divine Presence resides among them, etc."[105] The sign of the cloud hanging over the tent is that the same "household peace" that prevailed between Abraham and Sarah, will now prevail between Isaac and Rebecca, and she deserves all the blessings that came in Sarah's merit. In the Midrash[106] a fourth matter is mentioned: "As long as Sarah was alive, her house was wide open (to guests)." Rashi omitted this because it is not a precept particular to women as the first three are.[107]

---

[103]Gen. *Rabbah* 60:16.
[104]See Rashi on Numbers 12:8.
[105]*Sotah* 17a; *Pirke de Rabbi Eliezer* 12; *Pesikta Zutarti* Gen. 2:23.
[106]Gen. *Rabbah* 60:16.
[107]Further reasons cf. *Gur Aryeh, Levush Haorah.*

Toldot

26:2 *Al teireid Mitzraymah*—"Do not go down to Egypt."

RASHI: Because he intended to go down to Egypt as his father had gone down in time of famine, God said to him: "Do *not* go down to Egypt for you are a burnt-offering without blemish, and residence outside the Holy Land is not befitting you."[108]

COMMENT: A burnt-offering without blemish is in the category of "holy of holies," whereas countries outside of Israel are defiled on account of the idols abounding in them, and in the days of Yosi ben Yoezer and Yosi ben Yochanan[109], the rabbis decreed that the Lands of the Nations be considered as defiled[110]—whereas they did *not* decree defilement upon the Land of Israel. Therefore, it is not befitting that Isaac who was "holy of holies" should go out to a place of defilement.

One might even say that Isaac was in the category of High Priest who is the holiest of all, regarding whom it is stated: "He shall not go outside the sanctuary, etc." (Leviticus 21:12). Therefore Isaac was compared to a "burnt-offering," which belongs entirely to God (except for the skin), unlike other offerings of which the owner and the priest partake. The Land of Israel by comparison to other countries is like the Sanctuary!

---

[108]Gen. *Rabbah* 64:3.
[109]Second century B.C.E. in the time of the Hasmoneans.
[110]*Shabbat* 14b.

Vayeytzey

28:17 *V'zeh sha'ar hashamayim—*
"And this is the gate to heaven."

RASHI: A place of prayer where their prayers would ascend to heaven. The Midrash states that the Heavenly Temple is situated immediately opposite the Earthly Temple.[111]

COMMENT: Question: Why do they need a Temple in heaven; do they offer sacrifices in Heaven? It may be explained by the Talmudic statement: "Rav Gidal said in the name of Rav: This verse (II Chronicles 2:3, 'a permanent duty upon Israel') refers to the built altar upon which Michael, the Great Prince (the angel Michael) offers a sacrifice" (daily).[112]

Tosafot in *Menachot* 110a cite two opinions as to the nature of Michael's sacrifice: 1) He offers up the souls of the righteous and 2) Sheep of fire. Whatever the meanings of these "sacrifices" are, we learn from this that there are a Jerusalem, Temple, and "sacrifices," of sorts, in Heaven—even if they are *not* the same kind as ours below. We cannot here enter into a discussion as to the nature of Michael's "sacrifices."[113]

Another plausible explanation is that the Midrash refers to prayer and *not* to actual sacrifice of animals. According to King Solomon's prayer, the major *original* task of the Temple was to serve as a center for prayer for the Jewish People, as is stated, "May Your eyes be open day and night toward this House ... may You heed the supplications of Your servant and Your people Israel, which they will offer toward this Place..." (I Kings 8:29–30). That the Heavenly temple is *opposite* the Earthly Temple means that the angels and the "heavenly entourage" (souls of the pious, etc.) pray at the

---

[111]Hence the Temple at Jerusalem = Bethel is, in this sense, "the gate" to the "Heavenly Temple"—Gen. *Rabbah* 69.

[112]*Menachot* 110a. Compare *Chagigah* 12b: "Zevul wherein are Jerusalem and the Temple and an altar, and Michael, the Great Prince, stands and offers a sacrifice upon it."

[113]See, however, *Agadot HaMaharsha* in *Chagigah* 12b and *Menachot* 110a.

same place and at the same time that the Jews pray. What do they pray?
That the prayers of the Jewish People should be accepted by their Heavenly
Father. They also sing praises to the Lord, and their praises are similar to
the praises sung by the Jewish people in their prayers.

Vayishlach

32:16   *G'malim meinikot u'vneihem shloshim*—
"Thirty milch camels with their colts."

RASHI: Milch camels thirty and their colts with them (i.e., the word *shloshim*—
"thirty" is connected with *g'malim*—"camels," not with *u'vneihem*—"their
colts"—the number of which is not stated). A midrashic explanation of
u'vneihem is that it is the same as *u'vana'eihem*—"their builders" (those that
build them up), i.e., one male for each female. However, because the camel
is chaste in its intimate relations, Scripture does not state this plainly.[114]

COMMENT: According to "plain sense" the meaning of *u'vneihem* is literal:
"and their sons." Hence there were thirty mothers and thirty sons. According to the Midrash there were altogether thirty: fifteen males and fifteen
females. From the fact that the Torah did not mention the male camels
explicitly, we learn to what extent the Torah is considerate of the dignity
of creatures, thus: If animals—which are *not* normally bashful or embarrassed—nevertheless, since camels *are* chaste, the Torah is considerate of
their dignity—people who are created in God's image, and more especially
Jews, "the bashful ones,"[115] all the more so must one take great care to
consider their dignity and not embarrass them!

32:30   *Lamah zeh tish'al*—"Why do you ask?"

RASHI: We have no fixed names; our names change, all depends upon the
errand with which we are charged.[116]

---

[114]Gen. *Rabbah* 76—but employs a term from which it may be inferred.
[115]Cf. *Yevamot* 79a: "this nation (Israel) possesses three signs: they are merciful,
bashful, and act kindly."
[116]Gen. *Rabbah* 78.

COMMENT: Giving a name sometimes means assigning a task, as noted above on 15:5 regarding the change of Avram and Sarai's names to Avraham and Sarah; likewise in the statement: "See I have *called by name* Bezalel, etc." (Exodus 31:2, 35:30) at which point he was charged with making the vessels of the Tabernacle. Similarly: "He reckons the number of stars; to each He gives a name" (Psalm 147:4), the meaning of which is that each star has a specific task.

Accordingly the names of the angels are determined by the mission they are to accomplish during each errand. All this is true of the angels that are created for the moment, for the sake of fulfilling certain tasks. However, there are certain great angels, who are charged with *fixed* tasks, and therefore have fixed names, e.g.: Michael, whose main task is to serve as "guardian angel" of the Jewish People.[117]

32:32   *Va'yizrach lo hashemesh—*
"And the sun shone for him."

RASHI: This is an expression that people use: "When we reached such-and-such a place the dawn broke upon us." This is the "plain sense" (of this phrase). But the Midrash explains that *vayizrach lo* means "for *his* need"— to heal his lameness, as you read (a similar metaphor) in the verse: "The sun of righteousness with healing in its wings" (Malachi 3:20). The hours that the sun had set *before* its time for his sake when he left Beer-Sheba (comp. 28:11 Rashi), it now rose before its time for his sake.

COMMENT: The midrashic explanation can be understood in light of the Rabbinic statement: "For *this* is the whole of mankind" (Ecclesiastes = *Kohelet* 12:13), Rabbi Elazar said: "The Holy One Blessed Be He, said: 'The entire world was created *for this one* (who is God-fearing).' " Rabbi Abba bar Kahana said: "This one is equal (in value) to the entire world." Rabbi Shimon ben Azai; but others say Rabbi Shimon ben Zoma said: "The entire world was created to serve as *company* for this one (the God-fearing)."[118]

Who is as God-fearing as Jacob was? Hence, it is understandable that the sun set before its time for his sake—and *now* rushed to rise before its time for his sake. However, one must understand that in all this special "effort" of the sun, no damage was caused to anyone else, otherwise there would be no justice in it—and surely the Lord is described as: "A Just and Righteous One is He!" (Deuteronomy 32:40).

---

[117]See Daniel 10:21, 12:1.
[118]Cf. *Berachot* 6b.

Vayeyshev

38:26   *Mimeni*—"From Me."

RASHI: *("From Me")* is she pregnant. Our rabbis, of blessed memory, explained that a *Bat-Kol* (= voice from Heaven) came forth and said: *mimeni*—"from Me and through Me" (God) have these things happened: Because she was modest while she was in her father-in-law's house, I decreed that kings shall descend from her, and I have decreed that I will raise kings from the tribe of Judah.[119]

COMMENT: Question: What is the connection between Tamar's modesty and kingship that issued from her as a reward for it? This can be explained as follows: One of the precepts for the king to follow is: "He shall write for himself a copy of this Torah... and let him read it all his life... so that he may not act haughtily toward his fellows (brothers)" (Deuteronomy 17:18–20). Hence, the reward is "measure for measure": Since she was modest, she merited that kings should descend from her, whose duty is: "that he may not act haughtily toward his fellows."

Moreover, Tamar's modesty serves as an assurance that the kings who will descend from her will also behave modestly and humbly—since they will inherit her traits. However, there is no certainty in the matter, since every person has freedom of the will. Therefore, the Torah enjoined the king to have a Torah written for him, and to read in it all his life. We have here an example of what the rabbis dubbed: "through me and you the matter will be decided."[120] Applied here the meaning is: In the merit of *both* the inheritance of the traits of modesty and humility from Tamar, *and* by writing a Torah that he will read all his life—he will be capable of "not acting haughtily toward his brothers."

---

[119] *Sotah* 10b; Gen. *Rabbah* 85:11.
[120] *Pesachim* 88a; *Megilla* 14a.

40:23   *Va'yishkacheihu*—"But he forgot him."

RASHI: (But he forgot him) afterward. Because Joseph depended on him that he should remember him, he was doomed to remain in prison for two years. So it is said: "Happy is the man who puts his trust in the Lord and does not turn to (*re'havim*) the arrogant (Psalm 40:5), i.e., he does not trust in the Egyptians who are called arrogant.[121]

COMMENT: By telling the cupbearer: "Mention me to Pharaoh and take me out of this house" (= prison, 40:14), Joseph showed him that he relies on *him* entirely. Hence, he did not mention God's hand in saving him from prison. For a righteous man like Joseph this is considered a desecration of God's Name, and therefore he was punished to stay an extra two years in prison. For an ordinary person Joseph's request would *not* be considered a sin, as we have a rule that one is not to rely on miracles—one must do whatever one can without resorting to miracles. Thus the rabbis explained the verse: "The Lord your God will bless you *in all the works of your hands*": (Deuteronomy 14:29): "If man does, the works of his hands are blessed; if man does *not* do, the works of his hands are *not* blessed."[122]

However, a man like Joseph should have at least told the cupbearer that he puts his *main* trust in God, and he is making the cupbearer *only* God's *agent* in his salvation. Since Joseph did *not* say so, he was punished.

---

[121]Cf. Isaiah 30:7, where *rahav*—"arrogance" refers to Egypt.
[122]Comp. *Shochar Tov* on Psalm 136 with minor changes in wording; *Yalkut Shimoni* Deut. 808: "If man does, he is blessed; if not, he is not blessed."

Mikeyts

41:48 *Ochel s'dei ha'ir asher s'vivotehah natan b'tochah*—
"He put in each city the grain of the fields around it."

Rashi: For every district preserves its own produce; and people put amongst the grain some of the earth (in which it grew) and this prevents the grain from decaying.[123]

Comment: One may ask: "What power does the earth have to prevent the grain from decaying?"

Answer: There are chemical ingredients in the ground that preserve the fruit and grain. This fact is well-known in the food industry, which uses these preservative ingredients, and adds them to hundreds, and thousands, of food products! There is hardly a food product today that does not contain these additives, which are designed to lengthen the shelf-life or the freshness of the food product.

The Torah teaches us here that there is no need whatever to use *artificial* food preservatives, made of various chemical materials, produced by man in an entirely unnatural manner. There are completely *natural* means that can be used—as Joseph used them![124]

---

[123]Gen. *Rabbah* 90.
[124]See, however, *Levush Haorah*, who missed this point entirely, and amends the reading in Rashi unnecessarily; comp. also A. Berliner in *Zechor LeAvraham*.

Vayigash

45:9   *Va'alu el avi*—"And go up to my father."

RASHI: (He said "go up") because the land of Israel is higher than all the countries.[125]

COMMENT: One must understand this statement from a *spiritual* point of view, since from a *geographic*, physical point of view there are many countries that are *higher* than Israel. However, from a spiritual point of view Israel, which is the "chosen land," is indeed higher than all other countries. In this vein, too, the prophets Isaiah and Micah said about the Temple Mount: "*All nations* will stream to it... for from Zion will the Torah come forth, etc." (Isaiah 2:2–3; Micah 4:1–2).

46:6   *Asher rachshu b'eretz K'naan*—
"That they acquired in the Land of Canaan."

RASHI: But whatever he acquired in Padan-Aram he gave to Esau in payment for his share in the Cave of Machpelah. He said: "The possessions I obtained outside of Israel are of no value to me." It is to this that the words *asher kariti li*—"which I have *bought* for myself" (below 50:5) refer, meaning: "I obtained for myself by means of a *kri*—"pile." He placed before Esau piles of gold and silver like a heap *kri* and said to him: "Take these."[126]

COMMENT: In what way is the property acquired in Israel different than that acquired abroad? The answer is that the word *r'chush*—"property" as used *here* refers mainly to livestock and not to chattel. Since sheep, cattle, and other livestock get their sustenance from the ground; if, then, they grazed

---

[125] *Pesikta Zutarta.*
[126] In exchange for your share in the Cave of Machpelah—*Tanchuma.*

on the ground of Israel, they absorbed the holiness of Israel into their bodies—and surely the sages stated: "the air of Israel makes one wise and healthy."[127] Therefore Rashi continues: "He placed before Esau piles of gold and silver like a heap *kri* and said to him: 'Take these,' " in order to emphasize that Jacob did not want the gold and silver acquired abroad, because they did not absorb the air of Israel.

In *Pirke de Rabbi Eliezer*, Chapter 38, we read: "Esau said to Jacob: Let us divide everything that father left us into two parts, and I get the first choice since I am the first born." Said Jacob (to himself): "This wicked man (Esau) will not be satisfied with all the riches, as is stated: 'and his eye is never sated with riches'" (*Kohelet* 4:8). What did Jacob do? He divided into two parts: *All that his father left—one part, and Israel was the second part....* Now, Esau took whatever his father left, but Israel and the Cave of Machpelah he gave to Jacob, etc." According to this Jacob did not want even chattel (gold and silver) from *Israel* because they did not absorb the air of Israel, as stated above.[128]

---

[127]Comp. *Bava Batra* 158b and commentaries thereto.
[128]Comp. *Sotah* 13a; *Bereshit Rabbah* 100:5; *Shemot Rabbah* 31:8, *Tanchuma Vayechi* (Targum Jonathan *Vayechi* 50:5).

Vayechi

48:16   *V'yidgu*—"May they teem like fish."

RASHI: Like fish which are fruitful and multiply, and the evil eye cannot affect them.[129]

COMMENT: Question: What is the nature of "the evil eye" that harms a person? Either/or: If a person is liable for punishment on account of his sins, then he is liable even without the effect of "the evil eye"; if he is guiltless, then no amount of "evil eye" ought to harm him!

One might explain that the "evil eye" is a type of prayer: If the person who casts an evil eye is greatly distressed on account of another's great wealth or achievements, or on account of the other's successful children, and the like; if at the same time, the one who casts the evil eye is also a pious person and has many merits—then God does not wish to behold his anguish, and He deprives the other of the things that caused the righteous man all this anguish: sometimes it is his wealth at other times his children, etc.

48:19   *Gam hu yih'yeh l'am v'gam hu yigdal—*
"He too shall become a people, and he too shall be great."

RASHI: For of him will be born Gideon, through whom the Holy One, Blessed Be He, will perform a miracle.[130]

---

[129] *Berachot* 20a.
[130] *Tanchuma Vayechi* 6.

> *V'ulam achiv hakaton yigdal mimenu*—
> "However, his younger brother shall be greater than him."

RASHI: For Joshua will be born of him, who will make Israel to inherit the Land (of Canaan), and he will teach Israel Torah (ibid).

COMMENT: One may ask: Why did Rashi not explain that "his younger brother shall be greater than he" in that Joshua would one day make the sun and moon stand still (see Joshua, Chapter 10), which is a greater miracle that the one God will work for Gideon?

One may explain that the answer lies in the very question: True, Joshua's was a greater miracle than Gideon's—which was also a *miracle*, and not the result of Gideon's (spiritual) power. Yet making Israel inherit the land and teaching Torah to an entire People, are much greater merits—since these are *not* in the realm of miracles, but rather achievements for which one needs tremendous spiritual powers and great merits. Not everyone can hope to achieve these; to such an extent is this true, that even Moses was not granted both accomplishments (to teach Torah to the Jewish People *and* make them inherit the Land of Canaan)!

49:1 *V'agidah lachem*—"That I may tell you."

RASHI: He wished to reveal to them the end (of Israel's exile), but the *Shechinah* departed from him, and he began to speak of other things.[131]

COMMENT: Why didn't God want Jacob to reveal to his sons the end of the exile? One may ask similarly regarding the statement by the rabbis: "May the bones of those who calculate the end of the exile blow out (their marrow) rather wait for him."[132]

This may be explained as the Gemara there continues: "For people would say: Since the end (of the calculation) arrived and Messiah did not *come*, he won't come anymore. Rather wait for him." Meaning: Since Messiah's coming depends on repentance and good deeds, if people would calculate his coming and he would *not* come on the date that was calculated—because that generation was not worthy of him—people will despair altogether of future redemption and will say: "There is no Messiah and no future world," God forbid! If so, what need is there for us to toil in learning Torah and keeping its commandments? "Eat and drink, for tomorrow we die" (Isaiah 22:13)—there is *nothing* after death!

---

[131]Gen. *Rabbah* 98.
[132]Messiah, patiently. See *Sanhedrin* 97b and Maharsha thereto.

Such a trend of thought could cause, God forbid, a complete throwing off of the yoke of Torah and commandments—or, at least, profound sadness—which in itself is a grave sin, on account of which numerous curses visit Israel, as stated: "Because you did not serve the Lord your God in joy and gladness over the abundance of everything" (Deut. 28:47). In order to preclude such developments, "the end" was hidden.

49:7 Achalkeim b'Yaakov—"I will divide them in Jacob."

RASHI: I will separate them from each other in that Levi will not be counted among the tribes; thus they will be divided. Another explanation is: There are no poor, "scribes," and teachers of small children but from Shimon— so that they may be scattered (among the tribes). Whereas the tribe of Levi he caused to go around to the threshing floors to collect *Terumah* and *tithes*—he allotted his dispersion in a (more) honorable manner.[133]

COMMENT: Both explanations are necessary: According to the first, the word *b'Yaakov*—"in Jacob" does not fit (since Levi is *not* counted among the tribes of Jacob). According to the second explanation, "in Jacob" means that both tribes are scattered among the dwellings of Jacob (the tribes). However, the difficulty with the second explanation is the word *achalkeim*— "I will *divide* them"; he should have used the expression *afazreim*—"I will scatter them."

Shimon was punished more than Levi because he was the initiator in the sale of Joseph; he said to Levi: "Here comes the dreamer, etc." (above 37:19). We likewise find that Joseph treated Shimon more harshly: "He took from among them Shimon, etc." (42:24) "and not Levi."[134]

Sofrim—"Scribes" are the teachers of the nation, i.e.: the leaders of the People; whereas "teachers of small children"—*melamdei tinokot* are literally teachers of young children. Regarding Levi (above 29:34) Rashi wrote: "He called his name Levi." I wonder, in regard to all of them (the other children) it says: "She called" (the mother named the children), but with this one, it states "He called" (masculine)? There is a Midrash *Agadah* (homiletical Midrash) in the Book of Deuteronomy stating that God sent Gabriel (the angel), who brought him (Levi) to Him, and He (God) gave him this name (Levi) and gave him the twenty-four priestly gifts—and because He *livahu*—*accompanied* him with gifts He called him "Levi" (i.e., the one who was accompanied).

---

[133]Gen. *Rabbah* 98:5, 99:6.
[134]Comp. *Maskil LeDavid.*

One may ask: "If God gave him the twenty-four priestly gifts at his birth, how can one say that *Jacob* caused Levi to go around to the threshing floors to collect *Terumah* and *tithes*, which are *part* of the twenty-four gifts?" The answer is: Indeed, God gave the tribe of Levi the twenty-four gifts, and although the Levites began serving (in the Tabernacle and later in the Temple) instead of the first born only *after* the gold-calf episode, nevertheless, since God knows everything in *advance*, He knew already at the time of Levi's birth that he will receive twenty-four gifts. This is the meaning of: "He accompanied him with gifts."

Should you ask: "If God knew all of this in advance, then the firstborns *had* to sin with the golden calf and the Levites *had* to substitute for them; for should they *not*—because they had free will—then God's 'knowledge' would have turned out to be *faulty*, God forbid?"

This is no question, for it's an accepted truth that God's knowledge is unlike that of humans. Human beings have a past, present, and future; no person can think in concepts of time other than these. Whereas in God's frame of reference, the past, present, and future all occur simultaneously. Hence, whatever is to us in the "future," from God's point of view it is happening *now*, or already *happened*. The same applies to the human "past": as far as God is concerned the deed or event is occurring *right now!*

Such a grasp of "time" is beyond human ken, since man cannot function or fathom a type of "time" that transcends the tenses: past, present, and future. Therefore, although God foresaw the episode of the golden calf and that the Levites will one day substitute for the firstborns, nevertheless this does *not* contradict the principle of "freedom of the will"; God saw the event as if it had *already* occurred, even though in human conception of time at the birth of Levi, the event (golden calf, etc.) was still in the distant future.[135]

49:33 Va'yigva va'yeyasef—
"He expired and was gathered (to his people)."

Rashi: But "death" is not mentioned in his case; therefore our Teachers (the Sages) said: "Jacob, our father, did not die" (or: "is not dead").[136]

Comment: The Talmud asks: "Rav Nachman asked R. Isaac: 'Was it in vain that the eulogizers eulogized, and the embalmers embalmed Jacob (since

---

[135]Comp. Maimonides' approach to this question in *Laws of Repentance* 5:5. See also Ravad's objections and the defense of Rambam by the *Kesef Mishneh* [R. Joseph Caro]. See also: Tosafot Yom Tov to *Avot* 3:15; Responsa of Ribash No. 188.
[136]*Taanit* 5b.

he did *not* die)?' He said to him: 'I learn it (that Jacob did not die) from a verse: 'But you, have no fear, My servant Jacob… for I will deliver you from far away, and your children from their land of captivity, etc.' (Jeremiah 30:10)—he is compared to his children, just as his children are alive (the Jewish People is alive always), so also he is alive" (*Taanit* 5b). Rashi there explains: "Just as when He will gather Israel from the land of their captivity, He will gather the living (not the dead), so too is he (Jacob) alive, i.e., *God will bring him (Jacob) into exile so that he may redeem his children,* as we find in Egypt: 'And Israel saw,' which we interpret as '*Grandfather Israel.*' As regards the embalmers having embalmed him—he *seemed to them* as dead" (but *really he was not dead*).

Tosafot at *Tannit* 5b writes: "Jacob, our father, did not die—it appears so since it states: 'He *expired,*' but does not state: 'He *died.*' This is also apparent from *Sotah* 13a where it is explained that Jacob opened his eyes before his burial and laughed at his brother Esau, who was there."

"Torah Temimah" writes: "Were it not for Rashi's and Tosafot's explanations (see above), I would have said that the meaning of: 'Jacob did not die,' and the comparison: 'Just as his children are alive, etc.' is similar to the statement in *Bava Batra* 116a that *death* is not mentioned in regard to David, because he left behind a son as great as himself. Here, too, because Jacob left behind children that were righteous like himself, therefore death is not mentioned in his case—the rabbis expressed this idea figuratively by stating: 'Jacob, our father, did not die.' But according to Rashi and the Tosafot this Midrash exegetes very slight ancient allusions; it is more in the nature of esoteric allusions than plain sense…."

However, what is the meaning of whoever leaves behind a righteous son, it is as if he did not die; surely he *did* die and how does his son reflect on him? The son is righteous because even before he was born he was exhorted: "Be righteous, and don't be wicked, etc.!"[137]

The meaning is this: The accomplishment of a pious man in the world is to teach his followers a Torah-true life; to bring down Godliness in this world, and to make this world a fitting abode for the *Shechinah.* If the son follows in his ways, he fulfills the father's mission, and since a person's agent is considered like himself—it seems to the pious man as if he is *still* alive, and continues his blessed mission, which he could fulfill *only* while he was alive, but not after his death.

What is the meaning of Rashi's statement in *Taanit* 5b: "God will bring Jacob into exile to redeem his children"; surely the ingathering of the exiles is one of the tasks of the Messiah,[138] what need is there for Jacob to be brought into exile for this purpose?

---

[137] *Nidah* 30b. See a lengthy explanation of this statement in *Tanya,* Chapter 14.
[138] Rambam, *Hilchot Melachim,* Chap. 11:1,4.

The meaning is that Jacob has to serve as an example to his children. After Jacob devised a scheme by means of the sticks to greatly increase his livestock, it is stated: "The man grew *exceedingly* prosperous, and had large flocks, maidservants and menservants, camels and asses" (30:43). Now, even though he became *very wealthy*, he did *not* stay in exile with Laban, but returned to Israel (Canaan). Likewise, the Jews who will be alive in the generation of the redemption will have to return to Israel *despite* the great wealth that they amassed in exile—even if they will have to leave their fortunes behind, because they will not be able to carry it with them!

Exodus

Shemot

3:15 *V'zeh zichri*—"This is My appellation"
(= "the mention of Me").

RASHI: He taught him how the Divine Name shall be read (pronounced). Similarly David said: "O Lord, Your Name is forever (*shimcha l'olam*); O Lord, Your mention is throughout all generations (*zich'rcha l'dor vador*)" (Psalm 135:13).

RASHI: The original meaning of the root, *z'ch'r*, was to pronounce with one's lips, *not* to remember. This is the meaning of Rashi's comment: "He taught him how it is *read*," namely: God taught Moses how to *pronounce* the ineffable Name—*Y-H-V-H*, not the way we pronounce it, in the sense of "Lordship"—"Adon...," but as the High Priest would pronounce it during the Yom Kippur service. This is also the meaning of the verse that Rashi cites as proof, in which there is an exact parallel between the two parts of the verse: *shimcha-zich'rcha*—"Your name—Your mention"; *L'dor vador-l'olam*—"forever—throughout all generations." Surely, a name (mention) is not a name unless it is *read* or *pronounced.*

We ought to explain similarly the verse: "These come with chariots, and these come with horses; but we pronounce *nazkir* "the name of the Lord our God" (Psalm 20:8). Namely: The gentiles put their faith in chariots and horses, but we, the Jewish People, pronounce—mention the name of God in our prayers, and thus we are helped. This, too, is the meaning of Isaac's statement: "The voice is the voice of Jacob, but the hands are the hands of Esau!"—Genesis 27:22).

In light of the above one can understand the statement in the Talmud: "Our Rabbis taught: '(The verse) *Remember* (lit. *zachor*—"mention") the day of the Sabbath to sanctify it'" (Exod. 20:8)—*Remember* (= mention) it on wine when it starts...."[1] From here we learn that the sanctification of the Sabbath Friday night while reciting a blessing on wine is Torah ordained.

---

[1] *Pesachim* 106a.

65

Only by realizing that the Hebrew *zochreihu* means "mention" it, can the above be understood; for if *zachor* meant to "*remember*" in the *brain* (without pronouncing by mouth), nothing could be derived about the duty to *pronounce* a blessing on wine, which must be done by mouth, not merely "remembered" in the brain!

Another talmudic text can be understood in light of the above: "We learnt: If it had stated only *zachor* (that which Amalek did to you— Deuteronomy 25:17), one might think in the mind (= remember). However, since it says: 'Do not forget'—then forgetfulness of the mind (heart) is already mentioned. What then is the import of *zachor*? It refers to *bapeh*— 'the mouth.'"[2]

Here the Talmud rejects the meaning of the root *z'ch'r*—"remember" (in the brain) and goes back to the original meaning of *zachor*—"to pronounce." It is interesting to note that the Akkadian (ancient Babylonian) word *zakaru* = *z'ch'r* means "speak"! It is for this reason that most halachic authorities agree that the reading of the portion regarding Amalek's encounter with Israel (Deut. 25:17–19) *zachor* on the Sabbath before Purim is Torah-ordained, unlike the other special portions: "Shekalim, Parah, Hachodesh," that are read for Maftir during the month before Passover.

5:22   *Lamah hareiota la'am hazeh*—
"Why did you bring harm upon this People?"

Rashi: If You ask me: "What do you care?" I answer: "I complain that You have sent me."[3]

Comment: One may ask: How did it occur to Moses that God will ask him: "What do you care?" Surely we read in the beginning of this section how Moses suffered and commiserated with "his brothers" to such an extent that he put his life in danger by killing the Egyptian, and was forced to flee from Pharaoh?

We can explain the meaning of the question: "What do you care?" thus: If God should tell Moses: "True, you are their *brother* and you were rightly upset by their suffering. However, I am their *Father* and I called them: My *firstborn son* Israel! Surely then, as a "Father," I feel their suffering even more keenly than you, their "brother," since a father is closer to his children than one brother to another. If then, I allow them to suffer to such an extent that "it has gone *worse* with this People" (5:23), it is obvious that there is

---

[2] *Megillah* 18a.
[3] Tanchuma *Vaeira*; *Shemot Rabbah* 5:22.

a good reason for it, and that I have a plan in the matter. If so, what do you care—surely you cannot possibly care more than I do?!" Moses answered: "Indeed I realize that there must be some plan in the matter, but why did you send *me*? Why do *I* have to be the means by whom their lot should even deteriorate?"

Vaeira

6:13 *Vaytzaveim el Bnei Yisrael*—
"And instructed them concerning the Israelites."

RASHI: He instructed them (Moses and Aaron) to deal with them in a gentle manner and to be patient with them.[4]

V'el Par'oh melech Mitzrayim—
"And regarding Pharaoh, King of Egypt."

RASHI: He instructed them to show him respect in their speech. This is the midrashic explanation, but the "plain sense" is: He instructed them regarding Israel and his mission to Pharaoh....

COMMENT: According to "plain sense" this verse is very difficult, for it begins with: "The Lord spoke to Moses and Aaron *and instructed them concerning the Israelites*" and ends with: "to take out the Israelites from the land of Egypt." Now, surely He did *not* instruct the Israelites to take *themselves* out of Egypt! Furthermore, regarding Israel, God is *not* giving them *any new* mission in this verse, as he already gave them all the instructions earlier, as stated: "Moses spoke thus to the Children of Israel" (6:9). What is added here?

This verse, therefore, begs to be interpreted homiletically. Therefore, Rashi gives the midrashic interpretation first, *before* the "plain sense." With some imaginative daring, one might say that the Midrash understands the word *vaytzaveim*—"and he instructed them" not in the usual sense, but in the sense of *tzavta*—"company," namely: "attachment." Thus the import of the verse would be: God told Moses and Aaron that they should *attach* themselves to the Jewish People and empathize with them in their difficult situation—not stand aloof and unfeeling, as is the way of other leaders—consequently they will deal with them gently and will be patient with them.

---

[4]Exod. *Rabbah* 7.

As regards Pharaoh, God instructed them to show him respect. This, too, is impossible unless they would *attach* themselves to him and understand his point of view—although there is good reason to *distance* themselves from him and even be angry with him for his stubbornness.[5]

7:19   *Emor el Aharon*—"Speak to Aaron."

RASHI: Because the river protected Moses when he was cast into it, therefore it was not smitten by him neither at the plague of blood, nor at the plague of frogs, but it was smitten by Aaron.[6]

COMMENT: Similarly, Rashi explains below at 8:12: "Speak to Aaron"—The dust did not deserve to be smitten by Moses, for it protected him when he slew the Egyptian "and hid him in the sand" (above 2:12)" but it was smitten by Aaron."

Question: Surely both the river and the dust *were* smitten; what difference is there whether by Moses or Aaron? Answer: Had they been smitten by Moses, it would have been a show of ingratitude, since they saved him in time of trouble. The Torah wishes to *instruct* us[7] in good manners, to be grateful to *anyone* who deals kindly with us—be it even inanimate objects like the river or dust!

However, as far as the river and dust are concerned it is not called being "smitten," since through this "blow" they fulfill God's will in producing frogs and lice or turning the water into blood. On the contrary, they are happy to do the bidding of their Creator—and that is the sole reason for their creation! Therefore they do not feel that they were "smitten."[8]

---

[5]Parenthetically, in light of the above, one can explain the Rabbinic statement in *Avot* 4:2: "The reward of a mitzvah is a mitzvah," namely: the reward of a mitzvah is "mitzvah," i.e., by performing the mitzvah—"precept," one *attaches* (*mitzaveh*) oneself more and becomes closer to God.

[6]*Shemot Rabbah* 9:10.

[7]See above Gen. 1:1 where the point was made that Torah means "instruction"— to instruct us, guide us, on the proper path in life.

[8]Compare our explanation above Gen. 22:13 that the ram ran to Abraham in order to fulfill his mission, for which it was created—to serve as a burnt-offering instead of Isaac.

Bo

12:16   *L'chol nefesh*—"Every person."

RASHI: Even cattle. One might think that also (food may be prepared) for non-Jews! The Torah therefore states *lachem*—"for you" (but not for non-Jews!). [Other version: therefore it states: *ach*—"only," to limit (for you *only*, not for non-Jews).][9]

COMMENT: Rashi explained according to the opinion of Rabbi Akiva, even though it is *not* the law. This is how the *Baraita* has it:

"From the statement—*l'chol nefesh*—lit. "for every soul" I might derive that it refers even to the soul of an animal, as is stated: He who smites the *soul* of an animal shall pay for it' (Leviticus 24:21—where soul—*nefesh* is used with animal), it is therefore stated *lachem*—"for you," for *you* (humans), but not for dogs—these are the words of R. Yossie Haglili. R. Akiva says: Even the soul of an animal is meant (you may prepare food). If so, why does it state *lachem*—"for you"? For *you*, but not for idol-worshippers. What reason did you see to include dogs and exclude idol-worshippers? I include the dogs for whose sustenance you are responsible, but exclude idol-worshippers for whose sustenance you are *not* responsible."[10]

Tosafot in *Betzah* 21b states that the law is like R. Yossie Haglili, even though generally the ruling is like R. Akiva against *any* opponent,[11] yet we find an anonymous Mishna that agrees with R. Yossie Haglili.[12] Also Maimonides ruled likewise[13] and similarly in *Orach Chaim* 512:3.

It should be noted that according to Rashi's avowal: "I have come to explain only the plain meaning of Scripture, etc." (Gen. 3:8), it seemed to him that R. Akiva's opinion: "For you, but not for idol-worshippers" is closer to the "plain sense" than to exclude animals, as R. Yossie Haglili does.

---

[9] *Mechilta Bo* Chap. 9.
[10] *Betzah* 21a–b.
[11] *Eruvin* 46b.
[12] *Challah* 1:8.
[13] *Hilchot Yom Tov* 1:13.

Animals (dogs, cows, sheep, and other domesticated animals) are also part of one's "household or estate," and can well be included in the word *lachem*—"for you." Whereas idol-worshippers are *not* part of a Jew's household, therefore ought *not* to be included. In explaining the "plain sense" of a verse, Rashi is *not* bound to explain it necessarily according to the *halachic* ruling.

12:22   V'atem lo teitz'u, etc.—
"And none of you shall go out, etc."

RASHI: This tells us that when permission is given to the angel of destruction to do damage, he does not distinguish between righteous and wicked[14] and night-time is the domain of the forces of destruction, as it is said: "[You make darkness and it is night], when all the *beasts of the forest* creep" (Psalm 104:20—"the beasts of the forest" = forces of destruction).

COMMENT: Why, indeed, doesn't he distinguish between righteous and wicked; surely it was on account of this injustice that Abraham cried out to the Lord: "Far be it from You! Shall not the Judge of all the earth deal justly?" (Gen 18:25).

One may answer: In truth: "There is no man so righteous on earth that he (always) does good and never sins" (*Kohelet* 7:20 and comp. I Kings 8:46)—even totally virtuous people like Abraham, Moses, Rabbi Akiva, etc., but by comparison to a wicked man he is righteous. Therefore, in time of a plague (when permission is given to the angel of destruction), the righteous can be convicted even for the slightest sin—that at a time of peace and calm would be overlooked—*now*, one is particular with him even for the slightest misdemeanor.[15]

12:28   Ka'asher tziva Hashem et Moshe v'Aharon—
"Just as the Lord has commanded Moses and Aaron."

RASHI: This comes to declare Israel's praise—that they did not omit a single matter of all the commandments of Moses and Aaron. And what is meant by *kein asu*—"so they did"? Moses and Aaron too, did so.[16]

---

[14] *Bava Kama* 60a; *Mechilta*, Chap. 11.

[15] See also the explanations of *Torah Temimah* and Ramban's remark on Rashi's comment. Cf. also the kabbalistic explanation of *Maskil LeDavid.*

[16] *Mechilta*, Chap. 12.

In light of the above one may explain as follows: Since the placing of blood on the lintel and doorposts and eating the Paschal lamb in Egypt, etc., were all a *sign* that Israel was engaged in performing God's commands so that they should thereby merit redemption—one could argue that Moses and Aaron were not in need of a *sign*, since they were *entirely* dedicated to the service of God.

Similarly, on the Sabbath and Festivals one need not don phylacteries (*tefillin*), because phylacteries are a sign (that God is with us) and Sabbath and Festivals, too, are signs—and there is no need for a double sign ("a sign for a sign"). Hence one could have thought that Moses and Aaron really did *not* perform these precepts, which serve as signs. Therefore the Torah states: "So they did—Moses and Aaron too, did so," meaning: These *mitzvot* are not only for a "sign," but rather an integral part of the Passover requirements in Egypt.[17]

---

[17]A similar explanation is offered in *Zeh Yenachamenu*: "Since the reason that God commanded them to take a sheep was because the Jews then worshipped idols, including sheep and God wanted them to get rid of their idols, one might think that since this reason does *not* apply to Moses and Aaron (as they didn't worship idols), therefore they really did *not* do all this—hence the Torah teaches us that they too took a sheep, etc.—in order not be different than the rest."

Beshalach

14:7   *V'chol rechev mitzrayim*—"And all the chariots of Egypt."

RASHI: And with them (with the 600 chosen chariots) were all the other chariots. And where did these animals (for the chariots) come from? Should you say from the Egyptians, but it is stated: "All the cattle of the Egyptians died" (above 9:6). And if you say they were from the Israelites' cattle, but it says: "Our cattle, too, shall go with us" (10:26). Then whose were they? Of those (Egyptians) "who feared the word of the Lord" (9:20) (and saved their cattle during the plague of hail by bringing them into the houses). From here (on account of this fact) R. Shimon used to say: "The best of the Egyptians—kill him (otherwise he will afterwards pursue you), the best amongst the serpents—crush its brain"![18]

Comment: One may ask: What is the connection between "the best of the Egyptians" and "the best of the serpents," and why did Rashi cite the end of the statement: "the best of the serpents—crush its brain"—surely we are dealing with the Egyptians here, not with the serpents?

The connection between the two is in the idea expressed in the dictum: *Kabdeihu v'chashdeihu*—"Honor him, but beware of him,"[19] namely: One who is evil by nature, then even if he gives you advice, which on the surface appears to be for *your* good—look into it carefully, because he is incapable of saying or doing anything for *your* good. The serpent, who was evil by nature, advised Eve to eat of the Tree of Knowledge, with the pretext: "You will become like God knowing good and evil" (Gen. 3:5)—seemingly good advice. However, since he was evil *by nature*, he had only his own interest in mind—that Adam should eat *first* and die and he (the serpent) will then marry Eve (Rashi on Gen. 3:15). The same applies to "those who feared

---

[18] *Mechilta Beshalach*, Chap. 1; *Masechet Sofrim*, Chap. 15: "The best among the gentiles *at time of war*, kill him!" Comp. Tosafot *Avodah Zarah* 26b: "namely at time of war."

[19] *Kallah Rabati* 9.

the Lord" among the Egyptians: Since they were evil *by nature* in the end they chased the Israelites and wished to kill them.

15:17   *Mikdash Hashem*—"The sanctuary, O Lord."

RASHI: The accent on the word *mikdash* is a *Zakef Gadol* (a disjunctive, separating accent) to separate it from the word *Hashem*—"O Lord," which follows it, i.e., "The sanctuary which Your hands have established, O Lord." The Temple is beloved (by God), for the Universe was created by one hand, as stated: "My hand has laid the foundation of the earth" (Isaiah 48:13)— whereas the Temple by two hands (as stated here). When will it be built with two hands? At the time when "The Lord shall reign forever and ever" (verse 18)—in the future period when all the Kingdom will be His.[20]

COMMENT: It seems to me that the reason the Temple is more beloved than the entire Universe, and the meaning of the statement that the Temple "was created with two hands" is to emphasize that the Divine Presence (the *Shechinah*) resides in the Temple more so than in the rest of the world. It is worth comparing Rashi's comment to: "And God created man in His image" (Gen 1:27)—"In the mould that was made for him, for everything (else) was created by an order, whereas he (Adam) was created *by hands*, etc."

The meaning is that man is bestowed with special Divine Providence and the Lord shows a special interest in man, more so than in all other creatures. This is much like a dish a person cooks himself, or clothes that he/she sewed with his/her own hands (not bought in a store); these are especially dear to him. Similarly, the Almighty is closer, so to speak, to man than to all His creatures—since man is the work of His *hands*. The same applies to the Temple, which was created "with two hands," the Almighty makes His Divine Presence—*Shechinah* reside in it more so than in any other place in the world.

16:29   *Al yeitzei mim'komo*—"Let no one leave his place."

RASHI: These are the 2000 cubits of the Sabbath limit.[21] But this is not stated explicitly here, because the Sabbath limits were only instituted by

---

[20] *Mechilta,* Chap. 10.

[21] I.e., the limit one can walk to outside one's town, village, etc., See *Mechilta Vayasa,* Chap. 5.

the Rabbis (*Soferim*). But the verse itself is stated (only) with regard to the gatherers of manna.[22]

COMMENT: Question: If the "plain sense" does *not* refer to the Sabbath limits, why does Rashi cite the Midrash altogether? The reason is that Rashi is in the habit of citing *halachic* (legal) *midrashim* in order to relate laws to Scripture (to show how abstract laws are derived from certain verses). His statement: "because the Sabbath limits were only instituted by the *Soferim*" means the limits of 2000 cubits are rabbinic. However the limits of twelve mil (approximately nine miles)—the size of the Camp of Israel— is a Torah law (that one must not walk on Sabbath beyond this limit) according to *all* opinions—and one who violates it is liable to the thirty-nine lashes.[23]

Rashi's statement: *v'lo bimforash*—"not stated explicitly," means that the 2000 cubits are *not* derived from here, as if they were stated in the verse explicitly, but only as an allusion—since the 2000 dubits are only rabbinic in origin. The main intent of the verse is regarding the gatherers of manna, that they should not go out on Sabbath to gather it.

---

[22] *Sotah* 30b.
[23] Comp. *Sefer Hazikaron.*

Yitro

18:12   *Vayavo Aharon, etc.*—"And Aaron came, etc."

RASHI: But where had Moses gone? Was it not he who had gone out to meet him and was the cause of all the honor shown him? But (why is Moses not mentioned, because) he was waiting upon them.[24]

COMMENT: However, why did Aaron and the Elders of Israel agree that Moses—the greatest among them—should serve them? Moreover, the rule is "A king who forgoes his honor, his honor is *not* forgiven."[25] Moses was in the category of a king, so that he was not *allowed* to forgo his honor, how then could he wait upon them?

The answer is that Moses was in this instance the proprietor, and the rule is: "Whatever the owner tells you—do it," and indeed this *was* Moses' honor—to serve the Sages. Hence, he did *not* forgo his honor, because this *was* his honor! Rabban Gamliel, who was the President, emulated Moses when *he* served the Sages at a banquet. According to the *Mechilta*, Moses learned this practice from Abraham, who was a "prince of God" (Gen. 23:6). Abraham in turn learned this practice from God Himself, who constantly supplies sustenance to all creatures of the world. Surely, there is no greater service than that!

19:20   *Vayeired Hashem al Har Sinai*—
"The Lord came down upon Mount Sinai."

RASHI: One might think that He *actually* came down upon it? Therefore it states: "You have seen that I spoke to you from *heaven*" (below 20:19). This (apparent contradiction) teaches us that He bent down the upper and

---

[24]*Mechilta*, Chap. 1.
[25]*Ketubot* 17a.

79

lower heavens and spread them over the mountain like a bedspread over a bed, and the Throne of Glory descended upon them.[26]

COMMENT: What is the meaning of the phrase: "and the Throne of Glory descended upon them"; surely there was no physical descent since God "is neither body, nor has an image of a body,"[27] hence a physical "descent" pertaining to Him is inconceivable?

One may gain *some* understanding of this matter by citing the *Mechilta* in its entirety. It states the following:

"One might think that the Glory really came down upon Mount Sinai? Therefore it is stated: 'for from heaven (have I spoken with you'"—Exodus 20:19). This teaches that God bent down the lower and the uppermost heavens and spread them over the mountain, and the Glory came down— like a man who spreads a pillow at the head of the bed, and like a man who speaks from above the pillow, as it says: "As when fire kindles brushwood (*hamasim*); and fire makes water boil (*tiv'eh*—"bubble")—*To make Your Name known to Your adversaries*, so that nations will tremble at Your presence, when You did wonders, etc." (Isaiah 64:1–2).

The *Birkat Hanziv* (commentary on the *Mechilta*) remarks: "If he hadn't bent down the heavens, how would the nations know?" Hence, the whole purpose of spreading the lower and the uppermost heavens over Mount Sinai and the "descent" of the throne on it, as it were, was only to make a strong impression on the nations of the world (and upon Israel all the more so). Why was there a need for this?

To *show* the entire world that the Ten Commandments, which include within them the entire Torah,[28] were given by the Almighty. The majority of the Ten Commandments are precepts between man and man.[29] One might therefore argue that there is no need for a *Divine* command in order to observe them, since they are mandated by *human* intellect and morals. Therefore the Torah emphasizes that without an explicit *Divine imperative*— and this is the meaning of "the Throne of Glory came down upon them"— people would *not* observe even these basic moral laws, which serve as the foundation of all human society, such as: "Honor your father and mother; do not murder; do not commit adultery; do not kidnap, etc."

Similarly we find that Abraham said to Avimelech: "For I said, surely

---

[26]The heaven and the mountain—*Mechilta*, Chap. 4.
[27]As Maimonides states in the famous "thirteen fundamental principles," which many Jews recite after the morning service daily.
[28]As Rashi points out below 24:12 and see our commentary there.
[29]According to the version in Deuteronomy, Chap 5, even the commandment concerning Sabbath is a social one, as stated there in verse 14: "In order that your slave and maidservant may rest like you."

there is no fear of God in this place and *they will kill me* because of my wife"
(Gen. 20:11). Hence *human* morals alone were not sufficient to prevent the
Philistines even from murder! If so, there was definitely a great need to
bend down the lower and uppermost heavens, and the coming down of
the Throne of Glory upon Mount Sinai, etc., to make a very strong impression that these are *Divine Imperatives*—maybe, maybe then, they will be
observed.

20:1   *Et kol had'varim ha'eileh*—"All these words."

RASHI: This phrase teaches that God said the Ten Commandments in *one*
utterance, which is impossible for a human being to speak in this manner.
But if this is so, why does Scripture say again (the first two Commandments)
anochi and *lo yihyeh l'cha?* (Since only the first two Commandments were
said in the second person: "I am the Lord *your* God," "*You* (sing.) shall have
no other gods"; and also in the first person: "*I* am the Lord, before Me"—
whereas the rest were said in the third person: "Do not bear *the Name,*" not
"*My* Name." If so, how could all of them have been said in *one* utterance?)
Rashi answers: "that He expressly repeated, etc.," namely: The first two
Commandments we heard *directly* from the Almighty, and the other eight
from Moses. Therefore they are said in the *third* person, as if Moses speaks
on behalf of God to Israel.[30] Because He expressly repeated each of these
two Commandments by itself.[31]

COMMENT: Question: Why *did* God say the Ten Commandments in *one*
utterance; if it was to show His power, as Rashi seems to suggest: "which
is impossible for a human being to speak in this manner," surely He had
no need of that. The splitting of the Red Sea; the stopping of the sun and
moon in the Valley of Ayalon and in Gibeon (Joshua, Chap. 10); the
bringing down of manna; taking water out of the rock—and other similar
miracles—are much greater deeds and miracles than saying the Ten Commandments in one utterance—especially since the above miracles and their
like were urgently needed by the world—which was apparently *not* the case
in saying the Ten Commandments in one utterance?! Hence, we must say
that the world *was* in great need of this miraculous utterance. What was
the need?

Answer: The need for saying the Ten Commandments in *one* utterance
was to show the world that *all* the Commandments are equally important

---

[30]Cf. *Be'er Avraham.*
[31]*Mechilta,* Chap. 4.

and valuable for the world. Since the Ten Commandments include the *whole* Torah,[32] *all* of them are *equally* important—both those that are between man and God and those that are between man and man—all of them are one unit.[33]

20:22-23   *Va'tchalleha*—"You will have profaned it."

RASHI: Thus you may learn that if you lift up an iron (tool) above it, you profaned it; for the altar was created to lengthen man's days,[34] and iron was created (one of its uses is) to shorten man's days—it is not right that the one that shortens (man's days) should be lifted above that which lengthens.[35]

Another reason is: The altar makes peace between Israel and their Father in Heaven, therefore there should not come upon it anything that cuts and destroys. Now, surely it is a logical inference (lit. an "a fortiori—*kal va'chomer*"): If stones that neither see, nor hear, nor speak, because they bring about peace the Torah ordained: "Do not lift up an iron tool above them!"—One who makes peace between a man and his wife; between family and family; between one man and another—how much more certain is it that punishment will not come upon him (*Mechilta*).

Asher lo tigaleh ervatcha—"That your nakedness may not be exposed."

RASHI: Because of these steps you will have to take wide paces (and thus spread the legs). Now, although this is not an actual uncovering of one's nakedness (the genital parts), since it is written: "Make for them (the priests) linen breeches to cover their nakedness" (28:42), still taking large paces is close to uncovering one's nakedness (hence described as such here), and you would be treating (the stones of the altar) disrespectfully. Surely it is a logical inference ("a fortiori"—*kal va'chomer*): If stones that have no sense (feeling) to be particular about disrespect shown to them, the Torah said that since they serve a need, you should not treat them disrespectfully, your fellow man (friend) who is in the image of your Creator—and *is* particular about disrespect shown to him—all the more so (that you should not treat him disrespectfully)![36]

---

[32] See our comments above 19:20 and Rashi below 24:12.

[33] As the Sages said: "The Holy One, blessed be He, the Torah and Israel are all one"—*Zohar Parshat Acharei.*

[34] Because the altar atones for sins that shorten man's days—*Gur Aryeh.*

[35] *Mechilta,* Chap. 11; *Middot* 3:4.

[36] Mechilta, Chap. 11.

COMMENT: The phrase "and iron was created to shorten man's days" means that *one* of the uses of iron is to shorten man's life, since weapons are made from it, which kill people, but certainly not that this is the *main* use of iron!

Rashi's commentators have expressed surprise: Surely Rashi does *not* cite the Midrashic interpretations of the Rabbis unless there is a great need for them. What then forced him to cite the Rabbinic Midrashim here?

The author of *Be'er Mayim Chaim* explains as follows: "Although it is *not* Rashi's practice to cite *midrashim* in his commentary, nevertheless *this* Midrash is required for the plain sense, for Rashi's difficulty was: Why does the Torah give the reasons for these two negative commands (not to lift up an iron; not to go up to the altar by steps) more so than with other negative commands (whose reasons are *not* given by the Torah)? Therefore Rashi explains that the Torah comes to teach us how important it is to bring about peace between man and his fellow man, and also how severe would be the punishment of one who embarrasses another."[37]

We might add that although it is true that Rashi usually refrains from citing *midrashim* if they are not close to the plain sense, nevertheless if the Midrash carries an important moral lesson, he does not refrain from citing it. On the contrary, he sees it as one of his major tasks—the education of the young student[38] in good character traits and morals; and to teach us the correct way of life![39]

---

[37]Cf. "*Deek Tov*," who explains similarly.
[38]Who, according to the Mishna in *Avot* end of Chapter 5, begins studying *Tanach* at the age of five!
[39]See above "Introduction," principles 2–3.

Mishpatim

Introduction

The section of *Mishpatim* is a good example of an important rule in Rashi's commentary on the Torah, i.e., if a verse or part of it relates to the *law,* Rashi does *not* insist on explaining it in the strictly "plain sense" inherent in the words of that verse. He then cites the *halachic* Midrash to that verse, provided the Midrash is not too far from "plain sense." Even when the Midrash *is* far off from the plain sense, Rashi may cite it, but then he indicates that the Rabbis exegeted the verse so and so, but the plain sense is such and such. Or he may indicate that the law derived from the verse is only of Rabbinic origin (*Midivrei Sofrim*).

In this methodology we see clearly that Rashi assumed the role of "teacher of the People" in its most literal sense. Since "the 'word of the Lord'—this refers to *Halacha,*"[40], and considering the fact that a majority of the people is incapable of arriving at the law by means of the Talmud[41], or the "Laws of Alfasi,"[42] Rashi therefore saw a need to find references to laws in the verses—as far as possible by means of a commentary to the text, without violating too much the "plain sense" of a passage. In this approach he follows the example of *halachic midrashim*: *Mechilta, Sifra,* and *Sifrei.* Almost the entire section of *Mishpatim* is full of examples of the above general rule[43]. Here are a few out of many such examples exemplifying this methodological approach.

---

[40]*Shabbat* 138b and compare: "From the day the Temple was destroyed, the Holy One, blessed be He, has nothing in His world but the four cubits of *halachah* alone" –*Berachot* 8a and see Maharsha there.
[41]And the Code of Law of Maimonides; the *Tur Shulchan Aruch* and the *Shulchan Aruch* by R. Joseph Caro did not exist yet in Rashi's day.
[42]*Hilchot Alfasi* or the *Rif.*
[43]See our Hebrew commentary to *Mishpatim.*

21:2   *Ki tikneh*—"When you acquire (a Hebrew slave)."

RASHI: From the court that sold him for a theft he committed, as it is said: "If he does not have (money to pay), he shall be sold for his theft" (Exod. 22:2). Or maybe it is not so, but the verse refers to one who sells himself because he is destitute, while the one who was sold by the court shall not go free after six years! (This cannot be so for) when it says: "If your brother becomes impoverished with you and is sold to you... he should serve you up to the year of Jubilee" (Levit. 25:39–40). Surely this passage speaks of one who sells himself out of destitution. What then is the case intended by the words *ki tikneh*—"when you acquire" here? It refers to one who was sold by the court.[44]

COMMENT: This is obviously a *halachic* Midrash, for according to "plain sense" the words "When you acquire a Hebrew slave" refer to *any* form of acquisition; whether from the court, or to one who sells himself out of destitution, or from another person. Moreover, the verse Rashi cites as *proof*, is no proof, because in regard to one who sells himself out of destitution it is stated: "He should serve you up to *the year of Jubilee*" (Levit. 25:40), but we *exegete* it to mean "If Jubilee arrived *before* the six years were up, the Jubilee year frees him" (Rashi there). Whereas, according to "plain sense" he would really have to work up to the Jubilee year—whether it be close (less than six years) or distant (more than six years).

The words "When you acquire, etc." in our verse we would explain according to plain sense as referring to one who buys a Hebrew slave from another person, *not* from the court, since the section about the thief who is sold for his theft comes later (22:2). Why should we assume that *our* verse deals with this situation? We are forced to say that since this is a *halachic* Midrash, Rashi cites it, even though it is not the plain sense.

21:3   *V'yatz'ah ishto imo*—"His wife shall go out with him."

RASHI: But who brought her in (as a slave) that she should go out? But Scripture tells you (in this phrase) that he who acquires a Hebrew slave must provide food for his wife and children.[45]

COMMENT: This law is derived from one who sells himself, about whom it is stated: "Then he shall leave you; he and his children with him" (Levit.

---

[44] *Mechilta Nezikin*, Chap. 1; comp. *Kiddushin* 14b.
[45] *Mechilta, Mishpatim*, Chap. 1; *Kiddushin* 22a; comp. *Sifra, Behar*, Chap. 7.

25:41), thus: Just as with the slave who sells himself, the master is obligated to provide for his wife and children, so too in the case where the *court* sold him, is the master obligated to provide for his children. Now, just as when the court sold him, the master is obliged to provide for his wife—so too if he sold himself, is he obligated to provide for the slave's wife.[46] Even though the father is *not* obligated by the Torah to provide for their sustenance, the master *is* so obligated.

The above is true by midrashic derivation, but according to "plain sense" nothing is intimated regarding the slave's wife and children. On the contrary, the verse teaches a novel concept, namely: Although the master provided the slave's wife and children with sustenance for six years, and one might think that they must now pay for it by working for him extra time—the Torah tells us that this is *not* so, but: "His wife shall go out *with him*" and also: "*He and his children with him,*" namely they go out "with him" without additional work—but not that the master is *obligated* to provide food for his wife and children.

21:6   V'avado l'olam—"And he shall serve him forever."

RASHI: Until the Jubilee. Or perhaps it is not so, but "forever" literally? It is however stated (regarding the Jubilee year): "and each man shall return to his family" (Levit. 25:10). This tells us that fifty years are called *olam.* However, it does *not* imply that he has to work for him the *entire* fifty years; but rather he has to serve him until the Jubilee (the fiftieth year)—whether it is close or distant.[47]

COMMENT: Rashi at Leviticus 25:10 cites the Talmud: "Each man shall return to his family—this includes the slave whose ear was bored" (*Kiddushin* 15a). This, too, is a Midrash *halachah,* for according to plain sense *l'olam* means "forever" (i.e., for the rest of his life). As for Leviticus 25:10 ("and each man shall return to his family"), there is no *explicit* mention of the bored slave there. It would stand to reason that a slave who declares "I love my master, my wife and my children; I will *not* go out free" (21:5), should really *never* go free! Hence the exegesis *"l'olam—*until the Jubilee" is indeed a Midrash *halachah.*[48]

---

[46]See Rashi on Levit. 25:41 and *Kiddushin* 22a under: "He and his children."
[47]*Kiddushin* 15a; *Mechilta,* Chap. 2.
[48]See further examples of Rashi's citing *halachic* midrashim in our Hebrew commentary: *Be'ur setumot be-Rashi* on Exod. 21:7, 11, 24, 28, 29, 30, 32, 33, 34; 22:3, 12, 19, 23, 30; 23:2, 7, 11, 12, 21–pp. 190–204.

24:11   *Vayechezu et ha-E-lohim*—"And they beheld God."

RASHI: They gazed at Him intimately (or: with arrogant hearts), while eating and drinking. This is the explanation of Midrash *Tanchuma*.[49] But Onkelos does not translate the passage this way.[50]

COMMENT: Why does Rashi emphasize that Onkelos did *not* translate the passage this way?

Rashi wishes to teach us that Onkelos' translation is *not* the literal one according to plain sense but comes to *interpret* in a manner that would preserve the honor of Jewish leaders (in our case: Nadav, Avihu, the elders)—as is the methodology of the Targum generally. Had Onkelos' explanation been the plain sense, they would *not* have incurred the death penalty, as Rashi noted in verse 10 and also in this verse: "He did *not* stretch out His hand—this implies that they deserved that God should stretch out His hand against them."[51]

---

[49]*Tanchuma, Behaalotcha* 15.

[50]I.e., he does not translate in a *negative* sense that Nadav and Avihu and the elders acted improperly—but rather favorably. His translation is: "They beheld God's Glory and rejoiced in their offerings, which were accepted as though they were eating and drinking." Comp. *Berachot* 17a: "They were satiated from the radiance of the *Shechinah* as if they were eating and drinking."

[51]Levit. *Rabbah* 20; see also Targum Jonathan.

Terumah

25:31 *Tey'aseh hamenorah*—"The candelabrum shall be made."

RASHI: (The passive form: "shall *be made*"). Because Moses was puzzled by it (the making of the candelabrum), God told him: "Cast the talent of gold into the fire and it will be made of itself." Therefore it does not say here: *Ta'aseh*—"You shall make."[52]

COMMENT: The above explanation of the Midrash is problematic since in *Vayakhel* (below 37:17–24) the Torah states explicitly that Bezalel made the candelabrum and all its vessels. Many of the "supercommentaries" on Rashi struggle in their attempt to explain the apparent contradiction. (See, for example, the very lengthy and complicated explanation of Mizrachi, who attempts to explain away the contradictions between the Midrash *Tanchuma* and the Talmud *Menachot* 29a.)

In our opinion the explanation is as follows: At first Moses *was* puzzled by the making of the Menorah, and God told him: "Throw the talent of gold into the fire and it will be made of itself," and indeed he did so. However, *that* Menorah was *not* eligible (Kosher) for the Tabernacle service, since it was made by God *miraculously*, whereas the *Israelites* were commanded to make a Menorah—and with *this one* they did not fulfill God's command! Therefore the automatic Menorah served only as a *sample*, by which Bezalel (who was the agent of the entire People) made the Menorah.

The Maharal of Prague in his *Gur Aryeh* commentary on Rashi wrote in a similar vein: "It was absolutely necessary to show Moses (the Menorah) so that he should know its structure, for *Israel* was commanded to make it, not that it should be made entirely by God... *When Moses began to make it, God completed it for him.*" All deeds that come from Above, it is necessary for man to do (something) below. So with the splitting of the Red Sea—an act of God—it states: "Now you (Moses) raise your staff and split it." Similarly all the miracles in Egypt were done through Moses.

---

[52] *Tanchuma, Shemini* 8 and *Behaalotcha* 3.

89

In *our* opinion, the *entire* Menorah needed to be made by Israel, not only to *begin* making it, otherwise it could not be used in the Tabernacle—as it appears from 37:17–24 that *all* of it was made by Bezalel. However, the Menorah that was made "of itself"—by God, served (only) as a sample for Bezalel to be guided by it in his work—as pointed out above.

27:2   *V'tzipita oto n'choshet*—"And overlay it with copper."

RASHI: To atone for (sins committed with) impudence,[53] as it is said: "And your forehead is copper" (= brazen, Isaiah 48:4).[54]

COMMENT: Question: Why did Rashi find it necessary to explain the reason for overlaying the *altar* with copper more so than the overlaying of the other vessels in the Tabernacle?

Maskil LeDavid explains it as follows: "For if not for this reason (to atone for brazenness) he should have made the overlay of silver or gold since we have a rule: 'There is no poverty in a place of wealth.'[55] Therefore Rashi was obliged to find a reason here, more so than with the other overlays of the vessels."

One might ponder the reason why just the altar atones for impudence; why not the Headplate (*tzitz*) regarding which it is said: "and it shall be on Aaron's *forehead,* etc." (Exod. 28:38), we could then apply the following exegesis: Let the Headplate, which is placed on the *forehead,* atone for "impudence of the *forehead*"?

Answer: The copper altar, upon which most of the sacrifices were offered, such as: the sin-offering, the guilt-offering, etc., was a symbol of subjugation to God—which is the very opposite of impudence!

It is a known fact that before a Jew would bring a sin-offering, or a guilt-offering, or even a burnt-offering, he would first confess his sins—whether he transgressed positive commands or negative ones, or a command that carries the penalty of excision (*karet*), etc. Naturally then he would feel contrite and submissive before his Creator, which is the opposite of brazenness. It is therefore fitting that the copper altar should atone for impudence–brazenness.

---

[53]Lit. "with impudence of forehead," the Hebrew expression for impudence being "having a copper forehead."

[54]Comp. the English expression "brazen-faced," *Tanchuma, Terumah* 11.

[55]*Shabbat* 102b, namely: In the Temple—the House of God, who is *rich,* as the prophet says: "Mine is the silver and Mine is the gold says the Lord" [*Chagai* 2:8] it is improper to display signs of poverty—such as making the overlay of copper rather than silver or gold.

Tetzaveh

29:40 *B'shemen katit*—"Of beaten oil."

RASHI: Not as an obligation is it stated "beaten" but only to make it permissible. Since it states: "beaten for the light" (Ex. 27:20), which implies for the light, but *not* for the meal-offering. I might conclude to declare beaten oil unfit for meal-offerings; therefore Scripture states here "beaten" (that beaten oil *may* be used for meal-offerings). And "beaten for the light" is said only to exclude meal-offerings from the *requirement* of "beaten oil"— for even oil obtained from olives ground in a mill is permissible in meal-offerings.[56]

COMMENT: Rashi at *Menachot* 86b writes: "Because of economy or thrift (*chisachon*), i.e. "pure and beaten" are not required in meal-offerings, as they are for the candles.... Because meal-offerings are numerous and require very much oil, if one had to look for 'pure and beaten' oil for them there would be great loss as they would have to purchase it at a high price."

Actually, beaten oil is always of a better quality than ground oil, but the Torah did not require it out of economy. This is unlike the nature of a person, who reserves the *best* oil for food, and the rest for lighting. Here though, it was the opposite: the best oil for lighting and the more inferior for meal-offerings (altar food). This shows that God has no need of lighting, nor of food.[57]

One would be tempted to argue logically thus: If a person chooses the best oil for *his* food (beaten oil), all the more so should the best (beaten) oil be required for the food of the Most High (*achilat gavoah*)—the altar! Therefore the Rabbis inform us that He needs no food, nor light. However, this is a Midrash *halachah*, but according to "plain sense," beaten oil *is* required for meal-offerings, just as it is required for lights.

---

[56] *Menachot* 86b.
[57] See *Be'er Maim Chaim*.

However, whenever the plain sense *negates* the *halachic* Midrash, Rashi opts for the Midrash, because it is the law. But here there is an additional reason to prefer the Midrash, as it teaches us the important lesson: "He needs neither light, nor food," namely: All the commandments are the decrees of the King, and His nature is *not* that of human beings! (Hence beaten oil (best) is for lights, and ground oil for meal-offerings.)

29:43   *V'nikdash bichvodi*—"And it shall be sanctified by My Glory."

RASHI: For my Divine Presence (*Shechinah*) shall dwell in it. A Midrash *aggadah* states: "Do not read *bichvodi*—'by My Glory, but *bichvuday*—'by my Honored ones.'" Here God hinted to Moses the death of Aaron's sons on the day when the Tabernacle was erected. This is the meaning of what Moses then said: "This is what the Lord said: 'Through those that are near to Me I will be sanctified'" (Lev. 10:30). But where did He say this? In the words: "It shall be sanctified by My honored ones."[58]

COMMENT: The *Torah Temimah* asks: "This entire matter is puzzling: what was God's intention... to dedicate the Tabernacle with the death of these noble men (Nadav and Avihu)... and what is the meaning of Moses' statement to Aaron: 'Your sons died only in order to sanctify the Name of God'— what is the nature of this sanctification of the Name?" He replies that since the purpose of the Tabernacle and sacrifices was to atone for the sins of the Jewish people, "the *masses* should not think that there is no more a need to stay away from sin, for the sacrifices will atone. Therefore, God showed that the Tabernacle and sacrifices do *not* atone for those who transgress the Law *intentionally*, only for unintentional sinners. He showed this with the death of Nadav and Avihu, who *were* righteous and beloved by God. Nevertheless when they transgressed *willfully*,[59] the sanctity of the Tabernacle did not protect them, etc."

The above answers the question: Why did Rashi find it necessary to cite the Midrash? Surely the verse is fully understood according to the "plain verse" that Rashi offers first: "The Tabernacle will be sanctified by My Glory—that My *Shechinah* will dwell in it"? According to the *Torah Temimah*, Rashi cites the Midrash to teach an important lesson, namely: Sacrifices do *not* atone for willful transgressions, only for unintentional ones, or accidental sins.

As the educator of the People, Rashi saw a great need for teaching this

---

[58] *Zevachim* 115b.

[59] By bringing in "an alien fire which He had not commanded them"—Levit 10:1.

lesson even in our times when there are no sacrifices, so that the *masses* should not think, mistakenly, that since the prayers are instead of sacrifices, therefore they too atone for *both* willful and unintentional transgressions.

Moreover, surely "the Temple will be rebuilt speedily,[60] and Every day I await his (Messiah's) coming" (which we recite after the morning service, as one of the thirteen Principles of Faith by Maimonides—the so-called *Ani Ma'amin*—"I believe ... "). With the coming of Messiah we will have the Third Temple, and this lesson will become appropriate all the time.

---

[60] *Sukkah* 41a; *Sanhedrin* 22b; *Bechorot* 53b.

Ki Tisa

30:13   *Ze yitnu*—"This shall they give."

RASHI: He showed him a kind of coin of fire the weight of which was half a shekel, and He told him: "Like this shall they give."[61]

COMMENT: Question: Why did God show Moses specifically a coin of *fire*, not one of metal? One could answer that fire represents spirituality and the message is that when one gives "an offering to the Lord," it has to be done with *enthusiasm* like a burning fire, in the sense of: "Give Him what is His, for you and whatever is yours—are His."[62] And as God Himself is described as a *"consuming fire* is He."[63]

30:34   *V'echelbnah*—"And galbanum."

RASHI: A spice whose odor is bad, it is called "galbanum." Scripture numbers it among the spices of the incense to teach us that it should not be unimportant in our view to include among us in the assemblies of our fasts and prayers the sinners of Israel, that they should be numbered together with us.[64]

COMMENT: Rashi was bothered by the question: If the odor of galbanum is *bad*, why is it numbered among the *spices* whose odor is good and pleasing? Hence the Torah must have wished to intimate that although its odor is bad, it has a use no less than the rest of the spices whose odor is good— and it deserves to be called a "spice" and be numbered among the rest of the spices. We can derive from this fact a lesson to include among

---

[61]*Shekalim* 1:4; *Tanchuma, Ki Tisa* 9; *Naso* 11.
[62]*Avot* 3:37.
[63]Deut. 4:24, 9:3. See commentaries there as to the meaning of this phrase.
[64]*Kareitot* 6b.

us in our fasts and prayers the sinners of Israel (whose "odor is bad" spiritually).

One may add that not only does the community give the sinners the privilege of including them in their fasts and prayers, the sinners favor the community, for the community learns from them a religious lesson by applying the logical inference "a fortiori" (*kal v'chomer*) thus: If the "sinners of Israel" fast and pray (at least in time of trouble), how much more so should we fast and pray with broken hearts—and we are assured by "the sweet singer of Israel"[65] that: "A heart broken and humble, O God, You will not despise" (Psalm 51:19). This way the willful transgressions of the sinners of Israel become merits, since they fast and pray together with the entire community—thus they repent. In this matter, too, they are like the galbanum, which in itself has a bad odor, but by making it part of all spices, it is numbered with them and considered a "spice." Therefore Rashi emphasizes that galbanum is "*a spice* (even though) whose odor is bad"— and there is no contradiction between the two.

31:18   *K'chaloto*—"When He finished."

RASHI: *K'chaloto* is written as though *k'chalato*—"as his bride" (without a *vav* after the *lamed*), for the Torah was given to him as a gift (complete in everything) like a bride to the groom (supplied with all her needs), since he was not able to learn all of it in such a short time (forty days and nights on Mount Sinai). Another explanation: Just as a bride adorns herself with twenty-four ornaments—those mentioned in the book of Isaiah (Chap. 3:18–24)—so must a scholar (*talmid chacham*) be learned in the twenty-four books of Scripture.[66]

COMMENT: What forced Rashi to cite the midrashic explanations, which are obviously *not* the plain sense of the word? Surely there are many words in the Torah written without a *vav* and Rashi does *not* cite a Midrash each time to explain the defective writing![67]

Answer: Indeed, as far as "plain sense" is concerned, there was no need for Rashi to cite the midrashic explanations, since he did not claim that the word *k'chaloto*—"when He finished," or all three words: *k'chaloto l'dabeir ito*—"when He finished speaking to him" are superfluous—which they

[65]King David—II Samuel 23:1.
[66]Comp. *Tanchuma, Ki Tisa* 16; Exod. *Rabbah* 41:6; *Nedarim* 38a.
[67]Indeed, it is surprising that Rashi's great commentators, such as *Mizrachi, Gur Aryeh,* and *Divrei David* (the Taz) have nothing to comment on this Rashi!

seem to be. He only notes that *k'chaloto* is written without a vav and therefore he cites the midrashic explanations.

What prompted Rashi to cite the midrashim are the lessons to be derived from them, namely:

1) A bride is given to the groom after a short time, even though he did not yet manage to grasp her character, personality, and goodness sufficiently. The husband must learn to understand the character traits, goodness, and mannerisms of his wife during their lifetime together. The same applies to the Torah, as Rashi remarks: "for he could not learn *all of it* (i.e., all the details and nuances deriving from the 613 Commandments, which are delineated in the Oral Law) in such a short time (of forty days and nights on Mount Sinai).

2) A scholar (*talmid chacham*) must be fluent in all the twenty-four books of Scripture, not only in the Oral Law (Talmud), unlike many scholars who do not know a verse in the Bible. Indeed, Rashi showed his own astounding fluency in all the twenty-four Books, both in his commentary on the Bible and on the Talmud. With his commentary on this verse, Rashi fulfills one of the tasks he took upon himself—to be the educator of the People.[68]

luchot—"tablets"

RASHI: *Luchot* is written defectively (without a *vav*) between the *chet* and the *tav* as though the singular form *luchat*, for they were both equal (ibid).

COMMENT: What difference does it make whether they were both equal or not? We find in the Midrash: "Rabbi Chanina said it is written *luchat*—'one was not bigger than the other.'"[69] The commentary on the Midrash *Yefei Toar* writes: "This shows the greatness of the miracle, because it is beyond human power to make two things *exactly* equal."

We may further explain thus: Each of the two tablets had five Commandments. One tablet had the Commandments between man and God, while the other had the Commandments between man and man. With the statement "for they were both equal," the Midrash alludes to the fact that both types of commandments are equally important. One type of com-

---

[68]See our Introduction to *Mishpatim*.
[69]*Shemot Rabbah* 41:6

mandment has no advantage over the other—we heard *both* types from the Almighty. Rashi comes to teach us this fundamental truth with his brief commentary.

33:4   *Ish edyo*—"(And no man put on) his jewelry, finery."

RASHI: The crowns that were given to them at Horev, when they said (Exod. 24:7): "We will do and obey" (lit. "and hear").[70]

COMMENT: In *Shabbat* 88a we read: "Rabbi Simai propounded: When Israel preceded to state 'we shall do' before 'we shall hear' six hundred thousand angels came down. To each one of Israel they tied two crowns, one corresponding to 'we shall do,' and one corresponding to 'we shall hear.' When Israel sinned (with the golden calf) 1,200,000 destructive angels came down and removed them, as it is said: 'The Children of Israel stripped themselves of their jewelry from Mount Horev'" (Exod. 33:6). Rashi there explains: "Two crowns" from the radiance of the "*Shechinah* (Divine Presence)."

What is the nature of these "crowns"—surely they cannot have been physical crowns, since *angels* would have nothing to do with them? The author of *Be'er Yitzchak* declares rather despairingly: "The nature of this *spiritual jewelry* and its secret is above my understanding—I the simpleton (*ani hahedyot*)."

Secondly, even in the opinion of Rabbi Shimon ben Yochai that "All Jews are sons of kings,"[71] it is impossible that they were physical crowns, because only the king wears a crown, not his sons. Various attempts have been made by great commentators of the Talmud and Rashi to understand this difficult Midrash.[72]

We can find a basis for interpreting this puzzling Midrash in Rashi's two words in *Shabbat* 88a *miziv haShechinah*—"from the radiance of the *Shechinah*." Well-known is the statement: "A favorite statement of Rav was: The Future World will have neither eating nor drinking... but the righteous will sit with their crowns upon their heads *and will enjoy the radiance of the Shechinah.*"[73] Maimonides in *Laws of Repentance* 8:2 states: "What is the

---

[70] *Shabbat* 88a.

[71] *Shabbat* 67a; *Bava Metzia* 113b; *Zohar* III 28, 223, 255.

[72] See e.g. the heroic attempts at interpretation made *by Be'er Mayim Chaim* on Rashi and by Maharsha on Talmud *Shabbat*, 88a and refutations of same in our Hebrew commentary *Be'ur Setumot Be-Rashi*, Vol. I, pp. 236–237, which we cannot go into here.

[73] *Berachot* 17a.

meaning of: "and will enjoy the radiance of the *Shechinah?*—They will know and grasp the truth of the Holy One, blessed be He, that which they do *not* know whilst in the dark, lowly body."

In the introduction to Chapter *Chelek*[74] Maimonides elaborates as follows: "By saying: 'and they will enjoy the radiance of the *Shechinah,*' they mean: those souls (in the Future World) take pleasure in their grasping and knowing of the truth of the Creator, just as the *Holy Beasts* and other levels of angels take pleasure in grasping and knowing of His reality."[75]

In light of the above explanation of "radiance of the *Shechinah*," we can explain that the "two crowns," which according to Rashi were also "from the radiance of the *Shechinah,*" refer to two kinds of secrets of the Torah and knowledge of God, namely: "Works of Creation" (*ma'asey b'reishit*) corresponding to: (*na'aseh*—"We will do") and "Works of the Chariot" (*ma'asey merkavah*), corresponding to: "We will hear" (*nishma*). It is enlightening that when speaking about knowledge of the truth of the Creator, Maimonides states: "as the *Holy Beasts* take pleasure... in their grasping and knowing of his reality." But surely the "Holy Beasts" are an integral part of the "Holy Chariot" in Ezekiel Chapter 1.

That the word *nishma* corresponds to "Works of the Chariot" (*ma'asey merkavah*) is clear if we translate it as "we shall understand."[76] The "Works of the Chariot" are secrets of the God head beyond our understanding (as Rashi says in his comment on Ezekiel 1:27: "One is not allowed to ponder the meaning of this verse,") but they do *not* relate to God's acts in the world as the "Works of Creation," which refer to the secrets of Creation. It appears that by accepting the Torah with "We shall do and we shall hear," the Jewish People merited to grasp these two types of Divine secrets.

As to the need for *1,200,000* angels of destruction to remove the "crowns" after they sinned with the golden calf, Tosafot on *Shabbat* 88a writes: "Although a good attribute is greater than a negative–punitive one (*g'dolah midah tovah mimidat pur'anut*), here too it is greater since *one* good angel tied *two* crowns, whereas a destructive angel had the power to remove only *one* crown (hence the need for 1,200,000, not only 600,000)."

---

[74]*Sanhedrin* Chap. 11.

[75]See also Maimonides on the nature of the Future World in Chapters 2 and 4 of his "Epistle on Resurrection," *Igeret T'chiyat Hameitim.*

[76]As in the verse: "they did not know that Joseph understands (*shomeya*), because the interpreter was between them"—Gen. 42:23, or as in the Rabbinic statement: "The word *sh'ma* means in any language that you *shomeya*—understand"—*Berachot* 13a.

Vayakhel

35:34   *V'Oholiav*—"And Oholiav."

RASHI: Of the tribe of Dan, of the lowest tribes, of the sons of the maid-servants (namely Bilhah). Yet the Omnipresent *(ha-Makom)* made him equal to Bezalel with regard to the construction of the Tabernacle, although he (Bezalel) came from the greatest of tribes (Judah!) in order to fulfill what is stated: "He does not regard the rich more than the poor" (Job 34:19).[77]

COMMENT: Question: Maybe God made Oholiav equal to Bezalel because he was wise and an expert like him, but not "in order to fulfill what is stated, etc."?

The author of *Devek Tov* answers: Since Oholiav was with Bezalel, it should have stated: "He put into *their* hearts (= gave them the ability) to teach." Since it says "into his heart" it must refer only to Bezalel, meaning that Bezalel alone taught them how to do everything—whereas Oholiav was no different than the other craftsmen. If so, why was he singled out by name? Therefore Rashi explains: "He was from the tribe of Dan ... in order to fulfill what is stated, etc."

However, the main reason Rashi cites the Midrash is because verse 34 is not written in the proper order. This is how it should have been written: "And with him was Oholiav.... He filled them with a wise heart, etc." At the *end* it should have stated: "and He put into their hearts to teach." Since the verse emphasizes: "He and Oholiav ... from the tribe of Dan," this means that the Torah wishes to stress their equality. Now why was it necessary to emphasize their equality? To teach us this lesson that God shows no more regard for the rich than for the poor.

---

[77] *Tanchuma, Ki Tisa* 13.

Pekudei

38:21 *Hamishkan mishkan*—"The Tabernacle, the Tabernacle of."

RASHI: The word *mishkan* is written two times, as an allusion to the Temple which was taken as a pledge (*nitmashkeyn*)—"as a security-pledge for Israel's repentance"—by being destroyed twice for Israel's sins.[78]

Mishkan haeydut—"The Tabernacle of Testimony."

RASHI: A testimony to Israel that the Holy One, blessed be He, has forgiven (lit. *viteyr*—"forgone") them for the matter of the golden calf. He made His *Shechinah* dwell among them (by means of the Tabernacle).

COMMENT: One may ask: Wherein lies the similarly to a "pledge" here? A pledge is an object that the lender holds onto until the money is returned to him; if the money is not returned, he keeps the pledge forever. If so, in order that the simile should be valid, one must explain what "debt" Israel incurred toward God, and how could the Tabernacle–Temple serve as a pledge for a debt?

We may explain this by showing the equal aspects in both: Just as a pledge is equal in value to the sum of money that was loaned against it (sometimes it is worth more than the debt), so is there an equal value between the Jewish People and the Temple in God's eyes. This may be explained with the words of the prophet: "This people I have formed for Myself that they may declare My praise" (Isaiah 43:21), namely: The task of the Jewish People is to publicize the Name of God in all the world ("that they may declare My Name"). This is also one of the main tasks of the Temple—to publicize God's name in the world. Rashi on Duet. 33:19 states: "the people (tribes) will assemble at the mount." Another explanation is: Due to the business of Zevulun the gentile merchant would come to his

---

[78]*Tanchuma, Pekudei* 5; Exod. *Rabbah* 51.

land ... and they would say: Seeing that we have bothered to come up here, let us go to Jerusalem and see what is (the nature of) the God of this nation (Israel), and what is their conduct? They see that all the Jews worship one God, and eat one (kind of) food (= Kosher). Now among the gentiles, the deity of this one is not the deity of that one, and the food of this one is not the food of that one. And they say: There is no nation as worthy (lit. *K'sheyrah*—"Kosher") as this one, *and they convert there*, as stated: "There they slaughter offerings of righteousness."

It appears from the above that the Jewish People and the Temple are equal in the task of publicizing Godliness in the world. There is yet another equal aspect to both: Just as the borrower wants to get back his pledge, and as soon as he has the money he redeems it from the lender by paying the debt, so too the Jewish People want the Divine Presence to reside in the Temple, and is prepared to redeem it from the lender—God, by repenting their sins, on account of which it was taken as a pledge (destroyed—the Temple). However, as long as they have *not* repented, they cannot get their pledge—the Temple—back, since both have the task of publicizing God's name in the world. How could the Jews publicize God's name in the world if they themselves do not fulfill his wishes—this would be a contradiction in terms. But as soon as they repent and the *Shechinah* will once more reside in the Third Temple, may it be rebuilt in our days, the two—the Temple and Israel—will once more be able to fulfill their major function—to publicize God's name in the world.

> 38:22   *U'Vtzalel ben Uri etc., asah et kol asher tzivah*
> *Hashem et Moshe*—"And Bezalel, son of Uri, etc.,
> did all that God commanded Moses."

RASHI: "That Moses commanded" is not written here, but "All that *God* commanded Moses," i.e., even things which his teacher (Moses) did *not* tell him,[79] his own opinion was in agreement with what was said to Moses on Sinai.[80] [For Moses told Bezalel to make first the vessels and afterwards the Tabernacle. But Bezalel said to him: "It is customary for people (lit. the world) to make first a house and then they put vessels inside it." Moses said to him: "So, indeed, did I hear from the mouth of the Holy One, blessed be he." Moses (further) said to him: "In the shadow of God (*B'tzel ey-l*, similar to his name *B'tzalel*) have you been, for certainly God commanded

---

[79]Like the overlay of the pillars—*Chizkuni*.
[80]Jerusalem Talmud *Peah* 1:1; Gen. *Rabbah* 1.

me (to make the Tabernacle first). And thus Bezalel made the Tabernacle first and afterwards he made the vessels.][81]

COMMENT: Some of the greatest supercommentaries on Rashi went to great lengths to explain this in a way that it should not contradict the explicit statements in section *Terumah, Vayakhel* and *Ki Tisa* (where Moses was explicitly commanded to make the Tabernacle first).[82]

However, most fitting are the comments of "Torah Temimah" on the statement in the Yerushalmi. Here is a portion of his comments: "It comes to intimate that anything a person does with the intention of fulfilling God's will and for the sake of heaven," he is aided (from Heaven) to arrive at the very truth of the matter.... Since Bezalel did everything for the sake of Heaven in order to fulfill the wish of the Omnipresent (*ha-Makom*), his opinion concurred with that of God, even in things which he did not hear from Moses...."

It would seem that this is the *very* moral that Rashi meant to teach us by citing the statement of the Rabbis on this verse, since there is absolutely no difficulty here according to the "plain sense" of the verse. Here, too, Rashi is seen as the great educator that he was.

39:33   *Vayaviu et hamishkan, etc.*— "They brought the Tabernacle to Moses, etc."

RASHI: For they were not able to erect it. And since Moses had not done any work in (the construction of) the Tabernacle, God left him its erection, for no man was able to erect it, because of the heaviness of the boards, for no man had the strength to set them up—but Moses set it up. Moses said to God: "How is its erection possible by human beings?" God answered him: "Put your hand on it." It appeared as if Moses erected it, but (actually) it stood and arose by itself. That is why it says: "The Tabernacle *was erected*" (passive form, 40:17) i.e., it was erected by itself. That is a Midrash of Rabbi Tanchuma.

---

[81]The entire section in square brackets is missing in the Editio Princeps—the first printing of Rashi—1474–75. However, it is the statement of Rabbi Yochanan in *Berachot* 55a with minor changes in wording and an additional statement. Apparently, some student or printer added this statement on his own, in order to explain Rashi's statement: "Even things which his teacher did *not* tell him, his opinion agreed with what was said to Moses on Sinai."
[82]Cf. *Gur Aryeh; Levush Haorah; Divrei David; Be'er Mayim Chaim.* See also *Maskil LeDavid*, who offers a Kabbalistic explanation of our Rashi.

COMMENT: Question: Why was it necessary that Moses should do at least *some* work in the Tabernacle, to such an extent that God had to erect it by a miracle? We know that it is improper to resort to miracles, except in a dire need—usually for a communal purpose, not for an individual.[83] Why was there a dire need for a miracle?

One may answer in two ways: First, if Moses would have *no* part whatever in the building of the Tabernacle—not even in its erection—it could cause him great pain. A place that was meant to be the center of the Divine Presence on earth—and as the Rabbis expressed it: "the Holy One, blessed be He, *desired* to have a dwelling in the lower world,"[84] or according to another version of this idea: "God *desired* that *just as* He has an abode above, *so* should He have an abode below"[85] and Moses was the one who brought down the *Shechinah* "Below ten tefachim[86]—*l'matah mey'asarah t'fachim*—"he should have no part in the work of the Tabernacle"?!

We find that when it was decreed that Moses should not enter the Land of Israel, God told him: "Go up this mount of Avarim—Mount Nevo ... and see the land of Canaan ... for from a distance shall you see the land, *but you will not enter there*" (Deut. 43:49–52), and Rashi remarks there: "For I know that you love it (the land), therefore I tell you: Go up and see it." Here too: if Moses had no opportunity to do *anything*, for the Tabernacle, his pain would have been too great—and God does not wish the righteous to suffer so much.

Second, if Moses would not have the merit to do anything for the Tabernacle, it could cause a denigration of his honor in the eyes of the people—God forbid. They might have mumbled behind his back: "This son of Amram is not what he appears to be, for we simple folk merited to donate to the Tabernacle—wherein the Divine Presence resides—and even to construct it, whereas Moses had no part in it at all! Surely he isn't what he seems to be. Therefore God prevented him from having *any* part in the Tabernacle."

---

[83] See e.g., *Chullin* 43a; *Berachot* 60a. Cf. *Talmudic Encyclopedia* Vol. I, coll. 681.
[84] *Tanchuma, Naso* 7; See a lengthy explanation for this statement in *Tanya,* Chap. 36.
[85] *Tanchuma, Bechukotai* 3. The difference between the two versions is: According to the first statement: "God desired to have a dwelling *in the lower world,*" the main Presence of the *Shechinah* is here on earth. This is in accord with the statement in Gen. *Rabbah* 19:13: "the main *Shechinah* was *in the lower worlds.*" Whereas according to the statement: "God desired that *just as* He has an abode above, so should He have an abode below," the upper and lower worlds are equal in the matter of the Divine Presence.
[86] A "tefach" is the width of a fist, approximately $3^1/2$–4 inches, i.e., Moses brought down the *Shechinah* from heaven to earth.

We have a rule that if a Torah scholar is embarrassed, it is an embarrassment for the Torah itself. Who is there greater (in learning) than Moses? Why, the very Torah is called *Torat Moshe*—"The Torah of Moses"! Besides: "A king who forgoes his honor, his honor is *not* forgiven"[87] and Moses was in the category of a king. Indirectly it could even cause a desecration of God's Name, for some might harbor a grudge toward God complaining: "This is the man whom God chose to be our leader and to receive the Torah! We see that he is not even worthy of taking part in the work of the Tabernacle! It must be that God doesn't know him as well as we do." There is no greater desecration of God's Name than that!

We have a principle: "Where there is a desecration of God's Name, we do *not* give honor even to a master."[88] Now, all-the-more-so do we not *withhold* honor for the above reasons. Hence, there was a great need for Moses to have *some* part in the work of the Tabernacle, or at least in its erection—even though a miracle would have to be worked, since this was not *only* for the sake of the individual, but for the benefit of the entire community, and to prevent the desecration of God's Name.

---

[87] *Ketubot* 17a.
[88] *Berachot* 19b—in order to *prevent* a desecration of the Name.

Leviticus

Vayikra

1:1 *Leimor*—"Saying."

RASHI: Go and speak to them words of contrition *(divrei k'vushin)*, i.e., "It is for *your* sake that He speaks with me!"[1] For all the thirty-eight years, during which Israel was in the desert, as it were excommunicated—from the time of sending of the spies on—there was no *intimate* conversation (of God) with Moses, for it is stated: "When all the warriors among the people had died, the Lord spoke to me saying... (Deut. 2:16–17): "Only *then* did God speak to me again."[2]

COMMENT: Rashi's comment is difficult: Elsewhere Rashi remarked that speech expressed by the Hebrew root *a'm'r* is "soft speech," *not* admonishment, for in Exod. 19:3 on: "Thus shall you say *(tomar)* to the House of Jacob," Rashi writes: "To the House of Jacob, refers to the women—*tell* them *(tomar)* in *b'lashon rakah*—"soft speech?"

Answer: Indeed for Israel these are words of comfort: "For *your* sake He speaks with me" shows how beloved they are by God. Thus they can also serve as an admonishment: When they hear how much God approves of them, they will be inclined to return to Him in penitence. However, to Moses these are harsh words, for he did not merit an *intimate* communication from God *(dibur panim el panim)* in his *own* right, only thanks to Israel!

(Comp. "Face to face did God *speak* with you"—Deut. 5:4 and "Mouth to mouth do I *speak* to him"—Numbers 12:8. In both the root—*d'b'r*—"speak" is used connoting: "face to face/mouth to mouth").

RASHI: Another explanation of *leimor* (meaning: "to speak to God"): "Go and tell them My commands, and bring Me back their answer if they accept

---

[1]Rashi in *Taanit* 15a explains: *divrei k'vushin*—Words of contrition—that cause the hearts to be contrite and repent, namely words of admonishment."
[2]*Sifra*, Chap. 2:13.

them, as is stated: "Moses returned the words of the people to the Lord" (Exod. 19:8).

COMMENT: This second explanation seems to be closer to the "plain sense." If so, why did Rashi cite the Midrash first, unlike his usual manner to first give the *plain* sense? It would seem that the reason is that here Rashi wished to underscore how important Israel is in the eyes of God to such an extent that only in *their* own merit did God speak with Moses. This principle is more important than the plain sense; therefore Rashi cites it first.

1:17 *Lo yavdil*—"He should not separate it."

RASHI: It is stated (here) of a bird-offering: "a pleasing odor (to the Lord)," and it is stated of an animal sacrifice: a "pleasing odor (to the Lord)"— verse 13, to tell you: Whether one offers much (an animal) or little (a bird)—it is equally pleasing to God, provided he directs his heart to Heaven (= has the proper intention to serve God).[3]

COMMENT: According to "plain sense" the above inference is *not* absolutely required, since about a meal-offering (*minchah*) the words "a pleasant odor" are also mentioned (below 2:2, 9)—yet there Rashi does not comment at all because according to plain sense there is no difficulty. This inference is a moral lesson, which Rashi as an educator is interested in teaching us—not for the sake of the "plain sense."

3:1 *Sh'lamim*—"Peace-offerings."

RASHI: (They are called *sh'lamim*) because they bring peace (*shalom*) into the world. Another explanation: (They are called *sh'lamim*) because through them there is "peace" (lack of envy) to the altar to the priests and to the owner of the sacrifice (since all three receive a portion).[4]

COMMENT: Both of Rashi's explanations are from "Torat Kohanim = *Sifra*" (the *halachic* Midrash on Leviticus) 16:1–2, but one may ask:

1) What is meant by: "They bring peace into the world;" how is this accomplished by sacrificing peace-offerings?

---

[3] *Menachot* 110a; *Sifra*, Chap 9:6.
[4] *Sifra* 16:1–2 and comp. Rashi Exod. 29:22.

2) What is the advantage of peace-offerings over other sacrifices in this matter of bringing peace into the world?

"Maskil LeDavid" writes: "They bring peace, etc." Another explanation, etc.—for according to the first explanation (it is difficult), since *all* sacrifices bring peace into the world, as the intention is that *they cause the unification above of God and the Jewish People* (obviously a kabbalistic concept—P. D.) and that is peace in the world, and that is why they are called *korbanot*—for they bring close the attributes. "See Rabenu Bechayey, etc."

Now, Rabenu Bechayey writes on the verse: "If his sacrifice is a burnt offering from the herd" (1:13): "By way of a Kabbalistic explanation: the verse preceded the burnt-offering because it is a brick. Therefore the order of the sacrifices is: first the burnt-offering; then peace-offerings; then the ox of the three names (of God) in the Thirteen Attributes: The burnt-offering is above the attributes.[5] Peace-offerings is *the go-between them to complete them*; the sin-offering is for the Jewish People, etc."

According to the above we may say that the advantage of peace-offerings over other sacrifices is that they *go between* (compromise) the Attributes: Loving-Kindness and Might (*chesed-g'vurah*), just as the Attribute "Tiferet" compromises between them. According to Kabbalah "Tiferet" is the Attribute of Jacob, who was "the choice of the forefathers"; whereas the Attribute of Abraham is "Loving-Kindness," and that of Isaac is "Might." If so, peace-offerings have an advantage over other sacrifices since they correspond to Tiferet—just as Jacob was "the choice of the fore-fathers" and his image "is engraved under the Throne of Glory."[6] Hence, they bring peace into the world more so than other sacrifices all of which are brought to atone for a sin (even a burnt-offering, which atones for improper thoughts and for omitting a positive command), whereas "peace-offerings" bring only peace into the world.

4:17 *Et p'nei h'aparochet*—"In front of the curtain."

RASHI: But above (verse 6, in reference to the ox of the High Priest) it states: "in front of the Curtain of the *Holy*." The difference may be ex-

---

[5]See Rabbi C. D. Chavel's interpretation in his edition of *Rabenu Bechayey*, Mosad Harav Kook, 1981, Vol. II, pp. 396–97: "The burnt-offering is above the attributes; they are the three upper ones. *Peace-offerings is the go-between Tiferet*, sin-offering for the crown (of) the Jewish People. This is the opinion of the Ramban in *Ki Tisa*, portion of the Thirteen Attributes (Naftali)."
[6]Gen. *Rabbah* 82:2.

plained by comparing it to a king against whom the country revolted. If only a minority revolted, his council (familia) still exists, but if the whole country revolted, his council no longer exists (see *Zevachim* 41b and Rashi there). Here, too, if the High Priest *alone* sinned, the appellation of "sanctity" attached to the place still remains on the Temple. But when *all* of them sinned, *God forbid*, the "holiness" disappears. (I.e., the *Shechinah* departs from the Temple and the curtain is no longer *parochet ha'kodesh*—"Curtain of Holiness.")

COMMENT: Question: Since the Community sinned inadvertently, why should the holiness depart? The reason is because even an inadvertent sin is considered "a sin" and requires atonement. (See *Shevuot* 2b; Rashi Gen. 9:5: "for every man for that of his brother—i.e., whom he loves like a brother, and killed him accidentally, I will require of him if he does not go into banishment and begs forgiveness for his sin, for also an accidental sin requires atonement, etc.")

A *cheit*—"sin" means missing the mark, as in: "all these could sling a stone at a hair and *v'lo yachati*—"not miss" (Judges 20:16). A person who sinned, did not fulfill the wish of the Creator at that moment, even if it was accidental, so that he *missed* the target. Therefore he requires *kaparah*—"atonement," which is an expression of "wiping away and removing,"[7] namely: It is necessary to wipe away and remove the impression left by an act that was against the will of the Creator.

Rashi is precise in stating: "*God forbid* the holiness disappears." Similarly in *Zevachim* 41b Rashi writes: "Here, too, since the majority of the Community sinned *kivyachol*—as it were there is no holiness here," because in reality the *Shechinah* (holiness) does not *ever* depart from Israel completely—even in their impurity.[8] It is only "as it were" that there is no more Holiness.

---

[7]As Rashi points out in his comment on Gen. 32:21: "I will atone his face—*achaprah panav*—It seems to me that every expression of atonement—*kaparah* in reference to 'sin' or 'face'—all of them are a matter of wiping away and removal, etc."
[8]See Rashi Levit. 16:16: "Who resides among them within their impurity—even though they are impure, the *Shechinah* is among them (*Yoma* 57a)—and even in exile, which is a result of their sinning (as the Torah itself promises: 'But despite all this, while they will be in the land of their enemies, I will not reject them, nor spurn them, etc.' "—Levit. 26:44).

Tzav

8:36 *Vaya'as Aharon uvanav*—"Aaron and his sons did."

RASHI: It comes to tell their praise that they did not swerve to the right, nor to the left.[9]

COMMENT: Would it occur to anyone that such holy people would diverge an iota from God's command, that the Torah had to testify that they did *not* swerve to the right or left? Is it really a *praise* for people of their caliber?

We may arrive at an answer to the above questions if we pay attention to Rashi's precise wording: "that they did not *swerve* (*hitu*—"incline") to the right or left"; he did not write the usual expression: "to tell their praise that they did not *change* (*shinu*)." This wording is precise and deliberate, and may be understood by means of the following anecdote cited by the renowned writer S. Y. Agnon in one of his stories:

> The Rabbi of Zhitomir asked the Rabbi of Berditchev about the verse: "And Aaron did so," where Rashi explains: "It comes to tell us that he did not change." Now, is that possible? God told Aaron to light the candles, is it possible for him to change? If the Almighty commanded an *ordinary* person, would he change anything? What then is the praise of Aaron that he did not change? However (answered the Rabbi of Zhitomir) if God had told the Rabbi of Berditchev to light the candles, he would most likely have the greatest awe and enthusiasm, and while preparing to light, he would have spilt the oil on the ground, out of awe and enthusiasm, and would not manage to light them. But Aaron, who doubtless had the greatest awe and enthusiasm, when he came to light the candles, he fulfilled God's command exactly and managed to light without any change."[10]

---

[9]*Sifra, Tzav, Yalkut Shimoni* 519.

[10]Cf. All the Stories of Shmuel Yosef Agnon, Vol. II, Elu Vaelu, Shocken Books, Jerusalem 1960, pp. 140–41 (Hebrew).

According to the above, Rashi's precise wording "that they did not *swerve* (*hitu*)" is enlightening: Aaron and his sons were the owners of the sacrifices during the seven days of their initiation (*miluim*), whereas Moses served as the priest, as Rashi pointed out (Exod. 29:24, 33). As "owners" Aaron and his sons had to lay their hands on the heads of the sacrifices, and to waive them—as stated in this *parsha* (8:14, 18, 22, 27). Had they "swerved–inclined" their hands to the right or left, out of great enthusiasm and awe, they would not have fulfilled the mitzvah of laying the hands and waiving at all. As a result all their sacrifices would have become *invalid*, and they would not become initiated as priests for service in the Tabernacle, God forbid! When it comes to "laying hands and waiving" it is more fitting to say "they did not *swerve*-incline," since what is meant is the "swerving–inclining" of the hands "right or left." Hence Rashi's precise wording.

Shemini

11:2 *Zot ha'chayah*—"These are the creatures (that you may eat, etc.)."

RASHI: The word *ha'chayah* is an expression of life: because Israel cleave to God and deserve to be living (*zot ha'chayah* means: "This, O living nation, may you eat, etc."). He therefore separated them from what is impure (animals) and imposed commandments upon them, whereas to the (other) nations He prohibited nothing. This may be compared to a physician who came to visit a sick person, etc., as is mentioned in the Midrash of Rabbi Tanchuma.[11]

COMMENT: The parable in Tanchuma, *Shemini* 6 is as follows: "A physician came to visit *two* sick people. He saw that one of them was incurable, so he told his household: Give him any food he asks for. He saw that the other would live, so he told them: Such-and-such food he *may* eat, but such-and-such he may *not* eat! They asked the physician: "Why did you allow one to eat whatever he wishes, but the other you restricted?" He answered them: "The one who is destined to live, I told him: 'This you may eat, but that you shouldn't eat." But about the one who will not live (anyway), I said: 'Give him *whatever* he desires, for he won't live anyway'." Similarly, God permitted the nations the abominable creatures and creeping things. But Israel, who are destined to live, he told them: "Be holy for I am holy; do not abhor your souls; this you shall eat and this you shall not eat; do not defile yourselves by them, for you will become defiled." Why so? Because they are destined for life, as is stated: "But you who cleave to the Lord your God, are all of you alive today, etc." Rashi abridged this Midrash.

Rashi emphasizes: "as is mentioned in the Midrash of Rabbi Tanchuma," even though a similar, but briefer version is cited in Levit. *Rabbah* 13:2, because in the Levit. *Rabbah* version the reading is: "Similarly, the nations of the world who are not destined for *life in the Future World*, etc., but Israel who are destined for *life in the Future World*, these are the creatures that you

---

[11]Cf. *Tanchuma, Shemini* 6: Leviticus *Rabbah* 13:2.

may eat." Rashi wished to stress that refraining from eating impure animals, birds, creeping creatures, and fish is important even for life in *this* world, for they harm the body and stupefy and dull the soul. Israel must beware of anything that harms the body and dulls the mind and soul, in order to be able to fulfill the commands of the Creator without any physical or mental hindrance. Therefore, Rashi prefers the version in *Tanchuma*, because according to it Israel is destined for life also in *this* world—as the Midrash concludes with the verse: "But you who cleave to the Lord your God, are all of you alive *today*."

11:8   *Uv'nivlatam lo tiga'u*—"Nor shall you touch their carcass."

RASHI: One might think that ordinary Israelites (non-priests) are forbidden to touch a carcass (anytime)? It therefore states (regarding defilement by touching a corpse): "Speak to the priests, etc." (21:1)—priests are prohibited (from touching it), but ordinary Israelites are not forbidden. Hence, we can make the logical inference a fortiori (*kal v'chomer*): If uncleanness caused by touching a corpse, which is a severe kind of uncleanness, still the Torah forbids it only to priests, then surely uncleanness caused by a carcass—which is less stringent than a corpse (i.e., by touching a corpse one becomes defiled for seven days, but by touching a carcass only until that evening)—all the more so that only priests are forbidden! If so, why does it state here "nor touch their carcass?" It refers to a Festival (Passover, Shavuot, and Sukkot, when every male Israelite was obliged to appear in the Temple, and would therefore be in a state of cleanness).[12]

COMMENT: Since all Jews are obliged to come to the Temple on the three Pilgrimage Festivals to bring sacrifices, and if they touch a carcass they will not be allowed to enter the Temple, therefore even ordinary Israelites were bidden to remain clean during their pilgrimages. But the rest of the year they are allowed to defile themselves, if they so wish.

QUESTION: Why did Rashi find it necessary to cite a Midrash *halachah* here, which is *not* the "plain sense," according to which there is no mention of Festivals in the verse?
Answer: Rashi wished to teach two things:

1)   To set the minds of ordinary Israelites at rest, for they were *not* forbidden to touch a carcass most of the year. This was necessary

---

[12]See *Rosh Hashanah* 16b; *Sifra, Shemini* 4:8–9; and comp. Rashi on Deut. 14:18 and *Yevamot* 29b.

because the "plain sense" of the verse sounds as though *every* Jew is forbidden at *all times* to touch a carcass! This is something most people cannot adhere to. As the Teacher of the People par excellence, Rashi found it necessary to set the minds of the common folk at rest—they should not worry about not touching a carcass—a most difficult task for them (especially in a rural agricultural society where dead animals are common!).

2) On the other hand Rashi wished to teach that on a Festival *every* Jew should keep away from touching a carcass, for surely "The Temple will be rebuilt speedily,"[13] and it will be necessary once more to make pilgrimages to bring sacrifices.

From Rashi's commentary both here and in *Yevamot* 29b, it appears that he held that even ordinary Israelites must remain in a state of cleanness on the Festivals as a *Torah* obligation. This is also the opinion of Maimonides.[14] However, Ramban on this verse states explicitly that it is only an obligation ordained by the Rabbis.

However from Rashi's statement here: "One might think that ordinary Israelites are *forbidden* to touch a carcass?" It appears that they are not *forbidden* even on a Festival! But the statement: "Why then does it state 'nor touch their carcass'"? It refers to a Festival—is only good advice, so that they should be prepared to enter the Temple and partake of the sacrifices, since "the Temple will be rebuilt speedily" (any day now!).

11:43 *V'nitmeitem bam*—"Lest you become defiled through them."

RASHI: If you defile yourselves through them on earth, I will defile you (i.e., treat you as defiled) in the world-to-come and in the heavenly court (*bi'yshivat ma'lah*). In *Yoma* 39a, on which this Rashi draws, the last two words "in the heavenly court *bi'yshivat ma'lah*" are *not* mentioned. Neither did Mizrachi have them in his edition of Rashi. Most likely they are an addition of some copyist, who understood *Ani m'tamei etchem* as "I will *declare* you unclean," and therefore supplied the phrase *bi'yshivat ma'lah*—"in the heavenly court."

COMMENT: The end of this verse sounds self-contradictory: First it states: "You should *not defile* yourselves by them"; then it ends: *v'nitmeihem bam*—"You *will become defiled* by them"? Therefore Rashi explains that if you defile yourselves here on earth, the result will be that *I* will defile you in the world-to-come and in the heavenly court.

---

[13] *Sukkah* 41a; *Sanhedrin* 22b; *Bechorot* 53b.
[14] *Hilchot Tum'at Ochalin* 16:10.

From Rashi's wording in our printed editions: "In the world-to-come *and* in the heavenly court *ba'olam haba u'vishivat ma'lah*," it appears that they are different entities. One might say that the "heavenly court" refers to the world of souls after death, as it exists *now* before the advent of the Messiah and the life in the Hereafter. Namely, a person who defiles himself through various abominable creatures in *this* life, is rejected and banished from the world of souls (the heavenly court), for God—Who is Holy—and he cannot dwell together. The "world-to-come" refers to the period *after* the Messianic era, after the resurrection of the dead—everlasting life. A person who defiles himself by various abominable creatures is banished from these realms also (unless, of course, he repented before his death).

Tazria

12:2 *Ishah ki tazria*—
"When a woman conceives" (lit. "brings forth seed").

RASHI: Rabbi Simlai said: Just as the creation of man was after that of every cattle, beast, and fowl at the time of Creation, so also the law regarding man was set forth after the law regarding cattle, beast, and fowl.[15]

COMMENT: You might ask: Why wasn't Rashi satisfied with the "plain sense" of these words, and what does the Midrash of R. Simlai add to their meaning? Another difficulty: In *Sanhedrin* 38a are given a number of reasons why man was created last:

1) should he boast, one could tell him: "even a mosquito was created before you,"
2) so that he should enter into the mitzvah of the Sabbath immediately,
3) so that he should enter the feast immediately[16]—and other reasons, none of which apply here? Another difficulty: Woman was created *after* man, why then were the laws of defilement of a woman set forth *before* the laws of defilement of a *male* leper (which begins only in Chapter 14)?

The above may be explained as follows: The words: "When a woman conceives—*ishah ki tazria*" seem superfluous; the verse should have stated merely: *Ishah asher teileid zachar*—"A woman who gives birth to a male, shall be defiled, etc." The phrase *v'yaldah zachar*—"When she conceives (brings forth seed) and *will* bear a son" intimates that it is a sure thing that if a woman "brings forth seed," she will *definitely* bear a son—who is to guaranty

---

[15]Which was given in Chapter 11. Levit. *Rabbah* 14. Comp. *Sanhedrin* 38a; *Yalkut Shimoni* 547.

[16]He should find everything prepared for him and eat whatever he desired—Rashi.

121

that this will be the case? Therefore, Rashi explains that this is inherent in the superfluous words *ishah ki tazria*—"a woman who will bring forth seed," having in mind the rule: "If a woman brings forth seed (= climaxes during intercourse) first, she will give birth to a male child; if a man climaxes first, she will have a girl."[17] If so, why did Rashi not cite this rule explicitly, as in *Nidah* 31a, which derives this rule from our verse? His citing R. Simlai's Midrash leads one to believe that it is a general introduction to the *whole parsha*?

The answer is that Rashi emphasizes the word "Torah—instruction/ law" in R. Simlai's statement, meaning that this rule: If a woman climaxes first, she will give birth to a male child, etc., is "Torah—instruction for life."[18] Namely: Just as knowledge of the clean and unclean (= Kosher and non-Kosher) cattle, beasts, fish, and fowl is *Torah*—since the unclean animals, beasts, fowl, and fish are harmful to both body and soul, so is knowledge of intimate marital life, including the rule "If a woman climaxes first, she will give birth to a male, etc."—*Torah,* and needs to be studied.[19]

In light of the above the Torah *does* indeed mention matters pertaining to the *male* first: "If a woman conceives and gives birth to a *male*"—whose creation came before the females, and also because: "Happy is he whose children are male, etc."[20]—and this depends upon "When a woman brings forth seed (climaxes)," which is Torah = instruction. However, since giving birth to a male child causes defilement to the woman, the Torah proceeds to delineate the laws relevant to the defilement of the mother.

---

[17]*Nidah* 31a; comp. Rashi Gen. 46:15.
[18]Comp. our interpretation on Gen. 1:1 s.v.—*B'reishit, B'reishit bara*—when God was first creating.
[19]Cf. *Berachot* 62a that Rav Kahana used the expression: "It is Torah and I need to learn it" to justify his observation of his master Rav's conduct with his wife during intimate relations specifically.
[20]*Kiddushin* 82a.

Metzora

14:4   *T'horot*—"Clean ones."

RASHI: This word *t'horot* excludes an unclean bird (of a species that may not be eaten).[21] Because plagues (of leprosy) come as punishment for slander, which is done by chattering, therefore birds were required for his purification because birds chatter constantly with a twittering sound.[22]

COMMENT: Question: Why didn't Rashi give the reason for the requirement of birds on the word *tziporim*—"birds" in the verse, but rather on the word *tehorot*—"clean ones"—what is the connection between their being "clean" and their "chattering"?

It would seem that the idea behind this is: Just as for the purification of the leper, who was punished by leprosy because of his chattering slanderous tales, only *clean* birds are suitable,[23] so one must be careful that his "chattering" (= speech) should always be "clean," e.g., chattering words of Torah, prayer, etc., and not chattering that is "unclean" such as slander, gossip, lies, etc.

---

[21] *Chullin* 14a.
[22] *Arachin* 16b. Comp. Rashi on Isaiah 8:19: *ham'tzaf'tzfim v'hamahgim*. See also: Mizrachi (who takes issue with Rashi); Ramban.
[23] Even though some unclean birds also chatter.

123

Acharei Mot

14:4 *V'natati panai*— "I will direct My anger (lit. I will set my face)."

RASHI: *Panai* means: *pnai sheli*—"My free time," i.e., I will turn away (*poneh*) from all My affairs and will concern Myself (only) with him.[24]

COMMENT: The phrase *V'natati panai; etein panai*, or *v'samti et panai* appears three times in the Torah (here, and Levit. 20:3,5; 26:17). Each time Rashi explains: "My free time, I will turn away, etc.," whereas Onkelos translates each time: *v'etein rugzi*—"I will set My anger."[25] Why does Rashi differ from Onkelos, whom he often follows?

It seems that Rashi prefers here to follow the *Sifra*, which understands the word *panai* not as "My face" (*panim*), but from *pnay*—"My free time," as if the letter *alef* is missing.[26]

Rashi does not follow Onkelos "My anger" in order to avoid, as far as possible an anthropomorphism: "My free time" is even less anthropomorphic than "My anger." He could *not* leave the phrase *v'natati panai*—lit. "I will set My *face*" without any explanation, because the *literal* meaning of these words is highly anthropomorphic and is not befitting God. It could, God forbid, mislead simple folk into believing that God has a *face*.

17:13 *Asher yatzud*—"Who will hunt."

RASHI: From this expression I know only that the blood of *hunted* animals must be covered with dust. From where do I know that this applies also

---

[24]*Sifra*, Chap.7:4; cf. also Targum Jonathan.
[25]Comp. Ibn Ezra on Levit. 26:17—"My wrath, anger, etc."
[26]Comp. Exod. 10:21 Rashi: *v'yameish* is like *v'yei'ameish*. There are many words that have the *aleph* missing, because the *aleph* is not felt in pronunciation, therefore the verse is not particular about leaving it out." Rashi gives additional examples there.

to geese and fowls (which do not require hunting, but are kept in the house)? Therefore it states: (*asher yatzud*) *tzeid*—"who hunts a *hunted* thing"—under any circumstance (whether hunted now or before). If so, why does it state: *asher yatzud*—"who will hunt" at all (let it state only *asher yishchat*—"who will slaughter, etc."—since "hunting" is *not* a prerequisite for covering the blood)? But it uses the term "hunting" to teach that one should not eat meat except after such *toilsome preparation.*[27]

COMMENT: Rashi's comment is based on a *Baraita* in *Chullin* 84a: "Our Rabbis taught: 'Who will hunt'—from this I know only if he (actually) hunts (then he must cover their blood). Whence do I know those that are already hunted, such as geese and fowls? It therefore states *tzeid*—"hunted thing"—in any manner. If so, why does it state 'Who will hunt'? *The Torah teaches proper conduct*—(*limdah Torah derech eretz*) that a person should *not* eat meat except by such (toilsome) preparation." Rashi there explains: "As if he is hunting, and does not have it at hand, namely: He should *not* eat meat constantly so that he should not become impoverished."

Rashi deleted the phrase "the Torah teaches proper conduct," which appears both in *Sifra* and in the Talmud. Why did he do so?

It would seem he deleted these words in order to make the statement more forceful, namely: This is not only good advice—so that he should not become impoverished—but there are other reasons, e.g., for health reasons one ought not to indulge in such frequent meat-eating. Without the words "The Torah taught *proper conduct* (*derech eretz*), the matter carries greater force, sounding almost as a prohibition—not merely good advice.[28]

[27]As hunting requires. *Chullin* 84a; *Sifra* 11:2.
[28]See, however, *Maskil LeDavid* who writes: "The reason for this is so as not to waste. However, this applied only to the early generations, who were strong and healthy (in the time of the Talmud). But we, who are overcome by weakness, the wasting away of our bodies takes precedence," namely: for *us* it is healthy to eat meat constantly. Yet in *our* generation doctors advise to minimize the consumption of meat, because it is *unhealthy!* See also Chafetz Chaim on the *Sifra* 11:12.

Kedoshim

14:4   *B'tzedek tishpot amitecha*—
"With righteousness shall you judge your fellow."

RASHI: The phrase means exactly what it implies (i.e., strict justice). Another explanation is: Judge your friend with an inclination in his favor.[29]

COMMENT: You might ask: Where is the difficulty in the "plain sense," which Rashi calls here *k'mashma'o*—"as it implies" meaning: the *literal* meaning of the words, without any Midrash—since the verse speaks to the judges. Why then is there a need for "another explanation," which is the Midrash?

It appears that Rashi emphasizes the word *amitecha*—"your fellow (colleague)," i.e., only your "colleague" must you judge righteously, but not every person. In this context it is enlightening to cite Maimonides' interpretation of the statement by Rabbi Joshua ben Perachya: "Judge *every person* with an inclination in his favor".[30]

> "If you see a person, whom you do not know whether he is righteous or wicked, doing something, or saying something that—if you explain it one way, it will turn out good; but looked at another way, it will be bad—take it that he meant well, don't think evil of him. But if the person is known for his piety, and you see him doing something... it behooves you to take it in his favor—since it is possible that it *is* good. You must not suspect him. Regarding this they said: 'Whoever suspects the innocent, will be punished physically.'"[31]

---

[29]Instead of "your friend," *Sifra*, Chap. 4:4 has: "*every* person: *et kol ha'adam.*" This is also the reading in *Avot* 1:6. Cf. *Shevuot* 30a; *Shabbat* 127b; *Sanhedrin* 32a; *Yalkut* 611.
[30]Maimonides' commentary to *Avot* 1:16.
[31]*Shabbat* 97a.

Conversely, if you see a person who is known to be wicked doing something that *appears* to be good—beware of him and do not trust him that his act is a good one, since there is a *possibility* of evil. Regarding this it is stated: "Though his voice is ingratiating, do not trust him, etc." (Proverbs 26:27). However, if the person is unknown to you, and his deed is (also) inconclusive in any direction (good or evil), then as a matter of piety one must incline in his favor...." It seems that by writing "your colleague" and not "every person," Rashi had in mind such a situation as described by Maimonides.

Rashi follows the text of the Talmud, which is more legally binding than *Sifra* and the Mishna in *Avot*. In the Gemara we read: "With righteousness shall you judge your colleague...." Another explanation: "Incline in your *friend's* (*chavercha*) favor."[32] Rav Joseph taught: "With righteousness shall you judge—*amitecha*—the nation (*am*) who is with you (*she'itcha*) in Torah and *mitzvot*—try to judge him favorably" (Interpreting *amitecha* as a combination of *am* and *she'itcha*—the People who is with you): In *Shabbat* 127a-b we read R. Asi said that R. Yochanan said: "Six things a person eats (enjoys) their dividends in this world, but their capital remains for the world-to-come. These are: hospitality... and he who judges his *friend* favorably. One who judges his friend favorably, he too is judged favorably (in heaven), etc." As stated above, Rashi preferred the version in the Talmud that is *legally* binding (and not a matter of *piety* as the Tractate *Avot* says, therefore it states "*every* person") and at the same time explains the words *chavercha*—"your colleague."

20:2 *V'el B'nai Yisrael tomar*—"Say to the Children of Israel."

RASHI: One is punished for (violating) the *prohibitions (onshin al ha'azharot)*.

COMMENT: What is the difficulty in these words that Rashi had to explain them? How did he improve the sense with his comment, "One is punished for the prohibitions," which is an obscure statement and itself needs to be explained?

It seems that Rashi's problem with these words is the Torah already introduced all the sexual prohibitions and that of Molech with the general statement: "Speak to the Children of Israel and tell them, etc." (above 18:1) in the previous *parsha*. If so, what need is there to state again: "Say to the Children of Israel," it should have begun immediately: "Whoever of the

---

[32]*Shevuot* 30a, where Rashi remarks: "The verse does not deal with the law of litigants, but one who sees his friend doing something which can be judged as a sin, or favorably, do not suspect him of a sin."

Children of Israel, etc."? Moreover, punishments are the domain of the court, not of the People—what sense is there in stating: "Say to the Children of Israel"? Therefore, Rashi explains: "One is punished for the prohibitions," namely: Tell them in a general way that there is a punishment for each prohibition stated in *Acharei Mot.* For there it states: "You shall keep My decrees and My laws, which man shall do, and by which he shall live" (18:5). A person might think: "(This is merely) good advice" (but not binding). Therefore you should warn them explicitly: "One is *punished* for the prohibitions" and the details of the various punishments are delineated in this entire *parsha* (section).

Am ha'aretz—"The people of the land."

RASHI: The People for whose sake the earth was created (i.e., Israel. Cf. Rashi Gen. 1:1). The People who are destined to inherit the Land (Canaan–Israel) by observing these commands.[33]

COMMENT: Question: What difficulty is there in the words "the people of the land" according to their "plain sense" meaning?

Answer: It should have stated "the entire *congregation* (*ha'eidah*) shall stone him,"[34] or: "All the people of his town shall stone him"[35] or: "the entire community" (*kol hakahal*)[36] as in other places. Therefore Rashi gives a reason for this special designation "the people of the land."

In *Sifra* 4:4 Rashi's comments are divided into *two* opinions: "Another explanation: The people of the land—the People for whose sake the earth was created." Rabban Gamliel says: The People who are destined to inherit the Land through these things (i.e., by keeping these commands). Rashi combined the two opinions in the *Sifra*, as if they are one. Why did he do so?

It would seem that in Rashi's view there is no controversy between the two opinions; each one of them emphasizes a different trait of the Jewish People. This may be understood better by comparing it to other statements of the Rabbis, e.g., "Jerusalem is destined to become like the Land of Israel, and the Land of Israel like the entire world."[37] Also: "Israel is destined to rule over the entire world from corner to corner."[38] Judging by such and

---

[33] *Sifra* 4:4.
[34] Comp. Levit. 24:14,16; Numbers 15:35.
[35] As in Deut. 21:21.
[36] Comp. Ezek. 23:47.
[37] *Pesikta Rabbati Shabbat ve-Rosh Chodesh* 2; *Yalkut Shimoni* Isaiah 503.
[38] Levit. *Rabbah* 36:2.

similar Rabbinic statements, there really is no controversy between the two opinions: Indeed the entire world was created for Israel, and they are destined to rule the entire world—the same idea in different words. This is what Rashi means to stress by combining the two opinions into one.

20:15   *V'et ha'behaimah ta'harogu*—"And you shall kill the animal."

RASHI: If the man sinned, how did the animal sin (having no understanding of sin)? But because the man's stumbling (sinning) was caused by the animal, Scripture said: "Let it be stoned!" All the more so does this apply to a person, who knows to distinguish between good and evil, and yet causes evil to his fellow man by making him sin (he will surely be punished severely)!

Similarly you must explain: "You shall utterly destroy all the places" (Deut. 12:2). We can draw a logical conclusion: If in the case of trees, which neither see nor hear, since they were the cause of a person's sin (who worshipped them), the Torah said: "Destroy, burn, and exterminate them!" A person who causes another to deviate from the path of life (i.e., the Torah) to the path of death (= sin)—all the more so that he will be punished.[39]

COMMENT: Rashi's comment is problematic for a number of reasons:

1) He writes: "If the man sinned, how did the animal sin?"—implying that sin does not apply to animals for lack of understanding, whereas regarding the Flood he writes: "For all flesh had *corrupted*—even animals, beasts, and fowl mated with different species"[40]—implying that sinning *does* apply to animals, beast, and fowl?

2) What need is there for a *second* proof from the trees; why is the first reason not enough?

3) Rashi does *not* state what will happen to a man who causes his fellow man to sin, nor to the one who causes another to stray from the path of life to the path of death?

---

[39] *Sifra* 11:5–6; *Sanhedrin* 54a, 55a.

[40] Gen. 6:12 and comp. his comment there verse 7: "From man to animal – they too *corrupted* their ways."

4) Why does Rashi not cite the second reason for killing the animal cited in the Mishna: "Another reason: so that the animal should not pass by in the street and people will remark: 'This is the one through which so and so was killed?'"[41]

Let us try to answer the above questions in their order.

1. As for the possibility of animals "sinning," from the wording here it appears that the man is the initiator, for it states: "A man who will lie with an animal," not: "If an animal lies with a man." Hence the man causes the sin and the animal only follows his act, without *intending* to make him sin. (At most it intends only to satisfy its own desire.) However, regarding the generation of the Flood, the Torah testifies: "For *all flesh* has corrupted," and Rashi remarks: "They were (deliberately) mating with species other than theirs"—even though *their* species were there. They could have satisfied their desire *and* propagated with their own species. Whereas when they mate with other species, they do *not* conceive. Therefore the Torah calls it "corruption," for they were created to propagate; for although, admittedly, they did not "sin" in the normal sense, they did "corrupt" their ways.

2. The example of the trees comes to underscore the fact that by merely *causing* a man's sin, they must be destroyed, thus: Whereas in the case of an animal one might argue that it did some act to *arouse* the man to lie with it. Hence it is in a way responsible for his sinning and must die— it has an *active* part in the sin. This is not true of trees, which have no *desires* of their own; one cannot argue that they *aroused* the man to worship them! They are completely *passive*. Nevertheless: "Because they were the cause of a person's sin, the Torah said: 'Destroy, burn, and exterminate, etc.'" This example strengthens the argument.

3. Rashi cannot state what will happen to a man who causes his fellow man to sin, or to the one who causes another to stray, etc., because their punishment is meted out by Heaven, not by a human court. Only one who entices to idolatry is punished by a human court, but not one who causes another to stray in other matters. God has many ways of punishing the one who deserves it.

4. Rashi does not cite the second reason: "So that the animal should not pass by in the street, etc." because as an educator he is interested in stressing the educational aspect of this logical inference (*kal va'chomer*) from one who causes another to sin, etc. Moreover, from the reason, "So

---

[41] *Sanhedrin* 54a.

that the animal should not pass by in the street, etc." we derive the principle: "God is considerate of people's honor" (*chas ha'makom al kevod ha'briyot*), which Rashi cites in the matter of Bilam's donkey, which was slain by the angel for that reason[42]—so as not to cause great embarrassment for Bilam, if it remained living.

20:17   *Chesed hu*—"It is a disgrace (lit. a kindness)."

RASHI: In Aramaic the Hebrew *cherpah* ("a disgrace") is rendered *chisuda*.[43] The Midrashic explanation of *chesed* is: If you should say: "But Cain married his sister!" The answer is: The Omnipresent (*ha'makom*) did a kindness (by allowing him to marry his sister) in order to build His world through Cain, as is stated: "The world was built through lovingkindness"—*chesed*.[44]

COMMENT: Rashi was obliged to cite the Midrash and was not satisfied with the plain sense that *chesed* is equivalent to the Aramaic *chisuda*—a disgrace, because only in the prohibition of marrying a sister do we find the expression *chesed*, not in any of the other sexual aberrations.

In *Sanhedrin* 58b we read: "Come hear, why did Adam not marry his daughter? In order that Cain should marry his sister, as it says: 'For I said: Let the world be built up through loving-kindness (*chesed*).' " Rashi there explains: "The beginning of the world (population) was built by *chesed*, for He commanded Adam to deal kindly with his son, and forbade her (his daughter) to Adam and permitted her for Cain, so that the world should be built. This is what is meant by the verse: 'If a man takes his sister, daughter of his father it is a kindness (*chesed hu*)—My allowing Cain was a kindness that I dealt with him.'"

One ought to ponder: To whom did the Lord do a kindness, surely: "They decided by vote that it would have been better for man *not to have been* created, but now that he *has* been created, let him examine his deeds (and correct them[45])." If so, it is no kindness? One may explain this in two ways:

1) The first kindness was to Cain, as Rashi pointed out: "He commanded Adam to deal kindly with his son," namely: Cain was *already* born and most likely had sexual desires. If he had to wait until his father

---

[42]Cf. Numbers 22:33 Rashi.
[43]Cf. Onkelos on Gen. 34:14.
[44]Psalms 89:3; *Sifra* 11:11; *Sanhedrin* 58b.
[45]*Eruvin* 13b.

had a daughter (who was not a sister born *together* with him) and until she grew up enough for him to marry her, he would have suffered acute sexual deprivation (since there were as yet no other women besides his sisters).

2) One may also explain in consonance with the Rabbinic statement: "The Holy One, blessed be He, desired to have an abode in the lower world"[46] or: "The Holy One, blessed be He, desired that just as He has an abode above, so He should have an abode below."[47] Or as the prophet says: "This People have I created for Myself that they may tell My praise."[48] According to these statements the main purpose of the world is the Residence of the *Shechinah* in it, and surely there is no King without a People (therefore the world *must* be populated). We can therefore say that the kindness is, as it were, to God that the world should be populated quickly, so that His Presence may reside in it quickly.

---

[46] *Tanchuma, Naso* letter 7 and see a lengthy explanation of this statement in *Tanya*, Chapter 36.
[47] *Tanchuma Bechukotai* letter 3.
[48] Isaiah 43:21.

Emor

22:28 *Oto v'et b'no*—"It and its offspring."

RASHI: This law applies only to the female (although the masculine form (*oto*) is used), that it is forbidden to slaughter the mother and its male or female young (on the same day); but it does *not* apply to the male parent, and it is permissible to slaughter the father and the son (or daughter) in one day. "It and its offspring"—slaughtering the young first and then the mother is also implied.[49]

COMMENT: Ostensibly Rashi's explanation is against the plain sense, since the verse is couched in the masculine *oto ve'et b'no*—lit. "him and his son," not: "her and her daughter." How is it possible to ignore the "plain sense" entirely and say: "It does *not* apply to the males, etc."? Even if we should say that the masculine wording is not to be taken literally, even then one should not *exclude* the male, but at most only *include* the female?[50]

It would appear that Rashi wished to interpret this verse according to the Halachah and he rules in accord with the Rabbis against Chanania that the law applies only to the female parent, not the male. Since this law affects the *entire* people (not only priests or the learned who are diligent and would know the law), and it is almost a *daily* occurrence, Rashi found it necessary to teach the law to the common folk, so that even those who are *not* fluent in the Talmud and its commentaries should not mistakenly believe that the law applies only to the male parent, not the female—as it appears ostensibly from the wording (masculine). Therefore Rashi did *not* explain here in accordance with plain sense.

---

[49] *Sifra, Parshata* 8:11–12, Chap. 8:1–4; *Chullin* 78b, 82b.

[50] Thus Ibn Ezra writes: "The mitzvah applies to the male and female." This is also the opinion of Chanania in *Chullin* 78b. See also: Maimonides, *Hilchot Shechitah* 12:11; *Haktav ve-HaKabbalah*; *Gur Aryeh*; and *Be'er Maim Chaim*.

Furthermore, Rashi sees the *halachic* tradition of the Rabbis as the true meaning of the verse. In that sense it *is* the "plain sense" of the verse.[51]

22:32 *V'lo t'chalelu*—"You shall not desecrate (My holy Name)."

RASHI: By transgressing My commands willfully. Since it says already, "You shall *not* desecrate My name" (which implies that it must be hallowed), what is the meaning of *V'nikdashti*—"I shall be hallowed?" (It implies a *positive* act of sanctification of the Name): Abandon yourself (i.e., your life) and hallow My name! I might think even in private (when no other Israelites are present when the gentile demands he transgresses a Divine command upon threat of execution)! Therefore it states: Among the Children of Israel. When offering himself to martyrdom, one should offer himself even on the threat of death (to be ready to die in order not to transgress the Torah!), for he who abandons himself on condition of a miracle (= expecting a miracle will occur and he will *not* have to die)—no miracle will be wrought for him. Thus we find in the case of Chanania, Mishael, and Azariah that they did *not* offer themselves for martyrdom expecting a miracle will occur, as is stated: "[And God whom we worship is able to deliver us from the burning, fiery furnace, and He will deliver us out of your hand, O King]. "But if not, be it known unto you that we will *not* serve your gods, etc.—Whether He saves us, or does not save us, "be it known unto you (that we will not serve your gods)" (Daniel 3:17–18).[52]

COMMENT: There is a slight difficulty in that *V'nikdashti*—"I shall be sanctified" is a passive form, meaning automatically, i.e., If you do not desecrate My name, as a result I will be sanctified. If so, how do we learn from here: "Abandon yourself to martyrdom and sanctify My name," which is an *active* form of sanctification?

One might say that the passive form (*nifal*) comes here to indicate that the mitzvah of sanctification of the Name of God *is* to a certain extent *passive* in that one need not *look* for a chance to offer his life for martyrdom actively. On the contrary, a person must do all in his power to remain alive, in order to be able to fulfill His commandments, as is stated: "You shall

---

[51]We have remarked on several occasions that the *intent* of the verse is its "plain sense"—even if it may not be accepted to our *limited* understanding at first glance. Rashi rules like the Rabbis, not Chanania, in consonance with the rule that the law is like the majority against an individual authority.

[52]*Sifra*, Chap. 9:4–5. Cf. also *Tanchuma* 58:10; Levit. *Rabbah* 33:6; *Bamidbar Rabbah* 15:14; *Midrash Chazit* 2:30; 7:13; *Yalkut Shimoni*, Daniel 661.

keep My statutes and laws, which man shall do, and by which he shall *live*" (Levit. 18:15), meaning: He shall live by them—not die by them. However, if the mitzvah of sanctification of the Name comes to him *by chance*, as it happened to Chanania, Mishael, and Azariah—*without* searching it out *actively*, then surely it is a mitzvah even to die in order to sanctify God's Name in public.

23:22 *Uv'kutzr'chem*—"When you reap (the harvest of your land)."

RASHI: The Torah repeats the prohibition here (although it was already mentioned above in 19:9) in order to make one who transgresses this law (cutting the corner of the field, etc.) liable for *two* negative commands. Rabbi Avdimas, son of R. Joseph, said: Why did the Torah see fit to place this law (concerning the corner of the field) *between* the Festivals—Passover and Pentecost on one side of it, and Rosh Hashanah and Yom Kippur and "the Feast" (Tabernacles = Sukkot) on the other side of it? To teach you that he who gives to the poor the gleanings (*leket*), the forgotten sheaf (*shikchah*) and the corner of the field in the proper manner, it is accounted in his favor as if he had built the Temple and offered his sacrifices in it.[53]

COMMENT: Since Rashi did *not* introduce R. Avdimas son of R. Joseph's statement with the words: "Our Rabbis taught," or "The Midrash explains," etc., he apparently considers his statement to be the "plain sense" of the verse. What obliged Rashi to cite this Midrash and how does it foster our understanding of the verse? Moreover, what indeed is the similarity between the gifts to the poor and offering sacrifices in the Temple that "it is accounted in his favor as if he had built the Temple, etc."?

Answer: The mitzvah of the corner of the field and gleanings is a *glaring* interruption in the middle of the laws concerning the Festivals, and this is the meaning of the question: "What reason did the Torah see to place this law in *the middle* of the Festivals—surely it is such an interruption that surprises even a five-year-old who first begins to study Torah? Since the Torah nonetheless saw fit to interrupt in the middle of a subject, it must have meant to *teach* us an important lesson, which is therefore the "plain sense" of the verse.

As for the similarity between the gifts to the poor and offering sacrifices in the Temple, it behooves us to cite part of the explanation offered by "Gur Aryeh" who writes:

[53]*Sifra*, Chap. 13:12.

The reason is known: offering a sacrifice means he is giving part of it to God. Likewise he who gives gleanings, the forgotten sheaf and the corner of the field to the poor, gives of his own money to the poor, which is like a sacrifice to God—for gifts to the poor are considered as given to God, as is stated: "One who is gracious to the poor has lent to God" (Proverbs 19:17). Therefore it is accounted as if he built the Temple and offered a sacrifice in it, etc."[54]

---

[54]See also the lofty and uplifting exposition of this matter in *Maskil LeDavid*. It is, however, too lengthy to reproduce here.

Behar

25:1 *B'har Sinai*—"On Mount Sinai."

RASHI: What does the Sabbatical year have to do with Mount Sinai (that the Torah felt it necessary to state that the laws relating to the Sabbatical year were given at Sinai)? Surely *all* the commandments were given at Sinai! But, just as in the case of Shimittah (i.e., Sabbatical year) its general rules, its specific prescriptions, and its minute details were *all* stated at Sinai—so also with *all* the Commandments—their general rules, specific prescriptions, and minute details were *all* stated at Sinai. That is how it is taught in Torah *Kohanim*.[55] It seems to me that this is the explanation of the Midrash: Since we do not find in Deuteronomy that the law concerning the rest of the soil during the Sabbatical year was repeated in "the Plains of Moav" (where the laws contained in Deuteronomy were promulgated), we may infer that all its general rules and specific details were promulgated at Sinai. This verse therefore teaches us regarding *every* Divine speech that was spoken to Moses, that *all* of them came from Sinai—their general rules and minute details—and were (only) repeated in "the Plains of Moav."[56]

COMMENT: It is of the essence to point out that in his comment Rashi teaches us an important tenet in belief, namely: The Torah chose to teach us particularly with regard to Shimittah that its general rules and minute details were *all* given at Sinai—even though it may have been *more* appropriate to have given them in "the Plains of Moav" when they were on the verge of entering Canaan—where they were to have fields and vineyards to which the laws of Shimittah apply—in order to stress thereby that *all* of the laws were given at Sinai, both in their general rules and in minute details. Otherwise we might think, God forbid, that Moses said them of his own accord—as Scripture testifies regarding his welfare speeches at the

---

[55]The *halachic* Midrash on Leviticus, also called *Sifra*.
[56]*Sifra Behar* 1:1; see: *Zevachim* 115b; *Chagigah* 6b; *Sotah* 37b that this is the opinion of Rabbi Akiva that both general rules and details were stated at Sinai.

139

beginning of Deuteronomy: "These are the words that *Moses* spoke to all of Israel, etc.," and as the Talmud says that what he said in Deuteronomy was *mipi atzmo*—"of his own accord."[57]

Therefore Rashi emphasizes: "Every Divine speech that was spoken to *Moses* that they were *all* from Sinai... and were *repeated* (by Moses to Israel) in the Plains of Moav." This principle is most evident in the laws of Shimittah, "since we do not find that the laws concerning the rest of the soil were repeated in the Plains of Moav," we *must* say that both their general rules and details were all said at Sinai. From this we derived that *every* utterance that was spoken to Moses—all of them, the general rules and the details were from Sinai. We can therefore apply an inference a fortiori: If the laws of Shimittah, which they needed to know only after entering and apportioning the land, nevertheless were already given at Sinai, all the more so other *mitzvot* that applied *immediately*, certainly their general rules and minute details were given at Sinai.

The meaning of the words: "general rules, specific prescriptions, and minute details" is this: *k'lal*—"general rule" is a general statement without details, like: "The land shall rest a Sabbath to the Lord" (verse 2)—this includes all work in the fields and vineyards, without detailing. A "specific prescription" *p'rat* is an example of the general statement, like: "You should not sow your field, nor prune your vineyard" (verse 3). *Dikduk*—"A minute detail" is an inference from that which is written, but not stated *explicitly*, like: "Your *harvest* you shall not reap" from which we infer: "to keep it like the rest of the harvest (*katzir*), but it should be ownerless (*hefker*)—for everyone" (Rashi on verse 5).

25:25   *Mei'achuzato*—"From his estate."

RASHI: But not the entire estate. The Torah thereby teaches a practical rule (*derech eretz*) that one should always leave for himself a field (i.e., landed property—however needy he is).[58]

COMMENT: The inference is from the words: *ki yamuch*—"if he becomes impoverished," which are superfluous, for it should have stated merely: *ki yimkor ish*—"if a person should sell, etc." It therefore comes to teach that one should sell only when he is "impoverished" *ki yamuch*, not to put the money in his own money belt, or to buy cattle or tools, etc. (*Sifra*, i.e., one should not sell a field in order to buy cattle, tools, etc.)

---

[57] *Megillah* 31b.
[58] *Sifra* 5:1.

By stating "the Torah teaches a *practical rule*, etc.," Rashi teaches us that there is no absolute prohibition, since he is selling out of poverty. Hence, if he won't have food until he sells his *entire* property—he may do so. The Torah only teaches a "practical rule" that even in an impoverished state, a person should be as frugal as possible so that he may leave for himself some field (i.e., immovables).

25:38 *Asher hotzeiti, etc.*—"Who took you out, etc."

RASHI: I distinguished between those who were firstborn and those who were not firstborn (a matter hidden from human knowledge), I also know (the true situation) and will punish one who lends money to a Jew with interest, saying that it belongs to a non-Jew (who *is* allowed to lend money with interest).[59]

Another explanation: I brought you out of the land of Egypt so that you should take upon yourselves to fulfill My commands—even if they are hard for you.[60]

Latet lachem et eretz k'na'an—"To give you the land of Canaan."

RASHI: As a reward for accepting (to keep) My commands.

Lih'yot lachem leilokim—"To be your God."

RASHI: Because whoever lives in the Land of Israel—I am his God, but whoever leaves it is like one who worships idols.[61]

COMMENT: The question here is: What is the connection between the Exodus from Egypt and lending money with interest; how are they similar? Another difficulty: How does the Exodus serve as a reason for the prohibition against charging interest; was the Exodus predicated upon not lending with interest? Moreover, verse 36 states the motive of the prohibition with the words: "So that your brother may live with you"—what need is there for additional reasons?

[59]*Bava Metzia* 61b; cf. Rashi on 19:36 and Numbers 15:44.
[60]The words "even if they are hard for you" are not in *Sifra* 5:3 from which this explanation is taken. They are Rashi's additional comment.
[61]*Sifra* 5:3–4; *Bava Metzia* 61b; *Ketubot* 110b; and cf. Rashi on Gen. 17:8.

Therefore Rashi explains that verse 38 is not a *reason* for the prohibition of lending with interest, but rather as a warning: See who forbids it, I who brought you out of Egypt. How is this fact connected to lending with interest? That Rashi answers by saying: Just as I distinguished between those who were firstborns and those who were not, so will I know to distinguish the money of a Jew about which the lender says that it belongs to a non-Jew, namely: Me you will not be able to cheat, and from Me you will not be able to hide anything, just as the Egyptians could not hide their firstborn sons.

However according to this explanation it should have stated: "I am the Lord who smote every first born in Egypt" because this is the main part of the comparison, not the actual Exodus from Egypt? Therefore Rashi cites "Another explanation is... so that you should accept upon yourselves the fulfillment of My commands—even if they are *hard* for you." This explanation is especially appropriate to the matter of interest, which is a "hard" mitzvah, since the lender allows himself to charge interest because his money cannot earn money as long as it is in the hands of the borrower. The interest is therefore a kind of payment for the loss in earnings that he is suffering. Hence it is *hard* to refrain from charging interest.

Since Rashi explained "who took you out, etc.—so that you should take upon yourselves to fulfill My commandments, etc.," Rashi continues in this vein and explains: "to give you the land of Canaan—as a reward for accepting My commands." Lest we err in believing that "to give you the land of Canaan" is the *reason* for the Exodus from Egypt, Rashi explains that it is the *result* of accepting the *mitzvot*—not the reason for the Exodus.

After having mentioned the acceptance of the *mitzvot* and its reward, the words "to be your God" appear to be superfluous or redundant, for what could "to be your God" mean if not that you should accept My commands? Furthermore, the main reason for going out of Egypt must be "to be your God" as God told Moses: "When you take the People out of Egypt, you will worship God on this Mount" (Exod. 3:12). If so, the order of the words in that verse should have been reversed: "to be your God, to give you the land of Canaan." Why then is "to be your God written" after "to give you the land of Canaan"? Rashi answers: "For whoever lives in the land of Israel, I am his God, etc." Namely, the original intention (of God) was that the commands be fulfilled necessarily in the Land of Israel.[62] However, because we sinned we were exiled from our Land.

---

[62]Comp. Rashi on Deut. 11:18: *"You shall place My words—even after you are exiled, be distinguished by mitzvot . . . in order that they should not be like new to you when you return, etc."*

25:43   *Lo tirde bo b'farech*—
"You shall not rule over him with hard labor."

RASHI: Unnecessary work in order to afflict him, e.g., do not tell him: Warm up this glass (of drink) for me," and he (the master) does not need it; "Hoe under this vine until I come." You might say: Nobody knows the fact if it is necessary, or not, and I will tell him it *is* necessary! This is a matter that depends on the mind (lit. "his heart") of the master—therefore it is stated: "but fear your God."[63]

COMMENT: Question: Why didn't Rashi explain according to plain sense, as he explained the verse: "The Egyptians enslaved the Children of Israel with hard labor—with hard labor that breaks the body and crushes it,"[64] and as Onkelos translates here: "With harshness"? The reason is because in verse 40, Rashi explains: "Agricultural work, etc." Now field work is mostly hard labor that crushes the body, and the Torah permitted the master to give the servant such work. Hence the word *b'farech* here must mean *mental hardship*, not physical. Therefore, Rashi cites two examples of mental anguish.

The author of *Be'er Mayim Chaim* gives a psychological explanation: A person is by nature a free soul. Therefore any work that he does willingly, even if it be hard labor, it is easy for him. But if he does *not* want to do it, then even light work, such as "Warm this pot or glass for me"—he considers it hard work. As for: "Hoe under this vine until I come"—since he is waiting for the master's arrival all the time, he suffers anguish and heartache. But if he gives him a time limit: "Hoe until evening, etc.," he suffers no anguish.

The author of the *Torah Temimah* writes: "The reason Rashi cites the examples of warming up a glass of liquid and hoeing under a vine is because hard labor *avodat parech* has two ingredients: 1) work that is not really necessary, 2) work that has no time limit. Both of these are exemplified in these two examples.

25:55   *Ani Hashem elokeichem*—"I am the Lord your God."

RASHI: Whoever enslaves them (the Israelites) here below (on earth), it is as if he enslaves (Him) above.[65]

---

[63] *Sifra* 6:2; See Rashi on 19:32 with regard to the meaning of the expression *v'yareita mei'elokecha*—"but you should fear your God."
[64] Rashi on Exod. 1:13.
[65] *Sifra*, Chap. 9:4.

COMMENT: We read similarly in *Mechilta* (the Midrash *Halachah* on Exodus): "Whenever Israel is enslaved, it is as if the Divine Presence (*Shechinah*) is enslaved with them."[66]

The version in *Sifra* 9:4 is: "Why does it state: 'I am the Lord your God?' It teaches us that whoever enslaves them below, it is accounted to him as if he enslaved Above."

The Korban Aharon on the *Sifra* explains that the verse states that since He is our God, whoever enslaves him, it is as if he enslaves Him, blessed be He. S. D. Luzzato writes: "In the manuscript of Rashi in my possession it states: 'As if he enslaves Above.'"

In *Maskil LeDavid* he explains thus: "As if he enslaves them, etc., namely: "as if he enslaves the root (source) of their souls, which is from above in holiness (and subjugates them) under the external forces in the *klipot* (lit. "shells")."

From the above we learn that the meaning of the statement in *Sifra* and Rashi is that whoever enslaves any Jew, the Torah considers it as if he enslaved God, as it were. One may ask: What is the big deal? Why is it really considered as if he enslaves God? One may explain in light of the beginning of this verse: "They are My servants whom I have taken out from the land of Egypt," namely: Since God took out Israel from Egypt in order that they should become *His* servants, then he who *enslaves* them (beyond the time that the Torah permits to engage a servant: six years for one who was sold by the court, or until the Jubilee year for one whose ear was bored, or has sold himself on account of poverty and nobody redeemed him before Jubilee) wishes to void God's intention, showing thereby he does not need to consider God's plan—as if his power is greater than God's, God forbid! Therefore he is considered as if he is enslaving God, as it were—since the power of the enslaver is always greater than that of the enslaved one!

Another explanation: In *Likutei Amarim*[67] it is stated that the souls of the Jews are: "A portion of God from above[68] in *actuality*" (*cheilek e-lo-ha mima'al mamash*), as is stated: He blew into his nostrils a breath of life" (Gen. 2:7),[69] and we say: You blew it into me" (morning prayer: *e-lo-hai neshama*—"My God, the soul, etc."; *Berachot* 60b). As stated in *Zohar*. "whoever blows, blows from his innermost self, namely: the innermost life-force of a person he lets out when he blows with power, etc." Accordingly he who enslaves anyone of Israel, whose soul is an actual part of God from above, it is as if he enslaves the very Godhead, Heaven forbid![70]

---

[66]On Exod. Chapter 12.
[67]*Likutei Amarim—Tanya*, Chap. 2.
[68]Cf. Job 31:2 and comp. Psalms 16:5, 73:25; Jeremiah 10:16.
[69]See Ramban's explanation.
[70]Maybe that is what the author of *Maskil LeDavid* had in mind.

Bechukotai

26:4 *V'eitz hasadeh*—"And the tree of the field (will give its fruit)."

RASHI: It refers to the non-fruit-bearing tress (*ilanei s'rak*), and even these will bear fruit in the future.[71]

COMMENT: This Midrash is based on the superfluous word: *hasadeh*—"of the field," for it should have stated only—*V'ha'eitz yitein piryo*—"and the tree will give its fruit." The word *hasadeh*—"of the field" comes to include also non-fruit-bearing trees. Now Rashi is faced with a difficulty: The blessing has not materialized (non-fruit trees do *not* bear fruit)? Therefore he adds: "and they will bear fruit in the future," i.e., in Messianic times.[72]

Actually the entire phrase: *V'eitz hasadeh yitein piryo*—"and the tree of the field will bear fruit," is superfluous, since the words *v'natnah ha'aretz yevulah*—"the land will give its produce" include fertility of the trees too.[73] However the emphasis is on *v'eitz hasadeh*—"and the tree of the field" to indicate a tree that grows in the field, not in an orchard, i.e., non-fruit-bearing trees.[74]

26:9 *U'faniti aleichem*—"I will turn to you."

RASHI: I will turn away from all My occupations in order to pay you your reward. To what may this be compared? To a king who hired laborers, etc., as is stated *in Torat Kohanim*.[75]

---

[71]*Sifra*, Chap. 6.
[72]Cf. *Ketubot* 112b: "All the non-fruit-bearing trees (*ilanei s'rak*) in Israel will bear fruit in the future."
[73]Cf. the use of the word *yevul*—"produce in regard to fruit trees" in *Chabakuk* 3:17 *V'ein yevul ba'gfanim*—"There is no produce in the vines."
[74]See Mishna *Kil'ayim* 6:5.
[75]*Sifra*, Chap. 2:5. The parable states that one of the laborers distinguished himself by his excellent work. When they came for their wages the King said to him: "My

COMMENT: Several difficulties arise from this Rashi:

1) What is missing in the explanation: "I will turn away from all My occupations to pay you your reward" that Rashi is forced to add: "To what may this be compared? To a king who, etc."?

2) What does the parable: "To a king who hired laborers, etc." add to the explanation itself: "I will turn away from, etc."?

3) Why does Rashi allude to the parable without citing it fully, only stating, "as is stated in *Torat Kohanim*"?

The difficulty that motivated Rashi to explain: "I will turn away from all My occupations, etc." is that the words *Ufaniti aleichem*—"I will turn to you" are really superfluous, for they do not contain an additional blessing? Therefore Rashi writes: "I will turn away from *all* My occupations," namely: The merit of: "If you will follow my statutes *im bechukotai teileichu*, meaning: "that you will *labor* in my Torah" (Rashi verse 3) is so great that God, as it were, has to turn away from *all* His occupations to ponder and determine the reward that is appropriate for such a great merit.

The parable: "To a *king* who hired laborers, etc." adds the reason why the merit of "laboring in the Torah"—*ameilim baTorah* is so great, since it is similar to a *king* who hired laborers, namely: Ordinarily a king does not need to hire laborers at all; rather since he is the king and ruler of the land, all his subjects are *obligated* to fulfill his wishes and commands. Obviously then, this parable does not speak of matters that the citizens are *obligated* to do for the king and country, but about things they are *not* obliged to do. Therefore, if the king wishes these to be done he must *hire* laborers, since they are not an obligation of the citizens—and he must pay them high wages.

The simile is as follows: The *parsha* begins with: *Im bechukotai teileichu*— "If you will walk in My statutes," which Rashi explained: *she'tih'yu ameilim baTorah*—"that you will labor in the Torah," i.e., not merely fulfilling the obligation of studying Torah, but *much* more, to the extent that you will *labor* in the Torah. Such preoccupation with the Torah—above and beyond all obligation—is like a *king* who hired laborers, and requires a reward much greater than that for the mere fulfillment of the *mitzvah* of learning Torah. Therefore, "I will turn away from *all* my occupations to pay you your reward," namely: This phrase expresses the large reward due for "*laboring* in the Torah," so much so that God has to turn away from *all* his occupations to ponder the appropriate reward!

---

son, I must turn my attention to you—let me first reward those who have done little work and paying whom will not take me long. With you, however, I have to settle larger accounts, and this I wish to do at leisure, etc."

Rashi only alludes to the parable of the king, etc., with the words "as is stated in *Torat Kohanim*," because the *main* reason for the great reward is already expressed in the words "To a *king* who hired laborers, etc." The rest are only *details* of the parable, that do not add to the *reason* of the great reward. Whoever wishes to know all the details, can look them up in *Torat Kohanim*—therefore Rashi writes "as is stated in *Torat Kohanim*." Moreover, in *Torat Kohanim* there is a contrast between Israel and the nations regarding the *amount* of reward each of them will receive, whereas Rashi does *not* emphasize *this* contrast, but rather the contrast between studying Torah as an *obligation* and "*laboring* in the Torah." Therefore he does not cite the parable fully.

26:12 *V'hithalachti b'toch'chem*—"I will walk among you."

RASHI: I will walk with you in the Garden of Eden, like one of you and you will not be frightened of Me (lit. *mizda'azim mimeni*—"tremble before Me"). One might think you will not fear (i.e., *tir'u*—"be in awe") Me! Therefore it states: "But I will be your God."[76]

COMMENT: The difficulty according to plain sense is: How is it possible to say about God: "I will *walk* among you" in a literal sense? In the story of Adam and Eve where it states: "They heard the sound (lit. *kol*—"voice") of the Lord God *walking* in the garden, etc." (Gen. 3:8), one could explain that the word "walking" (or: "moving about"—*mithaleich*) refers to the "voice of the Lord"—that the voice was moving about.[77]

Now, the idea of walking in the Garden of Eden is a colorful metaphor for grasping and understanding secrets of the Torah and Godliness. Just as a person does not *walk* (or *atayeil*—"stroll") in a park with another person unless he knows him well and has a mental and spiritual affinity with him—so also "I will walk with you in the Garden of Eden *like one of you*" means: you will have knowledge and understanding of Godliness as if I was *one of you*, whom you know well and are close to mentally and spiritually, before you embark on a walk with him in the park.[78]

---

[76] *Sifra*, Chap. 3:34.

[77] Cf. Rashi there and comp. Gen. *Rabbah* 12:12: Rabbi Tachlifie said: We heard that walking pertains to voice, as stated: "They heard the voice of the Lord God walking"—whereas here "walking" is inappropriate. Hence Rashi explains: "I will walk with you in the Garden of Eden, etc."

[78] The matter of grasping and understanding the secrets of the Torah and Godliness is explained at length in *Tanya—Likutei Amarim*, chapters 39, 41; and *Shaar Hayichud V'ha'emunah*, Chap. 5; *Igeret Hakodesh*, chapters 4, 11, 17, 27.

The reason that grasping and understanding secrets of the Torah and Godliness were compared to a stroll in a Garden (of Eden) is because a walk–stroll in a park is a spiritual pleasure, not unlike the pleasure the righteous ones derive from the "Radiance of the Divine Presence" (ziv ha'Shechinah) in the (Upper and Lower) Garden of Eden, by virtue of their understanding the secrets of the Torah and grasping the nature of Godliness—which they could not grasp while they were alive in this world.[79]

The meaning of "and you will not tremble before me" is that you will not become confused by the deep secrets that you will grasp—as happened to some of the four who "entered the orchard."[80]

The question: "One might think that you will not fear Me?" means, since you will grasp the secrets of the Torah and Godliness, do not imagine, God forbid, that you can compare yourselves to Me and be on one level with Me—and were that to happen, you would not stand in awe of Me, Heaven forfend, as a person does not fear another whom he knows closely! Therefore it says: I will be your God (E-lohim), which is an expression of dominion and authority.[81] Namely, with all your grasping of the profoundest secrets, your intellect will still be limited, and there will still be a huge difference between Me and you—as there is a difference between a prince and judge[82] and the commonfolk. This is how I would explain Rashi's profound comments and would that I expressed his intention accurately.

One may further say that gaining an understanding of the secrets of the Torah and Godliness is the acme of all the blessings and their goal. It is for this reason that the matter of "I will walk with you in the Garden of Eden, etc." (as explained above) comes at the very end of all the blessings.

---

[79]Cf. Tanya—Igeret Hakodesh,"Chap. 5, p. 212. See Berachot 17b: "The world-to-come... the righteous sit with their crowns on their heads and enjoy (or: take pleasure in) the radiance of the Shechinah," which Maimonides in Laws of Repentance 8:5 explains thus: "What is the meaning of their statement: They take pleasure in the Radiance of the Shechinah? That they know and grasp the truth (i.e., true essence) of the Holy One, blessed be He, that which they do not know while they are in the dark, lowly body, etc."

[80]Shenichn'su la'pardeis—"A metaphor for delving into the profound secrets of the Torah." Cf. Chagigah 14b and see a lengthy interpretation thereto in Beer Yitzchak to our verse.

[81]Cf. Rashi Gen. 6:2 "The sons of God b'nei ha'e-lohim—"the sons of princes/ministers" (b'nei ha'sarim) . . . every expression—e'lohim in Scripture means authority (marut), etc.

[82]Meanings of the word e-lohim Rashi Gen 6:2.

26:32 *V'hashimoti ani et ha'aretz*—"I will make the land desolate."

RASHI: This was a demonstration of kindness (lit. "a good measure"—*midah tovah*) toward Israel, that the enemies would find no satisfaction in their (the Israelites') land, thus it would become desolate of its inhabitants (also of the enemies; therefore Israel might again take possession of it.)[83]

COMMENT: Question: If this is "a *good* measure for Israel," why is it written among the admonishments (which are curses)?

One may explain this by the principle: "Merciful in judgment"[84] namely: Although desolation of the land in *general* is a punishment, and therefore belongs among the admonishments, still one could find "a good measure" for Israel even in this, i.e., that the enemies will not endure in the Land because of its desolation. This fact will enable Israel to resettle the land upon their return (in both senses: "their return" to God in penitence, and their return from their exile). This is the meaning that God is "merciful in judgment," i.e., although desolation of the Land is *judgment,* nevertheless there is in it also a manifestation of *mercy* in that the enemies will not endure in the Land on account of its desolation. The import of this verse is thus: "I will make the Land desolate to such an extent that your enemies who settle in it will be desolate and will leave it, and you will be able to resettle it."

Furthermore, even if the enemies who settle the Land will *not* leave on account of its desolation, still they will not find satisfaction in it. This is "a good measure for Israel," for if the enemies *would* find satisfaction in Israel, the Jewish People would be greatly pained thereby, thinking: "Not only were we exiled from our Land, but our enemies come and find satisfaction in it."[85]

26:37 *V'chashlu ish b'achiv*—"They will stumble over one another."

RASHI: When they will run to escape, they will stumble against each other, because they will be in a hurry to run away . . . A Midrashic explanation of *V'chashlu ish b'achiv* is: "One will stumble on *account* of the sin of the other, for all Israelites are held responsible for each other (morally)."[86]

---

[83] *Sifra,* Chap. 6:5.
[84] Rashi in Deut. 3:24.
[85] See also: *Gur Aryeh; Devek Tov; Maskil LeDavid; Mizrachi.*
[86] *Sifra* 7:5; *Sanhedrin* 27b; *Shevuot* 39a

COMMENT: You may ask: 1) What is difficult with the "plain sense" of these words that forced Rashi to cite the Midrashic explanation? 2) In Deut. 24:16 we read: "Each man shall be put to death only for his own sins." If so, why would "one stumble on account of the sin of the other?"

Answer: According to the plain sense there is a slight difficulty; in the previous verse it is stated: "They will fall though no one is chasing." What need is there to say after that: "They will stumble over one another," if the intention is to *physically* fall by stumbling against each other? What difference does it make how they fall; surely the main curse is that they fall before their enemy. If the Torah meant to *heighten* the sense of "falling," it should have stated: "They will flee as one flees the sword, and they will stumble over one another, and they will fall though no one is chasing, etc." This would emphasize that the *falling* would be caused by stumbling against each other. The present order alludes to a different kind of falling, not to a physical, but rather a spiritual stumbling, i.e., "One will stumble on account of the *sin* of the other."

It would seem that the Rabbis understood the letter *beit* in the word *b'achiv* as a "causative" *beit*, namely: "because of, on account of the guilt of his brother," i.e., "One will stumble because of, on account of the sin of the other, etc."[87]

In *Sifra* 7:5 the reading is: "They will stumble one over his brother"— it does not say "One *before* (*mip'nei*) his brother" (this is the amended version of the Gaon of Vilna), but one *because* of his brother. This teaches that "all Israelites are responsible for each other." The commentary on *Sifra* "Korban Aharon" explains: "It does not say that one will stumble over another literally, for if so it should have said: *ish b'ish*—"man against man," why "one against his brother"? But it means one for the sin of the other, on account of the *brotherhood* between them, since they are "responsible for each other."[88] From all of the above it would appear that the Rabbis understood the *beit* in *b'achiv* as a "causative" *beit*, not in the physical, but spiritual sense.

As for "Each man shall be put to death for his own sin," the Talmud states that the statement in *our* verse refers only to a case where others could have protested another's sinning, but did not protest.[89] Moreover, even if we interpret, as the Midrash does, "One will stumble because of the sin of another," it still does not mean that he will actually *die* because of him. Maybe he will be liable to a different punishment, and there is no contradiction with: "Each man will be put to death for his own sin."

---

[87]Cf. Hosea 14:2: "Return, Israel . . . for you have stumbled because of your sin."
[88]Cf. *Gur Aryeh*, who explains in a similar vein.
[89]*Sanhedrin* 27a.

26:42   *V'zacharti et briti ya'akov—*
"I will remember my covenant with Jacob."

RASHI: In five places in the Bible the name *ya'akov* is written with the letter *vav* (*ya'akov*).[90] Jacob (as it were) took a letter (*vav*) of Elijah's name as a pledge that he should come and bring good tidings of his (Jacob's) children's redemption.[91]

"I will remember my covenant with Jacob"—Why are the patriarchs enumerated in a reverse order (from Jacob back to Abraham)? To say that Jacob, the youngest of the patriarchs, is worthy of this (that through his merits his children should be redeemed). Should he *not* be sufficiently worthy, then Isaac is with him (his merit is added). If he is not sufficiently worthy, then Abraham is with him, who is surely worthy enough! Why is the word "remember"—*zachor* not mentioned in connection with Isaac's name? Because (it is not necessary since) the ashes of Isaac (who was to become a burnt-offering) are always visible to Me (as though they were) heaped up and lying on the altar.[92]

COMMENT: A number of difficulties arise from Rashi's comments:

1) What is the meaning of taking a letter from Elijah's name as a pledge; does Elijah *not* wish to come and bring tidings of the redemption of Israel of his *own* accord, so that it was necessary to take a pledge from him to assure his coming?

2) Why does Rashi call Jacob "the small one"—*hakatan?* In what way is he smaller than Abraham and Isaac? On the contrary, we find that Jacob is called "the choice of the patriarchs" (*b'chir she'b'avot*).[93]

3) Rashi writes: "If he is not worthy, then Isaac is worthy; and if he is not worthy then Abraham is with him, *who is surely worthy.*" This sounds that Abraham is *surely* worthy, even in his *own* merit! Why is Rashi so certain that Abraham is more worthy than the other patriarchs?

---

[90]They are: 1) in this verse, 2) Jeremiah 33:26, 3) Jer. 46:27, 4) Jer. 30:18, 5) Jer. 51:19, and the name *E-liya-hu* without a *vav* in five places (*Ei-li-yah*). They are 1) Kings 1:3: *El-yah Hatishbi,* 2) Ibid, verse 4: *va'yeilech Ei-li-yah,* 3) Ibid. verse 8: *va'yomer Ei-li-yah,* 4) Ibid. verse 13: *va'ya'an Ei-li-yah,* 5) Malachi 3:23: *hinei anochi sholei'ach lachem et Ei-li-yah Hanavi.*
[91]Cf. Midrash *chaserot v'y'teirot*—"missing and extra letters."
[92]*Sifra,* Chap. 8:7–8 and comp. Levit. *Rabbah* 36:5.
[93]Gen. *Rabbah* 76:1; *Zohar* Part I, 119b, 163b; II 36a.

4) Toward the end Rashi states: "The ashes of Isaac are visible to Me heaped up and lying on the altar." Isaac was *not* burnt as an offering in the end. How then could *his ashes* lie on the altar?

5) Why was Elijah's name written without the letter *vav* in *five* places; for the sake of the pledge *one* place would suffice?

We shall try to answer the above questions in their order:

1) The letter taken from Elijah's name as a pledge is a kind of *oath* that Jacob made Elijah swear that he will bring the good tidings of the redemption of Israel. Similarly we find that God swore: "that His Name will not be complete, nor will His throne be complete until the name of Amalek will be eradicated and when his name *will* be eradicated, His name and His throne will become complete, etc."[94] The need for taking a pledge was due to Elijah being a prophet zealous for the Lord, as he himself testifies: "I have acted very zealously for the Lord, God of Hosts" (I Kings 19:10, 14).[95]

As one zealous for the Lord, Elijah would not have been prepared to bring the tidings of Israel's redemption until Israel repented completely. Therefore, Jacob made him swear that he will *not* wait for complete repentance, but when the time for redemption will arrive, he will come and bring the good tidings—whether they repented or not. Apparently therein lies the controversy between Rabbi Eliezer and Rabbi Joshua:[96] R. Eliezer says: If the Jewish People will repent, they will be redeemed; if not, they will not be redeemed; but R. Joshua holds they will be redeemed even without repentance and good deeds. At the end of that controversy it is stated: "R. Eliezer fell silent"—apparently giving in to R. Joshua. Here, too, Elijah was forced to agree with Jacob by giving him as a pledge a letter from his name.

Another insight into the parallelism between Jacob and Elijah on the one hand, and Rabbi Eliezer and Rabbi Joshua on the other hand is as follows: Jacob is the attribute of truth as stated: "You grant truth to Jacob" (Micah 7:20). God's seal is truth (*Shabbat* 55a) and He is "abundant in kindness and truth" (Exod. 34:6). Now, the Rabbis said: "The image of Jacob is engraved under the Throne of Glory."[97] Accord-

---

[94]Rashi on Exod. 17:16.
[95]Note that also regarding Pinchas it is stated: "when he acted zealously for My sake among them" (Numbers 25:11). "Pinchas is Elijah"—Rashi *Bava Metzia* 114b and cf. *Pirke de Rabbi Eliezer,* Chap. 47, *Shir Hashirim Rabbah* 2; *Yalkut Shimoni* beginning of section Pinchas.
[96]*Sanhedrin* 97b–98a.
[97]Gen. *Rabbah* 82:2.

ingly Jacob, like God, inclines toward kindness—whereas Elijah the zealous prophet is strict and assumes the attitude: "Come what may, strict law must prevail."[98]

As for the relationship between R. Eliezer and R. Joshua, we have the statement: "R. Eliezer is of the School of Shamai,"[99] whereas R. Joshua is of the school of Hillel. Therefore R. Eliezer was, most of the time, more stringent than R. Joshua. True, according to *absolute* truth it is possible that the law should be like the school of Shamai (strict), and like R. Eliezer. But all this will be in Messianic times, when the evil inclination will cease and we will be able to accept stringent rulings. But in our time the law is like the school of Hillel (and R. Joshua) mostly, because we have no strength to accept stringencies on ourselves.

2) Rashi calls Jacob the small one—*ha'katan* as a compliment, i.e., he holds himself small out of humility, as he himself said: "I have been diminished by all the kindnesses, etc." (Gen. 32:11). Similarly, "Samuel the little one" is so called not because he was "little," since he was worthy of prophecy, but his generation was not worthy,[100] but because he held himself small. Besides, the prophet calls Jacob "small": "How will Jacob survive, for he is small."[101]

Another explanation for the appellation "small" is that it signifies fondness, similar to the expression "the choice of the patriarchs." The Rabbis interpreted the above verse in Amos thus: "It can be compared to a king who had many sons, but he loved the smaller one, etc."[102] Accordingly the meaning of "Jacob the youngest (smallest) is worthy of this": since he is the most beloved and the choice of the patriarchs. However, the attribute of judgment is very strong on account of the many sins, and Jacob's merit is not sufficient, then Isaac is with him, etc.

3) The addition of the words "who is surely worthy—*she'hu k'dai* with Abraham can be explained according to the statement in *Sifra* 8:7 as the Gaon of Vilna amended the text there: "And why were the patriarchs stated backwards? But the deeds of Jacob are worthy (sufficient). If Jacob's deeds are not sufficient, then Isaac's deeds are sufficient. But if Isaac's deeds are not enough, then the deeds of Abraham are enough, "and each one of them is worthy."

In his commentary on the *Sifra*, the Chafetz Chaim explains, at great

---

[98] *Yevamot* 92b; *Sanhedrin* 6b.
[99] *Shabbat* 130b.
[100] *Berachot* 28b.
[101] Amos 7:2, 5.
[102] *Eliyahu Rabbah*, Chap.6; *Shochar Tov*, Chap.5.

length, that the deeds of Abraham are the worthiest of all because he
recognized God by his own powers—without having had any tradition
of monotheism as Isaac and Jacob had—and publicized the knowledge
of God in the world. Therefore he is worthy, on his own, to protect
Israel from evil.

4) The matter of Isaac's ashes lying on the altar may be understood according to the version in the *Sifra*: "And why is remembering
mentioned by Abraham and Jacob, but not by Isaac? But *we see* his ashes
as if heaped up and lying on the altar"—and remembering does not
apply to something that is seen constantly. According to this Isaac's
ashes are not *really* heaped up on the altar, but his merit always stands
before God's eyes, and it is *as if* his ashes are heaped up on the altar
= there's no need for remembering.

However, Rashi did not write "as if"; his wording sounds like he
meant that his ashes are *really* lying on the altar? We may suggest that
since the ram substituted for Isaac was indeed burnt and *its* ashes are
lying on the altar, therefore by the principle "A person's agent is like
himself"[103] one may say: "The ashes of Isaac are seen to Me heaped
up and lying on the altar" in reality.

5) The reason that *E-liya-hu* is written without a *vav* and *Yaakov*
with a *vav* in *five* places instead of one is that it is as if Elijah swore
by the Five Books of the Torah—just as the name Israel—*Yisrael*—is
written five times in one verse (Numbers 8:19 and see Rashi there)
corresponding to the Five Books of the Torah.[104]

27:7   *V'im mi'ben sheeshim shanah . . .*—
"And if from sixty years and up."

RASHI: When one approaches old age, a woman is close in importance to
a man, therefore a man decreases to less than a third of his original value
when he becomes old (his—*erech* between ages twenty-to-sixty was fifty
shekels—verse 3—and after sixty only fifteen, which is less than a third of
fifty), while a woman decreases to exactly a third of her original value (her
erech when young was thirty shekels—verse 4—and after sixty it is ten—one-
third), because people say: "An old man in the house is a snare (nuisance)
in the house; an old woman in the house is a treasure in the house and
a good omen in the house."[105]

---

[103]Mishna *Berachot* 34b; Rashi Exod. 12:6.
[104]See *Be'er Mayim Chaim; Be'er Yitzchak; Gur Aryeh; Divrei David; Mizrachi.*
[105]Cf. *Arachin* 19a and Rashi there.

COMMENT: Question: If "an old man in the house is a *snare* (nuisance), an old woman in the house is a *treasure* and a good omen," then the woman's value at old age should be *greater* than the man's, since she is a "treasure," whereas he is a "snare (nuisance)." But according to our verse the man's value at old age is still greater than the woman's—fifteen as against ten shekels?

I did not see any of the supercommentaries on Rashi addressing this question. However one may say that the reason is because of the principle: "Great is the dignity of the people, etc.,"[106] namely: If the value of a woman would be *greater* than a man's value, it would constitute a great embarrassment and shame to the man, who fell from his high value "to the pits"— from fifty to ten shekels, which is only one fifth of his original value. Whereas an old woman's value would be, by this calculation, fifteen shekels, which is half of her highest value! This would cause great anguish to the man, and we know that: "The Holy One, blessed be He, does not wish to pain (*l'honot*) any creature."[107] Therefore it is sufficient for a woman who approaches old age that she should be "close in importance to a man." This is an achievement for her.[108]

---

[106]*Berachot* 19b—many references there.

[107]Rashi's wording in Gen. 3:7.

[108]Cf. *Be'er Mayim Chaim*, who gives a reason why an old woman is a treasure in the house, whereas an old man is a nuisance.

Numbers

Bamidbar

3:1   *V'eyleh toldot Aharon u-Mosheh*—
"These are the offspring of Aaron and Moses."

RASHI: But the verse mentioned only Aaron's offspring, nevertheless they are called Moses' offspring because he taught them Torah. This teaches that anyone who teaches Torah to the son of his fellow man, Scripture considers it as if he had begotten him.[1]

B'yom diber Hashem et Mosheh—
"On the day the Lord spoke with Moses."

RASHI: These became his offspring, because he (Moses) taught them *whatever he learned from the Almighty.*

COMMENT: One may ask:

1) Surely Moses taught Torah to *all* Israelites, not only to Aaron's sons, why then were only Aaron's son called his offspring?

2) In his first comment Rashi states simply: "because he taught them Torah," but in the second comment he says: "because he taught them *whatever he learned from the Almighty*"—why the change in wording—is there a difference between them?

3) Rashi's comment negates the musical notations (*ta'amim*), which are also punctuation marks, according to which there is the sign *etnachta* which is a major pausal sign—under the word *Mosheh*—"and Moses," whereas Rashi connects the continuation: *Beyom diber Hashem v'go*—"On the day the Lord spoke, etc." with the words: "The offspring of Aaron and Moses"—

---

[1] *Sanhedrin* 19b; comp. *Bamidbar Rabbah* 2:21.

159

Toldot Aharon u-Mosheh. Why does Rashi negate these musical punctuation marks?

Let us answer the questions in order:

1. Since God *commanded* Moses to teach the People Torah, it is inappropriate to say that all of Israel are Moses' children—for where it not for Israel, the Torah would *not* have been given to Moses (alone). But his teaching the sons of Aaron much more than he taught the rest of the People, that came from Moses alone—he was not told by the Almighty to teach them *more*. In this extra teaching they are considered his offspring.[2]

2. Rashi's intent with the change in wording: "because he taught them *whatever* he learned from the Almighty" is to allude to this very fact that he taught Aaron's sons much more than he was commanded by the Almighty to teach all of Israel—He taught *everything* that he learned from the Almighty, not only the *mitzvot* and their meanings as he taught *all* of Israel.

In *Sanhedrin* 99b we read: "Resh Lakish said: Whoever teaches his fellow Jew's son Torah, Scripture considers it as if he *made* him, as is stated: 'The souls that they *made* in Charan' (Gen. 12:5 and Rashi there)." Rashi there explains: "Abraham converts the men and Sarah converts the women and Scripture considers it as if they *made* them." According to Resh Lakish, teaching another's son Torah is like converting him, since both are derived from the same verse! "A non-Jew who converted is like a newborn."[3] Perhaps Rashi had this in mind when he wrote: "They *became* his *offspring*," not only: *"as if he begot him"* as in the first comment.

3. The reason Rashi diverged from the punctuation marks (*ta'amim*) is because according to plain sense one cannot say that "on the day, etc." is a *new* matter, for if so, why are both in the *same* verse, and what does this have to do with the offspring of Aaron and Moses—as many commentators indeed ask?[4]

It would seem that the Masorites who placed a major pausal sign *etnachta* under the word *u-Mosheh* alluded to the Midrash: "And why does it state: The offspring of Aaron *and* Moses? In honor of Moses; not to diminish his honor." However Rashi did not feel this to be in Moses' honor. On the contrary, if you say "the offspring of Moses" and you do *not* mention

---

[2] *Gur Aryeh*; comp. *Devek Tov.*
[3] *Yevamot* 22a; *Bechorot* 47a.
[4] See: *Gur Aryeh*; *Devek Tov; Maskil LeDavid; Sefer Hazikaron; Siftei Chachamim; Mizrachi.*

their names, it diminishes his honor! That is why Rashi preferred the exegesis of the Talmud to that of the Midrash, besides the educational idea: "It teaches that whoever teaches the son of his fellow man Torah, etc."

3:38   *Mosheh ve'Aharon u-vanav*—"Moses and Aaron and his sons."

RASHI: And adjacent to them was the banner of the camp of Judah, and next to them were encamped Issachar and Zevulun—"It is good for the righteous, (and therefore) good for his neighbor!" Because they (Judah, Issachar, and Zevulun) were the neighbors of Moses who was occupied with the Torah they became great scholars in the Torah, as is said: "Judah is my lawgiver" (Psalms 60:9). "Of the children of Issachar, men with understanding of the times to know what Israel had to do, their heads were two hundred" (I Chronicles 12:33)—i.e., two hundred heads of the *Sanhedrin*— "and out of Zevulun came those who ply the scribal quill" (Judges 5:14).[5]

COMMENT: The difficulty in this verse is the difference between the manner of describing the encampment of Moses, Aaron, and his children, and the encampment of the children of Gershon, Merari, and Kehat: in the case of all the Levites, the names of the families are mentioned first and then where they should encamp, e.g., "*The families of Gershon* should encamp behind the Tabernacle to the west" (verse 23); "The chief of the father's household *of the Merari families* ... they should encamp on the side of the Tabernacle to the north" (verse 35)—whereas here the description is reversed: first the location is given: "and those who encamp in front of the Tabernacle ..." then the identification: "were Moses, Aaron, and his children." Had the verse meant to *assign* their place of encampment, it would have stated: "Moses, Aaron, and his children should encamp in front of the Tent of Meeting to the east, etc." Hence the intention is *not* to assign the location of encampment, but to *declare* their location. What is this declaration alluding to? Rashi explains it was meant to allude to the *importance* of those who encamped in front of the Tabernacle, etc., namely Moses, Aaron, and his children. It is therefore understood that those who were adjacent to them, i.e., the whole banner of Judah, the tribes: Judah, Issachar, and Zevulun would be influenced by their proximity to these righteous leaders, on the principle: "It is good to the righteous—good for his neighbor."[6]

Furthermore, Rashi comes to answer another question: Why does the

---

[5] *Tanchuma Bamidbar* 14.
[6] Mishna *Negaim* 12:6; *Sukkah* 56b.

Torah spell out the exact location of Moses, Aaron, and his children; they are part of the Kehat family and naturally they would encamp with the rest of the Kehatites. Besides, why is it necessary to know where they encamped, the Torah does *not* deal with *individuals* (Moses, Aaron, and his children), but rather with entire families of the Levites? Therefore Rashi explains that the Torah indicates the location of their encampment to hint that those who were adjacent to them were influenced by them and also became great Torah scholars.

There is however one difficulty: Why does Rashi point out that Zevulun too were great Torah scholars; surely Issachar and Zevulun struck a partnership where Zevulun would do business and support Issachar, whereas Issachar would sit and learn Torah—thereby Zevulun had a share in Issachar's Torah learning, since they enabled it.[7] It would appear then that Zevulun's main occupation was business; how did they become Torah scholars?

Answer: From here we learn the importance of a good neighbor: Although their major occupation was business, nevertheless their proximity to Moses, Aaron, and children had the effect that even the Zevulunites became Torah scholars!

---

[7]See Rashi on Deut. 33:18 and comp. Rashi Gen. 49:13.

Naso

5:10 *V'ish et kodashav lo yihiyu*—
"The sacred offerings of a person shall be his."

RASHI: Because the gifts due to the priests and Levites were stated (Deut. 18:1–8), one might think they may come and take them by force? Therefore it states here: "Every man's holy things shall be his"—this teaches that the—*tovat hanaah*—the pleasure of giving the gifts to *any* priest or Levite he wishes—is the owner's (they cannot be taken by force). Many other laws were exegeted from this verse in the *Sifrei.*[8]

An *Agadic* (homiletical) explanation of this verse is: Whoever keeps the tithes and does not give them to the Levite, only the tithes will be his, i.e., his field will yield no more than a tenth (= tithe) of what it used to yield (his *whole* possession will be equal to the gifts (tithes) he should have given to the priests and Levites).[9]

Ish asher yiten lacohen—"A man who does give to the priest."

RASHI: The gifts that are due to him.

Lo yihiyeh—"He shall have."

RASHI: Much money (riches).[10]

COMMENT: The difficulty Rashi is addressing is how is it possible that the *kodashav*—"holy things" that he consecrated *lo yihiyu*—"shall be his." Surely he must give them to the priests, altar or Temple, to whom he consecrated

---

[8] *Sifrei Naso,* sec. 6; *Chullin* 133a.
[9] *Tanchuma R'ey* 10; *Tosafot Taanit* 9a.
[10] *Berachot* 63a.

them? Rashi answers that they are his only to the extent that he may give them to whichever priest, Levite he chooses and they cannot take them by force. This privilege is called *tovat hanaah*: An Israelite may accept money from another Israelite for the privilege of giving his *terumah* or other "holy things" to his daughter's son who is a priest (rather than to another priest).[11]

The problem with this explanation is that the words *lo yihiyu*—"shall be his" do not refer to the "holy things"—*kodashav*, but to that privilege. Therefore Rashi cites the Midrash according to which "his holy things"—*kodashav themselves* "shall be his," i.e., "one-tenth." But according to the Midrash: "that his field will yield no more than one-tenth," how can one call this *kodashav* his—"holy things," this is his *entire* crop—not merely the *consecrated* part! Therefore Rashi gives both explanations.

The problem with the words: A man who gives to the priest he shall have" is if this refers to the "holy things," namely that *they* belong to the priest, the plural—*lo yihiyu*—"they shall be his"—should have been used? Therefore Rashi explains that—*lo yihiyeh*—"he shall have" (sing.) refers to the Israelite, i.e., "he shall have much money," if he gives the priest his dues.

The author of *Be'er Mayim Chaim* derives a beautiful moral from the Midrash *Agadah* that Rashi cites: The reason (for only one-tenth of the original crop) is that the entire world belongs to God, and in His mercy He gave Israel the land of the seven nations (Canaan), who are a tenth of the seventy nations of the world. God commanded Israel to give one-tenth of their crops—then He will establish them as the *owners* of the fields. But if they do *not* give tithes (a tenth), then God shows that *He* is the Owner of everything and takes for Himself nine parts, and gives the (human) owner one part, the tenth part, which belongs to the poor.

By the statement: "Many other laws were exegeted from this verse in the *Sifrei*" Rashi means that all the other explanations in the *Sifrei* are *far* from the plain sense. Only the Midrash that he cites is close to the plain sense; therefore he does not designate his first explanation as a Midrash—although it too is from *Sifrei*. Actually the "Midrash *Agadah*" he cites is also far from the "plain sense." However, it contains an important moral lesson (above), and helps explain the plural wording, as per above—therefore Rashi cites it.[12]

---

[11]Cf. *Nedarim* 85a; Maimon. *Hilchot Terumot* 12:15.
[12]See *Sifrei Naso* sec. 6, numerous Midrashei *halachah* that are far removed from the "plain sense."

5:12   *Ki tisteh ishto*—"Whose wife shall go astray."

RASHI: Our Rabbis taught: "Adulterers do not sin until a spirit of folly ("stupidity"—*shtut*) enters into them, as is written:—*ki tisteh*—"if she becomes foolish" reading *tishteh*, i.e., if she becomes a—*shotah*—"idiotic"). And it states about him (the adulterer): "He who commits adultery with a woman lacks understanding" (Prov. 6:32). But the plain sense of *ki tisteh* is if she deviates from the path of modesty and becomes suspect in his eyes like: "Turn away (*stey*) from it and pass by" (Prov. 4:15); "Let not your heart turn (*yeyst*) her way" (Prov. 7:25).

U-ma'alah vo ma'al—"and commits treachery against him"

RASHI: And wherein lies the treachery? *ve'shachav ish otah*—"If a man lies with her, etc."[13]

COMMENT: Rashi follows the Midrash, which states in connection with Prov. 6:32: "He who commits adultery lacks understanding"—From here we learn that a man does not go to a married woman unless he goes out of his mind, and so says the verse: 'Whoever is foolish, let him turn here. To him who lacks understanding she says: Stolen waters (= a married woman) are sweet, etc? (Prov. 9:16–17). Just as he is called "foolish," so is the harlot called "foolish," for she does not sin (sexually) until she goes out of her mind ... and so did Moses allude to her lack of understanding, as it says: "Any man whose wife goes astray (*tisteh*)—it states—*tishteh* with the letter *shin*, to tell you that she is not (sexually) unfaithful until a spirit of folly enters her. This is the meaning of *ki tishteh ishto*—"if his wife becomes foolish."[14]

The folly here is twofold, besides the general folly in *every* sin by which a person becomes separated from the Almighty at the time of sinning.[15]

First, both the woman and her lover place themselves in mortal danger, for just as the "bitter waters" examine the woman, so do they examine her lover, who is also included in the curse "to cause (your) stomach to distend and (your) thigh to collapse" (Rashi on verse 22). Second, the woman puts herself in danger of her husband's jealousy. Should he catch them in the act, it is possible that out of anger he might kill her—and maybe even her lover. All this could be the result of "a spirit" of folly (*ruach shtut*).

---

[13] *Tanchuma Naso; Bamidbar Rabbah* 9:6; *Sifrei Naso*, sec. 7.

[14] *Bamidbar Rabbah* 9:6.

[15] Cf. Isaiah 59:2; *Tanya* Chap. 24–25; *Igeret Hateshuva*, chap. 5; *Kontres Umayan*, Chap. 42 ff.; Discourse *Ba'ti Legani*, 1950 letter 10: Even though in most cases of sin the ill effect may be corrected through repentance, yet at the time of sinning he *is* separated from God.

The word *shtut*—"folly" is akin to *shoteh*—"a fool." A fool does not consider the results of his actions. He does not "foresee the outcome," which is the trait of the wise ("Who is wise, one who foresees the outcome"—*Tamid* 32a). The fool fulfills his desire at a *given moment* without consideration of the future. Like him, adulterers are interested only in satisfying their desire at the moment without regard for the physical or spiritual consequences—even if they endanger their life thereby.

Rashi's comment: "and commits treachery against him—And wherein lies the treachery? If a man lies with her, etc." comes to obviate an error; we should not think that these are *two* matters: 1) She commits treachery against him (in some way); 2) "and if a man lies with her." Hence Rashi explains that her "going astray" is the treachery, i.e., "if a man lies with her." The beginning is her deviation from the path of modesty, becoming suspect in his eyes. This can later lead to "a man lies with her," which is the heart of treachery. The treachery *ma'al* here is *not* that she stole something from him or denied something—which are the usual cases of treachery—but rather in her sexual misconduct. This is reflected also in the *Sifrei*: "Regarding a sexual matter. Or maybe regarding a monetary matter? Since the verse states: 'If a man lies with her *carnally* hence it is sexual, not monetary treachery."[16]

5:15 *Se'orim*—"Barley"

RASHI: And not wheat; she committed a bestial act, therefore her offering is that which is food for animals (barley).[17]

COMMENT: Rashi at *Sotah* 15b explains: "She committed a bestial act—she abandoned herself to having sex with one who is not her marital partner." This implies that an animal *does* have carnal relations with one that is not its partner, since there is no concept of "marriage" with animals; hence "partner" does not apply. This is indeed the case with regard to *some* animals. But many animals and beasts are loyal to their partners as long as they are alive. Domesticated animals like sheep, goats, and cows do mate with *any* animal with whom their owner mates them (and maybe Rashi meant such an animal). But undomesticated animals and beasts usually mate only with their partner (although occasionally, as with the lion, one male may have many female partners).

---

[16] *Sifrei Naso*, sec. 7.
[17] Mishna *Sotah* 14a, 15b; *Bamidbar Rabbah* 9:31; *Sifrei Naso*, sec. 8.

Question: On the verse "for *all* flesh had corrupted its way, etc." (Gen. 6:12) Rashi comments: "Even animals, beasts, and fowl mated with others than their kinds (species)," implying that it was accounted to them as a sin and therefore they were wiped out in the Flood (Gen. 7:23); whereas here it is implied that it is normal for an animal to mate with another that is not its partner, and not deplorable?

However, there is a difference between mating with one that is not "its partner" (*ben zugah*) and one who is not "its species" (*she'ainan minan*). Since there is no concept of marriage with an animal, there is no harm done if it mates with another that is not "its partner" (*ben zugah*). But people whom the Torah forbade to mate with one that is not one's "partner"—thereby elevating man from the level of animals—it is very deplorable if a woman abandons herself to one who is not her partner. By such an act she proclaims to everyone, as it were, that her level is not higher than an animal's (this is the meaning of: "a bestial act"—she behaves and considers herself an animal. Therefore her sacrifice is animal food [barley] for it is as though an animal brings an offering from that which it eats!

However, when animals, beasts, and fowls mate with those that are not their species, they disrupt God's plan, for an animal that mates outside its species—e.g., a lion with a wolf, etc.—does not procreate from this union. This is a disruption of God's command to them: "Be fruitful and multiply" (Gen. 1:22 and Rashi). Therefore it is considered a sin and corruption. This is why they were destroyed in the Flood.

6:9   *B'feta' pit'om*

RASHI: *B'feta'* means (that the Nazirite defiled himself) by accident. *Pit'om*—means "inadvertently." Some say that *Peta' pit'om* is *one* thing—an occurrence of suddenness (suddenly).

COMMENT: Rashi was faced with a difficulty: The Nazirite vowed "for the sake of Heaven" (Cf. Rashi verse 2 on:—*lehazir*) and he is termed *kadosh*—"holy" (verses 5, 8). If so, why wasn't he careful not to become defiled even unintentionally? Surely, even on committing a sin inadvertently one is called a sinner and requires forgiveness?[18] Therefore Rashi states that the *first* possibility of defilement the Torah mentions is *b'feta*—"by accident." However, since the Torah also mentions—*pit'om* one must say it refers to "inadvertent" defilement. Since the Nazirite is holy and vowed "for the sake of Heaven," it is closer to plain sense to say that if he *does* become defiled

---

[18]Cf. Rashi Gen. 9:5; *Shevuot* 2a.

at all, in most cases it would be by accident rather than inadvertently. In rare cases he will become defiled inadvertently—or even intentionally.

In light of the above explanation one can see the great love Rashi had for the Jewish People, since he diverged from the order stated in the Talmud and *Sifrei*, which is *peta'* means "inadvertently"; *pit'om* means "by accident," in order to express the idea that it is more likely that the Nazirite will become defiled by accident than even unintentionally—and certainly not willfully. All this is part of *plain sense!*

7:23   *U-lezevach hashlamim bakar shnayim*— "And for the peace sacrifice two oxen."

RASHI: Corresponding to Moses and Aaron who made peace between Israel and their Father in Heaven.[19]

Eylim, 'atudim, kevasim—"rams, he-goats, sheep"

RASHI: Three species corresponding to Priests, Levites, and ordinary Israelites, and corresponding to Torah, Prophets, and Writings. Three times "five" corresponding to "the five books" (of the Torah), and the five Commandments written on one Tablet and the five written on the other. Thus far is from the work (*Yesod*) of Rabbi Moshe the Preacher.

COMMENT: The numbers "two, five" in this verse: "two oxen, rams, he-goats, sheep-five" express the idea of equality, namely: two oxen corresponding to Moses and Aaron who are equal.[20] Same with "Three species corresponding to priests, Levites, and Israelites—who are also equal to each other." Also: "and corresponding to the Torah, Prophets, and Writings"—they too are equal, because they were said with Divine Inspiration as the verse states: "They were given by (from) One Shepherd" (*Kohelet* 12:11)—God. This is the meaning of "and corresponding to Torah, etc." namely: just as Priests, Levites, and Israelites are equal to each other, so Torah *and* Prophets *and* Writings are equal. The same applies to "three times five corresponding to the Five Books," namely: just as the three sets of five (animals) which correspond to Priest, Levites, and Israelites and to Torah, Prophets, and Writings—where all sets of three are equal to each other—so too are the Five Books equal to each other. No one should think: "Exodus or Leviticus

---

[19] *Bamidbar Rabbah* 13:20.
[20] Cf. Rashi on Exod. 6:26.

is more important than Genesis because it contains more commands," or conversely: "Genesis is more important because it relates the Creation of the world, the stories of the Forefathers, etc." Such arguments are invalid, for all Five Books are equally important.

This is also the meaning of: "and the five Commandments written on one Tablet, and the five written on the other," namely: Although on one Tablet were mainly the commands between man and God (the right Tablet: "I am the Lord, etc."), and on the second (the left) the Commandments between man and man, nevertheless the Tablets are equal to each other— one type of Commandment (between man and God, or between man and man) has no advantage over the other—we heard both types from the Almighty (cf. our interpretation of Exod. 31:18).

Behaalotcha

8:3   *Vaya'as kein Aharon*—"And Aaron did so."

RASHI: This comes to tell the praises of Aaron—that he did not change.[21]

COMMENT: One may ask: Would it occur to anyone that "Aaron the holy one of the Lord" (Psalm 106:16) should change, so that Scripture had to testify that he did *not* change? This may be explained with the following anecdote from one of S. Y. Agnon's stories: The Rabbi of Zhitomir asked the Rabbi of Berditchev regarding the statement "and Aaron did so," where Rashi comments: "It tells you that he did not change," is it possible? God told Aaron to light the candles, is it possible that he should change? If God had commanded an ordinary person, would he change; so wherein is the praise of Aaron the Priest that he did *not* change?

However, if God had told the Rabbi of Berditchev that he should light the candles, he would have been possessed of great enthusiasm and awe, so much so that when he came to light, he would have spilled the oil on the floor and would not manage to light on account of being overawed. But Aaron, although he had more awe and enthusiasm than any man, when he came to light the candles, he fulfilled God's command and lit them without change.[22]

The *Sfat Emet* explains thus: The meaning is that Aaron performed the mitzvah (of lighting) all his life with the *same* level of intention and will. The nature of a person is that at first he is enthusiastic, but later forgets (his erstwhile enthusiasm). In truth the *first* enthusiasm is the best. Therefore it is said about Aaron that he did not change, etc.[23]

---

[21]Cf. *Sifrei* 60; *Yalkut Shimoni* 719.

[22]*All the stories of Shmuel Yosef Agnon*, Vol. II; *Elu Va-Elu*, Shocken Books, Jerusalem, 1960, pp. 140–41. (Hebrew)

[23]*Sfat Emet*, 1875, cited in *Perushei Rashi al ha-Torah* by C. D. Chavel, Mosad Harav Kook, Jerusalem 1982, p. 430. Comp. "Minchat Yehudah" in Chumash *Mechokekei Yehudah*.

8:19   *Va'etnah v'go*—"And I assigned, etc."

RASHI: The expression "the children of Israel" is mentioned in this verse five times, in order to tell that they are beloved (by God), since they are mentioned five times in one verse corresponding to the Five Books of the Torah. Thus I saw written in Gen. *Rabbah*.[24]

COMMENT: Since "the Children of Israel" were mentioned in verse 18, all five mentions of "the Children of Israel" in our verse are superfluous; it should have stated: "I assign the Levites to Aaron and his sons to do their service in the Tent of Meeting and to atone for them, so that there may be no plague among them when they (the Israelites) approach the Sanctuary." Since the Torah does not contain a single extra word, or letter,[25] why are there five superfluous mentions of "the Children of Israel" in one verse?

Rashi replies: "to tell that they are beloved (by God)." If so, it is not superfluous. The reason Rashi had to cite this Midrash here is because in verse 17 Rashi mentioned that the Israelites erred in the matter of the golden calf. One might think that they are no longer beloved by God. Therefore he explains that God's love for them has not been removed, since they are mentioned five times in one verse, corresponding to the Five Books of the Torah—which is the "plaything" of the Almighty.[26]

9:1   *Bachodesh harishon*—"In the first month."

RASHI: The section at the beginning of this Book was not said until Iyar (the second month, cf. 1:1): hence you learn that there is no *order* of "earlier" or "later" (chronological order) in the Torah. But why did the Book not begin with *this* section (since it is chronologically earlier)? Be-

---

[24]This is *not* found in our edition of Gen. *Rabbah*, but there is a similar statement there (Gen. *Rabbah* 3:5) about the fivefold "or" mentioned in Gen. 1:3–5. Cf. *Yalkut, Bereshit* letter 4. But in *Vayikra Rabbah* 2:4 there is a statement very similar to Rashi's. Indeed the Yemenite MS of Rashi reads: "This I saw in *Vayikra* Rabbah." Cf. also: *Tanchuma, Tisa* 8; Aruch entry "chamesh," *Pesikta de Rav Kahana, Shekalim* 17:1.
[25]How far this is taken can be gauged from the statement in *Menachot* 29b that Rabbi Akiva deduced "from every single embellishment of the letters in the Torah-scroll *heaps and heaps of laws*."
[26]Cf. Proverbs 8:30: "I was His nursling; I was His plaything (or delight) every day." See the numerous Midrashim on this verse, e.g., *Avot de Rabbi Natan* Chap. 31; Gen. *Rabbah* 1:1, 8:2; *Tanchuma, Bereshit* 1, etc. See: *Torah Haktuvah ve-hamesurah* notations to this verse.

cause it is disparaging to Israel—that during the whole forty years that they were in the desert they brought only this single Passover sacrifice.[27]

COMMENT: Several questions arise from Rashi's comment:

1) The principle that there is no chronological order in the Torah has been stated many times *before* this verse—why does Rashi state it again here if there's nothing new added?[28]

2) Rashi himself states that there is no chronological order in the Torah; why then does he ask: "Why did the Book not begin with this section?"

3) If this section is "disparaging to Israel," why does the Torah write it at all; surely: "What was—was."[29] Is God a tale-bearer that He should slander Israel?[30]

The explanation of the above is:

1) The Torah emphasizes the chronological order at the beginning of this Book: "On the first day of the *second* month of their leaving Egypt," and here: "In the second year of their leaving Egypt, in the *first* month." Nevertheless these sections are set in a *reversed* order. From this we learn a new principle: Even when the Torah emphasizes the *time* of the commands, and one might think it means to relate the *order* of the commands and events—even then "there is no order of earlier or later in the Torah."

2) Although "there is no earlier or later in the Torah" *chronologically,* there is a different order of "earlier" or "later" according to the *importance* the Torah attaches to the events—which is more important than the chronological order, and therefore the Torah mentions certain events that happened later—earlier. One must therefore, look for the reason for this specific order, which necessitated the change in the chronological order. Rashi asks: "But why did it not begin with this section?" Why did it not begin the Book with this section on Passover (and the "second Passover")?" Moreover, the Torah mentions the "love of Israel by God" at the beginning of the Books: Exodus, Leviticus, Numbers.[31] If so, the Book should have

---

[27] *Sifrei* 64 and 87 and "Meir Ayin" there; Tosafot *Kiddushin* 38b s.v. hoil.
[28] Cf. Rashi on Gen. 6:3, 35:29; Exod. 19:11, 31:18; Levit. 8:2, etc. All these come before this verse. Cf. also Rashi Exod. 4:40.
[29] *Pesachim* 108a; *Yoma* 5b, 37a, *mai dehavah havah*—and one does not mention it!?
[30] Cf. *Sanhedrin* 11a; *Tanchuma, Vayeishev* 2.
[31] Cf. Rashi on Exod. 1.1; Levit. 1:1; Numbers 1:1—at outset.

begun with *this* section where the virtues and affection for Israel are mentioned, e.g., that they fulfilled God's command completely: "According to *all* that God commanded Moses, *so* did the Children of Israel" (verse 5). Even those who were "unclean" wished to fulfill God's command and asked "Why should we be less, etc.?" (verse 7). Their request was accepted by God and they were given the "second Passover" (in Iyar). Surely all this shows God's affection for them. Therefore Rashi asks: "Why did the Book not begin with *this* section"—which both expresses God's affection for Israel *and* precedes it in time? He answers: "Because it is disparaging to Israel," whereas the section, with which the Book begins shows only God's affection for Israel.

3) True, the Torah could have ignored this single Passover that Israel performed in the desert, and commanded regarding the "second Passover" as part of the commands about Passover in section "*Bo.*" However, Rashi himself remarks: "This section ought to have been said through Moses like the rest of the Torah, but these (the 'unclean' who asked: Why should we be less, etc." verse 7) merited that it should be said on their account, because '*Meritorious deeds are brought about by worthy men.*'"[32] In order to teach this lesson it was necessary to relate that Israel made only one Passover in the desert; there were "unclean" among them, who could not sacrifice and asked: "Why should we be less, etc." Thus it came about that the command of the "second Passover" was given. Without this story we could not learn this important lesson![33]

10:36   *Rivavot alfei Yisrael*—"The myriad thousands of Israel."

RASHI: This teaches us that the *Shechinah* does not reside in Israel if there are less than twenty-two thousand.[34]

COMMENT: Question: The Sages stated: "Whence do we know that if even *one* sits and studies Torah that the *Shechinah* is with him? For it says, etc."[35] If so, what need is there for twenty-two thousand?

The "Torah Temimah" answers: The statement in *Sanhedrin* refers to ten people who gathered to pray or study Torah, then the *Shechinah* is

---

[32]Rashi on verse 7. Cf. *Shabbat* 32a; *Bamidbar Rabbah* 13:7; *Sifrei* 68.

[33]As to what exactly was "disparaging to Israel" see: Tosafot *Kiddushin* 37b; *Amar Ne'ke; Gur Aryeh; Siftei Chachamin*—all of whom deal with this question.

[34]*Sifrei* 84; *Yevamot* 64a; *Bava Kama* 83a; *Yalkut* 731.

[35]*Berachot* 6a; comp. *Avot* Chap. 3:2, 6; *Sanhedrin* 39a: "At every gathering of ten the *Shechinah* resides (forever)."

among them as mentioned in *Berachot* 6a; whence do we know that if even *one* studies Torah the *Shechinah* is with him, etc., But our verse refers to the *Shechinah* residing *constantly*, even without prayer or Torah study. This is only in the presence of twenty-two thousand."

The author of *Tanya* makes the following distinction: The statement of the Gemara "that even if *one* studies Torah, etc." is supported by a verse only for *allotting a reward*, to an individual according to his achievement and to the many according to theirs. But as far as bestowing *God's Holiness* upon him, he cannot compare to the many. The difference between "bestowing" (*hashra'ah*) and "allotment of a reward" (*keviat sachar*) is that the Lord shines upon the soul that seeks Him, with the light of His Torah. Since the soul is limited in its powers, the light of God that illuminates it is also *limited* and *restricted* (*gevuli metzumtzam*), etc. But bestowing (His Holiness) means a *huge illumination* from God's light that illuminates it *without any limit*. It cannot embody itself in a limited soul, rather it surrounds it *from above* from head to foot, as the Rabbi's said: "Upon each gathering of ten the *Shechinah* resides, i.e., *above* them etc."[36]

In *Yosef Hallel* the author writes: "In the Alkabats version (of Rashi) there is the following addition: "For upon whom does He reside, upon the tribe of Levi who were not less than twenty-two thousand." The Maharsha writes[37] that the 22,000 corresponds to the "Camp of the *Shechinah*" above, which numbers 22,000 as stated: "God's entourage is twice ten thousand, thousands of angels ..." (Psalm 68:18). Similarly, in that generation there were 22,000 Levites—all of them righteous upon whom the *Shechinah* resided. They did not take part in any sin of the generation of the Desert. They were the very Chariot, for they carried the holy vessels upon which the *Shechinah* rests, etc. These are the very words of Rashi according to the Alkabats version at which the Maharsha arrived on his own.

In the Zamora printing (of Rashi) the reading is: "It teaches you that the *Shechinah* does not reside in Israel, *when Israel* is less than 22,000."[38]

According to these two versions the question does not even begin:

---

[36] *Tanya*, Part 4: *Igeret HaKodesh*, Chap. 23. Accordingly the difference between an individual and many is not only quantitative but qualitative: The individual is allotted a reward according to his value, but the many have a "huge illumination" from the light of God without limit. All this is "at each gathering of ten," where the light of God surrounds them *from above* and does not embody them. But with "twenty-two thousand" the *Shechinah* resides *within them* (embodies them), not only surrounds them—although they are not aware of it because their souls are finite, whereas the *Shechinah* is infinite. This is my understanding of the above citation—hopefully correct.

[37] At *Yevamot* 64a.

[38] *Yosef Hallel*, Part II, p. 136 and note 13.

According to the Alkabats version Rashi meant only *that generation* of the desert when the Levites were 22,000, and the context is the traveling of the Ark and its resting in the desert, as per plain sense of the verse. Hence there is no contradiction with the statements of the Sages.

According to the Zamora version the meaning is that the *Shechinah* does not rest even on an individual Jew when Israel numbers less than 22,000! Surely such a state, that the Jews would be less than 22,000 never existed. Hence the *Shechinah always* rests in Israel.[39]

11:5   *Asher nochal bemitzraim chinam—*
"That we ate in Egypt free of charge."

RASHI: If you say the Egyptians gave them fish for nothing, but does it not say: "No straw shall be given to you" (Exod. 5:18)? Now, if they did not give them straw for nothing, would they give them fish for nothing! What then is the meaning of—*chinam?* Free from (Heavenly) commands.[40]

COMMENT: Namely: in Egypt our food did not depend on our fulfilling commands, as the manna *is* dependent on that, as stated: "I shall rain down for you bread from Heaven ... so that I can test them whether they will follow My Torah or not" (Exod. 16:4). One cannot interpret *chinam* as "without payment," because the manna they also received without payment. If so, there's no contrast to the manna? Hence it must mean: "free from commands."[41]

One may ask: How are commandments *payment* for the manna, since for the fish, etc., they paid with *money.* If so, in order for the simile to be valid, there would have to be a common denominator between money and commands—since both serve as payment?

It would seem that the equal aspect in both is that both of them are attained through hard work and toil: Money is attained by toil in a literal sense. Commands (*mitzvot*) are also attained through toil, for in order to fulfill them properly one has to study Torah as stated: "If you will follow My laws" where Rashi explains: "That you should *toil* in Torah"; and "you

---

[39] I hope I grasped the true meaning of Rashi. Cf. also *Gur Aryeh.*
[40] *Sifrei* 87: Midrash *Agadah:* free from sexual prohibition—*chinam min ha'arayot.*
[41] Also Jonathan translates: *lelo tafkidata*—"without commands." Cf. also *Divrei David; Lifshuto shel Rashi.*

will observe My commandments"—Rashi—"you should toil for the sake of keeping and fulfilling, etc."[42]

11:17 *V'yarad'ti*—"I will go down."

RASHI: This is one of the ten descents written in the Torah.[43]

COMMENT: What is Rashi trying to teach us—what is the significance of the ten descents, and what are they?

The word *v'yarad'ti*—"I will go down" is superfluous. Besides, how could the expression "I will *go down*" be applied to God? Therefore Rashi writes: "This is one of the *ten* descents, etc." Namely: The meaning *here* is the same as its meaning in all *ten* descents written in the Torah—in all of which it is *not* literal, God forbid. *What* the ten descents are is not integral to the meaning of *v'yarad'ti*; therefore Rashi does not enumerate them.

The ten descents are "Ten descents did the Holy One, blessed be He, go down to earth: one in the Garden of Eden; one during the generation of Dispersion (Tower of Babel); one in Sodom; one at the (burning) bush; one in Egypt;[44] one at Sinai; one in the cleft of the rock;[45] two in the Tent of Meeting,[46] and one at the end of days (lit. "in the Future to come" *le'atid lavo*).[47]

As regards the significance of the descents the author of *Gur Aryeh* writes: "It is the ten descents in the Torah, *all* of which were written on account of their importance. Here it is written that God came down from His abode in Heaven for the sake of the Elders—to accord them importance."

"Divrei David" writes: "The meaning is we find at the destruction of

---

[42]Levit. 26:3. However, Ibn Ezra explained "*chinam*—cheaply as if it were free." The Ramban explained *chinam* literally: "free of charge"; cf. the argument of *B'er Maim Chaim* against him. See also: *Maskil LeDavid; Mishmeret HaKodesh; Emek Hanziv, Siftei Chachamim.*
[43]*Sifrei* 93.
[44]In *Zayit Raanan* it is explained: "Namely during the plague of the firstborn where it states: 'I will go through the land of Egypt on this night' (Exod. 12:12).
[45]Exod. 33:22: "When My glory passes, I shall place you in the cleft of the rock."
[46]One in *Shemini*; the second in *Behaalotcha* during the appointment of the Elders—*Zayit Raanan*, adding: "Although He spoke to Moses the entire forty years, maybe He did not go down *on earth*, but remained above ten hand-breadths (*lema'alah mey'asarah tefachim*)—"except for those times."
[47]This statement about the ten descents is cited, with some changes in *Pirke de Rabbi Eliezer*, Chap. 14 and *Avot de Rabbi Natan*, Chap. 34.

Jerusalem, when the *Shechinah* removed itself, that it ascended ten ascensions—from below—above.[48] Now this is the meaning of the ten descents, until it came down *in honor of Israel.*" Namely: Obviously there were no *physical* descents, which do not apply to God. But the Torah spoke in the manner of people—and all of them were in honor of Israel and its leaders.

11:22-24   *Hatzon u-vakar yishachet; 'atah tir'eh ha-yikrecha d'vari; vayeitzei Mosheh vaydaber el ha'am*—"Can sheep and cattle be slaughtered ... Now you will see whether what I have said happens to you ... Moses went out and spoke to the People ..."

RASHI: This is one of the four things[49] that Rabbi Akiva interpreted (in a certain way), but R. Shimon did not interpret like him: R. Akiva says: "Six hundred thousand footmen (is the people), and You said, 'I will give them meat and they will eat for a whole month' (verse 21), could sheep and cattle be slaughtered (to suffice them?)—all to be taken *literally*, would it suffice for them? *u-matza lahem* is similar in meaning to: *u-matza k'day geulato*—"and has sufficient for redeeming it." (Levit. 25:26. Here too: *u-matza lahem* is equal to: *u-matza k'day lahem*—"would it be sufficient for them?"). Which case is worse? This one, or (when Moses said): "Here now, you rebels?" (20:10).[50] But since he did not say it (his doubt) in public, Scripture (God) had mercy on him and did not punish him. Whereas the sin at Meriva took place in public, therefore God did not have mercy on him (but punished him, that he may not enter the land of Israel)."

Rabbi Shimon says: "God forbid! This (doubt) never entered the mind of that righteous man! He, about whom it is written: "He is faithful in all My House" (below 12:7) would say: "God cannot supply enough for us"?! But this is what Moses said: "Six hundred thousand footmen, etc., and You said: 'I will give them meat for a whole month'—and then You will kill such a great nation?! Should sheep and cattle be slaughtered for them, so that they may be killed, and this eating should suffice them forever (be their last meal)? Is this Your praise? Do people say to a donkey: Take this kor

---

[48]Cf. *Avot de Rabbi Natan*, Chap. 34:6: "Ten ascensions did the *Shechinah* remove itself from one place to another."

[49]Biblical passages. *Rosh Hashanah* 18b; Rashi there lists all four and gives the references.

[50]Obviously *this* case was a greater show of disbelief on the part of Moses, for at Meriva Moses did not doubt that God could supply enough water for all the people, but only whether *that one*, was the rock. Whereas here he doubted whether God could *at all* supply sufficient meat for everyone!

of barley (and eat it) and then we will cut off your head?! God replied to him: "But if I do not give them (meat), they will say that My hand is limited (lit. short). Would it be pleasing to you that it should appear to them that the hand of the Lord is short (i.e., incapable of supplying their needs)? Let them and a hundredfold like them perish, but let not My hand be short in their eyes even for one moment!"

R. Gamiliel son of R. Judah ha-Nasi said: Moses said: One cannot fathom a blabber! (*ee efshar la'amod 'al hatafeyl*). Since they are only looking for a pretext (to complain), You will never satisfy them; in the end they will always argue against You! If you give them meat of large cattle (oxen), they will say: "We wanted that of small animals (sheep)." If you give them meat of sheep, they will say: "We wanted meat of large cattle, or we wanted beasts and fowl; we wanted fish and locusts." God said to Moses: "If so (and I give them nothing) they will say that My hand is short (I cannot supply them)?" Then Moses said: "I will go to appease them." God said to him: "Now you will see whether what I have said happens to you (verse 23)— for they will not listen to you!" Moses went to appease them, saying to them: "Is God's hand short? (incapable of supplying your needs). Behold He smote the rock and the waters flowed ... surely he can give you also bread!" (Psalms 78:20, hence He can supply you with meat). They said: "This is (only) a compromise. He has no power to grant our request (for meat)!" This is why it says: "Moses went out and spoke to the People (the word of the Lord)." Since they did not listen to him, "He gathered seventy men (of the Elders of the People, etc.)" (verse 24).[51]

COMMENT: Verses 22–24 relate the dialogue between Moses and God, as a result of which Moses went to appease the People and gathered the seventy Elders, according to the Midrash that Rashi cites. Therefore we grouped them together, as one unit.

Several questions present themselves:

1) Why does Rashi preface his comments with: "This is one of the four things, etc."? He should have begun: "Rabbi Akiva says, etc." immediately. What did he improve with the prefatory remark?

2) In Rabban Gamliel's statement it says: "Moses went to appease them, saying to them: *Is God's hand short*, etc.?," implying that Moses said these words to the people, whereas verse 23 says explicitly the opposite; "The Lord said to Moses: Is the Lord's hand short." Rashi does not comment anything about R. Gamliel's statement, implying that he accepts it as

---

[51] *Tosefta Sotah* 6:4; *Sifrei* 95.

the correct explanation of the verse, although it is in direct contradiction to verse 23!

3) Why does Rashi mention the names of the Rabbis whose opinions he cites? He should have written: "Some of our Rabbis state ... and others say, etc." or, "Our Rabbis differ in its interpretation—some say ... others say, etc." We have a rule that Rashi does not give the names of the Sages, unless he wishes to allude to the consistent method of a certain Rabbi—as reflected in other statements by him.[52] If so, what does Rashi allude to by mentioning the names of Rabbis Akiva, Shimon, and R. Gamliel son of R. Judah ha-Nasi?

We may offer the following explanation, in order of questions:

1) Rashi had to preface: "This is one of the four things that R. Akiva interpreted, etc." for two reasons: 1) there is a rule: "The law is like R. Akiva against his colleague."[53] Therefore Rashi emphasizes that this rule applies only when R. Akiva said a *law*, but not when he makes a *homiletical* statement, (*doresh*) as in this case. Each one of the four statements by R. Akiva is introduced by "*darash* R. A"—*R. Akiva interpreted homelitically and R. Shimon concluded each one:* "I approve of my words more than of R. Akiva's." 2) Most of Rashi's statements are taken from the *Tosefta* and the *Sifrei*; and we have a rule: "An anonymous *Sifrei* is R. Shimon's statement, an anonymous *Tosefta* is R. Nehemiah ... *and all of them are in accordance with R. Akiva.*"[54] Therefore Rashi had to point out that this is one of the four things where R. Shimon does *not* interpret like him.

2) According to Rashi the words: "Is God's hand short?" were said twice: the first time by God to Moses as implied in verse 23; the second time by Moses to the People. The meaning of verse 24: "He spoke to the People *the words of God* "is" Is God's hand short?," which is what God said to *Moses.* This is Rashi's intention with the statement: This is why it says: Moses went out and spoke to the People the words of the Lord," namely: the words of appeasement he said to them: "Is the Lord's hand short? Behold He smote the rock and waters flowed, etc.—these are the *very* words of God.

3) Rashi does indeed allude to the consistent methodologies of the Rabbis he cites: Rabbi Akiva follows the "plain sense" of the verse, e.g., 1)

---

[52]Cf. *Klalei Rashi*, pp. 61–62, parag. 1, 3, 6.
[53]*Eruvin* 46b; *Pesachim* 27a; *Ketubot* 21a.
[54]*Sanhedrin* 86a.

Commenting on the words: *ha-yarey verach halevav*—"one who is fearful and faint-hearted"—who is one of those who go home from the battlefield—Rashi says: "R. Akiva says *as the words sound* that he cannot stand battle and see an outstretched sword."[55] 2) In the matter of ransom: "He shall pay as a redemption for his life" (Exod. 21:30), says Rashi: "The value of the one damaged—the words of R. Ishmael, R. Akiva says: the value of the damager.[56] According to plain sense—*pidyon nafsho* means the value of the damager, since he is redeeming *his* soul (life), not of the one damaged. Besides, this verse speaks of the damager: "If a ransom is laid *upon him*," i.e., the damager.[57] In our verse too, Rashi comments on R. Akiva's statement: "all to be taken *literally* (*hakol k'mashmao*)." Therefore he cites R. Akiva first because it is the plain sense.

However, it is difficult to impute such harsh words to the "Master of the Prophets" (Moses) concerning whom it says: "He is faithful in all My House." Hence Rashi cites R. Shimon's milder view.[58]

R. Shimon follows the *motives* of Scripture,[59] and here too he explains the "reason" in Moses' words that he meant it in God's honor. The main thing is: "Should sheep and cattle be slaughtered for them, so that they may be killed and this eating should suffice them forever"; is this *Your praise?* Surely this will cause a desecration of God's Name, Heaven forbid! God answered him: "But if I do not give them, they will say my hand is short, etc.!" Namely: There will result a greater desecration of God's Name if I do not give them meat, than if I give them and then kill them out. Therefore Rashi mentions R. Shimon's name, because here too, as in other places, he interprets the "reason, motive" of the verse.

There remains a difficulty according to both opinions: How does the latter part of verse 23: "Now you will see whether what I said will happen to you" connect with the foregoing; what did God say will happen to Moses? Therefore Rashi cites Rabban Gamliel's statement, the gist of which is: "He told Him: I will go to *appease* them. God said to him: Now you will see, etc., Moses went to appease them, etc.": Rashi mentions the name R. Gamliel son of R. Judah ha-Nasi because his statement here is in line with his statement elsewhere: In the "Ethics of the Fathers" he says: "Annul your

---

[55]Rashi Deut. 20:8; *Sotah* 44b. R. Yossi ha-Glili gives the Midrashic interpretation: "One who is fearful of his sins, etc."

[56]Rashi Exod. 21:8.

[57]Cf. our Hebrew supercommentary *Be'ur Setumot be-Rashi*, Part I, pp. 193–94 as to why Rashi gives R. Ishmael's opinion before R. Akiva's even though R. Akiva's is the plain sense.

[58]Yet, although R. Shimon praised his own opinion: "I approve of my words more than of his," Rashi held that R. Akiva's is closer to plain sense. Hence he cites him first.

[59]*Yoma* 42b; *Yevamot* 23a; *Bava Metzia* 115a.

wish on account of His wish, so that He may annul other people's wish on account of your wish,"[60] meaning: When Moses went to *appease* them he said: "You are only looking for a pretext since you have enough meat."[61] If so, annul your will on account of God's will, Who wished to feed you manna, because: "The Torah can be expounded properly only by those who eat manna,"[62] so that he may annul the will of others on account of your will."[63] This is the meaning of: "I will go to *appease* them," namely: I will make their view concur with God's view. To that God replied: "Now you will see whether what I said will happen to you," i.e., they will not listen to you. Hence Rashi writes: "Since they did not listen to him," he gathered seventy men, etc.[64]

12:15   *V'ha'am lo nasa*—"And the People did not travel."

RASHI: The Omnipresent showed her this honor (as a reward) for the single hour she lingered for Moses' sake when he was thrown into the river, as is stated: "His sister placed herself far off: (i.e., she was waiting—Exod. 2:4).[65]

COMMENT: A number of questions arise from this comment:

1) What difficulty is there in the verse that Rashi needs to explain?

2) According to this explanation the People did not travel *only* as a reward for Miriam because she tarried for one hour, etc., Would they have traveled without Miriam otherwise? They had the well for the entire forty years in Miriam's merit[66]—would they have traveled without the well?

3) The verse states: "and the *People* did not travel until Miriam was brought in," implying that the People accorded her this honor, whereas Rashi states: "The *Omnipresent* showed her this honor" implying that *this* was the reason for lingering, not the People's gesture. Where did Rashi get this from?

---

[60] *Avot* 2:4.

[61] Cf. Rashi on verse 4.

[62] *Yalkut Shimoni, Beshalach* 226–27. Cf. *Be'ur Setumot Be-Rashi*, Part I, pp. 159–60, note 3 for an explanation of this statement.

[63] The will of Balak, Bilam, Amalek, etc.

[64] See the lengthy explanation of the *Sifrei* in *Emek Hanziv*, commentary on the *Sifrei*.

[65] *Sotah* 9b.

[66] Rashi Numbers 20:21; *Taanit* 9a.

Let us answer:

1) The phrase: "The People did not travel until Miriam was brought in" is apparently superfluous, since verse 16: "Afterwards the People traveled, etc.," and this verse begins with: "So Miriam was shut out, etc." Obviously then, the phrase in question is superfluous? Rashi answers that it comes to emphasize that the People did not travel in Miriam's honor.

2) Of course they would not travel without the well, but it stopped only when Miriam *died*.[67] Had she only been absent from camp for seven days, the well would continue to roll along with them.

3) Rashi's difficulty here was: Why does this verse attribute the delay in traveling to the *People*? Surely it depended on the Cloud, as it says: "Whenever the Cloud lifted from the tent ... then the Children of Israel traveled, etc." (above 9:17)? Therefore Rashi explains: "The *Omnipresent* showed her this honor," i.e., God held back the Cloud from lifting, so that the People should not travel. Hence Rashi attributed the honor to Miriam to God, for He caused that the People did not travel.

However, the *Sifrei* to verse 16 implied that the Cloud had already lifted and the People began to travel; and *then* tarried in honor of Miriam, quote: "Afterward the People traveled from Chatzerot—were there *two* Chatzerot, that they traveled from one and encamped at the other? But, as soon as Israel *journeyed* they did not manage to walk when they heard that Miriam became leprous, and *they returned backwards and encamped.* Therefore it states: And afterwards the People traveled from Chatzerot."[68]

However, their returning backwards and encamping was also by God's command, for had He not told them to go back, they would have continued traveling, even without Miriam. However, it is surprising that they did not complain that they had to go back after having started on their journey— even though it delayed them coming to the Land of Israel? It would seem therefore that it is for *that* reason that Scripture attributes it to the People: "The *People* did not journey until Miriam was brought in"—the People showed her this honor, and did not complain about the delay, but did it willingly.[69] However, the Rabbis and Rashi attribute the merit to God, for *He* was the major cause of the People not traveling.

---

[67]Which is implied by the proximity of the verses: "Miriam died there, etc., and there was no water for the congregation" (Numbers 20:1–2).

[68]*Sifrei* end of sec. 106, cf. *Emek Hanziv* on the meaning of *Sifrei*'s question and answer.

[69]The Mishna at *Sotah* 9b also emphasizes: "Miriam waited for Moses one hour, etc., therefore *Israel* lingered for her sake for seven days."

In light of the above we may explain a puzzling matter in regard to the Passover Festival: In the Torah this Festival is always called "the Festival of matzot" (E.g., Exod 34:18; Levit. 23:6; Deut 16:16). "Passover—Pesach" is the name of the sacrifice: "the sacrifice of Passover—korban Pesach" (Exod. 12:1 where Rashi says: "The sacrifice is called Pesach on account of the *skipping—haPesicha;*" Levit. 23:5; Deut. 16:1–2, 5–6). Whereas the Jewish People call the holiday "Pesach—Passover" or *Chag HaPesach*—"the holiday of Passover," and *never* "the holiday of matzot—*Chag HaMatzot*"?

The reason is God praises the Jewish People for having left Egypt with only the unleavened cakes ... nor had they made provisions for themselves (Exod. 12:39) without complaining: "How shall we go out into the desert without provisions, but they believed and followed Moses."[70] Therefore the prophet praised them: "I recall for you the kindness of your youth, the love of your nuptials, your following Me into the Wilderness, into an unsown land" (Jeremiah 2:2). Therefore the Torah calls this Festival always the Festival of Matzot (i.e., unleavened bread)—*Chag HaMatzot*, which mentions the praise of Israel and their faith.

On the other hand, Israel calls the Festival "Passover—Pesach" in order to mention the kindness the Omnipresent showed us: "Who *passed-over* the houses of the Children of Israel in Egypt when He smote the Egyptians, but He saved our households" (Exod. 12:27). Similarly here: The Torah attributed the merit to the Jewish People: "the *People* did not travel, etc." Whereas Israel (Rashi and the Sages) attribute the kindness to God: "the *Omnipresent* showed her this honor, etc."

---

[70] *Mechilta, Bo,* sec. 14 and Rashi Exod. 12:39.

Shelach

13:18 *Et ha-aretz mah he*—"The land—how is it?"

RASHI: There are countries that rear strong people, and there are countries that rear weak people; there are countries that produce a large population, and there are those that produce a small population.[71]

COMMENT: Question: How does one discern that "there are countries that rear strong people, etc." by examining the *land* without looking into the people?

It would seem that by the words: "You should see the *land—how it is?*" The Torah means what is the *nature of the land* itself, *without* considering the People. Moses' intention with these instructions to the spies was to convince them that "the Land is very, very good" (14:7) as Joshua and Calev said. For this purpose it was necessary to point out qualities the Land possessed that *everyone* could appreciate. Matters such as climate and scenery are not things that everyone can enjoy—what is good for one, is hard on somebody else. But "a country that rears strong people; that produces a large population"—these are qualities that *everyone* can enjoy: Each family wanted many strong and healthy children, for this is a great blessing, as is evident from the verse: "Behold! The heritage of the Lord is children ... like arrows in the hand of a warrior, so are the children of youth."[72] Happy is the man who fills his quiver with them" (Psalms 127:3–5).

As to the question how does one discern these qualities without examining the people, one might suggest that these qualities are, so to speak, embedded in the soil and its makeup. By the *nature* of the land one can discern if it rears strong or weak people, and produces a "large or small population." On the verse: "These are the sons of Seir the Horite who were *the inhabitants* (or settlers) *of the land*" (Gen. 36:20) Rashi comments: "Our Rabbis interpreted that they were expert in settling the land ... they would

---

[71]Cf. *Tanchuma Shlach* 6; *Bamidbar Rabbah* 16:12.
[72]Namely, children one had while young are healthy and strong.

taste the dust and know which plant is suitable for it." Thus we see that one who specializes and is expert at knowing the *nature* of the land, knows what it is capable of producing. Likewise in our case—by the composition or makeup of the land they knew if it is capable of rearing strong or weak people, and a large or small population. This knowledge is arrived at by observing and pondering. This is what the Midrash emphasizes: "Moses told them: *observe Eretz Israel.*, etc."

14:22   *Vay'nasu*—"They tried."

RASHI: Literally.

zeh eser p'amim—"These ten times."

RASHI: Twice at the Red Sea; twice regarding the Manna, and twice in the case of the quail, etc., as stated in Tractate *Arachin* (15a).

COMMENT: We must understand:

1) What mistaken interpretation of *Vay'nasu*—"they tried" did Rashi try to obviate by stating "literally"—what could have come to mind without this comment?

2) Why doesn't he cite all ten trials, but writes "as stated in Tractate *Arachin*"? If he does not wish to enumerate them, he should have stated simply: "They are all enumerated in Tractate *Arachin*," and not mention them at all.

3) In Tractate *Arachin* we read: "Two at the Red Sea, *two at the waters*, two with regard to the Manna, two in the case of the quail"—why did Rashi leave out "two at the waters"?

We may explain as follows:

1) Rashi wishes to preclude the understanding of *Vay'nasu* as an expression of "raising up, greatness," as in: *harimu neys*—"raise a banner" (Isaiah 62:10), as Rashi himself explained *l'va'avur nasot etchem*—"in order to elevate you" (Exod. 20:17). Indeed God's name became *raised* and great due to all the things that He supplied them upon their request (or demand). But such an understanding is mistaken, since *Vay'nasu oti 'eser p'amin* is stated as a *rebuke*, whereas by this explanation it is to their *credit*

that they caused an *upraising* of God's name by their wicked deeds. It is unbefitting to attribute *merit* to wicked deeds! Therefore Rashi states "literally," i.e., an expression of testing and lack of belief.

2) Rashi enumerated only those trials that exhibit lack of faith, where there was a clear miracle and at *the very same time* a lack of faith, e.g., at the Red Sea: At *the time* of the splitting of the Sea (miracle), the Israelites complained: "Just as we are coming up (from the Sea) on this side, so are the Egyptians coming up from the other side and will chase after us."[73]

"Two with the Manna:" the falling of Manna—an open miracle, and in that itself they tried God: 1) They were forbidden to leave over for the next day, yet they did; 2) They were told not to go out to collect on the Sabbath, yet they did.

"Two with the quail": When they said: Who will give us meat to eat?, they had *at that time* plenty of meat, yet tried God to see if He will supply them with more meat![74]

3) In the two trials at the water—at Mara (Exod. 15:23–25), and Refidim (Exod. 17:1–7)—the lack of faith was not so noticeable, because, ostensibly, they had a legitimate complaint: at Mara: "They could not drink the water of Mara because it was bitter" (Exod. 15:23); at Refidim we read: "and there was no water for the People to drink" (Exod. 17:1). Therefore Rashi leaves out the trials with water, since he is interested in highlighting the lack of faith in God, in line with his explanation of *vay'nasu*—"literally," which is a matter of lack of faith in God.

15:32 *Vayi'hyu ... bamidbar vayimtzeu—*
"(The Children of Israel) were in the Wilderness and they found."

RASHI: Scripture speaks to the disparagement of the Israelites, i.e., they kept only the first Sabbath, and on the second this man came and desecrated it.[75]

COMMENT: Several questions need to be answered here:

1) Why does the Torah speak disparagingly of Israel? Is God then a tale-bearer that he should slander Israel?

---

[73]Rashi Exod. 14:30; *Mechilta*, Chap. 6.
[74]Cf. Rashi Numbers 11:4.
[75]*Sifrei* 113; *Yalkut* 749.

2) How do we know that they kept only the first Sabbath; it does not state on *which* Sabbath this episode occurred? Maybe they didn't keep even *one* Sabbath and this episode occurred on the first Sabbath they were in the Wilderness?

3) What is the meaning of: "First/second Sabbath"—first, second by which count: from the Exodus; from the arrival in the Sinai Desert; after giving of the Torah?

Answers:

1) Indeed it is disparaging to Israel that they did not manage *all of them* together to observe more than one Sabbath. Although the wood-gatherer (*mekosheysh*) was an individual, and possibly everyone else kept the Sabbath properly, yet there is no *completeness*, since "All Jews are responsible (lit. guarantors) for each other."[76] However, through their censure one can hear their praise: out of some three million or more Jews who were then in the desert[77] only *one* desecrated the Sabbath—the wood-gatherer. This is a huge praise for the nation. If today there were only *one* desecrator of the Sabbath in the entire Nation, we would expect the Messiah to come.[78]

Furthermore, although they did not know what his judgement should be, yet they did *not* cover up for him; those who saw him gathering wood did *not* say: Why should we get involved and possibly be the cause of his death.[79]

2-3) Questions 2-3 are interdependent: If we know what Sabbath is called "first," and what "second," we could determine which Sabbath the wood-gatherer desecrated and how many Sabbaths they kept. A number of commentators hotly debate these issues.[80]

---

[76] *Shevuot* 39a and Rashi *Sanhedrin* 27b; *Sifra Bechukotai* 26:37, etc.

[77] It is a simple computation: From Egypt came out "About 600,000 *footmen*, men besides children" (Exod. 12:37). "Footmen" means infantrymen, men aged twenty-to-sixty. This doesn't include children under twenty—each family must have had several such—women and girls of *all* ages, and men above age sixty. Hence one must multiply the number 600,000 by at least five. Thus we arrive at three million, if not more.

[78] Cf. "If Israel would keep two Sabbaths according to law—they would be redeemed immediately"—*Shabbat* 118b. Comp. Yerushalmi *Taanit* 1:1; Exod. *Rabbah* 25:16—even *one* Sabbath!

[79] Have his blood on our hands? Cf. *Sanhedrin* 37b—Mishna.

[80] Cf. e.g., *Sefer Hazikaron; Be'er Yitzchak; Devek Tov; Be'er Mayim Chaim; Amar Neke; Maskil LeDavid; Divrei David; Gur Aryeh; Torah Temimah; Siftei Chachamim; Mizrachi.*

Thus the author of *Sefer Hazikaron* writes: "Scripture speaks of the disparagement of the Israelites ... the Rabbis arrived at this since it states: 'The Children of Israel were in the Desert.' Don't we know that they were in the Desert for forty years? It comes to tell you that at the *beginning* of the sojourn in the Desert this episode took place, for the Torah was given on the Sabbath, and *that* Sabbath they surely kept. Then it states: 'The Children of Israel were in the Desert.' Now, the Torah means to be explicit, not vague. Since it does not say when (exactly) this happened, you may say that at the *beginning* of their coming into the Desert 'They found a man gathering wood, etc.' Since on the first Sabbath they were at Mount Sinai, you are bound to say it was on the *second* Sabbath. The Rosh was asked about this and replied at length, but what I have written is the gist of his statement."[81]

The above position is self-evident: It is impossible to assume that the "first, second" Sabbaths relates to the Exodus, for then the Torah had not yet been given—until the third month—(Exod. Chap. 19), and the "gatherer" could not have been liable to the death penalty, since it was not yet said: "Whoever desecrates it shall surely be put to death" (Exod. 31:14). Rashi could not have written: "They knew that one who desecrates the Sabbath is punishable by death" (comment on verse 34)—how did they know?

One cannot argue that they had been commanded about the Sabbath at Marah *before* the giving of the Torah, for Rashi is precise in stating: "At Marah He gave them some *section of the Torah that they may apply themselves to them (parshiot shel Torah sheyitasku bahem)*: Sabbath, the Red Cow, Legislation" (Rashi on Exod. 15:25). Namely: He informed them and taught them the laws, for God was *about* to command them. This is the meaning of *that they may apply themselves to them*—that they should learn and know them.[82]

If so, they were not *commanded* yet regarding the observance of Sabbath, only to *study* the *mitzvot* relating to Sabbath. Hence, since the wood-gatherer incurred the death penalty, it was after the giving of the Torah, and the "first" Sabbath means the first Sabbath, on which the Torah was actually given—since all authorities agree that it was given on the Sabbath.[83] It is plausible to assume that that Sabbath all of them kept, and on the second one the wood-gatherer desecrated it.[84]

---

[81]Cf. *Maskil LeDavid; Divrei David* who wrote similarly, with some important changes.
[82]Cf. Ramban there. Cf. our commentary *Be'ur Setumot Be-Rashi*, Part I, pp. 169–70.
[83]*Shabbat* 86b.
[84]Cf. *Divrei David* and *Maskil LeDavid*, who go to great lengths to prove the incident occurred during the second year after the episode of the spies.

15:41   *Ani Hashem, Elokeychem*—"I am the Lord, your God."

RASHI: "I am the Lord" (means)—I am trustworthy to pay reward; "your God" (means)—I am trustworthy to exact punishment.[85]

Asher hotzeyti etchem—"Who has brought you out."

RASHI: On this condition have I redeemed you that you should take upon yourselves My decrees (that I should be your God).

Ani Hashem, Elokeychem—"I am the Lord your God."

RASHI: Why is this stated again? So that the Israelites should not say: Why did God say (*Ani Hashem*—"I am the Lord"); was it not that we should do (the commands) and receive reward? We would rather not do them, and not get reward! (Therefore it states again) Even against your will, I am your King (you *must* accept My commands!). Similarly it states: "Surely with a strong hand will I rule over you" (Ezekiel 20:33). Another explanation: Why is the Exodus from Egypt mentioned (in connection with fringes? As much as to say) I am the one who distinguished in Egypt between one who was a firstborn and one who was not.[86] I will also distinguish (discover) and punish one who attaches indigo-dyed wool (which looks like *t'cheylet*) to his garment and says it is *t'cheylet*.[87]

From the work of Rabbi Moses the Preacher I copy the following: Why is the section of the wood-gatherer next to the section on idolatry? To tell you that whoever desecrates the Sabbath it is like he worships idols, for Sabbath too (like the law of idolatry) is equal in importance to *all* the commandments. So too is it stated in Ezra.[88]

---

[85] *Sifrei* 115 end.

[86] Cf. Rashi Levit. 19:36.

[87] Rashi *Bava Metzia* 61b *t'cheylet* is expensive for it is dyed with the blood of the *chilazon*, which comes up from the sea only once in seventy years.

[88] In Rashi's time the Book of Nehemiah was still regarded as one with Ezra. It is in Nehemiah 9:13–14 although the wording is not *exactly* as quoted by Rashi. Possibly Rashi or R. Moses the Preacher quoted by heart—with slight changes. Cf. the section of Musaph of Rosh Hashana beginning with the words "Atah nigleita": *"You came down on Mount Sinai and gave Your People the Torah and commandments, and You made known to them Your holy Sabbath."* Also this section on fringes (*tzitzit*) was placed next to those (idolatry and Sabbath), because it too is equal to the commandments, as it says: "and do *all* My commandments" (verse 40 in section on *tzitzit*).

"On the borders (lit. *canfei*—"wings") of their garments"—corresponding to "I carried you on the wings of eagles" (Exod. 19:4). "On *four* corners,"
but not on a garment of *three* corners;[89] also not on a five-cornered garment.[90] This corresponds to the four expressions of redemption stated
regarding deliverance from Egypt: "I shall bring out" *vehotzeyti;* "I shall
deliver" *vehitzalti;* "I shall redeem" *vega-alti;* "I shall take"—*velakachti.*

"A thread of blue-purple"—*petil t'cheiletan*—an allusion to the bereavement of the firstborn, for the Targum (Aramaic) for *shickul* (bereavement)
is *tichla* (similar to *t'cheilet*), that plague was at night, likewise the color
t'cheilet is similar to the color of the sky when it darkens at night.[91] The eight
threads in the *tzitzit* allude to the eight days the Israelites waited from the
time they left Egypt until they sang the Song of Praise at the Red Sea.

COMMENT: A number of problems need to be addressed:

1) Why is there a need for *two* explanations for the mention of the
Exodus?

2) Why does Rashi resort to the Midrashic explanation of R. Moses the
Preacher?

3) Why does he explain *here* "on the four corners—not on three, etc.,"
since the words *arba' kanfot* are mentioned in the portion *Ki Teitsei* (Deut.
22:12)—not here—and the student is not up to there yet?

4) The recitation of the Song of Praise took place on the seventh day
of Passover, as Rashi himself explained (Exod. 14:5). Why then does he
write: "the *eight* days they waited ... until they sang praise at the sea"?

5) Why does he mention the allusion of the "eight threads in the *tzitzit*
correspond to the eight days, etc."—the eight threads are not mentioned
in this verse?

We may explain as follows:

---

[89]If he rounded off one of the four corners and made it a three-corner garment
it has no obligation of fringes.
[90]Cf. *Zevahim* 18b where there is a controversy among Tanaim about such a garment.
Rashi, following R. Moses the Preacher apparently ruled that a five-corner garment
has no obligation of *tzitzit* at all. Cf. also *Tur Orach Chaim*, Chap. 6 in *Beit Yosef, Orach
Chaim* 10:1 and *Tzeydah Laderech* here.
[91]*Menachot* 43b.

1) Ostensibly this entire verse is superfluous. If it came only to emphasize: "I am trustworthy to pay reward," and "trustworthy to exact punishment," verse 40 should have ended with the words *Ani Hashem, Elokeychem*—
"I am the Lord your God"—leaving out verse 41 entirely. Why then does
it come? Explains Rashi that it was written to underscore that the purpose
of the Exodus was that we should accept His decrees upon us. This is the
meaning of *lihiyot lachem Laylokim*—"to be to you your God (Master)," which
signifies *authority*, as Rashi explains elsewhere (Gen. 6:2).

The problem with this explanation is the Exodus was an essential
condition for *all* the commandments; why then is it mentioned in connection only with fringes? Although the mitzvah of fringes leads to the remem-
brance of *all* the commandments and to their fulfillment as stated: "In
order that you should remember and do *all* My commandments" (verse
40)—nevertheless, *tzitzit* is only *one* commandment. He should have rather
mentioned the Exodus in connection with idolatry, which is "like *all* the
commandments" (Rashi above, verse 22).

The difficulty with the second explanation is it should have stated: (I
am the Lord ...) "who smote the firstborns in Egypt," not "Who brought
you out of Egypt," since this explanation relates *only* to the plague of the
firstborns, which was *before* the Exodus. Besides, it is hard to say that "I am
the Lord your God" refers *only* to one who cheats on the matter of *t'cheilet*,
which is only one detail in the commandment of *tzitzit*.

2-3) Rashi resorts to the Midrashim of R. Moses the Preacher because
the fundamentals of the commandment of *tzitzit* are expressed in them, i.e.,
that it is equal in importance to all the *mitzvot*, as Rashi explains: "Who
brought you out of Egypt—it is on this condition that I redeemed you, that
you should accept upon yourselves My decrees"—specifically in the mitzvah
of *tzitzit*. However in the Midrashim it is explained that also Sabbath and
idolatry are equal to "all the *mitzvot*," why then does he state: "It is on *this*
condition that I redeemed you" only in connection with the mitzvah of
tzitzit?

Therefore Rashi continues to explain that *all* the details of the mitzvah
of *tzitzit*: "On the corners of your garments," "on *four* corners (not three,
etc.); "a thread of *t'cheilet*"; the eight threads—*all* of them related to the
Exodus—"alluding" to the various aspects of the Exodus. Therefore he
explains: "Four corners—not a garment of three," etc., here.

4-5) Rashi counts "eight days" until they sang praises at the Sea because
he counts the Exodus from the 14th of Nisan in the evening, when they
slaughtered sheep, the "deity of Egypt" as a Passover sacrifice and did not

fear that the Egyptians would stone them.[92] This is, therefore, the beginning of the redemption, and from then until they sang praises at the Sea
eight days passed. Although: "On the day after the Passover-offering (i.e.,
the 15th of Nisan) did the Children of Israel *go out* with an upraised hand
before the eyes of all Egypt (Numbers 33:3), and from *that* moment only
seven days passed until they sang praises."

Therefore Rashi mentions the allusion of the "eight threads" here—
because it is an important aspect of the Exodus, perhaps even its climax—
reciting the Song of *Praises* at the Sea which is the task of the Jewish People
and the raison d'etre for its becoming a nation, as the prophet states: "This
People that I have created for Myself that it should tell My Praises" (Isaiah
43:21), namely: The task of the Jewish People in the world is to publicize
God's Name and tell His praises in the world.[93]

---

[92]Cf. Exod. 8:22 where Moses asks Pharaoh: "Surely, if we were to slaughter the deity
of Egypt to the Lord *our* God will they not stone us?"

[93]One might add that this task is included in the statement: "That you should accept
upon yourselves My decrees." See also: *Be'urim le-Ferush Rashi al ha-Torah,* Part II,
pp. 218-20; *Be'er Yitchak; Gur Aryeh; Yosef Hallel; Lifshuto shel Rashi; Maskil LeDavid;
Sefer Hazikaron; Amar Neke, Mizrachi; Torah Temimah.*

Korach

16:27 *U-n'sheihem u-v'neihem v'tapam*—
"And their wives, children and infants."

RASHI: Come and see how terrible (a sin) dissension is: for an earthly tribunal (lit. "a court below") does not punish until a person has two hairs (i.e., signs of puberty); the Heavenly tribunal (lit. "the tribunal above") not before he is twenty years old—whereas here even the suckling (babies) perished![94]

COMMENT: Question: How does Rashi know that even sucklings are punished in a dissension; in this verse the punishment is not mentioned yet—only their brazenness, that they went out to scorn and curse?

Answer: Rashi was bothered by the mention of the infants in the verse. Surely they have no understanding, and one cannot say that they went to blasphemy and curse? If so, it should have stated merely: "They came out and stood ... and their wives and children"—especially as "their children" includes also very small children. But if we cannot apply the word *tapam*— "their infants" to refer to "scorn and curse," we can apply it to juxtapose it to "the earth opened its mouth and swallowed them up, etc.,"—including the infants. Hence we can make the deduction: "Come and see how terrible a sin dissension is, etc." namely: Even though infants do not blasphemy and curse, nevertheless since they stood together with the adults, they too were punished.[95]

---

[94]*Tanchuma Korach* 3; *Bamidbar Rabbah* 18:4. In the Yemenite MS and in the Alkabat printing there is an addition as follows: "They, their wives and infants—all gathered against him (Moses) to anger him—even day-old babies in their cribs. As they stood—big and small, so were they swallowed up ..." Also A. Berliner in his *Zechor le-Avraham?* cites this addition from a manuscript.

[95]Cf. *Gur Aryeh.* It would seem that this is the intention of the Yemenite manuscript and the Alkabats printing addition: "even day-old babies in their cribs. *As they stood big and small,* so they were swallowed up...." For verse 32 does *not* state: "It swallowed up them, their wives, their children *and their infants*," rather: It swallowed up them

18:9   *Asher yashivu li*—"Which they shall return to Me."

RASHI: This refers to property robbed (stolen) from a proselyte.[96]

COMMENT: How does Rashi know according to "plain sense" that this refers to property stolen from the proselyte, who is not even mentioned in the verse?

Because the Torah uses an expression of "returning" that is applicable to theft, as stated: "He shall return the robbed item which he robbed" (Levit. 5:23). One cannot interpret that "which they shall return" refers to the "meal-offerings, sin-offerings, and guilt-offerings" in the verse, for the expression of "returning" would not apply to them. It should have stated rather: "which they shall give, sacrifice." Also above in *Naso*, referring to theft from a proselyte it states: "the returned debt shall go to the Lord, for the priest (Numbers 5:8) and Rashi there explains: "To the Lord, for the priest—the Lord has acquired it and gave it to the priestly watch of that week."

We have here expressed the idea: "the earth is the Lord's and all there is in it" (Psalm 24:1), namely: *Everything* belongs to God, and He in His great Kindness allows man to use temporarily things that belong to God -and even to bequeath them to His children. This is how it is ordinarily when a person dies and leaves behind relatives who inherit him. But in the case of the proselyte who died, since he has no inheritors, his property reverts to its original owner—God. Hence it states: "which they shall return to *Me*." Now, the Lord gladly gives the property to the priestly watch of the particular week when the proselyte died.

---

and their *households*, etc." The addition emphasizes that the verse mentions the *infants* to include them in the swallowing explicitly—thereby stressing the moral "Come and see how terrible dissension is, etc." As for the reason why infants are also punished in a dissension see *Gur Aryeh*, who expounded on the matter at length, showing that it is appropriate by law.

[96]Who is considered not to have heirs by Jewish law, since his former family are non-Jews. Therefore his property goes to the priests; cf. Rashi on verse 8. *Sifrei* 117; *Chullin* 132b.

Chukat

19:22 *Vehanefesh hanoga'at*—"And the person who touches."

RASHI: The one who becomes unclean through a corpse, "shall be unclean until the evening." Here we learn that a corpse is the progenitor (lit. *Avi*—"the father") of primary sources (*Avot*—"fathers of") uncleanness: One who touches it (the corpse) becomes a primary source of uncleanness, and can make a person unclean. This is the explanation (of this chapter) according to its literal meaning and according to its laws (*halachot*). I have copied a Midrash *Agada* (homiletical explanation) from the work of R. Moses the Preacher, as follows ...

COMMENT: Rashi's remark: "I have copied a Midrash *Agada*, etc." means: indeed what follows is *not* the plain sense of the verses. However, since they express God's love for Israel and lofty moral ideas, it is worthwhile copying these statements. Following are several examples of these ideas:

1) "A red *cow*"—it may be compared to a handmaid's child who dirtied the king's palace. They said: Let his mother come and wipe up the excrement. Similarly, (since Israel became defiled by the golden calf) *let a cow* (its mother) *come and atone for the calf.* Herein is expressed God's love for Israel, since He Himself suggests how to "wipe up," i.e., atone for the sin of the golden calf.

2) "*Perfect—temimah*"—an allusion to Israel who were perfect (without blemish) and became blemished through the calf: Let this (perfect cow) come and atone for them and *they will return to their state of perfection.*" Here, too, is expressed God's deep love for Israel, namely: God *desires*[97] Israel to be *perfect* (without blemish) and righteous, so that He may be able to make

---

[97]Cf. the statement: "the Holy One, Blessed be He, *desires* to have an abode in the lower world (*batachtonim*)"—*Tanchuma Naso* 16; *Bechukotai* 3. See a lengthy explanation in *Tanya*, Chap. 36. Comp. our interpretation in *Be'ur Stumot Be-Rashi*, Part I, p. 248, note 11.

His *Shechinah* reside among them. Surely "perfection and without blemish (*tmimut vetamut*) are great praises, since in praise of Noah and Jacob we read: "Noah was a righteous, *perfect* man, etc." (Gen. 6:9); "Now Jacob was a *whole/perfect* (*tam*) man dwelling in tents" (Gen. 25:27).

3) "Cedar wood and hyssop and crimson (*'eitz erez ve'eizov u-shni tola'at*)"—these three species correspond to the three thousand men who fell (died) on account of the golden calf. The cedar is the highest of all trees and the hyssop is the lowest of all—this is a *symbol* that one of high position who *was haughty and* (therefore) *sinned*, should lower himself as the hyssop and the worm (*tola'at*) and he will gain atonement."

Pride is a very grievous sin and the Rabbis expounded at length on its severity, to the extent that they made pronouncement such as: "Whoever is boastful causes anger in the world";[98] "If he became proud, God will lower him;[99] "Any person who has haughtiness (*gasut ruach*) it is as though he worshipped idols"; as if he denied the *Main* Cause (i.e., God), etc."[100]—and many similar statements.[101]

We wish to throw light on some more points in R. Moses the Preacher's Midrash in the order of verses:

19:2   *V'yikchu eylecha*—"They shall take to you."

RASHI: From their own (money): Just as they divested themselves of their golden earrings for the calf of their own (gold), so shall they bring this cow (which is a calf-like animal) of their own money as an atonement.

COMMENT: Why should we think that they should *not* buy the red cow from their own money—from whose then? Since Scripture call the cow *chatat*—"a sin offering," and it is a communal sacrifice, I might have thought that it should be brought from the communal treasury in the *Temple* (*terumat halishka*), just as all communal sacrifices. Therefore the Midrash states "from their *own* (secular) money"—the red cow requires a *special* collection from their *own* money.[102]

---

[98]*Taanit* 8a.
[99]*Megilla* 13b.
[100]*Sotah* 4b.
[101]See the numerous pronouncements against pride by the Rabbis in *Otzar Ha-Agadah* by R. Moses David Gross, Part I, pp. 149–51.
[102]*Maskil LeDavid* infers: "They shall take *to you*—just as they sinned toward Moses by saying: 'For this man Moses, we do not know what happened to him'" (Exod. 32:1), so should they take the cow *to you*—as an atonement.

Parah adumah—"A red cow."

RASHI: It may be compared to a handmaiden's child who dirtied, etc.

COMMENT: The sin of the golden calf is regarded as dirty, as Jacob said: "Perhaps after You promised me *I dirtied myself through sin* and it will cause me to be delivered into Esau's hands."[103]

Besides the reasoning: "Let the cow come and atone for the calf" because the cow is the mother, there is another allusion, namely: "Let the cow come and atone for Israel who were at that moment: 'Like a wayward *cow* has Israel strayed'" (Hosea 4:16).

Lo alah aleihah 'ol—"Upon which a yoke never came."

RASHI: Just as they cast off themselves the *yoke of Heaven.*

COMMENT: A *yoke* represents complete subjugation without thought or reasoning: a cow (and horse, donkey, etc.) usually submits to carrying a burden (or to pull a cart, etc.) without any complaint or calculations, but it trusts that its master will supply all its needs. Whereas Israel did complain: "Rise and make us a god, for this man Moses—we don't know what happened to him," i.e., they did not have faith in Moses and cast off themselves the yoke of Heaven and put their faith in the Calf. Therefore let the cow come and teach them a lesson how one is to accept the yoke of Heaven—above thought or reason.[104]

19:3   *El Elazar ha-cohen*—"To Elazar the priest."

RASHI: Because Aaron made the calf, this rite was not given to him (that Aaron should perform the rite of the red cow), because "a prosecutor cannot become the counsel for defense."[105]

---

[103]Rashi on Gen. 32:11.

[104]A yoke also represents innocence, without rational inquiry. Cf. Rashi on: "You shall be perfect (*tamim*) with the Lord your God" (Deut. 18:13)—walk with Him innocently and await Him (for His help, salvation), but *do not inquire regarding the future,* but whatever happens to you accept innocently (*betmimut*), and then you will be with Him and His share."

[105]Cf. *Rosh Hashana* 26a, i.e., having made the Calf Aaron became as though a prosecutor against Israel hence he cannot now atone for it with the Red Cow, thereby as though becoming the counsel for defense.

COMMENT: It is very likely that "because a prosecutor cannot be a counsel for defense" Israel were not commanded to take a red *calf*. It is *not* similar to the fig leaves from which Adam and Eve sewed themselves loin cloths, regarding which it was said: "That was the tree from which they ate; by the very thing by which they were corrupted, were they rectified."[106] For they had not eaten fig leaves, but the fruit of the fig tree. But here they sinned with the calf itself, not with the cow. Had they taken a calf, it would have really been a case of a prosecutor becoming a counsel for defense.

The same holds true for Aaron: Although he tried to delay them (from making the calf), hoping that in the meantime Moses would return,[107] nevertheless in the end corruption came about by his very actions (the calf was actually made by Aaron). Hence it is appropriate to invoke the principle: A prosecutor, namely one through whose action came about prosecution of Israel, cannot become a counsel for defense—an atoner.

20:1   *Vatamot sham Miryam*—"Miriam died there."

RASHI: Why is this section on Miriam's death juxtaposed to the section on the Red Cow? To tell you: Just as sacrifices atone, so also the death of the righteous atones.[108]

Also she died with a kiss and why is it not stated about her: By the *mouth of God*" (by a Divine kiss, as it does state about Moses and Aaron)? Because it is not a respectful way of speaking about the most High (God) (as this is the way of speaking about a woman). But of Aaron it says in *Mas'ei*: "By the mouth of the Lord."[109]

COMMENT: Although Rashi does not usually ask why one section in the Torah is juxtaposed to another, where such a juxtaposition is problematic, he does ask. The problem here is the section on the Red Cow was said in the *second* year after the Exodus, on the day the Tabernacle was erected,[110] whereas Miriam died in the *fortieth* year. If so, why were the two matters juxtaposed?

Several questions arise:

---

[106]Cf. Rashi on Gen. 3:7; *Sanhedrin* 70b.
[107]Rashi Exod. 32:5.
[108]*Moed Katan* 28a; *Yalkut* 763; Midrash *Agada*, where the reading is: Just as the Red Cow atones.
[109]Cf. Numbers 33:38; see *Bava Batra* 17a.
[110]Cf. *Gittin* 60a; Rashi above 5:2.

1) In *Moed Katan* 28a the Talmud states: "Just as the *Red Cow* atones, also the death of the righteous atones"; why did Rashi change to: "Just as *sacrifices* atone, etc."?

2) What is death "with a kiss"?

3) Why does Rashi add: "But of Aaron it says in *Mas'ei*: 'By the mouth of the Lord'—how does that relate to Miriam's death with which we are dealing here?"

Answers:

1) Rashi was obliged to change to "just as sacrifices atone," because according to *plain sense* the Red Cow does not atone for anything. The ashes only *purify* one who was defiled by a dead body, but do not atone for any sin. Only according to the Midrash does the Cow atone for the golden calf. Therefore he writes: "Just as *sacrifices* atone." But, since "according to its laws Scripture called it a sin-offering to state that it is *like sacrifices*, etc."[111]— one can juxtapose to it Miriam's death and infer: "Just as sacrifices atone, etc."[112]

2) Just as a real kiss is a cleavage of two bodies to each other—mouth to mouth, etc.—so is "dying with a kiss" a stronger cleavage to the *Shechinah* than was possible during the lifetime of the righteous person.[113]
The Talmud states: "R. Elazar said: 'Here it states: Miriam died, and below it states: Moses died (lit.) on the mouth of God' (Deut. 34:5) just as there it was upon the mouth of God, here too it was upon the mouth of God. Why does it not state regarding her upon the mouth of God? Because it is unseemly (*genay*) to state thus. Hence neither the angel of death, nor worms had power over her."[114]
"Torah Temimah" explains the above: "Upon the mouth of God means not by the angel of death, nor through pains. This is derived from Moses" ... The *Sifrei* states: When God takes the soul of the righteous, He takes it gently, the Rabbis termed such a death as "death with a kiss."

---

[111]Rashi above 19:7.
[112]Why was Miriam's death not juxtaposed to real sacrifices? Because, just as the Cow is not a real sacrifice on the altar, so is the death of the righteous not a real sacrifice—yet both atone (cf. *Siftei Chachamim*). See *Tanya, Igeret HaKodesh*, Chap. 28, pp. 294–96 for a Kabbalistic explanation of why Miriam's death was not juxtaposed to an "internal" sin-offering.
[113]Cf. *Be'er Mayim Chaim*.
[114]*Bava Batra* 17a.

Obviously the expression "upon the mouth of God" is not to be taken literally, since God has no mouth. However, in order not to give scoffers an excuse to scoff,[115] the Torah did not state by Miriam "upon the mouth of God."

3) The words: "But of Aaron, it says upon the mouth of the Lord" are proof of his statement: "She too died with a kiss,"thus: One may suppose that Miriam was Aaron's equal, at least in prophecy. She may have even felt that both of them are equal to Moses and therefore argued: "Did God speak *only* to Moses; surely He spoke to us too!" (above 12:2), until God corrected her error, stating: "If there be prophets among you, I, God make Myself known to him in a vision, in a dream do I speak with him. Not so is my servant Moses, etc." (ibid. verses 6–7). Hence, even God accorded them equal status with the word "your prophets." If so, why does it not state by Miriam: "upon the mouth of God," since she *was* equal to Aaron, and by him it *does* say so? Answer: because it is not a respectful way of speaking, etc. Hence, it is because it stated by Aaron: "upon the mouth of God" that we know that also Miriam "died with a kiss."

One may still ask: Why indeed, do the death of the righteous, and even sacrifices atone? What is the connection between the death of the righteous, or the animal that is sacrificed and the sin? We venture to offer the following explanation:

Both the death of the righteous and sacrifices atone because they arouse the individual or the entire nation to repentance, thus: Whoever offered a sacrifice had to lay his hands on the head of the animal (cf. Levit 1:4; 3:2, 8,13; 4:4, 15, 24, 29, 33, etc.). During the confession of the sin he would say: "May it be the Will, etc., as if my blood, fat and flesh are being sacrificed on the altar, etc." Thus he surely did penitence at that moment. Therefore sacrifices atone, as they bring about repentance.

Same with the death of the righteous: When a very righteous person like Miriam dies, the ordinary people apply to themselves a logical inference: If a pious person such as X died, and his piety was of no avail, "because there is *no* man who does not sin" (I Kings 1:46; comp. *Kohelet* 7:20)—all the more so do *I* have to examine my deeds (and correct them). That is why Solomon said: "It is better to go to the house of mourning than to go to a feasting, for that is the end of all man—*and the living should take it to heart*" (*Kohelet* 7:2), i.e., should repent. Perhaps this is another reason why Rashi wrote: "Just as *sacrifices* atone, also the death of the righteous atones," and did not write: "Just as the Red Cow atones, etc." The common

---

[115]This is the meaning of the statement: "It is not a respectful way of speaking about the Most High," namely: "upon the *mouth* of God" could cause a denigration of God's honor, God forbid.

denominator is between *sacrifices* and the death of the righteous—not between the Red Cow and the death of the righteous, as per above.

20:23   *Al gevul Eretz Edom*—"On the border of the land of Edom."

RASHI: This tells us that because they became close to the wicked Esau, their ranks (lit.—*ma'aseihem*—"works") were breached and they lost this righteous man.[116] Thus the prophet says to King Yehoshafat: "Because you joined Ahaziah, the Lord made a breach in your works" (II Chronicles 20:37).

COMMENT: One may ask:

1) Maybe Aaron died because his time to die came, not because they became close to the wicked Esau?

2) Just because Israel became close to Esau the wicked, Aaron must be punished and die?

We can reply as follows:

1) The Torah juxtaposed the words "on the border of the land of Edom" to the words: "May Aaron be gathered to his people" (die). It were more fitting to write "on the border of the land of Edom" in the previous verse where the name "Hor Hahar" is first mentioned—were it not for the reason Rashi gives here. Accordingly the word—*'al* must be understood as *biglal*—"because of," namely: because they became close to Esau, Aaron died.[117]

2) The death of a righteous man is bad for the generation, because the righteous protect their generation.[118] Moreover, by their suffering the righteous atone for their generation, as the prophet states: "Indeed he bore our ills, and carried our pains ... He was pained because of our rebellious sins, and oppressed through our iniquities" (Isaiah 53:4–5). Hence it is not a punishment for Aaron for his deeds.

---

[116]Aaron. *Tanchuma* 14; *Bamidbar Rabbah* 19:16; *Yalkut* 764.
[117]Comp. *lo yumtu avot 'al banim*—"Fathers shall not die on account of children"— Deut. 24:16, where 'al means "*biglal*—because of."
[118]Cf. *Zohar*, Part III, 71, 114: "The righteous protect the world while they are alive, and after they die even more than when they lived."

21:8   *Kol hanashuch*—"Whoever is bitten."

RASHI: Even if a dog or donkey bit him, he would be harmed and continued to grow weaker and weaker; but the bite of a snake kills quicker, therefore it stated here *vera-ah oto*—"when he sees it"—a mere glance (sufficed to heal him). But regarding a snake's bite it says *vehibit*—"if he gazed"—"if a serpent bit a man, when he *gazed* (at the copper snake), he lived"—for a serpent's bite was not quick to heal, unless he gazed intently. Our Rabbis said "Did the copper snake really cause death or life? But when the Israelites (while gazing at the snake) looked up (to God) and subjugated their hearts to their Father in Heaven, they would be healed—but if not, they pined away (lit.—*nimokim*—"disintegrated")."[119]

COMMENT:

1) How does Rashi know that even if a dog or a donkey bit him, he would be harmed, etc.—in this section only "fiery serpents" are mentioned.

2) Why, indeed, was there a difference between the dog and donkey bite and a snake bite?

It seems that from the superfluous word *kol*—"all" (who were bitten), all types of biting were included: dog, donkey, etc., bites, for it would have sufficed to state: "the one who was bitten, etc." If so, why does it state: "if a *snake* bit a man, he would gaze ... and live," implying that *only* a snake bite would heal? Therefore Rashi explains that it does not exclude other types of bites; rather it emphasizes that a snake bite requires an intent gazing before healing is attained, whereas with other kinds of bites a mere glance is sufficient.

A snake bite alluded to the fact that they behaved like the serpent, thereby sinning doubly: 1) they slandered the Manna just as the serpent slandered God;[120] 2) they were ungrateful in regard to the Manna[121]—just as the serpent was ungrateful. Therefore a snake bite was quick to kill, and one did not heal, "unless he gazed *intently*," i.e., until the one bitten realized that he behaved like the serpent and his sin is twofold.

Rashi's statement: Did the copper snake really cause death or life, etc., is in answer to the question: If all depends on the subjugation of one's heart to the Father in Heaven, what need was there for a copper snake and its

---

[119]*Tanchuma* 19; *Bamidbar Rabbah* 19:23; *Rosh Hashana* 29a; *Yalkut* 754.
[120]Cf. Rashi Gen. 3:5.
[121]Cf. Rashi on verse 6: "Let the serpent to which all kinds of food have *one* taste" (i.e., earth, cf. Rashi Gen. 3:14, *Yoma* 75a), come and punish these ingrates to which one thing (manna) had the taste of many different dainties (Rashi 11:8).

suspension on a pole? Rashi replies that the snake and the pole were the means for looking above and subjugating one's heart. For while they were looking above, they would be reminded of the One "who dwells in Heaven" (Psalm 2:4), and would subjugate their hearts, etc.

The reason God told Moses to make a *copper* snake was that it was "a miracle within a miracle," because whoever is harmed by anything—it is dangerous for him to look at the object that harmed him. Physicians too are careful not to mention to the one harmed the object that harmed him. Whereas God said: "If a snake bites a man, let him gaze at the copper snake and he will live"—which is contrary to nature! This comes to teach us that the snake does not kill; rather sin kills.[122]

21:9   *Nechash nechoshet*—"A copper serpent."

RASHI: Moses was not told to make it of *copper* (only), but Moses said: God calls it *nachash*; I will therefore make it of *nechoshet*—a play on words (lit. *lashon nofel 'al lashon*—"one term fitting the other term").[123]

COMMENT: Questions:

1) God did *not* call it *nachash*, but *saraf*; why then did Moses say God calls it *nachash*?

2) What is the significance of "a play on words"?

The explanation is:

1) Moses didn't say: God *told me nachash*, but "*calls* it *nachash*" as stated, "God sent among the people fiery *nechashim*" and according to Rashi's explanation: for they burn man with the poison in their teeth (verse 6), the word *haserafim*—"that burn" is a description of the snakes, namely: the snakes that burn—but not that there were *two* types: *nechashim* and *serafim*.[124] Now, since Moses was commanded: "Make for yourself a *saraf*" after the statement: "God sent against the people the *nechashim haserafim*," it is apparent that the expression saraf is an adjective, i.e., "burning" (not a new type of snake). Hence, God must have told Moses "Make for yourself a *nechash* saraf"—a burning snake. Moses abbreviated it to *'aseh lecha* saraf (leaving out the word *nechash*).

---

[122]Cf. the lengthy explanation of the Ramban to verse 9; *Gur Aryeh*.
[123]Gen. *Rabbah* 31:8; Yerushalmi *Rosh Hashana* 3:9; Midrash *Agadah*.
[124]Contra: *Amar Neke* and *Maskil LeDavid*. Cf. *Mizrachi, Siftei Chachamim*.

2) The importance of "plays on words" can be gleaned from the statement of the Yerushalmi to our verse: *nechash nechoshet*. R. Yossi said: The
expression "Make for yourself *aseh lecha*" is mentioned in four places, in
three of these it is explained (understood) in one it is not explained: 'Make
yourself an ark of Gofer wood' (Gen 6:14); 'make yourself two silver trum-
pets' (Numbers 10:2); 'make for yourself flint knives' (Joshua 5:2). But,
'Make yourself a saraf' is not clear. Moses said: Isn't the *main thing* a
snake?[125] Therefore "Moses made a copper snake." From here R. Meir
deduced the importance of "examining names."[126]

The Torah informed us that Moses made the snake from copper to
teach us that "plays on words" apply to practical law: "From *here* R. Meir
deduced the importance of examining names" that have a play on words.
Thus we find that R. Meir called a man "wicked" on the basis of his name,"
Kidor, because of the verse *ki dor tahapuchot haymah vego'*—"for they are
a generation of reversals, etc." (Deut. 32:20, cf. 83b).

It would seem that on account of a play on words Moses understood
that he ought to make it out of copper, for God told him *saraf* (burning)
and Moses understood from this that the snake had to be of a shining
material, looking as though burnt in fire, as Ezekiel states: "glittering like
burnished copper," which Rashi explains the "purified and burnished in
fire copper" (Ezekiel 1:7). Therefore he made a copper snake, namely
purified in fire, thus *nechash nechoshet* is a play on words.

One might further explain that Moses made the snake of copper (not
any other material) in order to speak in defense of Israel. Thus, true the
Israelites adopted the habit of the primeval Serpent by speaking evil of the
manna, and were ungrateful like the Serpent. On the other hand they
offered almost all their sacrifices on the *copper* altar, and the priests wash
their hands from the *copper* sink. Therefore, let the merit of the copper altar
and sink come and atone for the serpent—like acts they committed.[127]

Furthermore, the sink was made of "the mirrors of the legions" (Exod.
38:80), which were of copper, "to make peace between husband and wife,
to make a woman whose husband suspected her (of adultery) and she
secluded herself drink from the water of the sink."[128] By making the snake
of copper, Moses desired to make peace between God—"the husband" and
His wife—the Jewish People, according to the Midrash of Rabbi Akiva about
Shir Hashirim (the Song of Songs).[129]

---

[125]I.e., surely God told him to make a snake—*nachash*, while saraf is an adjective,
as explained above.
[126]Yerushalmi *Rosh Hashana* 3:9.
[127]This last insight I was privileged to gain from my learned, modest daughter Gitty,
may she be granted a happy and healthy long life.
[128]Rashi on Exod. 38:8 and *Tanchuma Pekudei* 9.
[129]Cf. Tractate *Yadayim*, Chap. 3, Mishna 5 and Rashi on *Shir Hashirim* 1:1.

Balak

22:10   *Balak ben Zipor vego'*—"Balak the son of Zipor, etc."

RASHI: Even though I am not important in Your eyes, I *am* important in the eyes of Kings.[130]

COMMENT: Two questions need to be answered:

1) How do we know that *this* was Bilam's intention with the words: "Balak the son of Zipor, etc."

2) What use is it to Bilam if he is important in the eyes of kings, if he is *not* important in the eyes of God?

We may explain as follows:

1) Since Bilam mentioned "the king of Moav" beside "Balak, son of Zipor" it indicates that he emphasizes the fact that he was important in the eyes of kings. If not, why does he emphasize "the king of Moav"—even the second emissaries of Balak did not describe him as "the king of Moav" only "Balak son of Zipor" (verse 16). Hence this was his intention. By saying: "I am important in the eyes of kings" Bilam meant: Since I am important in the eyes of kings, do not embarrass me in front of them and let me go with them.

2) In answer to this question it is worth citing the enlightening remark of "Be'er Yitzchak," at least briefly.

"It is indeed remarkable that Bilam should boast to God that he is important in the eyes of human kings, who is but an insignificant creature (lit. "a small creeping thing"—*remes katan*). Likewise what Rashi wrote: "God came to delude him, etc." (Rashi verse 9). How could a man of Bilam's stature think that God does not know everything? I believe that the

---

[130] *Tanchuma Balak* 5; *Bamidbar Rabbah* 20:9.

Rabbis felt that Bilam only had a strong imagination, which *could* have brought him to prophecy, had he had the traits which the Sages considered as prerequisites for a prophet: 1) Very wise intellectually; 2) Physically strong and able to subjugate matter to intellect; 3) Rich, i.e., being satisfied with his means—which Bilam did *not* possess, for he was lustful and haughty as Rashi stated in verses 13, 18.[131] He was neither strong, nor rich, nor wise—thus not worthy of prophecy at all ... He was a great magician and deceived the people of his generation, claiming that he was God's prophet.

However, in a temporary manner only, when Balak called him to curse Israel, because God loves his People, He inspired Bilam with His *Shechinah* (made him prophesy) in order to publicize the fact that Israel are the Children of His beloved (Abraham) and thus His children—so that all nations of the world should see that this wicked man (Bilam) will himself bless them against his will and will prophesy their greatness and the ruin of the nations. After God's plan was fulfilled, the Spirit of God left him and he became a magician as before. It is therefore no wonder that Bilam erred in believing mistaken ideas and boasting before God that he was important in the eyes of kings and believing that not all is known to Him ...."

According to the above it was *no* use to Bilam to say: "I am important in the eyes of kings"—it was only an error, a mistaken opinion. One might also assume that Bilam in his mistaken ideas, thought God was only the God of Israel—as was the belief of other nations that each nation had its own deity that somehow protected it.[132] Therefore he said: "Even though I am not important in *Your* eyes (who are the God of Israel), I am important in the eyes of kings," namely, the deity of these people will support me and I will be able to curse Israel, God forbid. When God apprised him of his error, namely that He is the God of the *entire* world and hence no nation has any power over Israel, he said: "I cannot transgress the word of my God, etc." (verse 39).

22:26   *Vayosef malach Hashem*—
"The angel of the Lord went further."

RASHI: Went further in front of him—it went so as to be in front of him in another spot. It is similar to: "and he passed in front of them" (Gen. 33:3). There is a Midrashic explanation in *Tanchuma*: What reason did he have to *stand* in three places? The angel showed Bilam symbols referring to the three patriarchs.[133]

---

[131]Cf. *Nedarim* 38a; Ramban, *Hilchot Yesoday Ha-Torah*, Chap. 7.

[132]E.g., Kemosh—the deity of Moav; Milkom—deity of Amon; Ashtoret—deity of Zidon, etc.

[133]*Tanchuma* 8; Midrash *Agadah*; *Yalkut* 765; *Bamidbar Rabbah* 20:14.

COMMENT: What are the symbols of the patriarchs that the angel showed Bilam? The first place: "The angel of the Lord placed himself in the way" (verse 22)—there was still room on either side, as it states: "and the donkey turned aside out of the way" (verse 23). The symbolical meaning is that had Bilam wished to curse the seed of Abraham, he could have found on either side the children of Ishmael and Keturah.[134]

The second place the angel stood was in a land between the vineyards: "and she (the ass) pressed herself against the wall" (verse 25) meaning: Had Bilam wished to curse Yitzchak's children, he would have found one side to curse—Esau.[135] The third place the angel stool corresponded to Jacob: "He stood in a place so narrow that there was no room to swerve right or left" (verse 26), namely: There was no blemish or imperfection in any of Jacob's children. Hence, a curse on them had no chance of taking effect.

Rashi points out that this is a "Midrash *Agada*," i.e., is not the plain sense of the verse. If so, why does he cite it? Because it answers a question in the mind of the student: Why didn't the angel reveal himself to Bilam immediately the first time—just the ass saw him on the first time, and as the Midrash wonders: "Why did he (the angel) precede him three times before he revealed himself to him?" Hence this is a type of "*Agada* that order the words of Scripture in a very plausible manner," which Rashi does utilize in his commentary besides the "plain sense."[136]

22:28   *Zeh shalosh regalim*—"These three times."

RASHI: He hinted to him (by the expression *shalosh regalim*): You wish to uproot a nation that celebrates these festivals annually (Passover, Shavuot, Sukkot)?![137]

COMMENT: In what way is the power of the three Festivals greater than all other commandments, that the angel attributed the merit of Israel to their celebrating the three Festivals annually?

We suggest that the reason the three Pilgrimage Festivals (Passover, Shavuot, and Sukkot) are so beloved by God, is because through them the Jewish People would publicize the Name and Kingship of God in the entire world: During these three Festivals a majority of the People would go on

---

[134]He would have found an imperfection in either of these and possibly the curse would take effect upon them.
[135]Both he and his children were blemished.
[136]See his statement in Gen. 3:8. Cf. *Be'er Yitzchak; Be'er Mayim Chaim; Levush Haorah.*
[137]*Tanchuma* 9; *Bamidbar Rabbah* 20:14.

a pilgrimage to Jerusalem. When the non-Jewish merchants saw that all of Israel worships one God, they were full of admiration for the Jewish People and for God and converted.

Thus Rashi writes on the verse: "Nations assemble at the mount" (Deut. 33:19). Another explanation: Through Zevulun's trading, the merchants of the nations come to his land ... and they say: "Since we have troubled ourselves to come up to here, let us go to Jerusalem and see what is (the nature of) the God of this people and what are His doings?" They see all Israel serving one God and eating one kind of food (only kosher food). For as regards the other nations, the god of one is not the god of the other, and the food of one is not the food of the other, so they say: "There is no nation as worthy as this one," and they convert (to Judaism) there, as it is said: "There shall they offer sacrifices of righteousness."

Now, this public realization that all Israel worships one God, etc., was the greatest of all especially during the three Pilgrimage Festivals, since "In a multitude of people is the King's (God's) glory" (Proverbs 14:28). Thereby Israel fulfilled their mission in the world, which is to publicize the Name of God in the world, as the prophet states: "This nation (Israel) have I created for Myself, so that they may tell My praises" (in the world—Isaiah 43:21), i.e., I created the Jewish People *in order* that they should tell my praise in the entire world.

> 23:7   *Arah li Ya'akov u-lecha zo'amah Yisrael—*
> "Curse Jacob for me, come bring anger upon Israel."

RASHI: By both their names (Jacob, Israel) Balak told him to curse them, lest one of them is not distinctive (enough to assure him that he means to curse Israel and no other nation).

Two questions need to be addressed here:

1) From where does Rashi know that Balak told Bilam to curse them by *both* their names; perhaps the mention of both names comes only as a "complementary parallelism"—where both parts, "Jacob—Israel," refer to the *same* thing, and used only as a figure of speech?[138]

---

[138]Just like the verbs *arah—zo'amah* "curse—bring anger," which mean the same and therefore Rashi does not comment at all on the change of the verb. Thus Ibn Ezra writes: "The meaning is double (i.e., the same) ... it is changed only for emphasis." Hence *arah ... zo'amah* are two words with one meaning.

2) What is the meaning of "distinctive" (*muvhak*) or "not distinctive" relative to God; surely before Him everything is revealed? Moreover, *both* names are distinctive, for even *after* Jacob's name was changed to "Israel" God continues calling him "Jacob"?[139]

a) Bilam understood that Balak asked him to curse them by both names from the fact that he did not mention the name of the (Jewish) people. He only said: "Behold *a people* came out of Egypt ... curse me *this people*" (verses 5–6). Why did he not mention their name? Surely he was not sure which is their distinctive name, thus hinting to Bilam that he should curse them by *both* names—so that the curse should take effect on whichever happens to be the distinctive name.

b) The matter of a "distinctive" name may be explained in accordance with the statement of *Be'er Yitzchak*[140] that Bilam was not at all worthy of prophecy, but was rather a great magician, etc., Certainly Balak was no prophet, but a magician like Bilam.[141] As magicians/diviners it was important to them to curse by the "distinctive" name only, because a curse by magic can take effect, in their erring opinion, only upon a distinctive name. In their mistaken opinion Balak and Bilam thought that God's power is no greater than their magical powers, Heaven forfend, by which they curse.[142] The fact that God continues calling Jacob by *both* names does not mean that both are distinctive. On the contrary, if both names are distinctive all the more so is it necessary to curse them by *both* names.[143]

---

[139]He is even called *both* names in one verse, e.g.: God said to *Israel* in a night vision, He said, "Jacob, Jacob(Gen 46:2).

[140]See our commentary above (22:10).

[141]He was even a greater diviner than Bilam as Rashi explains below on 23:14, s.v. *Rosh hapisgah*: Bilam was not a magician like Balak, etc.

[142]Cf. Rashi above 22:9 on: "Who are these people with you ... Bilam said (thought): Sometimes not everything is revealed to Him. His knowledge is not always equal. I too will find a time when I can curse without His Knowledge" (i.e., without God discerning that I cursed Israel). Thus we see that Bilam compared God's knowledge to the knowledge of the powers of defilement (*kochot hatumah*)—and even intended to overcome God's Knowledge, according to his erring opinion!

[143]R. Wolf Heidenheim in his *Havanat Hamikra* on Rashi cites here a rather lengthy addition from Rashi MS, and so does A. Berliner in his *Zechor Le-Avraham* conjecturing that it comes from R. Joseph Kara. However, interesting as this addition may be, as it is *not* directly related to the illucidation of *our* Rashi, we only allude to it without citing it in full.

23:10   *Mi manah 'afar Ya'akov vego'*—
"Who has counted the dust of Jacob, etc."

RASHI: The meaning is as its Aramaic translation: the infants of the House of Jacob.[144] The Aramaic *meyarba mashiryata* means: "who can count ... even one" of the four (*rova'*—"a fourth") banners (a group of three tribes under one banner). Another explanation of *afar Ya'akov*—"the dust of Jacob": They practice countless commandments in connection with dust: "Do not plough with an ox and donkey together" (Deut. 22:10); "Do not sow your field with two kinds of seeds" (Levit. 19:19); the ashes of the Red Cow (Numbers 19:9ff.); the dust used in the case of a woman suspected of adultery (Numbers 5:17); and similar cases.[145]

COMMENT: According to Targum Onkelos the meaning of the verse is "Who can count the little ones (*d'adkaya*) of the House of Jacob, regarding whom it is stated that they shall multiply like the dust of the earth (cf. Gen. 13:16)? Or (who can count) one of the four camps (banners) of Israel? By this rendition *rova'* means *reva'*—"a quarter."
This explanation is difficult on two counts:

1) There is a repetition in the verse, although according to Onkelos "the dust of Jacob" refers to small children, whereas "a quarter of Israel" refers to grown-ups. How did Rashi arrive at this distinction?[146]

2) There is no inner connection between this verse and the previous, which speaks of the merits of Israel?
Therefore Rashi offers: "Another explanation—they perform countless commandments in connection with dust, etc." According to this explanation our verse is an example of: Behold, it is a nation that dwells in solitude and is not reckoned among the nations" (verse 9), namely: There is no nation with so many merits as Israel has—since they practice countless commandments with the dust alone, besides many other commandments.
The difficulty in the second explanation is that there is no connection between "the dust of Jacob," which relates to commandments, and "the quarters of Israel," which refers to the actual children. It therefore seems inappropriate to state concerning both *together* "who has counted," since

---

[144]Who are compared to the dust of the earth in Gen. 13:16.
[145] *Tanchuma* 12; *Bamidbar Rabbah* 20:19.
[146]Cf. *Maskil LeDavid*, who asks: "When Abraham was told: 'Likewise your children shall be counted,' it was said about *all* of Israel (small and big). How does Rashi know that the little ones too will be countless?"

they refer to two different matters entirely. Hence both explanations are necessary.

23:23   Ka'eit yeiameir le'Ya'akov vego'—
"Even now it is said of Jacob, etc."

RASHI: There will yet be a time like this time (*ka'eit*) when the love that God has for them will be revealed to all (nations), for they (Israel) sit before Him and learn Torah from His mouth (i.e., directly from Him), and the place assigned to them will be more inward than that of the ministering angels (closer to the *Shechinah*) and the angels will ask them: "What has God wrought?" This is the meaning of what is said: "Your eyes shall see your Teacher" (Isaiah 30:20). Another explanation is that *yeiameir le'Ya'akov* ... is not an expression of the future, but the present, namely: They need no enchanter or diviner, for every time it becomes necessary to tell Jacob and Israel what God has wrought, and what are His decrees on High, they do not resort to enchantment or divination; rather it is told to them (*yeiameir le'Ya'akov*) through their prophets what is the decree of the Omnipresent (*mah pa'al e-l*) or the Urim and Tunim tell them. But Onkelos did *not* render thus.[147]

COMMENT: A number of questions arise out of Rashi's explanations:

1) According to the first explanation, what is the connection between *ka'eit yeiameir le'Ya'akov vego'*—"Even now it will be told to Jacob, etc." and *ki lo nachash be'Y'akov* ...—"for there is not enchantment in Jacob, nor divination in Israel" mentioned at the beginning of this verse?

2) Where in the verse is there an allusion to Rashi's statement: "For they sit before Him and learn Torah from His mouth, and the place assigned to them will be more inward than those of the ministering angels"?

3) Why does Rashi add: "This is the meaning of what is said: "Your eyes shall see your Teacher"?

4) According to the first explanation: Since we are dealing with Israel's virtue in the *future*, there is no reason not to curse them *now*?!

---

[147]Cf. *Tanchuma* 14: "The ministering angels ask them: "What did the Holy One, blessed be He, instruct (Israel)." See also: *Bamidbar Rabbah* 20:20; *Yerushalmi; Shabbat* 6:9; *Nedarim* 32a, and cf. Ran there s.v. *man dkapid;* Deut. *Rabbah* 1:12; *Yalkut* 769; Midrash *Agadah.*

5) According to the second explanation: Since the verse deals with a *constant* situation, why is the future tense used—*yeiameir*—"it *will be* told"? Also, what is the meaning of *ka'eit*—"as now"?

6) How does the section in Rashi: "and what are His decrees on High ... what is the decree of the Omnipresent" belong here?

7) Why does Rashi add: "But Onkelos did *not* render thus "? Surely, Rashi neither disputes Onkelos, nor explains his opinion!

What need is there to stress that "Onkelos did not render thus"?

We may explain as follows:

In this entire prophecy Bilam attempts to justify his inability to curse Israel, whether because God does not agree that he should curse them, as he states in verse 20: "Behold, I have received (an order) to bless, etc."— where Rashi comments: "I have received from Him to *bless* them" (not to curse them)—or because they are worthy of a blessing.[148] In verse 21 Bilam praises Israel highly and describes how beloved they are by God, e.g., "He perceives no iniquity in Jacob,"—Rashi: "When they transgress His words, He does not deal strictly with them, to pay attention to their iniquities, etc."; "and the friendship (*uteru'at*) of the King is in him"—Rashi: "It is (*teru'at*) an expression of love and friendship." In this verse he continues praising Israel highly: "For there is no enchantment in Jacob, etc.," namely: Not only do they not deserve to be cursed, but they are worthy of a *blessing*, because there are no enchanters, or diviners among them.

In light of the above one must explain that the words—*ka'eit yeiameir le'Ya'akov vego'* allude to Israel's virtues and God's love for them. How so? The word *ka'eit*—"like the time" points to a famous time in history when God's love for them was at its highest level, i.e., during the giving of the Torah to them, when Israel was very beloved by God, as stated: "You shall be to Me the most beloved of all peoples" (Exod. 19:5, cf. Rashi). Now, since our verse speaks in the *future* tense (Even now it *will be* told to Jacob, etc.), Rashi explains: "There will *yet* be a time like this ... when they sit before Him and learn Torah from His mouth," just as at the time of giving the Torah they learned Torah from His mouth (the Ten Commandments).

Rashi continues: "and the place assigned to them will be *more inward* than that of the ministering angels, and *they* will ask them: "What has God wrought?", since we are dealing here with the God of Israel, and their virtue as during the giving of the Torah—whereas the nations

---

[148]As stated in this verse: "For there is no enchantment in Jacob, etc.," and Rashi explains: "For they are worthy of a blessing because there are no enchanters or diviners among them."

do not recognize Israel's virtues, neither in the present, nor in the future.[149] Hence, it *must* refer to the angels; they will ask Israel: "What has God wrought?" If so, obviously the place of Israel will be *more inward* than that of the angels, who will require Israel's assistance!

Rashi adds: "Your eyes will see your Teacher," because of the difficulty. During the giving of the Torah, Israel did *not* wish to hear it directly from the Mouth of God, but said to Moses: "You speak with us and we shall hear, and *let not* God speak with us lest we die" (Exod. 20:16)? Therefore Rashi states: "The prophet (Isaiah) promises that in the Future, God Himself will be Israel's Teacher and they will not tremble before Him, rather: "Your eyes will *see* your Teacher," i.e., their virtue (achievement) will be even *greater* than at the time of giving the Torah!

Since such a glorious future is promised them that they will reach even greater heights than at the time of giving the Torah, and the place assigned to them will be closer to the *Shechinah* even than that of angels—it is impossible that God should agree to curse them, for surely: "God is not a man that He should be deceitful, nor a son-of-a-man that he should relent" (verse 19).

According to the second explanation—*ka'eit* means "at any time that will be necessary to tell Jacob, etc."—in every generation one can ask Jacob (Israel): "What has God wrought and what are His decrees, etc."—regarding *each* generation one may say—*ka'eit*—"as at *this* time."[150] Since we are dealing with a *constant* situation, one can use the future tense, for thus it was in the past, and thus will it be in the *future.*[151]

According to the second explanation: *Ka'eit yeiameir le'Ya'akov vego'* is a continuation of the beginning of the verse, i.e.: They do not need an enchanter or diviner to know "What are His decrees on High, since the prophets tell them "What is God's decree," even before they ask, since they are so beloved by God. Hence no curse will be of any avail, for they are aware of the decree and will do their best to nullify it by penitence and good deeds. This serves as negative grounds for not cursing them—besides the positive reason: "Behold I have received (an order) to bless, etc."—verse 20.

The reason Rashi adds: "But Onkelos did *not* render thus" is because here Onkelos translates according to the *plain sense* of the verse, unlike his

---

[149]For had Balak and Bilam recognized their love and virtue in the eyes of God, they would not attempt to curse them. The prophecies stating that in the Future the nations will serve Israel, e.g., "Foreigners will build your walls and their Kings will serve you" (Isaiah 60:10)—this will be *against* their will.

[150]Comp. Rashi on Gen. 24:14 *asher yeiameir hayom.*

[151]Cf. Rashi's explanation of Exod. 15:1, s.v. *va'yomru laymor ashirah laHashem.*

manner in other verses in this section, where he gives *homiletical* explanations. Therefore in other verses in this section Rashi states: "As the Targum renders it *ktargumo*."[152] Here, however, Onkelos gives the *literal* sense; neither the first, nor the second explanation given by Rashi.

24:3   *Sh'tum ha'ayin*—"With the open eye."

RASHI: His eye was bored and extracted, and its eye socket looked open. The word *sh'tum* "boring a hole" is a Mishnaic usage: "Enough time to bore a hole (in a cask) and stop it up *(kedei sheyishtom veyistom)* and it can dry."[153]

Our Rabbis said: Because Bilam said: *u-mispar et rova' Yisrael*—"and the number of a fourth of Israel" (23:10) meaning: that God sits and counts the sexual issues of the Israelites, (asking) "When will come the drop (of semen) from which the righteous man will be born?" He therefore said to himself: "He who is holy and whose ministers (angels) are holy should look at such things?!" On this account Bilam's eye was blinded.[154]

Some explain *shtum ha'ayin* "open-eyed," as Onkelos translated ("who can see well"). Since it says in the singular *shtum ha'ayin*—"open-eye," not *shtum ha'ainayim*—"open-eyes"—we learn that he was blind in one eye.[155]

COMMENT: According to *both* interpretations of *shtum ha'ayin*, the words *u'gluy 'ainayim*—"but his eyes are open" (verse 4) in the *plural*, i.e., as he was *before* one eye was blinded or extracted.

Question: Ostensibly Bilam's complaint: "He who is holy and His servants are holy should look at such things?!" is a valid argument. If so, why was one of his eyes blinded—as a "measure-for-measure" punishment?

The reason Bilam was punished was because he attributed to God the same drives and motives as humans have for *their* behavior. The *real* meaning of the Rabbis' statement: "God sits and counts the sexual issues of Israel (asking): When will come the drop *from which the righteous man will be born?*" is that God looks forward to the birth of the righteous because by their life

[152]Cf., e.g., verses: 22:24; 23:9,10,21; 24:7,9, etc.

[153]*Avodah Zarah* 69a. The context is about a wine store, if the Jew leaves the store, while the non-Jew remains. Rashi explains: "If the Jew stayed away a length of time sufficient for the non-Jew to bore a hole in the stopper of the barrel and stop it up again (with a clay stopper) and it dries—then the wine is forbidden to a Jew."

[154]*Nidah* 31a.

[155]Cf. *Sanhedrin* 105a and Rashi s.v.—*sh'tum ha'ayin*; Tosafot *Nidah* 30b s.v.—*sh'tum ha'ayin*; *Yalkut* 766.

and Torah they publicize God's name in the world. In like fashion the
Rabbis said: "God *desires* the prayers of the righteous," meaning: By their
prayers, the righteous express the idea that man is totally dependent upon
God, and therefore must be ever grateful to Him for His kindness toward
him.[156]

Similarly the Rabbis said: "The righteous are the Chariot of the
Omnipresent,"[157] meaning: Just as a chariot brings its rider to wherever he
wishes to go, so too do the righteous bring God—so to speak—to every
place in the world, by publicizing His Name in the entire world—both by
way of a personal example they serve for others, and by instructing the
People in the right way in life. Thus they serve as an instrument in the
hands of God, as a chariot serves as an instrument for its rider to get to
wherever he wishes to go.

24:5 *Mah tovu ohalecha*—"How good are your tents."

RASHI: He said this because he saw that the entrances of their tents are not
exactly facing each other (cf. Rashi verse 2). *Mishkenotecha* means: "Your
encampments," as Onkelos translates it.

Another explanation: "How good are your tents"—How good are the
tent of Shiloh and the Temple, when they flourished—where sacrifices
were offered to atone for you. *Mishkenotecha*—even when they are destroyed, because they were taken as a pledge (*Mashkon*, similar to
Mishkenotecha) for you—and their destruction is an atonement for *the souls*,
for it is said: "The Lord brought His fury to an end" (Eichah 4:11). By what
means did He bring it to an end? "He kindled a fire in Zion" (He destroyed
the Temple).[158]

COMMENT: Several points in Rashi's comment require an explanation:

1) Since he explained *Mishkenotecha*—"as Onkelos translates," why did
he not explain also *ohalecha*, as the Targum does: "your land"?

2) The context implies that the words "How good" refer also to "your
encampments Israel," i.e., "How good are your encampments Israel"—what
is the *good* in Israel's encampments?

---

[156]Cf. *Yevamot* 64a and Maharsha there. Comp. our Hebrew commentary: *Be'ur
Setumot be-Rashi*, Part I, pp. 31, 63–64.
[157]Cf. Rashi Gen. 17:22 and our commentary thereto.
[158]Cf. *Tanchuma Pekudei* 5; Rashi Exod. 38:21 s.v. *HaMishkan Mishkan*; *Yalkut* 771.

3) According to "Another explanation," how can one call the Temple (lit. "your *eternal* House"): "Your *tents*"—it was *not* a tent!

4) Why does Rashi emphasize: "and their destruction is an atonement for the *souls*, which "souls" does he have in mind?[159]

5) According to the second explanation, why didn't Rashi mention also the Tent of Meeting (*Ohel Mo'ed*), which was with them at the time Bilam blessed them?

We may explain thus:

1-2) Rashi did not wish to explain "your tents" as Onkelos does "your land," because that would be similar to *Mishkenotecha*—"your encampments," namely: the camp of Israel in their *permanent* encampment that is the Land of Israel.[160]

Moreover, Rashi explains *this* verse as he explained verse 2, where it says: "He saw Israel dwelling according to its tribes," and Rashi explains: "He saw each tribe dwelling by itself, not intermingled; he saw that the entrances (of the tents) were not exactly facing each other, so that one should not peep into the other's tent"[161] therefore: 'The Spirit of God was upon him'—he decided not to curse them" (to comply with the will of God—*Ruach Elokim*). Accordingly Rashi explains here—which is an introduction to the *blessings* (instead of curses): "How good are your tents Jacob—that the entrances of the tents were not exactly facing each other"; *Mishkenotecha*—"Your encampments," namely: "Each tribe dwelling by itself." Therefore they are worthy of *blessings* not curses.

The "good" in Israel's encampment is that each tribe dwells by itself and they are not intermingled.

3) The Temple may be called a "tent," for we find a number of places where a "tent" designates a place of residence, not always relating to a tent made of canvas curtains, e.g., "If I enter the tent of My *house*" (Psalm 132:3 referring to My *house*); "they went to their tents joyous" (I Kings 8:66); "the *house* of the Tent (of Meeting) in shifts" (I Chronicles 9:23).[162]

---

[159]At Exod. 36:21 Rashi explains: *"HaMishkan-Mishkan*—twice, it is an allusion to the Temple that was taken as a pledge during two destructions, because of Israel's sins." There he does *not* state that "their destructions are an atonement for the souls." Why does he emphasize this here?

[160]Cf. *Maskil LeDavid*.

[161]*Bava Batra* 60a.

[162]See many more such usages of *ohel* in *A New Concordance* by A. Even Shoshan, Kiryat Sefer, Jerusalem 1988, pp. 20–21 (Hebrew).

4) Above verse 1 Rashi wrote that Bilam said: "God wants and does not want to curse them. I will mention *their sins* (*avonoteihem*) and the curse will take effect upon the mention of their sins. 'He set his face toward the *wilderness*'—as the Targum has it.[163] The expression *avonot* refers to intentional sins, among them sins for which one is liable to premature death (below age sixty *karayt*) and capital punishment, such as the Golden Calf— for which sacrifices do not atone. Therefore Rashi adds: "and their destruction atones for *the souls*," as he explained the verse "these sinners against their souls—who became *willful* transgressors against their own souls, because they rebelled against God."[164] Hence: The destruction of the Temple atones even for very severe sins, such as for which one is liable to premature death and capital punishment.

5) Rashi does *not* mention the "Tent of Meeting" in his explanation of "your tents," because this entire parable implies that it is a prophecy for the Future, e.g., "Who sees the vision of the Almighty" (verse 4); "and his king will be more exalted than Agag" (verse 7); "He shall eat up the nations—his adversaries" (verse 8). Therefore the phrase: "How good are your tents, Jacob; your dwellings, Israel" is also a prophecy for the future. Therefore Rashi writes that it refers to the tent of Shiloh and the Temple.

24:6 *Kinchalim nitayu*—"They stretch out like brooks."

RASHI: Which lengthen and draw out to extend far out. Our Rabbis said: From the blessings of that wicked man we can learn how he had in mind to curse them, when he turned his face toward the Wilderness (cf. verse 1). When God turned the words in his mouth, he uttered blessings corresponding to the curses which he wished to pronounce, as is related in the chapter *Chelek.*[165]

COMMENT: In *Sanhedrin* 105b the Talmud enumerates ten curses with which Bilam wanted to curse Israel: Rabbi Yochanan said: From the blessings of that wicked man you learn what he had in mind: 1) He wanted to say that they should not have synagogues—"How good are your tents, Jacob";

---

[163]Onkelos explains: "He set his face toward the Calf that Israel made in the *Wilderness.*"
[164]Rashi on Numbers 17:3.
[165]*Sanhedrin* 105b. Rashi there states: "From his blessings you learn—for it states: 'God turned for your sake the curse into a blessing'" (Deut. 23:6). He wanted to curse them that they should have no synagogues, but He did not allow it, and Bilam said (instead): "How good are your tents, Jacob."

2) That the *Shechinah* should *not* rest upon them—"and your dwellings (*Mishkenotecha*) Israel"; 3) That their Kingdom should *not* be lasting—"They stretch out like brooks"; 4) They should *not* have olive trees and vineyards—"like gardens beside a river"; 5) That they should *not* exude a good odor[166]—"like aloes planted by the Lord"; 6) That they should *not* have lofty kings—"like cedars beside the water"; 7) They should *not* have a king son of a king—"Water shall flow from his wells"; 8) His kingdom should *not* rule over nations—"His seed shall be by abundant water"; 9) That their kingship should *not* be strong—"Their king shall rise *above* Agag"; 10) That there should be no fear of their kingdom—"Their kingdom shall be exalted."

Rashi's statement: "Which lengthen and draw out to extend far out" is the plain sense and refers to: "Your dwellings—your encampments," which lengthen and draw out to a distance like brooks.[167] In reference to brooks (rivers) one uses the expression "extension," as in: "Behold, I will extend peace to her like a river" (Isaiah 66:12).

Rashi continues: "Our Rabbis said: From the *blessings* of that wicked man," etc., in order to emphasize that this verse does not merely describe the length of Israel's encampment, but also contains "blessings," as the Rabbis state. All this underscores the honor of Israel.

25:5   *Hirgu ish anashav*—"Let each man kill his men ..."

RASHI: Each one of the judges of Israel killed two men (*anashav*—"his men," plural), and the judges of Israel were *eighty-eight* thousand as is related in *Sanhedrin*.[168]

COMMENT: Why didn't the Torah state the number killed by the judges, as it stated the number who died in the plague: "Those who died in the plague were twenty-four thousand" (below verse 9)?

It would seem that the Torah stated the number who died in the

---

[166]Rashi: "exude a good odor"—from commandments.

[167]Israel's camp in the Wilderness extended to twelve mil (approx. nine miles. Cf. *Berachot* 54b; *Sanhedrin* 5b. This is indeed "far out.")

[168]*Sanhedrin* 18a states: "Thus the judges of Israel were *seventy eight* thousand six hundred." The same number is given in Yerushalmi *Sanhedrin* 1:4; 10:2. This entire comment by Rashi is missing in the first printing of Rashi (1474-75) and in the Yemenite manuscript of Rashi—possibly because of the numerical discrepancy.

plague, because it was a relatively small number. We find that during the plague that broke out after David ordered a census of the People to be taken, within a short time of a day, or half a day,[169] 70,000 people died! But here *only* 24,000 people died.[170]

However, the judges killed 157,200! Had the Torah given their number, it would have been disparaging to Israel. Therefore, God was, so to speak—sensitive and considerate of the honor and dignity of the Jewish People. Besides, since we know the number of judges and that each of them killed two people, we thereby also know how many were killed—which is not the case with the plague.

---

[169]Cf. Rashi, Targum Jonathan, and Radak on II Kings 24:15 as to the time lapse.
[170]Especially if we give credence to the popular interpretation of "*vayihyu hameitim bamagefah*," lit. "Those that *were dead* (*hameitim*) were in the plague," i.e., those who were about to die anyway, even without a plague, were included among the 24,000. According to this explanation, the number of *healthy* people who died in the plague was much less than 24,000.

Pinchas

26:5   *Mishpachat hachanochi*—"The Chanochite family."

RASHI: Because the heathen nations spoke slightingly of Israel, saying: "How can they trace their descent by their tribes; do they really believe the Egyptians did not have relations (lit. *shelo shaltu*—"did not have power over") with their mothers? If they had power over their very bodies, surely they did so over their wives!"[171] Therefore, God set His name upon them: the letter *Hey* on one side of the name, and the letter *Yod* on the other side (*hachanochi*) to state: "*I* (God's Name *Yod-Hey*) testify for them that they are the sons of their fathers (and not of Egyptians). This is explained by David: *Shivtei Yod-Hey Eydut le'Yisrael*—"the tribes of *Yod-Hey* (i.e., God's Name) is testimony for Israel" (Psalm 122:4), namely: This Name *(Yod-Hey)* bears testimony regarding their tribes (i.e., that they are justified in tracing their descent to the tribes). Therefore in the case of all of them it is written *Hachanochi, Hapalui* (the letter *Hey* at the beginning and *Yod* at the end to form God's Name *Yod-Hey*). But in the case of *Yimnah* (verse 44) it was not necessary to state "the family of *HaYimni*," because the Divine Name is already attached to it: the *Yod* at the beginning and the *Hey* at the end (*Yimnah*).[172]

COMMENT: Question: If the name *Yod-Hey* testifies for them, why didn't God set His name upon them in the proper order—letter *Yod* preceding letter *Hey* as in the name *Yod-Hey*? Maskil LeDavid answers: The Rabbis stated: "If man and his wife merit it, the *Shechinah* is among them"[173]—the letter *Yod* in the word *ish*—"man," and letter *Hey* in *ishah*—"woman." The Rabbis also said: "In the merit (lit. *bischar*—"as a reward") of the righteous women were

---

[171]Who were the mothers of the present generation; hence they cannot trace their pedigree by their mothers.
[172]*Shir Hashirim Rabbah* 4:12; *Pesikta de Rav Kahana, Beshalach*; Levit. *Rabbah*, Chap. 23; *Yalkut* 772.
[173]*Sotah* 17a.

our fathers redeemed from Egypt.[174] Therefore he preceded the *Hey*, which is the wife's part. This explains also why a *Hey* is written with the name *Yimnah Mishpachat HaYimnah.* One might ask: Why is a *Hey* written, seeing that his name already has the name *Yod-Hey* in it: *Yimnah?* It should have written *Mishpachat Yimnah?* However, in his name the *Yod* comes first, and the Torah is particular to write *Hey*, first also in his case as in all cases to allude to what was stated above.[175]

If one asks: Why didn't He set His name upon the tribes also in other censuses, to dispel the slander of the nations: It is because here this is particularly appropriate—since those who failed (the test) in the episode with the daughters of Moav died in the plague. Therefore Scripture testifies for the Israelites that remained alive that they were "Kosher" (untainted) both in their genealogy and in their deeds—that there was no licentiousness among them.

26:54   *Larav tarbeh nachalato—*
"For the numerous one you shall increase its inheritance."

RASHI: To the tribe that had a large population they gave a large portion. Although the portions were not equal in area, because they assigned the portions according to the size of the tribe in each case—yet they did so only by the lot, but the lot was by the Divine Spirit, as is explained in *Bava Batra* (122a): Elazar the Priest wore the Urim and Tumim and would say by the Divine Spirit: "If such-and-such tribe comes up, such-and-such a territory shall come up with him" (from the lottery). The names of the tribes were written on twelve slips, and those of twelve districts on twelve slips. They mixed them in an urn, and the head of a tribe inserted his hand in it and took out two slips. In his hand came up a slip with the name of his tribe on it, and a slip with the district declared by the Urim and Tumim for that tribe on it. The lot itself cried out: "I the lot have come up for such-and-such a district for such-and-such a tribe," as is stated: "By the *mouth* of the lot (shall the possession thereof be divided"—Verse 56).

The land was not divided by measurement (alone), because one district is superior to another, but it was divided by estimate: An inferior piece of land enough to sow a kor was considered the equivalent of a good piece of land enough to sow a seah (one-thirtieth of a *kor*)—all depended on the value of the soil.[176]

---

[174] *Sotah* 11b; *Shemot Rabbah* 1:16.

[175] I.e., "that because of the merit of the righteous women ... and: If man and his wife merit it, the *Shechinah* is among them ..."

[176] *Bava Batra* 122a; *Tanchuma Pinchas* 6; *Sifrei* 132; *Bamidbar Rabbah* 21:9; *Yalkut* 773, cf. *Ramban.*

COMMENT: Two points need clarification:

1) If the land was divided by the lot, it is quite possible that for a *large* tribe the lot should fall on a *small* portion of land, not always on "a large portion" as Rashi suggests?

2) What is the meaning of: "The lot itself cried out, saying etc."—is it possible that the lot *spoke?*

1) We must explain that *before* they cast the lot, they divided the land by the size of the tribes. The lot only *confirmed* the division, which was also done by Divine Spirit. This is the meaning of the statement: "Elazar the Priest wore the Urim and Tumim and *would say by the Divine Spirit:* If such-and-such tribe comes up—such-and-such territory shall come up.[177]

2) That the lot "cried out, saying" is no surprise, since there were miraculous events with the lot. We find, similarly at the giving of the Torah that the boundary spoke, as Rashi explained: *leymor* ("saying") means: the border said to them: Be careful not to ascend from here on.[178] Rashi writes likewise in verse 56: "By the *mouth* of the lot"—the lot spoke, as I explained above, etc."[179]

28:3 *Shnaim layom*—"Two a day."

RASHI: According to its plain sense: two lambs for each day. But *mainly* it comes to teach that they should be slaughtered (at a spot), opposite the day (i.e., sun)—the regular morning offering (i.e., *tamid shel shachar*) at the west, and that of the evening at the east of the rings.[180]

COMMENT: Because these words: "two a day" are really superfluous—since verse 4 already states "the one lamb ... and the second lamb, etc.," we know

---

[177]Cf. *Tanchuma* 6: "*Before the lot would come up,* Elazar would say by Divine Spirit: The lot for such-and-such tribe came up, that he should take in such-and-such place. Joshua would stretch out his hand and it came up." In the Editio Princeps (1474–75) the reading is: "They did *not* do (the division) by the lot, but the lot was by Divine Spirit." This version proves our interpretation above.

[178]Rashi on Exod. 19:12. Comp. the opposing views regarding the speech of the boundary in *Divrei David*—did not speak; and *Zedah Laderech*—did speak; miraculously.

[179]Also *Tanchuma* states: How do we know that the lot spoke? As it states: "By the *mouth* of the lot."

[180]That were fixed in the ground, in which the animal's feet were inserted. Cf. *Sifrei* 142; *Tamid* 31b; *Yoma* 62b; *Yalkut* 777.

that there were two—therefore the Rabbis say that the Torah wrote these words that we should derive from them "that they should be slaughtered opposite *the day* (sun)."[181]

Rashi calls this the *main* meaning, because it expresses the *halacha* (law regarding these lambs, where they should be slaughtered) and "From the day the Temple was destroyed, the Almighty has nothing in His world but the four cubits of *halacha* alone"[182]—and as the Rabbis said: "Speedily the Temple will be built"[183] and we will have to know the practical law (where to slaughter the two daily lambs).

As for the reason why the Torah required the daily sacrifices to be slaughtered *opposite* the sun, commentators of Rashi wrote that it is because the daily sacrifice (*tamid*) comes to nullify the worship of the sun twice daily—at sunrise and at sunset: In the morning sun-worshippers would turn to the east; at night they would turn to the west. Therefore the Almighty required that two offerings be sacrificed to Him daily; and that the morning sacrifice be slaughtered in the *northwestern* corner (of the altar), and the evening one in the *northeastern* corner—the *opposite* of the sun-worship.[184]

28:15   *U-se'ir 'izim vego'*—"And a male goat, etc."

RASHI: All the *Musaf* goats[185] came to atone for causing uncleanness to the Temple or its holy things (sacrifices)—as explained in Tractate *Shevuot* (9a). The goat of the New Moon differs from other goats (brought as additional sacrifices) in that the word *laHashem*—"for God" is stated in regard to it (i.e., it is a sin-offering for the Lord—so to speak). The Talmudic explanation of this is: It comes to teach you that this goat only atones (for uncleanness) where there is no knowledge (of having caused uncleanness) either before or after (it has been done),[186] so that no one knows of the

---

[181]Rashi *Yoma* 62b s.v. *keneged ha-yom:* "opposite the shining of the sun. The word— *yom* in the sense "sun" (not "day") we find in Malachi 3:*19 v'lihat otam hayom haba—* "and that coming day (i.e., sun) will burn them ... " Cf. the homiletical exegesis of this verse in *Nedarim* 8b; *Sanhedrin* 10b; *Avodah Zarah* 4a.

[182]*Berachot* 8a.

[183]*Sukkah* 41a; *Sanhedrin* 22b; *Bechorot* 53b.

[184]Cf. *Torah Temimah. Be'er Mayim Chaim* adds: "For this reason the *Shechinah* was mainly in the west, where the sun is *weak* and sets—not in the east where it rises" (and is strong).

[185]Musaf—the *additional* offerings brought on the Sabbath, Rosh Chodesh [the New Moon = month,] and all holidays, besides the two daily sacrifices.

[186]Cf. Rashi on Levit. 16:16.

sin except the Holy One, blessed be He, alone.[187] The other goats learn
from this one.[188]

But its explanation in the *Agada* is as follows: The Holy One, blessed
be He, said: "Bring an atonement for Me (on the New Moon), because I
diminished the size of the Moon."[189]

COMMENT: Why does Rashi cite two explanations—what is difficult in each
one of them?

The difficulty in the first explanation is that we must take *lchatat* to
mean *lchet*—"for a sin," not as the sacrifice whose name is *chatat*, i.e., "a
sin-offering." This is a rather unusual usage of the word. By this interpretation, it should have stated: *lchatat lachet laHashem*," namely: "this goat is
a sin-offering for a sin which is only (known) to God." Therefore Rashi cites
a second explanation, which is the Midrash of Resh Lakish in *Chullin* 60b,
according to which *laHashem* means "*for* God."[190]

The difficulty in the second explanation is why should God require
"atonement"? What sin did He commit? In the marginal column known
as *masoret hashas*—lit. "the tradition of the Talmud," it is remarked at *Shevuot*
9a: "This is one of the secrets of the Kabbalah, which ought not to be taken
literally, God forbid, for: "Every honorable princess dwelling *within* (Psalm
45:14).[191] Hence both interpretations are necessary.[192]

---

[187]Hence it is called *chatat laHashem*—a "sin-offering" for a sin known only to God.
[188]I.e., the other goats also atone for the same kind of sin; we derive that law from
this goat.
[189]Cf. the legend in Rashi Gen. 1:16; *Shevuot* 9a and *Alfasi* thereto; *Chullin* 60b; *Pirke
de Rabbi Elizer*, Chap. 46; *Yalkut* 782.
[190]Comp. Gen. 41:36 *v'hayah haochel l-pekadon*—"The food will be for a reserve";
Hashem yilachem lachem—"The Lord will do battle *for* you" (Exod. 14:14). In both
these cases the letter *lamed* means "for the sake of."
[191]Namely, it is the honor of God not to reveal this secret in public. *Maskil LeDavid*
states in this regard: "Verily this statement (of the Rabbis) is *one of the secrets of the
Torah*, and it is explained in the writings of the Kabbalists." (Cf. *Zohar* I, 252; II,
271; III, 247.)
[192]Maimonides in *Guide for the Perplexed,* Part 3:46 writes the reason why by the goat
of the New Moon it says "*laHashem*—for the Lord" is because the Egyptians used
to sacrifice to the Moon on the New Moon (Rosh Chodesh) day. The Torah feared
lest people say that also the sacrifice that Israel brings on the New Moon is to the
Moon. Therefore the Torah calls it *laHashem*—for God. Although the Rabbis gave
a different reason (which Rashi cites), Maimonides did not hesitate to give a
different reason—based on logic, for Maimonides already stated in *Commentary on
the Mishna, Nazir,* Chap. 5:6 that in places where there is no practical difference as
to the law, it is permissible to interpret as one is inclined to do logically—as long
as it does *not* contradict a law in the Gemara. Cf. *Torah Temimah.*

However, the Rif (Alfasi) in the beginning of *Shevuot* explains: "An atonement *for Me*" (*Kaparah 'alai*) like *lifanai*—"before Me," quote: "Since God told her (the Moon): 'to rule during the day and at night' and she was *not* appeased, He then told her: 'I will do you an honor that will appease you for having diminished you. What is this? That Israel should each month offer a sacrifice to atone for their sins. Therefore God said: 'Bring a sacrifice *before* Me on the New Moon to atone for you, so that you may compensate for Me with this sacrifice, the honor I decided (lit. said) to do to the Moon for having diminished her. 'This is the meaning of: 'Bring a sacrifice to Me for having diminished the Moon.' "

The *Sefer Hazikaron* writes regarding the above: "The best explanation of this *Agadah* is that given by Rabbi Alfasi (Rif) in the first chapter of *Shevuot* (9a)."

28:19   *Parim, ailim, kevasim*—"Oxen, rams, sheep."

RASHI: "Oxen" alludes to Abraham, as is stated: "And to the bullocks ran Abraham" (Gen. 18:7). "Rams" alludes to the ram of Isaac (Gen. 22:13). "Sheep" alludes to Jacob, as stated: "Jacob separated the sheep" (Gen. 30:40). I saw this explanation in the work of Rabbi Moses the Preacher.[193]

COMMENT: One may ask:

1) What is the meaning of "alludes to/corresponding to" Abraham, Isaac, and Jacob—what is the significance of these allusions?

2) Why did Rashi not make the same comment with regard to the Musaf sacrifices of the New Moon, where there were also two oxen, one ram, and seven sheep (verse 11)?

One might say that "corresponding to" *keneged* is in the sense of "merit," i.e., in the merit of Abraham, Isaac, and Jacob we offer these Musaf sacrifices on Passover, which allude to the redemption (from Egypt) that came in the merit of the forefathers.

The reason Rashi did not make the same comment with regard to the Musaf sacrifices of the New Moon is because only Passover is connected with the forefathers, thus: Abraham had the vision of "the covenant between the pieces *brit bein habtarim* on Passover, the angels came to Abraham on Passover; Isaac was born on Passover; Jacob went down to Egypt on

---

[193]Comp. Rashi above 7:21; cf. *Midrash Tadshei*, Chap. 10: "One ram corresponding to Isaac who was redeemed by a ram; one sheep corresponding to Jacob, as it is said: 'A scattered sheep is Israel'" (Jeremiah 50:17).

Passover. However, there is no such connection between the New Moon and
Passover.

Similarly in *Emor* on the verse: "You shall bring a fire-offering to God"
(Levit. 23:8), which deals with the Musaf sacrifices of Passover, Rashi explains: "In any event, if there are no oxen, bring rams; if there are neither
oxen, nor rams—bring sheep." Why just on Passover did the Torah stress
that one should bring rams and sheep *in any event?* The reason is that since
three kinds of animals came as an allusion to Abraham, Isaac, and Jacob,
I might have said: If one of them is missing, the set is broken and the
symbolism in them is void, since there were *three* forefathers not two—and
he should not bring *any.* Therefore Rashi explains: "in any event." But in
the case of other Festivals, that are not necessarily connected to the forefathers, obviously he should bring whatever there is.[194]

29:18   *U-minchatam v'niskeyhem laparim*—
"And their meal-offerings and their libations for the bulls."

RASHI: The Bullocks brought on Sukkot are seventy (in all) corresponding
to the seventy nations of the world, and they gradually decrease in number
each day, this is an omen of annihilation to them. But at the time of the
Temple (when these Bullocks were offered) they protected them (the
nations) from suffering. *V'lakvasim*—"and for the sheep"—corresponds to
Israel who are called: "A scattered lamb" (Jeremiah 50:17). The lambs are
of a fixed number (fourteen each day).[195] Their total is ninety-eight, to
avert from Israel the ninety-eight curses stated in Deuteronomy (28:15 ff.).

On the second day of Sukkot it says *v'niskeyhem* (verse 19) in reference
to the two daily offerings.[196] The Torah changed the term to *v'niskayhem*
(in plural) to deduce from it some teaching, as our Rabbis said: "On the
second day it is said *v'niskayhem* (an extra final *mem*); on the sixth day
u'nsachaheyha (an extra letter *y*); on the seventh day *kmishpatam* (an extra
final *mem*). The additional letters are: *mem* and *yod* and *mem*, which together
spell: *mayim*—"water"—an allusion to the libation of water on Tabernacles
from the Torah.[197]

---

[194]Cf. *Yayin Yashan*, p. 111; *Maskil LeDavid,* who explains at great length the symbols
of the Musaf sacrifices of the Festivals.

[195]A symbol that the Israelites are also fixed, indestructible.

[196]Whilst the usual term is *v'niskah*—"its libation," corresponding to—*u-minchatah*
preceding it—both in singular.

[197]Cf. *Taanit* 2b; *Sukkot* 55b; *Shabbat* 103b; *Tanchuma* 16; *Sifrei* 147; Midrash *Tadshei*
Chap. 1; *Bamidbar Rabbah* 21:24; Midrash *Agada; Yalkut* 781.

COMMENT: Question: On the one hand Rashi states: "The seventy nations, who gradually decrease in number, it is a sign of *annihilation* to them." On the other hand he says: "During the time of the Temple they *protected* them from suffering." These two statements appear to be incongruent with each other—either "annihilation" or "protection"?

Answer: Rashi is precise in stating: "It is a *sign* of annihilation to them"—it is only a *sign* that the bullocks were sacrificed "as an allusion to the seventy nations *that gradually decrease,*" namely: *in the end* they will be annihilated. However, "during the time of the Temple"—in the distant past, *before* they began decreasing, the bullocks protected them from suffering.

In his work *Imrei Shefer*, R. Shlomo Kluger writes: "It seems that Rashi's intention is: Our Rabbis said: "Whoever studies the section (in the Torah) about the burnt-offering (*Olah*), it is as if he actually sacrificed an *Olah*.[198] Therefore, in our time when we mention the sacrifices in prayers, it is as if we sacrifice real bullocks. Hence the intention does not apply equally, thus: Nowadays that we are in exile in *their* hands, and they (nations) live in tranquility, this serves as a sign *for us* that the decrease (in the bullocks) is a sign of annihilation to them (nations)—indicating that although they are tranquil, nevertheless they *will* decrease—and this serves as a good sign for us. However at the time of the Temple, when *we* were above them, we didn't need this sign. Then it was the opposite (the bullocks came) to pray for them, to protect them from suffering—so that the world should not be destroyed because of them. Understand this because I wrote briefly, etc."[199]

---

[198]Cf. *Menachot* 110a with a slight change: "Whoever studies the laws of the sin-offering *chatat*, it is as he sacrificed a *chatat*, etc."

[199]*Imrei Shefer*, Lemberg 1895, p. 100. Cf. Rashi *Sukkah* 55b s.v. *Shiv'im parim:* "Corresponding to the seventy nations *to atone for them* so that it may rain in the *entire world*, since on Sukkot we are judged regarding water." Accordingly the "suffering" refers to the withholding of rain from the nations, which Festival bullocks averted. Cf. *Gur Aryeh* and *Torah Temimah*, who expounded at length on the reason for the libation of water on Sukkot and why this is alluded to especially on the second, sixth, and seventh days. Cf. *Be'er Maim Chaim:* "Corresponding to nations—therefore Scripture punishes them for not observing the holiday Sukkot more so than any other holiday, as we find in Zechariah (Chap. 14), because the bullocks of Sukkot used to atone also for them, as I have explained. Therefore they are worthy of punishment for not observing Sukkot."

Matot

31:8   *Bacherev*—"By the sword."

RASHI: He came against Israel exchanging his métier (forte) (the sword) for their métier (the mouth), for they conquer only through their mouth—through prayer and petition, and he came and took hold of their craft to curse them with his mouth. Therefore, they too came upon him, exchanging their craft for the craft of the nations who come with the sword, as is said: "And by your sword shall you live" (Gen. 27:40).[200]

COMMENT: Those who generally cite Rashi's sources[201] did not cite any source for this comment. However it would seem that his comment here relies on his explanation above 22:23—and his comment there is based on *Tanchuma Balak* 8. Therefore there is no need to look for a source of his comment here.

Ostensibly one might question Rashi's statement: "He came against Israel, *exchanging his craft (forte) for their craft, etc.*": Surely Bilam was a prophet.[202] As such his métier is also his mouth, as that of any prophet, and he did *not* exchange his craft for theirs?

However, this is no question, for the task of a prophet is not to curse a nation, but rather to make the People repent and better their ways.[203] Came along Bilam and used his mouth to *win* in battle—which is the craft of Israel, whereas "the nations come with the sword." In this manner he exchanged his craft, which is the sword in battle, for their craft, which is the mouth.

---

[200]Cf. Rashi Numbers 22:23 s.v. *v'charbo shlufah beyado*.

[201]Such as: A. Berliner in his Hebrew edition of Rashi: *Rashi al ha-Torah*; C. D. Chavel in his edition: *Perushei Rashi al ha-Torah*; and R. Judah Krinski in his glosses: "Mekorei Rashi" in the *Chumash Mechokkei Yehudah*.

[202]See Rashi above 22:5 implying that he was a prophet, not only a diviner.

[203]As Rashi states, ibid.: "If you should ask: Why did God make his *Shechinah* (Divine Presence) reside upon a wicked gentile? (Bilam). So that the nations should have no argument, saying: *'If we had prophets, we would have bettered our ways, etc.'"*

The word *Bacherev*—"by the sword" is apparently superfluous, since verse 7 already stated: "They killed all males," and the beginning of verse 8 states: "And the kings of Midian they killed along with their slain ones, etc." The majority of those killed in battle, are killed by the sword. If so, why does the Torah emphasize especially with regard to Bilam that he was killed by the sword? Besides, why do we need to know by what kind of weapon he was killed? Therefore Rashi explains that the word *Bacherev*—"by the sword" comes to allude to the fact that he exchanged his craft for their craft, etc.

32:16   *Nivneh l'mikneynu po*—"We shall build for our cattle here."

RASHI: They had greater pity on their property than on their sons and daughters since they mentioned their cattle before their children. Moses told them: Don't do so! Rather, make the main thing as the main, and the secondary, as secondary, namely: First build yourself cities for your small children, and afterwards folds for your flocks (cf. verse 24).[204]

COMMENT: Maybe they put their cattle before their children on the principle "The last but not the least"[205] and not because they had more regard for their property than for their children. This is likely, as in verse 17 they do not mention the cattle at all, only: "Let our small children stay in the fortified cities, etc."?

If they would have put the cattle first on account of "The last but not the least" principle, why did Moses change the order and told them: "Build yourself cities for your small children and folds for your flocks"? This shows that Moses felt that they regarded their property more than their children and rebuked them for such an approach, and therefore he changed the order.

In *Tanchuma* 7, which is the source for Rashi's comment, the rebuke to the tribes of Gad and Reuven is much sharper:

"Abundant livestock" (32:1)—this is what the verse says: 'The heart of the wise is to his right, but the heart of the fool is to his left' (*Kohelet* 10:2). The heart of the wise—refers to Moses; the heart of the fool—refers to the sons of Reuven and the sons of Gad; who made the main thing—secondary, and the secondary thing—the main. Why so? Because they *loved* their property *more than themselves* in that they said to Moses: "Folds for the flocks

---

[204] *Tanchuma* 7; *Bamidbar Rabbah* 22:9; Midrash *Agadah*.
[205] The Hebrew corresponding idiom *acharon acharon chaviv*—"the most last is the most beloved" is even more telling.

shall we build for our cattle here," *first* here, and *then* "cities for our children." Moses told them: don't do so; first do the main thing: "Build cities for your small children and *afterwards* folds for your flocks." Hence, the heart of the wise is to his right—that is Moses, and the heart of the fool is to his left—that is the sons of Reuven and the sons of Gad, etc."

It should be pointed out that just as the sons of Reuven and Gad had pity on their property, so is Rashi considerate of the honor of the tribes in two ways: 1) He didn't attribute to them the verse "and the heart of the fool is to his left," 2) He does not say about them that they *loved* their property more than *themselves* (i.e., their bodies), only that they *had pity* on their property, etc. But surely even "Righteous men, their money (i.e., property) is *more beloved* to them than their bodies."[206] By changing the statement of the Midrash Rashi defended their honor somewhat. However, they nevertheless acted improperly and therefore Moses rebuked them.

---

[206] *Chullin* 81a; Exod. *Rabbah* 1:25—said about Jacob!

Mas'ei

31:8 *Machlah, Tirtzah vego*—"Machlah, Tirtzah, etc."

RASHI: Here the Torah enumerates them according to their superiority one over the other in years, and they married in the order in which they were born. But everywhere else in the Bible they are enumerated according to their wisdom: This tells us that they were equal to each other.[207]

COMMENT: The very fact that sometimes this daughter is mentioned first and at other times another one comes first, comes to tell us that they were equal. For if they were not equal, the Torah should have counted them *always* either by the degree of their wisdom, as in *Pinchas*, or by the order of their birth as here. But if they were enumerated in *every* place according to their wisdom or by the order of birth, we would not have known that they were equal.[208]

QUESTION: Since Rashi states: "But everywhere else in the Bible they were enumerated according to their wisdom," this makes it clear that they were

---

[207]Cf. *Bava Batra* 120a: "The school of Rabbi Ishmael taught: the daughters of Tzelofchad were equal, as is stated *vatihyenah*—"they became"—one becoming to all. Rashbam there: "They were equal—therefore sometimes one is mentioned before the other, and sometimes vice-versa, as we interpret (*Megilla* 13): "He is Aaron and Moses—he is Moses and Aaron"—this teaches that they were equal. The word *vatihyenah*—"they became" is superfluous, for it could have written: *"Benot Tzelofchad livney dodeyhen ...*—The daughters of Tzelofchad (became) their cousins' wives." See Rashi on 27:1; Midrash *Agadah.*
[208]Cf. *Gur Aryeh.* Even though our verse relates their marriages, and it is the proper way that the older should marry before the younger daughter, as stated: "It is not the practice in our place to marry off the younger before the older" (Gen. 29:26) -nevertheless if the verse here had enumerated them according to their wisdom, as always, we would have said: This enumeration is only by the degree of their wisdom, but one must suppose that they married in the order of their birth—and then we would not know that they were equal.

not equal in the degree of wisdom. How then does Rashi say: "This tells us that they *were* equal to each other"?

True, they were not *exactly* equal in wisdom, but in their *own* eyes they were equal, for each one respected the other for *her* particular qualities, e.g., the older one respected the one who was wiser than her, although she was younger, and vice versa. They may have respected each other for other desirable qualities too, e.g., humility, piety, modesty, etc.

One may ask:

1) What difference does it make *to us* to know in what order the Torah enumerates them, and in what order they married?

2) Moreover, why should *we* care if they were equal, or not—surely: "What was—was."[209] The Torah is not merely a history book but rather a Torah for life"[210]—"Torah" meaning "instruction"?

We ought to explain this as per above: the Torah tells us that they married in their chronological order, and that they were equal—although they were not *quite* equal in wisdom, but respected each other *as if* they were equal. By this description the Torah comes to teach us a way in life— how brothers and sisters should behave toward each other: out of love and mutual respect, not out of jealousy and hatred. Therefore they married in order of their birth, although the wiser ones among them undoubtedly had earlier and more chances of marrying than their less wise, but older, sisters! Nevertheless, they showed respect for each other and married according to their age. Such a lesson is indeed "Torah and I need to learn it."[211]

---

[209]Cf. *Pesachim* 108a; *Yoma* 5b.

[210]As we say in the blessing *sim shalom* of the "Eighteen" blessings: "*Torat Chaim*— A Life-Torah." Comp. Proverbs 13:14.

[211]Cf. *Berachot* 62a; *Megillah* 28a.

Deuteronomy

Devarim

1:5   *Bey'ayr et Ha-Torah*—"To explain this Torah."

RASHI: In the seventy languages (of the ancient world) he explained to them the Torah.[1]

COMMENT: One may ask:

1) From what does Rashi derive that Moses explained the Torah in seventy languages?

2) Surely the Jewish People spoke Hebrew then, not seventy languages?

1) A number of supercommentaries on Rashi write that the "seventy languages" are arrived at by "verbal analogy" (*gzeyrah shavah*) thus: Here the word *beyayr*—"to explain" is used, and regarding the writing of the Torah on stones it says: *baayar heyteyv*—"well-explained" (below 27:8). Just as there it means in seventy languages,[2] also here it means in seventy languages.[3] That the Torah was written on stones in seventy languages is derived through numerical values (gematria) of the word *heyteyv*—"well" as follows: *hey* = 5; , *hey, yod* = 15; *hey yod tet* = 24; *hey yod tet vet* = 26—All together = 70.

One is obliged to say that the Rabbis had a tradition that Moses explained the Torah in seventy languages, since in *this* verse there is no allusion to this fact at all—even the word *heyteyv* is not stated *here*, and in the word *beyayr* alone there is no allusion to seventy languages—even by resorting to the use of "gematria."

---

[1] *Tanchuma, Devarim* 2; Gen. *Rabbah* 49:2; Midrash *Agadah.* Cf. *Sotah* 32a and Rashi on 27:8.

[2] See Rashi there and Mishnah *Sota* 32a.

[3] Cf. *Be'er Mayim Chaim' Devek Tov, Maskil LeDavid, Amar Neke, Siftei Chachamim.*

2) Moses explained the Torah in seventy languages by way of prophecy (or at least premonition) regarding the future: When Israel will go into exile among the nations and might, God forbid, forget Hebrew, they should know the meaning of the Torah in all the (then known) seventy languages. They should not have to rely on the translations of the Torah made by *other* nations into their languages—because such translations may be suspect of heretical tendencies.[4]

> 1:28   *a'rim gedolot u-vtzurot bashamayim*—
> "Great cities, fortified to the heavens."

RASHI: Verses (sometimes) are stated in unrealistic terms (*lashon ha-vay*).[5]

COMMENT: According to Rashi's explanation in *Chullin* 90b that *lashon ha-vay* means: "language of *ordinary* people" (*hediot*), it is especially appropriate to our verse, since it is used to describe the spies and the "complainers" (see verse 27), who at that time were "ordinary" people—not on the exalted level they were when Moses chose them as spies.[6] Since *lashon ha-vay* is not an outright lie, but one "who is not very particular in his speech, etc.," and sometimes exaggerates, the Torah does not refrain from using such expressions of exaggeration. This is akin to the statement: "the Torah speaks in the language of people."[7] The difference between the two expressions is apparently that: While "the Torah speaks in the language of people" usually refers to double expressions—in the same root—such as: *hocheyach tochiach* (*et a'mitecha*)—"You should surely reprove (your neighbor)" (Levit. 19:17);

---

[4]As indeed happened, with various non-Jewish translations during our exile. Perhaps for that reason they inscribed the Torah on the stones in seventy languages, in order that they should know the *correct* meaning in every language they happen to speak.
[5]*Chullin* 90b where Rashi explains: "*lashon ha-vay* means language of an ordinary person (*lashon hediot*) who is not very particular in his speech and (sometimes) utters something which is not so; not that he *intends* to lie, only he is not particular;" Cf. also *Sifrei* 25; *Yalkut* 805; and comp. *Tamid* 29a: "Do you really mean (fortified) to the *heavens*? But it is an exaggeration." The reading of Editio Princeps (1474–75), and the Alkabats and Zamora Printings is: *Diber Ha-catuv*—the *verse*—spoke, etc." This reading is preferable to our printed editions *dibru ha-ctuvim*—"the verses (pl.) stated, etc.," since Rashi is explaining *this* verse, not all such verses in the Torah, saying that *this* verse spoke in exaggerated terms. Cf. *Yosef Hallel*, Part II, pp. 211–12.
[6]See Rashi Numbers 13:3.
[7]*Berachot* 31b—numerous references listed there.

zachor tizcor—"Be sure to remember" (Deut. 7:18); *shamor tishmerun*—"Make sure to keep" (Deut. 6:17) and many others like them—*lashon ha-vay* refers specifically to exaggerations.[8]

1:44   *Kaasher ta'senah ha-dvorim*—"As the bees do."

RASHI: Just as the bee when it stings a person it dies immediately, it was the same with the Amorites, when they touched you, they died immediately.[9]

COMMENT: Question: If, as Rashi says: "when they touched you, they died immediately," then this is a *consolation* to Israel, whereas this entire section deals with Moses' *admonishment* to Israel?

The commentary *Devek Tov* writes: "This too is part of the rebuke, for you said: 'Because God hates us (He took us out of Egypt).'[10] Regarding this he said: Even at the time of anger, He gave you revenge from your enemies."

Ostensibly, this does not answer the question, for this too is a consolation. However, we may understand it with the words of the verse: "If your enemy is hungry, feed him bread; if he is thirsty, give him water to drink, for you will be scooping coals onto his head" (Proverbs 25:21–22), namely: If you deal with your enemy beyond the call of duty, and repay his evil to you with kindness—you will cause him great embarrassment that will burn within him, and it will be tantamount to having scooped coals upon his head. The same applies in our situation, namely: Although you sinned toward God, nevertheless He dealt kindly with you to such an extent that no sooner did the Amorites touch you than they died. If so, you should be thoroughly ashamed of your wicked deeds. Surely this is a rebuke!

2:5   *Ad midrach caf ragel*—"So much as a foot can tread on."

RASHI: Even a *midrach caf ragel*, i.e., "even a foot-tread" (even a single step); I do not allow you to pass into their land without permission. But the Midrash *Agadah* explains: (I will not give you of their land) until there will come the day of the treading of the sole of the foot on Mount Olive (i.e., the Messianic period), as it says: "And his feet shall stand (on that day upon

---

[8]All the examples of *lashon ha-vay* cited in *Chullin* 90b from the Torah, from Prophets and from Rabbinic statements are enormous exaggerations.
[9]*Bamidbar Rabbah* 17; Midrash *Agadah*.
[10]Verse 27; Rashi remarks there: "But He loved you, but *you* hate Him, etc."

the Mount of Olives, etc.") (Zechariah 14:4).

COMMENT: According to "plain sense" this phrase is all-inclusive,[11] i.e., I will not allow you to pass through their land *at all;* even a single footstep will I not allow you in their land without permission.[12]

Why does Rashi resort to the Midrash *Agadah* at all; the verse seems clear according to plain sense?

The reason is that one could mistake the meaning of *ad*—"until" as *not inclusive* (*ad velo ad bichlal* in Hebrew) i.e., I will not give you a *real* part of their land, but a "foot-step"—to pass through their land—you are allowed even against their will. Therefore Rashi explains that one *could* explain the phrase in this way, but not for now, only during the Messianic era. According to the Midrash: *Ad midrach caf ragel* is not inclusive—*ad velo ad bichlal.*

May we suggest that the Torah deliberately uses the ambiguous "*ad,*" not writing *gam midrach caf ragel* "also not a foot-step" to imply the double meaning: according to plain sense and the Midrash.

Rashi cites the Midrash *Agadah* because it is a consolation for Israel in *all* generations,[13] namely: True during the time of the Exile (at present) the sons of Esau-Edom rule over you. But there *will* come a day when you will have your revenge of them, i.e., the day of the treading of the foot on the Mount of Olives, regarding which it is said: "Behold, a day is coming for the Lord, when your spoils will be divided up in your midst... The Lord will go out and wage war with those nations, as He waged war on the day of battle" (Zechariah 14:1–3).

2:31   *Hachiloti tet lefanecha*—"I have begun to deliver before you."

RASHI: God bound the guardian angel of the Amorites, who was above, under Moses' feet and made him (Moses) tread on his neck.[14]

COMMENT: The word *hachiloti*—"I began" is problematic, since God began and also *completed* delivering Sichon into Israel's hand, for they destroyed him completely and inherited his land? Therefore the Rabbis, and Rashi,

---

[11]Known in Hebrew as—*Ad ve-ad bichlal.*

[12]Rashi adds "without permission" to obviate the question: Why did Moses request the king of Edom to allow them to pass his land, since God commanded that they should *not* pass through it? Therefore Rashi states "without permission," but *with* permission they were allowed to pass through.

[13]And especially Rashi's own generation that suffered so much from the sons of Esau-Edom during the notorious crusades.

[14]*Tanchuma Buber,* addition to *Devarim.*

applied the expression: "I have begun" to the downfall of the guardian angel of Sichon, which marks the beginning of the downfall of Sichon and his people. Thus we find that when God punishes a nation, He first casts down its guardian angel, who protects that nation. The Rabbis interpreted in this vein the verse: "The Lord will punish the hosts of heaven in heaven (*first*), and the kings of the earth on earth (*afterwards*)" (Isaiah 24:21).[15] We find similarly in Daniel that Michael, who is the guardian angel of Israel is fighting the guardian angel of the Persian Kingdom (Daniel 10:13, 20–21).

Obviously the anthropomorphic expressions: "He *bound* the guardian-angel of the Amorites... and made him tread on *his neck*" do not apply literally to a guardian *angel* who is incorporeal. They are only intended to emphasize that God subjugated the guardian angel of the Amorites and his nation before the Israelites.

---

[15]Cf. Rashi on Isaiah 13:13; *Makkot* 12a; Exod. *Rabbah* 9:10; *Mechilta* Exod. 15:1.

Vaetchanan

4:2 *Lo tosifu*—"You shall not add."

RASHI: For instance, to put five chapters in the *Tephillin* (instead of four), to combine five species (of fruit and plants to fulfill the commandment) of Lulav; to put five *tzitzit* (fringes) on one's garment (instead of four). The same applies to *velo tigr'u mimenu*—"You shall not diminish from it" (not to put three chapters in *Tephillin*; three species in Lulav; three fringes on the garment).[16]

COMMENT: Rashi was obliged to interpret: "For instance, to put five chapters in *Tephillin*, etc." because according to plain sense one might err and explain that one is not allowed to add *anything* to the 613 *mitzvot* that are written in the Torah. This would include all the enactments, decrees, and preventive measures instituted by the Rabbis—also the seven Rabbinic commands, God forbid. Obviously this is wrong. Therefore Rashi explains that one is not called a *mosif* or *gorea'* unless one adds or diminishes from the integral part of the mitzvah, such as *five* chapters in the *Tephillin*, etc.

4:6 *U-shmartem, va'asitem*—"You shall keep, and do."

RASHI: "You shall keep"—this refers to study (mishna) of the laws; "and do"—means literally (i.e., "do" the commands).[17]

COMMENT: The difficulty in the plain sense of "you shall keep" is that the verse does not specify the *object* of keeping—what is to be kept? It should have said at least "keep and do *them*" (the commandments mentioned earlier). But according to the Midrash the meaning is: "You shall keep = study," and then "and do—you will know what to do." This way the con-

---

[16] *Sifrei, Re'ei* 82 and Rashi below 13:1.
[17] Comp. Rashi below 12:28 and *Sifrei, Re'ei* 79.

tinuation of the verse connects well, thus: "For it—namely the Mishna[18] is your wisdom and understanding, etc."

Also below on: "Safeguard and hearken to all these words, etc." (12:28), Rashi comments: "This refers to Mishna, which you must keep in your belly, that it should not be forgotten, as it says: 'For it is pleasant if you guard them in your belly.'[19] Now, if you studied, it is possible that you will hear and observe. However, he who does not study, cannot do." Accordingly, *U-shmartem*—"You shall keep" is a negative command[20] not to forget learning.[21]

4:25 *venoshantem*—
"And you will have been long-established (in the land)."

RASHI: With the word *venoshantem* he intimated to them by allusion that they would be exiled from the land at the end of 852 years, which is the numerical value of *venoshantem*, but He sent them into exile earlier, after 850 years. He exiled them two years earlier than the numerical value of *venoshantem*, so that the prophecy: "You shall be utterly destroyed" (verse 26) should not be fulfilled. This is the meaning of: "The Lord *hastened* to bring the evil upon us, for the Lord our God is a *Tzadik*" (Daniel 9:14), namely: He acted charitably (*Tzdakah* from *Tzadik*) with us in that He brought the evil two years before its time.[22]

COMMENT: The words *venoshantem ba-aretz*—"you will have been long-established in the land" present a number of difficulties:

1) They are completely superfluous for if they will beget children and grandchildren, obviously they will be established in the land for a long time.

2) Because they will be long-established, they will "become corrupt"—what is the connection between the two?

---

[18]The word Mishna refers to the Oral Law in general and does not exclude Gemara, etc. The Oral Law both before and after it was committed to writing is called Mishna; comp. *Sefer Hazikaron.*

[19]Proverbs 22:18, whereas verse 17 there states: "Incline your ear and hear the words of *the wise,*" namely the Oral Law.

[20]Wherever it says any of these words: *hishameyr*—"take heed"; *pen*—"lest"; *al*—"do not"—they mean a negative command—*Eruvin* 96a; *Shevuot* 7a—many references.

[21]See *Yayin Yashan,* p. 118 at length.

[22]*Sanhedrin* 38a; *Gittin* 88a.

3) The expression "*venoshantem*" is very uncommon in Scripture; it should have rather said "*veta'arichun yamim*"—"you will live long" (on the land), etc.

Therefore Rashi explains that with the word *venoshantem* the Torah wishes to allude to the number of years they will stay in the land before they are exiled. This allusion is an expression of God's kindness, that they should know in advance the decree (of exile), perchance they will repent of their evil ways and avoid the decree altogether.

The calculation of 850 years is as follows: At the end of 480 years after the Exodus from Egypt, Solomon built the Temple, as is written: "In the four hundred and eightieth year after the Children of Israel's exodus from the land of Egypt... he built the Temple for the Lord" (I Kings 6:1). The first Temple stood for 410 years. Hence, they were exiled at the end of 890 years after the Exodus. Deduct from them forty years they stayed in the Desert. Hence they remained in the Land only 850 years—two years less than the numerical value of *venoshantem*.[23]

4:28   *Va-a'vadtem sham e-lohim*—"There you will serve gods."

RASHI: This is to be understood as Onkelos translates[24]—since you will serve those who worship idols, it is as if you worship them (idols).

COMMENT: Rashi was bothered with the question: If God will scatter them among the nations, does that mean that they *must* worship idols? Besides, there *is* free will—maybe they won't worship idols? Also, this verse, which is a continuation of verse 27 speaks of the punishment, not of the sin?

Therefore Rashi explains that *e-lohim*—"gods" here means the *worshippers* of idols.[25] Still this is not the "plain sense" of the verse, according to which the verse means that in exile they *will* worship idols—and this is part of the punishment. However, the boundless love and respect that Rashi had for the Jewish People obliged him to explain "as the Targum (Onkelos) explains." It is inconceivable, according to Rashi, that God who is "Merciful even in judgment"[26] should impose on His *Children*[27] a punishment requiring them to worship idols that are *hateful* to Him.[28]

---

[23]See *Maskil LeDavid*, who wrote at length explaining the reason for the number of the word *venoshantem*—852.

[24]You will serve those nations that worship idols.

[25]Comp. Rashi below 28:64.

[26]Cf. Rashi above 3:24 s.v. *Hashem Elokim—rachum badin*.

[27]As the verse states: "You are the children of the Lord your God"—14:1.

[28]For even a "pillar"——*matzeyvah* He hates, even for the purpose of sacrificing on it to Him—below 16:22 and Rashi there. All the more so does He hate the idols themselves!

4:41   *Az yavdil*—"Then (Moses) set aside."

Rashi: He paid attention to be zealous about the matter—to set them aside. And although these cities could not serve as cities of refuge, i.e., they would not absorb the accidental killer, until those of Canaan (on the western side of the Jordan) were set aside, Moses said: "A mitzvah (precept) that is possible to fulfill (now), I will fulfill it."[29]

Comment: Already at Exod. 15:1 s.v.: *az yashir Mosheh*—"Then Moses sang" (lit. "will sing") Rashi explained after citing a number of examples, "We learn from here that the letter *Yod* (i.e., the future form: *yashir* instead of the past *shar*) is used in reference to *intention* to do a thing." Here too the use of the future tense *yavdil* instead of *hivdil* in the past alludes to paying attention or thought.[30]

Rashi changed slightly the statement of the Talmud at *Makkot* 10a— and for good reason (see below). There we read:

"Rabbi Simlai expounded: That which it says: 'He who loves money (silver) will never be satisfied with money...' (*Kohelet* 5:9)—this refers to our Master Moses who knew that the three cities (of refuge) in the east of Jordan would not absorb (the killer) until the three in Canaan were selected, yet he said: 'A mitzvah *that came into my hand*, I will fulfill it,' etc." Instead of "that came to my hand" Rashi wrote: "that is possible to fulfill." The reason for the change is because the precept of setting aside cities of refuge was not given to Moses alone, but to *all* of Israel, as written: "Speak to the *Children of Israel* ... you should designate cities for yourselves, cities of refuge shall they be ... Three cities shall you (pl.) give on the other side of the Jordan (to the east), and three cities shall you give in the land of Canaan, etc." (Numbers 35:10–14).

It should be pointed out that the major lesson for future generations lies in the fact that Moses was very diligent in the performance of the mitzvah, saying: "A mitzvah that it is possible to fulfill, I will fulfill it (now)." Meaning: Every Jew must say to himself: Even though this mitzvah "can be fulfilled" also by someone else—since it was not given *only* to me, nevertheless let *me* fulfill it.

5:12   *Shamor*—"Safeguard (or observe)."

Rashi: But in the first Ten Commandments (Exod. Chap. 20) it says "Remember (the Sabbath day)"! Both of them (*Zachor* and *Shamor*—"Remem-

---

[29] *Makkot* 10a and cf. Rashi on Numbers 35:13.
[30] Cf. our Hebrew commentary to Exod. 15:1 in *Be'ur Setumot Be-Rashi*, Part I, p. 165.

ber" and "observe") were spoken as one utterance and as one word, and were heard simultaneously. *Caasher tzivcha*—"As (the Lord your God) commanded you" before the giving of the Torah—at Marah.[31]

COMMENT: Several questions need to be answered:

1) Why does Rashi emphasize: "as one *utterance* and as one *word*," since "safeguard" and "remember" are only one word each; obviously if they were spoken as "one utterance" then it must have been only one *word?*

2) How do we know that "as He commanded you" refers to before the giving of the Torah, at Marah; maybe it refers to the first Ten Commandments?

3) If "as He commanded you" is before the giving of the Torah, why does it not state "as He commanded you" also in *Yitro?*

Explanation:

1) In the Alkabats and Zamora printings of Rashi the reading is: "In one utterance were they spoken, and as one word were they *written,* etc." namely: Not only were they spoken and heard as one word, but they were even written as one word. The meaning of "as one word were they *written*" is not that both words *zachor* and *shamor* were written as one word, without a break between them: "*zachorshamor,*" for there is no miracle involved in this—any *person* could do the same! Rather, the meaning is that only one word was written, but this single word could be read as two: *zachor shamor.* This, indeed, is miraculous.

The significance of this fact is to emphasize the positive commands regarding the Sabbath, such as: Kiddush, the enjoyment of Shabbat and the like; and the negative commands, i.e., the thirty-nine major "works" forbidden on the Sabbath and their derivatives, the Rabbinic prohibitions, etc. All these are of *equal* importance; neither side has any advantage over the other.[32]

2) In *Beshalach* after the Israelites came to Marah it says: "There he established for it (the nation) a decree and an ordinance" (Exod. 15:25).

---

[31] *Mechilta Bachodesh, Parshah* 7; *Shabbat* 87b; *Sanhedrin* 56b; *Seder Olam,* Chap. 5; *Yalkut* 257; Midrash *Agadah.*

[32] Cf. our commentary at Exod. 31:18 s.v. *luchot* where this matter is explained in greater detail.

Rashi explains: "In Marah He gave them some *sections of the Torah to engage in* them: Sabbath, the Red Cow, and Legislation."[33] The Talmud states:

"We have learnt: Ten commandments were Israel commanded at Marah, seven that the Sons of Noah (i.e., all the nations of the world) had already accepted, and they added: Legislation (i.e., the duty to set up courts of justice throughout the land), Sabbath and honoring one's father and mother as is written: 'as the Lord your God commanded you.'" R. Judah said: "as commanded you" means "at Marah." Rashi explains: "The words: 'as the Lord your God commanded you' are written in the latter Com-mandments regarding Sabbath and honoring one's father and mother. Where did He command you? We cannot say that Moses told them in the Plains of Moav: 'as He commanded you at Sinai,' because Moses did not teach them Deuteronomy and exhorted them to keep the command-ments *on his own,* but only *as he received it,* he repeated it to them; *and everything that is written in the latter Commandments, was written on the Tablets,* and that is how he heard at Sinai." Hence, that also in the first Command-ments at Sinai Moses was told, and it was written on the Tablets "as He commanded you" (already before) regarding Sabbath and the honor of father and mother. Thus "as He commanded you" must refer to Maran and not to Sinai.[34]

3) As explained above, the words "as He commanded you" were said also in the first Commandments and were inscribed on the Tablets. How-ever, since *Yitro* describes the *actual* revelation at Sinai, and not Moses' review of it—it is not appropriate that God should tell them at the very time of giving the Torah: "As the Lord your God *commanded you"*—surely He is commanding *at this very moment,* and what reason is there to say: "as He commanded you"?[35]

---

[33]Cf. there our explanation of the expression "to engage in them" *sheyit'asku bahem* and comp. *Be'ur Setumot Be-Rashi,* Part I, pp. 169–70.

[34]Cf. Rashi *Sanhedrin* 56b. Comp. *Be'er Yitzchak; Torah Temimah.*

[35]Especially as we explained in Exod. 15:25 the difference between: "*sections of Torah* that they should engage in," and if Rashi had written: "He gave them some *mitzvot,*" which would have implied that Sabbath, Red Cow, and Legislation had already taken effect *before* the giving of the Torah, as *commandments.* This is not so, for they did *not* take effect as *mitzvot,* but they were to engage in the *study* of the motives, etc. of these "sections of Torah." Accordingly it is inappropriate to state in *Yitro:* "as He *commanded* you," because at Marah there was as yet no *command* to keep Sabbath and honor of father and mother. Only at Sinai were these stated as a *commandment.*

6:4   *Hashem Elokeynu Hashem Echad*—
"The Lord is our God, the Lord is One."

Rashi: The Lord is now (only) our God, and not the God of the nations (of the world); He will in the Future be the One (sole) Lord, as it is said: "For then I will turn to the Peoples a pure language, that they may all call upon the name of the Lord" (Zephaniah 3:9), and it also says: "In that day shall the Lord be One and His name One" (Zechariah 14:9).[36]

Comment: According to "plain sense" that the verse proclaims that the Lord our God is One in the world *at present*, the words "the Lord our God" are superfluous. It should have stated only: "Hear, O Israel: the Lord is One"—and no more.

Moreover, according to plain sense *this entire* verse is superfluous, since it was already stated above: "You have been shown in order to know that the Lord, He is the God. *There is none* beside Him!" (in the present; above 4:35). Besides, is He our God alone; surely He is the God of the entire universe?!

Therefore Rashi explains that this verse was said about the future: Now the nations do not accept the Unity of God in the world, but sometime in the Future they will admit to it. Therefore Rashi cites the verse in Zephaniah: "For then (in the Future to come) I will turn... that they may *all* call upon the name of the Lord."

Question: Why does Rashi cite *two* verses, especially since in *Sifrei*, which is the source for Rashi's comment, only the second verse: "In that day the Lord will be One, etc." is cited?

Answer: The verse in Zephaniah alone is not enough, for we could err and explain "so that they may all call by the name of the Lord" to mean: "Each nation will call *its idol* by the name of the Lord." If so, the Lord will *not* be one even "then"—in the Future to come. Therefore Rashi cites the verse: "In that day *the Lord will be One*, etc." However, this verse alone is also not enough, for one could explain it mistakenly thus: True, God *will be* One, but the nations will *not* recognize the fact. Therefore he cites: "That they will *all* call by the name of the Lord." Hence, both verses complete each other.

---

[36]Cf. *Sifrei, Vaetchanan*, end of Sec. 31, where the verse in Zephaniah is not cited. Neither does the Ramban cite it when quoting Rashi—only the verse in Zechariah. Comp. also *Mizrachi.*

6:7   *L'vanecha*—"To your children."

RASHI: These are the disciples. We find everywhere that disciples are called "children," as is stated: "You are the children of the Lord your God" (14:1); and it says: "The sons of the prophets who were in Bethel" (II Kings 2:3). Likewise, we find with Hezekiah who taught Torah to all of Israel and called them "children," as it says: "Now, my sons, do not be negligent" (II Chronicles 29:11). And just as disciples are called children, so the teacher is called "father," as it says: "My father, my father, the chariot of Israel, etc." (Elisha referring to his teacher Elijah by these words—II Kings 2:12).[37]

COMMENT: Several questions arise from the above:

1) Why doesn't Rashi explain the word *l'vanecha*—"to your children" according to plain sense, that a father has to teach his children Torah?

2) Why does he bring proof from *three* verses that disciples are called children?

3) Why does Rashi go on to prove that the teacher is called "father"; what does this proof add to the meaning of *l'vanecha*, whose meaning Rashi is trying to explain?

The explanation of the above is:

1) If we would explain that *l'vanecha* means literally "to your children," it would mean that every father is obligated to teach his son Torah *himself*, and should not hire a teacher, or send his son to a yeshiva! But surely it is an everyday practice that children are sent to a yeshiva to study Torah. The five-year-old, who is beginning to study Torah, could ask: "Why does my father *not* teach me by himself, as it says: 'Teach them thoroughly (*veshinantam*) to your children'?" Therefore one must explain *l'vanecha*— "these are the disciples." Hence, a father is allowed to hire a teacher, and does not have to teach his son himself.

However, Rashi does *not* mean that *l'vanecha* refers *only* to disciples, not to sons, because: a) The "plain sense" *always* applies and this would be the opposite of plain sense, b) If so, a father would not be obligated to teach his son Torah, but we learned explicitly: "Our Rabbis taught: A father is obligated to teach his son Torah, to circumcise him, to redeem him, etc. Whence do we derive to teach him Torah, as is written: 'You shall teach

---

[37]Cf. *Sifrei, Vaetchanan* 34; *Yalkut* 841.

them (the words of the Torah) your children, etc.'"[38] Rashi means only that *also* students are included in the name "children."

2) Rashi cites *three* verses because all of them are needed: Against "You are the children of the Lord your God" one may ask: Maybe it means only that Israel is beloved by God like real children. Or perhaps He called them children because He supplied their needs in the Wilderness for forty years and watched over them as a father watches over his children and supplies their needs—not because they are His disciples?[39]

Therefore Rashi cites proof from "The sons of the prophets, etc."[40] Against this one may ask: Maybe they were the sons of the prophets, not their disciples;[41] or perhaps they were called "sons of prophets" on account of their occupation as prophets? Therefore Rashi proves from Hezekiah who taught all of Israel Torah and called them "children." But that alone is no proof, for perhaps he called them "children" as a mark of affection, as: "Is this your voice *my son* David?" (I Samuel 24:16). Therefore the first two proofs are also needed. From all three together we conclude that the disciples are called children. That is why Rashi writes: "We find in *every place*," i.e., in the Torah, Prophets, and Writings, that disciples are called children.

3) Rashi goes on to prove that also the teacher is called "father" to teach us how much a teacher must devote himself to his students, namely: Just as a father does everything for his son, so must the teacher make the utmost effort in teaching the Torah to his students—his "children." That is why Rashi emphasizes: "*Just as* the disciples are called *children*"—which obligates them to honor their Master as though he was their real father— "*so* is the teacher called father"—this title then obligates him to devote himself to his disciples as a father does to his son.

7:7 *Lo meyrubchem*—"Not because you are more numerous."

RASHI: To be understood according to the plain sense. But the Midrashic explanation is: Because you do not consider yourselves "great" when I shower goodness upon you ("taking"— *lo meyrubchem* in the sense of "not

---

[38] *Kiddushin* 29a-b.
[39] Or perhaps because the souls of Israel are a veritable part of God from above, as the prophet says: "Have we not all one Father? Did not one God create us?" (Malachi 2:10).
[40] Targum Jonathan: *talmidey n'viyaya*—"the students of the prophets."
[41] Since Ovadiah hid a hundred prophets in two caves (I Kings 18:13). Maybe these were their sons.

because you make yourselves great"), therefore: "The Lord desired you, for you are the fewest (*ha-m'at*)—meaning: You regard yourselves as small (*m'at*), as Abraham who said: "For I am dust and ashes" (Gen. 18:27), and as Moses and Aaron who said: "For what are we?" (Exod. 16:7). Not as Nebuchadnezzar who said: "I will be like the Most High" (Isaiah 14:14) and Senacherib who said: "Who among all the gods of these countries (that saved their countries from me") (Isaiah 36:20), or Chiram who said: "I am a god, I sit in the seat of God" (Ezekiel 28:2).[42]

COMMENT: Two questions must be answered:

1) Why wasn't Rashi satisfied with the "plain sense" and cited also the Midrashic explanation?

2) Why does he bring *two* examples of humility from Israel (Abraham, Moses–Aaron) and *three* from other nations (Nebuchadnezzar, Senacherib, Chiram) and does not cite *all* the examples mentioned in the Talmud from Israel and the nations?

Answers:

1) Rashi's problem with the plain sense (alone) is twofold:
a) How could Israel have imagined that God desired them because they were "numerous," that He had to tell them that they were really "few." Such a thought flies in the face of reality—they would never claim that they were "numerous"?!
b) According to plain sense the verse seems to contradict itself: It begins with: "Not because you are more 'numerous' than all the nations did God desire you," implying that you *are* more numerous than other nations, but this was *not* the reason God desired you. The verse ends with: "For you are the *fewest* of all the nations"—if so, you are *few*?

Therefore he cites the Midrash showing that the verse does not deal with Israel being either numerous or few, but rather with their qualities— that they are not proud, but to the contrary behave humbly, even when God showers them with much goodness.[43] According to the Midrash *meyrubchem* is in the sense of *rav* = *gadol* "great" as in: *Ki chain yisad ha-melech 'al col rav*

[42] *Chullin* 89a; *Yalkut* 845; Midrash *Agadah*; *Tanchuma Buber, Ekev* 4.
[43] As expressed in *Chullin* 89a: "God said to Israel: I desire you, because even when I bestow *greatness* (*gedulah*) upon you, you humble yourselves before Me." Comp. Targum Jonathan here.

beyto—"for so the King ordered every officer (*rav*) of his house" (Esther 1:8), i.e., all the *great* in his palace; similarly: *Har Tzion ... Kiriat Melech Rav* "Mount Zion... city of the great (*rav*) King" (Psalm 48:3); *ve-rav ya'avod tzair*—'The greater (*rav*) one shall serve the younger" (Gen. 25:23).[44]

2) Rashi left out some of the examples brought in the Gemara for good reason: a) King David's statement: "I am but a worm (i.e., lowly) not a man" (Psalms 22:7) was not made when God showered goodness upon him, since at the head of that chapter he says: "My God, my God, why have You *forsaken me* ... My God, I call by day and *You do not answer*, etc." (Psalm 22:2–3). b) Rashi does not mention Nimrod (as in the Talmud) because the Torah does *not* state who said: "Let us build a city for ourselves," only: "*They* said: Let us build, etc." c) Also, in Pharaoh's statement: "Who is God?" we do not see much pride, since he continues: "I do not know God (and therefore), and I will not send out the Israelites." Whereas in the case of Nebuchanezzar and Chiram the pride is very evident.

Still Rashi points out that this is only a Midrash, but the "plain sense" is: "Because you are numerous"—literally. However, this seems to contradict reality; ostensibly the Midrash is here the plain sense?

This can be explained in accordance with the statement: "You are today like the stars of heaven in abundance"; although Rashi himself asks: "Were they really like the stars of heaven on that day; they were only six hundred thousand—what is meant by: You are today, etc?" And Rashi answers: "You are compared to the day (the sun, which exists forever), etc." (above 1:10 and Rashi)—Moses blessed them: "May the Lord, the God of your forefathers, add to you a thousand times as (many) as you are."[45] There is no doubt that Moses' blessing will one day be fulfilled, even if it was not fulfilled "on that day."

Hence, Israel *will* one day be more numerous than all nations. They could therefore have imagined that God chose them because of their large numbers, like a human king who desires a large population, and as is stated: "In a multitude of people is a King's glory" (Proverbs 14:28). Therefore the verse states that this is not the main reason, as *now*: "You are the *fewest* of all the peoples"—and God already chose you! But the real reason is as stated in verse 8: "Rather, because of God's love for you and because He keeps the oath that He swore to your forefathers, etc.

---

[44]Cf. further examples in Biblical Concordances s.v.—*rav*.

[45]Verse 11. Rashi there states that the Israelites complained to Moses: You are setting a limit to our blessing (only *a thousand* times!). Moses appeased them, saying: "This (a thousand times) is *my* blessing but God should bless you as much as He promised you!"

Ekev

7:12　*V'hayah e'kev tishme'un*—
"It shall come to pass if you obey. . . ."

RASHI: Also (*af*) ["if"—*im*][46] the lighter commands which a person treads on with his heels (i.e., treats lightly, disregards) you will listen to *v'shamar Hashem v'go*—"then God will keep, etc."—He will keep for you His promise.[47]

COMMENT: You may ask:

1) Why didn't Rashi explain simply *e'kev* in the sense of *ya'an, biglal*—"because" as Onkelos rendered *chalaf di tkablun* as below: *e'kev lo tishme'un v'go*—"because you would not listen, etc."[48]

2) How did Rashi improve with this comment: "He will keep for you His promise":—this is stated explicitly in the verse?

From the *Tanchuma* it would seem that the reading *af*—"also, even"—is preferable to *im*—"if." Thus we read:

"Blessed be the name of the Holy One, blessed be He, who gave Israel a Torah that contains 613 *mitzvot*—some of which are light and some severe. Because some of them are light and people do not pay attention to them, but cast them under their heels—meaning that they are light—therefore David was afraid of the day of judgment and said: 'Master of the Universe, I am not afraid of the severe commands, because they *are* severe. What am I afraid of? Of the light commands, lest I have transgressed any one of them ... because it was light.' But You said: 'Be as careful with a light command as with a severe one'.[49] Therefore he said: 'Why should I fear in the days

---

[46]In MS, *Mizrachi* and other of Rashi's commentators the reading is: *im*—"if." The reading *af*—"also" is given by A. Berliner and C. D. Chavel.

[47]*Tanchuma, Ekev* 1.

[48]8:20—there too Onkelos renders *chalaf.* In most occurrences in the Bible *e'kev* means "because"; Cf. Biblical Concordance s.v. *e'kev.*

[49]*Avot* 2:1.

of evil? The sin of my heels (i.e., the commands I trod upon with my heels) will surround me' (Psalms 49:6)—this is meant by *v'hayah e'kev tishme'un.*"

According to the above it is clear that it is harder to keep the lighter commands than the more severe ones. This is what *af*—"even/also" conveys: Even the light commands that a person treads under his heels will you keep, then you will deserve all the rewards that are enumerated in the following verses.

1) Rashi did not explain *e'kev* in the sense of "because," since the entire first half of the verse seems superfluous, thus *Vaetchanan* concludes with "You should keep the laws and the statutes, etc." This should have been followed immediately with: "And the Lord, your God will keep for you the Covenant, etc." At most it should have said: "If you will keep *them,* the Lord will keep, etc." Therefore Rashi explains that the verse comes to enjoin the keeping of the light commands no less than the severe.

2) With his comment: "He will keep for you His promise" Rashi comes to answer a possible question that arises: Ostensibly this verse implies: If you will keep the laws, etc., God will also keep the oath He swore to your forefathers—but if not, He will *not* keep His oath—God forbid?! It is sacrilegious to say so, for He *must* keep the oath, even if you will *not* listen, etc. because: "Every single utterance that came out of God's mouth for the good, even if it was on condition—He did *not* retract it."[50] If so, the second part of the verse from: "He will keep" till the end is superfluous; it should have stated merely: "He will love you, etc."?

Moreover, the verses appear to contradict each other: The previous verse (11) ended with: "Today to do them," which Rashi explained: "But tomorrow, in the future world to receive their reward," as the Rabbis state: "There is no reward for *mitzvot* in *this* world."[51] Whereas *all* the promises in this section, beginning with *this* verse, refer to good things in *this* world?

To answer all of the above Rashi writes: "He will keep for you His promises," namely: All the good things detailed in this *parshah* are not as reward for keeping the *mitzvot,* which is reserved for the *future* world. Rather, they are in *addition,* because He so promised the forefathers, and He *must* fulfill His promise.

Rashi does not give examples of the "light" *mitzvot,* because every person knows in his own heart which commands he considers "light." What one considers "light," another considers "severe," e.g. for one communal prayer (in a synagogue with a quorum *tefillah b'tzibur*) is a "light" command

---

[50] *Berachot* 7b.
[51] *Kiddushin* 39b.

and he is negligent in this regard. Whereas someone else considers this as a "severe" command and he is very particular to keep it. Similarly, slander, gossip, not studying as much Torah as possible (*bitul Torah*), etc., are *mitzvot* that are considered "light" by one, but "severe" by another.[52]

8:4   *Simlatcha lo valtah*—"Your garment did not wear out."

RASHI: The clouds of Divine Glory used to rub (the dirt off) their clothes and polish[53] them (they looked) like bleached, ironed clothes. Their small children, too, as they grew, their clothes grew with them—just like the clothes (i.e., shell) of a snail which grows with it.

Lo vatzeykah—"(Your feet) did not swell."

RASHI: Like dough (*batzeyk*) as is usual with those who walk barefoot—their feet are swollen.[54]

COMMENT: A number of questions arise out of Rashi's comments:

1) Why is it necessary to say that "the clouds of Glory would rub their clothes, etc.," since these verses point out the various acts of kindness that God bestowed upon Israel in the wilderness. Just as: "He gave you Manna to eat" was *only* due to God's kindness, and no other cause, so too the fact that "Your garments did not wear out" was also a mark of God's kindness—and there is no need to resort to the Clouds of Glory at all?

2) The "Clouds of Glory" were special clouds that came only in *honor* of Israel, and not to supply their needs.[55] Why then does Rashi say that the "Clouds of *Glory* used to rub their clothes ... and also their small children, as they grew, their clothes would grow with them." This is the greatest form of supplying their needs?!

---

[52]*Devek Tov* adds these two examples: 1) To go and accompany a person (who visited), 2) To do a kindness, which does not require an effort.

[53]Or: "bleach, iron," cf. *A'ruch hashalem*: s.v. *ghatz*; M. Jastrow: *Dictionary* s.v. *ghatz*; A. Even Shoshan, *Hamilon HeChadash ghatz.*

[54]*Yalkut, Ekev* 850; *Pesikta de Rav Kahana, Beshalach* 91:1.

[55]Wherever Rashi speaks of the practical, material use of the clouds, he writes "clouds, cloud" (without "Glory": Exod. 17:9, 19:4; Numbers 20:22; Deut. 25:18). But when he does not speak of their usefulness, he writes "Clouds of Glory" (Levit. 23:43; Numbers 20:29, 26:13; 33:40, and in our verse).

3) Why does Rashi add: "Their small children too, as they grew, their clothes grew with them"; how is this connected with the Clouds of Glory, and how is this derived from "Your garments did not wear out"?

4) What need for "bleached clothes" did they have in the desert? Surely no person insists on that during their travels!

5) From Rashi's comment it seems they walked barefoot in the desert, yet it states explicitly, below 29:4: "and your *shoe* did not wear out from *above* your foot"—hence they *did* have shoes?

We may explain as follows:

1) Had their clothes not worn out during *forty* years in the desert, without any external cause as the Clouds of Glory, it would have been even a greater *open* miracle than the Clouds of Glory rubbing and polishing them—and one ought not to use *open* miracles without a dire need for them.[56] But since the Clouds of Glory rubbed and ironed their clothes the miracle was not an "open" one, for one could argue that they contained chemicals that could wash clothes through rubbing them.

2) They could have cleaned their clothes even without the Clouds of Glory in an ordinary, natural way. The Clouds of Glory only served to save them the slight effort involved. This indeed is a mark of honor—it shows how dear Israel is to God, and to what extent He honors them.

3) Rashi adds: "Their small children too ... their clothes grew with them" to obviate a difficulty: True, adults could wear the same clothes for many years since "Your garments did not wear out"; but how could little ones, who are constantly growing, wear the *same* clothes? Answer: "Their clothes grew with them." True, there is no direct connection with the Clouds and the miracle of their clothes growing with them. This is *another* miracle, having to do with the *bodies* of the Israelites (not the Clouds). Therefore Rashi concludes: "like the clothes of a snail which grows with it."

4) The meaning of: "and polish them (*U-mgahatzim otam*) like ironed clothes" (*caylim mguhatzim*) here is "they washed and bleached them." This

---

[56]Such as the Ten Plagues, splitting of the Red Sea, bringing down the Manna, etc., since: "If a miracle is performed for him, it is deducted from his merits" (i.e., reward—*Shabbat* 32a).

is implied by R. Elazar son of R. Shimon's question to his father-in-law R. Shimon ben Lakonia regarding the clothes: "Did they not require laundering?" He answered: "The Clouds of Glory bleached (*megahatzin*) them."

5) Apparently they *did* have shoes (as the verse cited states), but without *soles*, so that they walked barefoot underneath. Therefore verse 29:4 states precisely: "and your shoe did not wear out from *above* your feet," i.e., the *upper* part of the shoe *above* the sole did not wear out, but *under* the sole did wear out, or had no sole at all.[57] Nevertheless: "Your feet did not swell." Accordingly, there is no contradiction between Rashi and Verse 29:4.

9:10   *Luchot*—"Tablets."

Rashi: This word is written *luchat* (without a *vav* before the *tav*, so that it may be read *luchat*—"singular—one tablet"), because both of them were equal.[58]

Comment: In *Tanchuma, Ekev* 10 we read:
    "Rabbi Chanina said *luchat* is written, for they were not one bigger than the other, but both were equal, and both were carved out (quarried) together." According to this the meaning of "both of them were equal" is equal in size. This emphasized their great superiority as Divine objects, as stated here: "written by the finger of God":

a) Two objects made by man cannot be *exactly* the same, to the last iota.

b) One tablet had the first five Commandments written on it, while the other had the second five Commandments.[59] Now, the first five Commandments had *many more* words and letters than the last five[60]—nevertheless they were "both equal."[61] This fact stresses that they were of Divine, exalted nature—not human.

---

[57]Cf. at length: *Divrei David; Be'urei Maharia; Maskil LeDavid.*

[58]*Tanchuma, Ekev* 10. Cf. Rashi on Exod. 31:18 and our commentary thereto.

[59]Cf. Numbers 7:23.

[60]In *Yitro* the first five Commandments have 147 words, while the second five have only twenty-six. In *Vaetchanan*, the first five Commandments have 162 words, while the second five have only twenty-seven!

[61]And one must assume that the size of the letters, and separations between words and between letters was equal in both Tablets—*not* that on one Tablet the letters were small, while on the other they were very large.

Question: Would anyone doubt that "He who spoke and the world came into being"[62] could make them both *exactly* equal, despite the huge difference in the number of words and letters between them? Why is it necessary to emphasize this fact especially? Surely, the creation of the world is a much greater source of wonderment?

We therefore venture to suggest that the main idea behind the statement "Both of them were equal" is that both Tablets were equal in importance. As is generally known, on the first Tablet were inscribed the Commandments "between man and God," while on the second Tablet the Commandments "between man and man." The allusion in the Midrash that "both were equal" is that both kinds of Commandments are equally important. One type of *mitzvot* has no advantage over the other—we heard both kinds from the Almighty—and we are not allowed to give preference to one kind over the other.[63]

11:13   *Le'ahavah et Hashem*—"To love the Lord."

RASHI: You should not say: I will learn, so that I become rich; so that I may be called Rabbi; in order to receive reward. Rather, whatever you do, do it out of love (for God), and ultimately the honor will come.[64]

COMMENT: Rashi artfully combined the *Sifrei* and the statement in the Talmud into one unit:

In the *Sifrei* we read: "To love the Lord, your God"—you might say: I will learn Torah in order to become rich, and in order to be called Rabbi, and in order to receive reward? Therefore it says: "To love the Lord your God, whatever you do, do it for nothing else but love."

In the Gemara we read: "We have learnt: 'To love the Lord your God,' to listen to His voice and to cleave to Him' (below 30:20). A person should not say: "I will learn Bible, so that people should call me 'wise'; I will study Mishnah so that they may call me Rabbi; I will study Talmud in order to become a savant and head of an academy. Rather, study out of love, and at the end honor will come, as it says, etc."[65]

Rashi was bothered with the following questions:

---

[62]"He who spoke, etc."—a widely used phrase by the Rabbis referring to God, e.g.: *Eruvin* 13b; *Megillah* 13b; *Kiddushin* 32b; etc.; widely used in Midrash.

[63]Cf. our commentary to Exod. 31:18.

[64]*Sifrei Ekev* 41, *Nedarim* 62a.

[65]*Nedarim* 62a.

1) How is it possible to *command* regarding the love of God; surely love is an *emotion*, not an action that could be commanded. If so, why does it state: I *command* you ... to love the Lord, etc."?

2) Love is possible between two people who are close to each other mentally and spiritually. None of this applies to the relationship between God and His creatures?

Therefore Rashi explains that love here means to do the commands of one's Creator out of love.[66] Namely, there is no *command* to love God, for one cannot command this, but to fulfill the *mitzvot* out of love of God, not for reward, etc.

It would seem that Rashi chose the wording of the *Sifrei* mainly—adding only three words at the end: "And ultimately honor will come" (*v'sof hacavod lavo*) from the Gemara, because the words of the Gemara refer to the verse below (30:19)—where no command is mentioned, but only as a continuation of the good counsel of the previous verse, namely: "You should choose life ... to love the Lord your God, etc."[67] Whereas here it states immediately before: "I *command* you today to love, etc."

---

[66]Rashi explained similarly above 6:6: "These words which I command you today, shall be upon your heart"—And what is the love? "These words shall be, etc., for thereby you will recognize the Holy One, Blessed be He, and will cleave to His ways."
[67]Cf. Rashi below 30:19: "You should choose life—I instruct you that you choose the portion of life, etc."

R'ei

12:17 *Lo tuchal*—"You may not (eat. . . .)"

RASHI: This verse comes to add a negative command to this matter (of eating: *ma'aser*, *bchor*, etc., outside the walls of Jerusalem. The positive command was stated already in verse 11).

Lo tuchal—literally "you cannot (eat, etc.)"—Rabbi Joshua son of Korcha said: You *can*, but you are not allowed to. A similar case (where *lo yachol* means "not allowed," not "unable") we find in: "As for the Jebusites, the inhabitants of Jerusalem, the Children of Israel *could not* drive them out" (Joshua 15:63); they *could* but were not allowed, because Abraham made a covenant with them when he bought from them the Cave of Machpelah (that they would be spared at the conquest of the Land). They were not really Jebusites, but Hittites,[68] but were called Jebusites after the city the name of which was Jebus. So it is explained in *Pirke de Rabbi Eliezer* (Chap. 36).

This is what it says (that when David was about to drive out the Jebusites from Jerusalem, they said to him): "Only if you take away the blind and the lame" (II Samuel 5:6)—(By "the blind and the lame" they meant) the idols upon which they had written the oath (which Abraham had sworn to their forefathers when he purchased the Cave of Machpelah).[69]

COMMENT: Two questions must be answered:

1) Rashi does not usually mention the name of the Rabbi who made the statement that he cites.[70] Why does he emphasize here: "Rabbi Joshua son of Korcha said"?

2) That the meaning of *lo tuchal* is "You are not allowed" and not any physical inability is obvious, since there is freedom of the will and a person

---

[68]As is evident from Gen. Chap. 23 at the purchase of the Cave.
[69]*Pirke de Rabbi Eliezer* Chap. 36; *Makkot* 19b; *Sifrei* 72; *Yalkut* 883
[70]Cf. *Klalei Rashi* (Rules in Rashi), p. 61, parag. 6; p. 62, parag. 6–7.

can do as he pleases—even against the will of God. Hence, there is nothing new in Rashi's explanation. Why then did he cite R. Joshua son of Korcha's statement?

Answers:

1) Rashi cites the name of "Rabbi Joshua son of Korcha" to indicate that his statement here is in line with his statement elsewhere regarding the Bible, in this case in Tractate *Berachot,* thus:

"Rabbi Joshua ben Korcha said: Why does the section of *Shema*—'Hear,' etc. (Deut. 6:4-9) precede that of *Ve'hayah im shamo'a*—'It will be that if you listen, etc.' (Deut. 11: 13–21)? In order that one should accept upon himself the yoke of the Kingdom of Heaven" (i.e., *Shema* stating "Hear, O Israel, the Lord is our God, the Lord is One") first, and afterwards he should accept the yoke of commands."[71] Hence, whoever accepts upon himself completely the yoke of the Kingdom of Heaven *cannot* oppose God's will. One may therefore say about him: "You *cannot* (or will not be *able*) to eat within your gates, etc."

2) The novelty about Rabbi Joshua ben Korcha's statement is in the psychological approach to the fulfillment of Torah and *mitzvot,* namely: Since the Torah forbade it, it is in the realm of "You will not be able"— as if there is a *physical* restraint in the matter. Although Rashi already explained in the verse: "The people *cannot* ascend Mount Sinai" (Exod. 19:23)—"they cannot ascend because they have no permission"; also on: "You *cannot* see My face," Rashi comments "I do not give you permission" (Exod. 33:20)—one cannot learn from them:

Regarding the ascent to Mount Sinai it says: "Beware of going up the mountain ... Whoever touches the mountain shall surely die!" (Exod. 19:12). I might have thought that they will not *be able* to ascend, because they will die before they manage to go up. Similarly about seeing "the Face of God" it says: "for no man can see My face and live"—if so, the expression there *lo tuchal*—"you cannot" could also be understood *literally.* Therefore Rashi cites the Midrash of Rabbi Joshua ben Korcha stating that *lo tuchal*—"you cannot" *here* means: You have no permission.

13:6 *Ve'hapodcha mibeyt 'avadim*—
"And Who redeems you from the house of slavery."

RASHI: Even if He had no other claim on you, but that He redeemed you, it would be enough for Him (to demand your obedience).[72]

---

[71]Mishna *Berachot* 13a.
[72]*Sifrei* 86; *Yalkut* 886.

COMMENT: We must understand:

1) In *Sifrei* there is yet another Midrash: "Who took you out of the land of Egypt—even if He had no other claim on you, but that He took you out of Egypt—it would be enough." Why didn't Rashi cite also that part of the Midrash?

2) If God had not done *any* other kindness, only delivered us from slavery, it would really *not* be enough! How would we have become the *People* of Israel in Egypt; it is unthinkable?!
We may explain:

1) Rashi left out the Midrash referring to "Who took you out, etc.," because it implies that it would be possible to have taken them out of Egypt and not redeem them, so that they would be slaves wherever they went. This is far from the plain sense!

Besides, the words "and Who redeems you from the House of slavery" appear to be superfluous, since it states before: "Who takes you out of the land of Egypt." As soon as He delivered them, they are *free*, because taking out implies redemption. However, redemption alone does *not* imply taking out (of Egypt), for it would be possible for them to have been redeemed from slavery and remain in Egypt as free men—and that too would be sufficient! Therefore Rashi stresses the Midrash on "Who redeems you, etc.," but left out the part on "Who takes you out of the land of Egypt."

2) One must understand the word *dayo*—"it would be enough for Him" in the same sense as: *Kamah ma'alot tovot lamakom 'aleynu*—"For how many kindnesses must we thank the Almighty," which we recite at the Seder on Passover, namely: Had He not done for us any other kindness, except redeemed us from slavery—it would be sufficient for us to thank Him and accept His yoke upon ourselves and obey His commands. It does *not* mean, God forbid, that it would be enough *for us*, and we would not lack anything. On the contrary, we would miss a lot: receiving the Torah; being chosen as God's "treasured people" (*am segulah*); residing of the Divine Presence (*Shechinah*) in our midst; and many other kindnesses He bestowed upon us.[73] It means only that this act of kindness *alone* (redeeming us from slavery) would be enough to accept His yoke upon us.[74]

---

[73]Namely all the numerous kindnesses listed in that poem "Oh how many kindnesses has God shown us for which we must thank Him"—*Kamah ma'alot tovot* mentioned above.
[74]Comp. *Be'er Yitzchak; Be'er Mayim Chaim; Mishmeret HaKodesh.*

13:17   *LaHashem El-ohecha*—"For the Lord your God."

RASHI: For (the honor of) His name and for His sake.

COMMENT: What did Rashi add or clarify by his two-word comment; the verse *itself* states that the burning of the city and its spoil is "for the Lord your God"?

Answer:

Rashi is replying to an inherent question: "What *need* does God have for the burning of the city and its spoil; surely nobody benefits from this destruction?" Moreover; true, the *inhabitants* of the city may be liable for annihilation because they worshipped idols and maybe even the animals are liable, for perhaps they were worshipped as idols. But the city itself and the movable objects within it—which have no intelligence:[75] In what way did they "sin" that they should be liable for burning? Rashi replies: "For Him and for His sake," i.e., it is a decree of the King (God) and we have no permission to question it.

Similarly, Rashi explains: "Let them take *for Me* a portion—For me: *for the sake of My name*" (Exod. 25:2 and Rashi). There too one might ask "What need does God have of 'a portion' (*truma*)? Surely, 'Mine is the silver and Mine is the gold, says the Lord'" (Chagai 2:8). Likewise, on the verse: "They should make a Sanctuary *for Me*," Rashi comments: "Let them make *for the sake of My name* a House of holiness" (Rashi on Exod. 25:8), for there too one may ask: "Behold, the heavens and the highest heavens [lit. "the heavens of heavens"] cannot contain You, surely not this Temple ...?" (I Kings 8:27). Also, on the verse: "The land shall observe a Sabbath [i.e., Sabbatical year] *for the Lord*," Rashi remarks: "For *the sake* of the Lord" (Rashi on Levit. 25:2), for there too one may ask: "What use or advantage does *the Lord* have from the land's resting?"[76]

---

[75]Even though the animals have no intelligence either, and have not "sinned," nevertheless they *are* liable, because they were the cause of man's downfall—so that people should not say (after the inhabitants are destroyed), "This animal is the one that caused so-and-so to be stoned" (*Sanhedrin* 54a). Cf. Rashi on Levit. 20:15 and our interpretation thereto.

[76]Cf. Be'er Mayim Chaim who adds pointedly: "If he hated the inhabitants of that city (that worshipped idols), he should not have in mind when killing the inhabitants that he is doing it as revenge, rather for the sake of His name."

14:21   *Lo t'vashel g'di—*
"You shall not cook a kid (in its mother's milk)."

RASHI: Three times (is the prohibition, in this *same phrase,* "You shall not cook, etc." stated in the Torah: Exod. 23:19, 34:26, and our verse), excluding [three species]: a wild beast, fowls, and unclean beasts [from this prohibition]).[77]

COMMENT: In *Chullin* 113a, the Mishna states: "Rabbi Akiva says: Wild beasts and fowls are not forbidden (to be cooked in milk) from the Torah, as it says: You shall not cook a kid in its mother's milk three times—comes to exclude beasts, fowls, and unclean animals." Rashi there explains "To exclude fowls, beasts, and unclean animals—'a kid'—to exclude fowl, which is not an animal; 'a kid'—to exclude a beast, which is not an animal (not domesticated)." Although the term "beast" is included in the term "animal."[78]

Rashi cites this exegesis here to explain why the Torah states the prohibition of *cooking* a kid in its mother's milk in the section that deals with the prohibition of *eating* unclean beasts and fowl. Rashi explains that according to Rabbi Akiva, whose ruling prevails against another opponent,[79] the Torah speaks here too about *eating* (not just cooking) and it comes to exclude beasts, fowl, and unclean animals. All this is derived from the word 'a kid' (*gedi*). But the reason for writing three times the words "You shall not *cook*," Rashi already explained in *Mishpatim* and in *Ki Tisa:* "Once to forbid eating; once to forbid benefiting, and once to forbid cooking (meat and milk together)."[80]

Rashi did not explain here: "As the Targum translates—'You shall not *eat* meat with milk,' " because Onkelos renders thus *all* three times—which is *not* according to the tradition of the Rabbis, which Rashi himself cites (above). Had he stated here: "As the Targum has it," we could err in believing that only *eating* meat with milk is forbidden, whereas cooking or having other benefit from them *is* permitted. Rashi as the Teacher of Generations par excellence could not allow such a mistake to arise in the

---

[77] *Sifrei* 104; *Chullin* 113a.

[78] Cf. Rashi Levit. 11:2: 'These are the beasts (*hachayah*) that you may eat out of all the animals (*habeheymah*)'—This teaches that *beheymah* (animal) *is* included in *chayah* (beast), this superfluous verse comes and excludes it; 'a kid'—but not an unclean animal. But a clean animal which is *not* a kid, like a cow and a ewe *are* included from verses (that they are forbidden to be cooked in milk) as the *Baraita* in the Gemara teaches (below—114a)."

[79] *Halacha K'R. Akiva Meychavero*—cf. *Eruvin* 46b; *Pesachim* 107a; *Ketubot* 21a.

[80] Cf. Rashi on Exod. 23:19, 34:16.

minds of the simple folk, who are not fluent in law, and rely on his commentary to the Torah![81]

16:3 *Lechem 'oni*—"Bread of affliction."

RASHI: Bread that reminds one of the affliction that they were subjected to in Egypt.

Ki vechipazon yatzatah—"For in haste did you go out."

RASHI: And the dough did not manage to become leavened, and this (eating unleavened bread) will be a reminder for you. The haste was not yours, but of the Egyptians, for so it states: "The Egyptians urged the people on, to make them leave in haste" (Exod. 12:33).[82]

Lema'an tizcor—"So that you may remember."

RASHI: By eating the Passover sacrifice and the matzot (you will remember) "the day when you went out" (of Egypt).[83]

COMMENT: Question: Why does Rashi add: "The haste was not yours, but the Egyptians', etc."; what does that add to the understanding of the verse?

Answer: Rashi interprets in honor of God and in honor of Israel, for had they left on account of *their own haste*, it would not be in honor of God

---

[81]As for Onkelos translating in all three places "You shall not *eat* meat with milk," not mentioning anything about not *cooking* or *benefitting* from them, cf. the commentary on Onkelos, *Netinah Lager* (by R. Nathan Adler) on Exod. 23:19: "The correct reason is as I write below Levit. 23:15: *The translator did not bother to render the verses everywhere according to Rabbinic tradition, only wherever the deniers* (of the tradition of the Rabbis) *oppose it.* Hence in this case that they argue that *only cooking* is forbidden, Onkelos rendered "You shall not *eat* meat with milk." Also, *vehayu letotafot*, he rendered—"they shall be as Tephellin (phylacteries);" also: *pre eytz hadar*—he rendered etrogim, etc." (Because in these cases the "deniers of tradition" reject the interpretation of the Rabbis—hence Onkelos emphasizes it.)

[82]There could not have been haste on the part of Israel for, as Rashi pointed out in verse 1, Pharaoh asked them to leave at night, but they did not leave until next day.

[83]*Sifrei* 130; *Mechilta, Bo* 87; *Berachot* 9a; *Pesikta Zutarti*.

or of Israel that they were *forced* to leave in a hurry, and *could not* stay even for the short time that it takes to bake bread properly due to pressure from the Egyptians.

But now that the haste was on the part of the Egyptians, the meaning is: "*We* have plenty of time, for we are sure that God will take us out at a time that is convenient for *us*." However, "The *Egyptians* urged the people on, etc." namely: "We will do *you* a favor when *you* are in trouble and leave right away upon your request (even without baking bread fully!). We will not be like you, who afflicted us, for four hundred years." This is indeed a great honor to Israel![84]

---

[84]In *Berachot* 9a there is a controversy: Rabbi Elazar ben Azaria holds it was the Egyptians' haste, while R. Akiva holds it was Israel's haste. However, Rashi there writes: "Everyone agrees—even R. Akiva admits that at night—*from midnight on it was the Egyptians' haste* to send them out of the land." Hence, Rashi's statement in our verse is a unanimous opinion, since here is mentioned "the day of your *going out* of Egypt," and the "going out" was by day in everyone's opinion.

Shoftim

16:19 *Ve'lo tikach shochad*—"You shall not take bribes."

RASHI: Even to judge justly.[85]

Ki hashochad ye'aver—"For the bribery blinds."

RASHI: As soon as he receives a bribe from him, it is *impossible* that his (the judge's) heart should not incline in his favor.[86]

Divrei tzadikim—"Just words."

RASHI: Righteous words, i.e., judgments of Truth (uttered on Sinai).[87]

COMMENT: The following questions require answers:

1) What caused Rashi to state "Even to judge justly"; a judge who takes bribes does it in order to *distort* justice in favor of the one who bribed him; he does *not* intend to "judge justly"?

2) Rashi explains "As soon as he receives a bribe from him, *it is impossible* for him not to incline his heart in his favor." Surely the judge has

---

[85] *Sifrei* 144; *Yalkut* 907; *Mechilta, Mishpatim* Sec. 20.
[86] *Ketubot* 105a; *Tanchuma Shoftim* 8; Midrash *Agadah.*
[87] The word *Tzadikim*—"Righteous ones" is thus a description of *divrei*—"words of." Comp. Onkelos: *Pitgamin Tritzin*—"upright words." *Mechilta* states likewise: "He changes righteous words that were uttered at Sinai" (*Mishpatim* 20). The first edition of Rashi (1474–75) reads: "Righteous words, judgment of truth, *bribery changes and distorts to lies.*" This addition is correct, for thereby Rashi explains also the word *visalef*—"distorts." The bribe changes the true judgment (in sing. not plural "judgments" as in our printed editions) to distortion and lies.

free will; how can one say with certainty: "*It is impossible* that his heart should not incline, etc."?

3) Why doesn't Rashi explain simply: *divrei tzadikim*—"words of the righteous," i.e., the words of the judges, who are *usually* "righteous" people, but if they take a bribe it distorts their words and causes them to distort justice?[88]

The explanation is as follows:

1) If "You shall not take bribes" means in order to distort justice only, which is the *usual* intention of a judge who takes bribes, this is already included in "You shall not pervert judgment" at the opening of this verse— hence, "You shall not take bribes" is superfluous? If so, it must express a new idea, not included in "You shall not pervert judgment"—it must mean "even to judge justly." How does one take a bribe and yet judge justly? If the judge thinks: "I will take money from him just to calm him down, he should not be afraid and become tongue-tied, etc. But *I* will judge justly come what may!" Concerning such a case the Torah warns: Nevertheless— do not take bribes—for it is *impossible* for you *not* to pervert judgment.

2) The Talmud states: "Rava said: What is the reason for bribes?[89] As soon as he received a bribe from him, his mind became closer to the giver, so that he became (in the judge's eyes) like *himself,* and a person does not see a convincing argument against himself."[90] The import of the above is: True, the judge *has* freedom of the will, but since he received a bribe, the giver becomes "like himself"—it is therefore his *choice* to acquit the giver— since he is, so to speak, judging *himself.* A person cannot convict himself, for it is against human nature.

3) Rashi is disinclined to interpret the word "righteous" *tzadikim* "words" as referring to the judges, who are *usually* righteous, since when they took bribes they are *wicked.* Even if before they *were* righteous, the Torah would not term them "righteous" after they took a bribe. Likewise, one cannot interpret *tzadikim*—"righteous" as referring to the litigants:

---

[88]In this way he would explain the *entire* verse as dealing with the judges, as explained in the *Sifrei* 144. Comp. *Sefer Hazikaron* on Exod. 23:8, and cf. Ibn Ezra there who states: "*divrei tzadikim*—refers to the litigants."

[89]Rashi: "Why is it forbidden to take a bribe to *acquit* the innocent?"—*Ketubot* 105b.

[90]Rashi there: "His mind does not incline toward conviction of himself, *even if he intends to judge according to the truth,*" loc. cit.

"Who are righteous in their *case*, although not in performance of commandments."[91]

17:8   *Vekamta ve'alita*—"You shall rise and go up."

RASHI: This (you shall *rise*) teaches that the Temple is the highest of all places.[92]

COMMENT: Rashi changed the statement of the Rabbis (in both its versions as quoted above), because it does not agree with the geographic reality of the world—it is impossible that in its original statement(s) it should be the "plain sense" of this verse.

Even in Israel itself the Temple is *not* higher than *all* of Israel—only than *most* of Israel. According to the Gemara in *Zevachim* (54b) David wanted at first to build the Temple in Ein Eitam because it is higher than Jerusalem. Therefore Rashi's statement: "the highest *of all* places" means: higher than *almost* all places—and only in Israel.

But one may ask: Why did Rashi, who is always very exact in his wording[93] write here in such a vague manner: "higher than *all* places," without explaining that he means that the Temple is higher than *almost* all places—and only in Israel? Moreover, why did the Rabbis express themselves in a manner that is contrary to geographic reality?

One may explain this according to the *Sifrei* in *Ekev* which states: "Thus it is stated: 'Let me sing for my Beloved; my Beloved's song concerning His vineyard' (Isaiah 5:1)—'Just as this ox has no higher place than its horns, so is the Land of Israel higher than all lands ... it comes to teach you *that whatever is higher than the other, is superior to the other*. Now, Israel, therefore, because it is higher than everything, it is superior to everything. *The Temple which is higher than all—is superior to all*, as is stated: You shall rise and go up, etc.'"[94]

---

[91]So explains Ibn Ezra in Exod. 23:8, since both of them are *not* righteous in this case; how could the Torah call *both* of them "righteous"? Therefore Rashi explains that righteous—*tzadikim* refers to "judgments of truth"—*mishpatei emet*—"trustworthy and righteous," as is stated: "Righteous laws and statutes" (Deut. 4:8).

[92]In *Sifrei* 152 the reading is: "It teaches that Israel is the highest of all lands and the Temple is the highest (place) in the Land of Israel." In *Kiddushin* 69a, *Sanhedrin* 87a, and *Zevachim* 54b the reading is: "It teaches that the Temple is the highest place in Israel, and Israel is the highest of all lands." Cf. other versions in C. D. Chavel's edition: *Peirushei Rashi al ha-Torah*, p. 555, note 16 and *Yosef Hallel* to this verse.

[93]See: *Klalei Rashi*, Chap. 12: "The language of Sages," especially pp. 77–78.

[94]*Sifrei* Ekev, end of section 37.

It is therefore clear that the Rabbis' statement was meant to praise Israel and the Temple: Israel is higher than all lands in a spiritual, not geographic sense. The same applies to the Temple, which is higher than all places in Israel also in a spiritual sense. Accordingly, Rashi's statement: "that the Temple is the highest *of all places*" is correct: in *spiritual* height the Temple is indeed the highest of *all* places in the world! Hence Rashi was precise in his statement here as everywhere else.

20:2   *V'dibeir el ha'am*—"And he (the priest)
shall speak to the people."

RASHI: In the Holy Language.[95]

COMMENT: You may ask:

1) *How* is it implied in these words that the priest spoke in Hebrew?

2) *Why* does he have to speak necessarily in Hebrew—what is the significance therein?

We may reply:

1) That the priest spoke to the People in Hebrew is stated in the Mishna: "He shall speak to the People—in the Holy Tongue." The Gemara explains: "What is the Mishna saying?[96] This is what the Mishna says: It says here: *vdibeir* "and he *shall speak*" and below it says: Mosheh *y'dabeir veha-Elokim ya'anennu bekol* "Moses would speak and God would answer him with a voice," (Exod. 19:19)—just as there it was in Hebrew, here too in Hebrew."[97]

There are superfluous words in this verse: "He shall speak to the People and say to them, etc." It should have stated simply: "The priest shall approach and say: Hear, O Israel, etc." since the verse opens with the words: "When you *draw near* to the battle," obviously then he is speaking *to the People?* However, the verse comes to allude to the above verbal analogy (*gzerah shavah*) *vdibeir*—*y'dabeir.* Rashi only cites the ruling of the Mishna (in Hebrew), without analyzing how it is derived—which is not part of the "plain sense" of the verse—only *alluded* to in the verse (as a verbal analogy).

---

[95]Hebrew. *Sotah* 42a; *Yalkut* 923.

[96]Rashi: How do we derive from these words the Holy Tongue? *Sotah* 42a.

[97]*Sotah* 42a. Cf. Tosafot there s.v. *Hachi Ka'amar* who cite other derivations from the Yerushalmi.

2) The significance of the Hebrew language is that the world was created in that language, as Rashi derives from the verse: *l'zot yikaray isha ki mayish lukachah zot*—"This one will be called woman for she was taken from man," Rashi: It is a play on words. From here we derive that the world was created in the holy language (Gen. 2:3). Also, the Torah was given in Hebrew.[98] Therefore the Sages said: "When a child begins to speak, his father should speak with him in Hebrew and teach him Torah.[99]

Hebrew was the language of the People when it was settled on its Land. It is also called *Yehudit*—"Judean," for it was the language of the *People* settled in *Judea*—in contradistinction to the king's officials who spoke and understood "Aramaic—*Aramit*."[100] Therefore our verse states: "The priest shall approach and speak *to the People*," i.e., in the language of the People—words that will enter the hearts of the common folk—not in the formal royal language *lingua franca*—which was not always Hebrew. It appears that Hebrew is the purest of languages. Therefore the world was created by it and the Torah was given in it.[101]

One might add that therefore Rashi adds the words "to the people" in his caption, not only *v'dibeir*—"he shall speak," even though the Talmud derives from the verbal analogy of *"v'dibeir—y'dabeir"* alone that the priest spoke in Hebrew—without using the words: *el ha'am*—"to the people" at all. Rashi wishes to emphasize "to the People"—the priest should speak in the language *of the People*, not in the language of the royal officials! The language of the Jewish People in its Land is necessarily the Holy Language—Hebrew.

20:3   *Shema Yisrael*—"Hear, O Israel."

RASHI: Even if you have no other merit than that of "Reading the *Shema*," you deserve that He should help you.[102]

COMMENT: The difficulty here is that the two words being in the *singular* are out of context with what precedes them and with what follows them—words couched in the plural: "When *you* (pl.) approach the battle" ... he shall say to *them* ... *you* (pl.) *are* approaching ... against *your* (pl.) *enemies,*

---

[98] *Sanhedrin* 21b; Gen. *Rabbah* 31:8; *Yalkut* 24.

[99] Rashi Deut 11:19; *Sifrei Ekev* 46; *Kiddushin* 29b.

[100] Cf. II Kings 18:26 = Isaiah 36:11.

[101] Cf. *Be'er Mayim Chaim* who goes to an extreme; thus: "There is no *speech only* in Hebrew, for the other languages are *strange unintelligible jargon* and not considered speech."

[102] *Sotah* 42a.

etc.,—all in plural. Therefore Rashi explains that these words (*Shema Yisrael*) are an allusion to the portion of "*Shema*" in *Vaetchanan* (above 6:4–9). In addition to the above, these two words are entirely superfluous and do not add anything to the content of this section. Surely then, they come to allude to the Midrash cited by Rashi.

In *Sotah* 42a we read: "Why particularly *Shema Yisrael?*[103] Rabbi Yochanan in the name of Rabbi Shimon ben Yochai said: The Holy One, blessed be He, said to Israel: "*Even if you haven't fulfilled anything, but the reading of the Shema in the morning and evening, you will not be delivered into their* (the enemies') *hands.*"

One must question: Why did Rashi change the wording of the Gemara? He didn't even save on any words: in God's words to Israel and in Rashi's wording there are twelve words in each version. If so, why did Rashi change?

We venture to suggest that Rashi wished to emphasize the *merit* of reading the *Shema*, without mentioning at all the non-fulfillment of the other commands. Therefore he refrained from writing: "Even if *you did not fulfill* anything but, etc.," which would imply that the Jewish People does *not* fulfill any mitzvah except "Reading the *Shema*," God forbid! Also, the expression "you *deserve* that He should help you" is more positive than: "You will not be *delivered* into their hands."[104] All this demonstrates the great love Rashi had for the Jewish People.

---

[103]Rashi there explains: "Why does the priest begin with this expression?" Namely, as explained above, since the entire context is in the plural, why are these two words in the singular?

[104]Which implies: True, you will not be *delivered* into their hands, but it *is* possible that the enemies will plunder you. Whereas "You *deserve* that He should *help you*" implies that you will not come to *any* harm at their hands.

Ki Teitsei

22:8 *Ki yipol hanofeil*—"If anyone falls from it."

RASHI: (The words mean: If he that is *meant* to fall (*hanofeil*) falls ...) Meaning: This one deserved to fall (and die, on account of some crime he committed), nevertheless his death should not be brought about by you (not having made a parapet); for meritorious things are brought about by a meritorious person, but liabilities are brought about by evil men.[105]

COMMENT: Rashi skillfully abridged the *Baraita* and also explained it. Thus we read in *Shabbat* 32a:

"The school of Rabbi Ishmael taught: 'If anyone falls from it'—this one was destined to fall from the time of Creation[106] since he did not fall yet and the verse calls him 'the one who is falling'—*hanofeil*[107] but (the reason is) because a merit is brought about by one who is meritorious, but a liability only by one who is evil (or: liable).[108]

Rashi added to the Gemara the words: "Nevertheless his death should not be brought about through you," because of the question: If he deserves to fall, why does the owner transgress the command: "You shall not put bloodguilt in your house" if he did not make a parapet—surely, it was *decreed* that he should fall?[109] Rashi replies: Nevertheless his death should *not* be brought about through you, etc.—since in the end a person died through you and a liability was caused by a person who is liable (you).

---

[105] *Sifrei* 229; *Shabbat* 32a; *Yalkut* 930.

[106] Rashi: "As is written: 'Who proclaims the generations from the start' (Isaiah 41:4), namely: The generations are revealed to Him and all their deeds and time of punishment."

[107] Rashi: When the Torah was given, this one did not fall yet, but the verse calls him: "the faller."

[108] Rashi: "By one who is liable—namely, this house-owner who did not fulfill the mitzvah of 'a parapet.'"

[109] One may even argue: On the contrary, he performed a *positive* act (mitzvah) by aiding the Decree to be carried out against the one it was decreed upon!?

This principle (meritorious things are brought about, etc.) is similar to the verse: "It is not good *for the righteous* to punish" (Proverbs 17:26), regarding which the Rabbis said: "He through whom another person *is punished*, is not brought into the Presence of the Almighty. We know this from here: 'It is not good for the righteous to punish'—it is 'not good' means: it is bad, etc.' "[110]

The reason it is bad for the righteous to punish is, because if a person is punished on his account, the deeds of the "righteous" are examined (in Heaven), to determine if he is worthy that so-and-so should be punished because of him. The sages said: "The Holy One, blessed be He, is particular with the righteous to *a hair's breadth*.[111] Therefore, when his deeds are being examined, it is very easy to find the "hair's breadth" of misdemeanor for which the righteous too deserves punishment. Hence, "Punishing—is not good *for the righteous*."

Rashi had to explain: "This one *deserved* to fall, etc." because the wording of the verse, lit. "For the faller *will* fall" implies a certainty that he will fall. Had there been a doubt, the verse would state: "*If* a person should fall from it." We must observe that this exegesis is based on all three words: *Ki yipol hanofeil*—"For the faller will fall," not only on *hanofeil*— "the faller," as is implied in the Gemara—for had that been the case, Rashi would have cited in the caption *only* the word *hanofeil*—"the faller" and no more.[112]

24:19   *Lema'an yevarech-cha—*
"So that (the Lord your God) may bless you."

RASHI: Even though it came into his (the stranger's or orphan's) hand without the owner intending it (since he forgot it in the *field*). The logical inference (*kal vechomer*) is: One who gives charity intentionally will certainly be rewarded (blessed). Hence you may say: If a sela (large coin) fell out of his hand and a poor man found it and supported himself with it—he will surely be blessed on that account.[113]

COMMENT: The question here is: Why does it state *only* in the case of forgetting (and leaving) a sheaf in the field "so that He may bless you, etc.," and not in regard to other precepts—especially so since in the *mitzvot* of *Pe'ah* (a quantity of fruit to be left for the poor) and gleanings—tender

---

[110]*Shabbat* 149b; cf. *Berachot* 7a; *Sanhedrin* 105b in the incident of Rabbi Joshua ben Levi.

[111]I.e., extremely particular for the slightest misdemeanor, cf. *Yevamot* 121b.

[112]See *Klalei Rashi*, p. 50.

[113]*Sifrei* 283; cf. Rashi on Levit. 5:17 end.

grapes *olelot*—to be left for the poor (verses 20–21)—no reward is stated, although they too are charity?

Rashi replies that the Torah wishes here to teach regarding the command of charity, which came about *unintentionally*, i.e., the owner did not have in mind to benefit the poor, since he *forgot* the sheaf, and when he remembered, he wants to go back to take it, but the Torah forbids that to him—nevertheless it says: "So that the Lord your God may bless you." "Hence, you may say: If a sela fell out of his hand, etc."—since also the poor man found the sela *immediately* when it fell, before the owner discovered his loss, and he did not have in mind to benefit the poor man—exactly like the forgotten sheaf. This is the major inference, whereas the statement: "All the more so (*kal vechomer*) one who gives charity intentionally, etc." is an additional logical inference.

25:14-15   *Lo yihyeh lecha*—"You shall not have."

RASHI: If you did so (had false weights) you will have nothing.[114]

Even shlemah vatzedek yihyeh lach—
"A perfect and honest (just) weight shall you have."

RASHI: If you did so (had just weights and measures), you will have a lot (of money).[115]

COMMENT: It would appear that Rashi (and the *Sifrei*) derive from the superfluous expressions: "You shall not have" and "You shall have" since these two phrases are written twice in verses 13–15. It would have sufficed to write: "There shall not be in your bag different weights and in your house diverse measures—big and small. Perfect and just weights; perfect and just measures shall you have," and no more. Therefore we interpret one "You shall not have" *not* in reference to "a weight and a weight; a measure and a measure," but in an *absolute* manner: "You shall have nothing." Similarly, one "You shall have" is absolute: "You shall have a lot."

Now, although one could argue that these phrases are *not* superfluous at all, for: "The Torah spoke in the style (lit. language) of people"[116]—

---

[114]You will become poor, deprived of your property just as you deprived others of their money by having false weights.

[115]*Sifrei* 294.

[116]Who use repetitive language and superfluous words, cf. *Berachot* 31b—many references for this principle there.

nevertheless, since these are highly *ethical* midrashim, Rashi saw fit to derive them from the verses.[117]

25:18   *Asher karcha baderech*—"Who happened upon you on the way."

RASHI: The word *karcha* is an expression of *mikreh*—"a sudden happening" (i.e., he came upon you by surprise). Another explanation: It is an expression of *keri* and *tum'ah*—"nocturnal emission (of semen) and uncleanness," i.e., Amalek polluted them with pederasty (sexual relations of male with male). Another explanation: It is an expression of *kor vechom*—"cold and heat," i.e., Amalek made you cold and lukewarm from your (previous) boiling state. For all the nations were afraid to wage war against you, and Amalek came and began (to wage war against you and thereby) showed a way for others (to battle with you). This may be compared to a boiling-hot bath, into which no living creature could go down. Then a good-for-nothing (or: scoundrel) came and jumped into it. Even though he scalded himself, he made it appear cold to others![118]

Vayzanev becha*—"And he cut down."

RASHI: The word *vayzanev* (from the word *zanav*—"tail") means: a blow to the *tail* (which hangs down), namely: Amalek cut off the membra (penis) and threw them up (provocatively) toward Heaven (God).[119]

Kol hanecheshalim acharecha*—"All the stragglers in your rear."

RASHI: *Necheshalim* means "those who were weakened on account of their sins[120] whom the Cloud had expelled (from the protection it provided Israel)."[121]

COMMENT: We need to explain:

---

[117]Cf. further our statement in *Be'ur Setumot Be-Rashi*, Part II, Introduction, p. ix, parag 3.
[118]Comp. *Sifrei* 196; *Tanchuma, Ki Teizei* 9.
[119]The First Edition of Rashi (1474–75) reads: "He would cut the penis and throw it."
[120]Understanding *necheshalim* as *nechelashim* —"weakened," like *cesev* for *ceves.*
[121]*Tanchuma, Ki Teizei* 10; *Pesikta Rabbati, Zachor; Yalkut* 938.

1) Why the need for three interpretations of the word *karcha*—what does each add not contained in the others?

2) What is the meaning of: "He cut off the membra and threw them up toward Heaven"; if it means literally, why did Amalek not kill the stragglers, only throw up their membra? If it doesn't mean literally, what does this despicable act symbolize?

3) Rashi explains *Kol hanecheshalim acharecha*, i.e., "those weakened on account of their sins, etc." Why not simply: weakened by the hardships of the journey?

The explanation is:

1) The difficulty with the first explanation is the verse: "Amalek *came* and *battled* Israel in Refidim" (Exod. 17:8) implies that it was *not* a chance encounter; rather Amalek came deliberately to provoke Israel. Rashi himself explains that the war with Amalek came as a punishment for Israel's complaint: "Is the Lord in our midst or is He not?" (Exod. 17:7).

Therefore Rashi cites a second explanation from the *Tanchuma*: "Rabbi Judah says *karcha* means "he defiled you." The difficulty with this explanation is that the verse in Exodus states explicitly "He *battled* Israel." Our verse too states: "He *cut off* (the stragglers) among you"—which is a matter of war—what is the connection between *warfare* and *karcha* if that means "he *defiled* you?"

Therefore, Rashi cites a third explanation: "An expression of cold and heat, etc." But this explanation *alone* is not enough, for according to this it should have stated in the Hifil (causative) form: *hikrecha*, i.e., "he cooled you off for others," as is evident from the parable Rashi cites, whereas *karcha* in the Kal form is *not* causative.

2) The meaning of "He cut the membra and threw them up, etc." is that Amalek denied the Covenant between the Lord and Israel, and also the election of Israel.[122] This is implied in *Tanchuma*'s statement: "What did the Amalekites do? They cut off the membra of the Israelites and threw them up to Heaven, and said: 'This is what You *chose*, take what You chose!'" "This is what is meant by what is written: "their disgrace with which they have disgraced *You*" (Psalms 79:12; *Tanchuma, Ki Teitsei* 10). This is a challenge to God; therefore, our verse ends with the words: "and he (Amalek) did not fear God" on which Rashi comments: "Amalek did not fear God, to refrain from harming you."

---

[122]As God said to Abraham: "You shall circumcise the flesh of your foreskin and that shall be the sign of the covenant between Me and you"—(Gen. 17:11).

3) The rabbis (and Rashi) interpret *necheshalim* like *nechelashim*—a "metathesis" (change of the place of letters within a word), like: *cesev—ceves*; *salmah—simlah*; *naakah—anakah*; *'alvah—'olah* and the like.[123] Rashi's statement: "Weakened on account of their sins, for the Cloud expelled them" is an abridgment of the *Tanchuma* and *Sifrei*, thus:

Tanchuma: The Rabbis say the stragglers were the tribe of Dan, whom the Cloud ejected. They were all idol worshippers, as is said: "and you were tired and weary and he did not fear God."[124] *Sifrei* 296 reads:

"This teaches that Amalek killed only people who tore themselves away from the ways of the Omnipresent and were expelled from under the wings of the Cloud."

The reason Rashi did not explain simply: weakened by the hardships of the journey, is because if so, *all* Israelites were equally tired and weary, not only: "the stragglers *in your rear*"—at the end of the Camp of Israel? Therefore Rashi explains: "the stragglers in your rear as a *spiritual* weakness, on account of their sins, etc."—whereas "tired and weary" is to be understood literally.

The above explanation of the three interpretations of the word *karcha* is according to the plain sense. However, according to "the wine of the Torah,"[125] we venture to suggest that with the three interpretations of the word *karcha* Rashi alludes to three types of disbelief (or "denial"—*kefirah*) that Amalek wished to instill in Israel. They are:

a) "An expression of chance," namely: The world and its events are all a matter of chance. There is, God forbid, no Master of the Universe and no Guide. As it were: "God abandoned the Earth" (Ezekiel 8:12, 9:9). He does not concern Himself with the world and its creatures. This is the very opposite of what we say in our morning prayers: "He who renews by His goodness, every day, *always* the works of Creation."[126] If everything is *hap-*

---

[123]See a long list of such interchanges in *Torah Temimah* to our verse.

[124]Accordingly the tribe of Dan "did not fear God." However, Rashi holds that this phrase refers to Amalek, not Israel. In *Sifrei* 296 we read: "You were tired and weary—Israel"; "and he did not fear God—Amalek," exactly like Rashi, not *Tanchuma*. So also Targum Jonathan. It is difficult to refer "and he *did not fear God*" to Israel, for if so, God would not avenge Himself so zealously of Amalek (thereby saving Israel), since Israel would have been deserving of punishment for not fearing God. Moreover, if so, it should have said: "and *you did not fear* God," just like: "and *you* were tired, etc." Cf., however, Tosafot *Kiddushin* 33b, s.v. *v'aima*.

[125]That is what the *Shalah* calls Rashi's commentary on the Torah—the inner meanings.

[126]Namely, not only once a day, but *always*—every single moment God renews Creation.

penstance, God forbid, then there is no reward, or punishment—and there is no good reason to fulfill the Torah and its commandments. Is there a greater apostasy (*kefirah*) than this?! Therefore Rashi brings this as the *first* interpretation, because it is the greatest of disbeliefs.

b) "An expression of nocturnal emission and uncleanness, i.e., Amalek polluted them with *pederasty* (*mishkav zachur*—"male with male relations")," meaning: Amalek wished to put to naught God's plan for the world! How so? The first commandment in the Torah is: "Be fruitful and multiply" (Gen. 1:28) and the prophet proclaims: "He did not create it for emptiness; He fashioned it to be inhabited" (Isaiah 45:18), i.e., it is a great mitzvah to take a wife and beget children and settle the world. Comes along Amalek and argues that there is no need for all this; one could engage in *pederasty,* which does *not* bring children into the world, and for which sin the Torah metes out the *most severe* of all punishments—death by stoning.[127] Is this not a disbelief that boasts: "The plan of the Lord will *not* prevail"—God forbid![128]

c) A third type of disbelief—denial Amalek wished to instill within the Jewish People is "an expression of *cold* and heat," namely: If he could not tear the Jew away from Torah and *mitzvot* at *any* cost, because: "They are our life and length of days, etc."[129] then at least let us try and instill a *coldness* in the study of Torah and fulfillment of commands, to cool them off from their boiling state—to turn Torah study and performance of *mitzvot* into acts done with a *coolness,* without enthusiasm or warmth, as a routine or chore.[130]

This too, is the complete antithesis of what is required of us by the Torah: "To love the Lord your God, to walk in all His ways and *to cleave* to Him" (Deut. 11:22), which we explain to mean to cleave to His ways: "Just as He is merciful, you too be merciful; just as He practices lovingkindness, you too practice it" (Rashi Deut. 11:22). It is written: "For the Lord your God is a consuming *fire*" (Deut. 4:24), which, from the point of view of the requirement to *cleave* to His ways, must mean that one has to fulfill the Torah and *mitzvot* with enthusiasm and heat—as if they were *fire.* Amalek came and attempted to instill a *coldness*—denial into the fulfillment of Torah and *Mitzvot.* All these types of denial—apostasy Amalek attempted

---

[127]See *Sanhedrin* 54a—Mishna and the discussion in Gemara there, pp. a–b.
[128]In direct opposition to the statement in Proverbs 19:21 "Many designs [or: plans] are in a man's mind, but the plan of the Lord *it alone* will prevail."
[129]As we say in the Maariv service every night.
[130]One is reminded of the Chasidic saying: "Between coolness and disbelief—denial (*kefirah*), the difference is very tenuous," i.e., coolness leads to disbelief.

to instill into the life of the Jewish People. No wonder the Torah commanded: "You shall blot out the memory of Amalek[131] from under heaven"
(verse 19), for: "I (= God) and he cannot reside in the world together."[132]

---

[131]Cf. Rashi to what extent: "Both man and woman; infant and suckling; ox and
sheep"—comp. I. Samuel 15:3 stating how the Amalekites were to be destroyed.
[132]*Arachin* 15b.

Ki Tavo

26:16   *Veshamarta ve'asita otam—*
"You shall keep them and do them. . . ."

RASHI: A voice from Heaven (*bat kol*) blesses him (the one who brought the first fruits) saying: "You have brought the first fruits today, you should have the privilege to bring them also next year!"[133]

COMMENT: Two questions may be asked:

1) Why does Rashi not explain according to the plain sense: "The Lord commands you to perform the statutes ... therefore, you shall keep and do them," as an exhortation: Take heed to keep them and do them with all your heart and soul! From where did Rashi derive that here is expressed a *blessing* of a "Voice from Heaven"?

2) "You brought the first fruits today, etc."—actually Rashi should have explained that the "blessing" refers to the tithes, which *are* spoken of in the previous verses, not to first fruits, which are mentioned in the section *before* the section on tithes?
The explanation is as follows:

1) Rashi was bothered with this expression, for two reasons:
   a) If "You shall keep them and do them" is a command or exhortation it is superfluous, as it just stated (in this verse): ("This day the Lord your God) *commands* you (*metzavecha*) to do these statutes and laws,"[134] why then repeat: "You shall keep and do?" Hence it must be a blessing.
   b) The words *veshamarta ve'asita* which are grammatically "past tense turned future" by aid of the letter *vav* that turns the past into future

---

[133] *Tanchuma, Ki Tavo* 1.
[134] And as Rashi points out in Levit. 6:2: "The expression *tzav*—'command' is nothing but an exhortation, immediately and for future generations."

287

(the "vav conversive"—*vav' hahipuch*) imply that there is a promise that you will *certainly* keep and do the laws and statutes. But surely there *is* free will; how then can one *promise* the performance of commandments? Hence, they are not a promise but a blessing.

2) The section: "When you finish tithing all the tithes, etc." (verses 12–15) deals with "the time for removing (the tithes from the house—*bi'ur*) and confession on the eve of Passover of the fourth year ... *and whoever delays his tithes* until then, Scripture required him to remove them from the house."[135] Namely, this is not the *desirable* situation, which is to separate tithes and give them *each year* to whomever they belong—and *not* wait till the fourth year! Hence the Torah describes here an *accidental* case; "whoever *delayed* his tithes Scripture required him to remove them" in the fourth year.

It does not seem appropriate that "a voice from Heaven" would confer a *blessing* on someone who performed an "accidental" act—although under the circumstances, he did perform a mitzvah. However, bringing the first fruits to the Sanctuary is a *desirable* act, and is an expression of gratitude to God.[136] For such an act it is appropriate to confer a blessing.

28:64   *Ve'avadta sham elohim acheirim—*
"There you will serve other gods."

RASHI: As the Targum renders it[137] not actual idol-worship, rather they will have to pay tribute (taxes) and poll taxes (head tax) to the priests of the idols.

COMMENT: We must understand:

1) Surely Rashi's interpretation: "They will pay tribute and poll taxes to the *priests* of the idols" is *not* as the Targum Onkelos who renders: "You will *serve* there *peoples* that worship idols." Paying tribute and poll taxes is *not service* to the peoples themselves. Why then does Rashi say "As the Targum renders"?

---

[135]Rashi above, verse 12.

[136]See Rashi above, verse 3: "and say to Him—that you are not ungrateful."

[137]I.e., "You will serve *peoples* that worship idols." The First Printing of Rashi (1474–75) and the Zamora printing leave out the word *ketargumo*—"as the Targum renders."

2) Why doesn't Rashi explain simply that in Exile the Jewish People will *actually* worship idols—which is the plain sense of these words? One may explain:

1) Because of this question one must accept the reading of the First Printing of Rashi (1474-75), which deletes the word *ketargumo*—"as the Targum renders," for Rashi's explanation does not really agree with that of Onkelos.[138]

2) Rashi cannot explain according to plain sense that in exile Israel will worship idols, because Rashi himself explained at the end of *Behar*: "You shall not make idols for yourselves"—this refers to the one who sells himself to a gentile that he should not say: "Since my master worships idols, I will do like him, etc."[139] Accordingly, even a slave, who is *completely* in his master's power and is dependent upon him for sustenance and everything else—is not allowed to worship idols. All the more so, one who is *not* a slave, but is in exile among the nations—surely then the Almighty would not be happy were he to worship idols! How is it possible that the Torah should tell each individual Jew (namely the *entire* nation): "The Lord will scatter you among all the nations... and there you will worship other gods, etc." This would imply, God forbid: "It serves you right, for you did not listen to the Voice of the Lord." Would God really be happy were we to worship others besides Him—Heaven forfend?![140]

And besides all the above, there is freedom of the will (to worship idols or not). It would not be to the honor of God, or of the Jewish People, to state categorically that they *will* necessarily worship idols in exile, God forbid! Therefore Rashi explains in a manner that preserve the honor of God and the honor of the Jewish People.

---

[138]Unless we assume that Rashi had a version of Onkelos that differed from ours, which coincided with his explanation. For that we have no proof. Therefore it is preferable to delete the word *ketargumo*—"as the Targum renders."

[139]Rashi on Levit. 26:1. Cf. our commentary at length in *Be'ur Setumot Be-Rashi*, Part II, pp. 193–95.

[140]Surely the prophet cried out in the name of the Lord: "It shall not be! As for what you say, 'we will be like the nations... to worship wood and stone,' as I live—says the Lord God [I swear that] I will rule over you with a stong hand and with an outstretched arm and with outpoured wrath!"—Ezekiel 20:32-33.

Nitzavim

30:3   *V'shav Hashem Eloke'cha et sh'vutcha*—
"Then the Lord your God will bring back your captivity."

RASHI: It ought to have been written (in the *causative* form) *v'heishiv et sh'vutcha*—"He will (cause to) return your captivity."[141] Our Rabbis learnt from this that—if one can say so of God—that the *Shechinah* (Divine Presence) dwells *with* Israel in the misery of their Exile, and when they will be redeemed (i.e., when God speaks of their redemption in the Torah) He *caused* "Redemption" to be written of Himself—that He will return (from exile) with them.[142]

It may be said further (to explain the strange form *v'shav ... et*—"He will return ...")—that the day of gathering in the exiles is so great and so difficult that it is as though He Himself has to take hold with His very Hands (dragging) each individual from his place (so that God Himself returns with the exile), as is stated: "And you will be gathered one by one, Children of Israel" (Isaiah 27:12). And also in connection with the gathering of the exiles of other nations we find the same expression, e.g., *v'shavti sh'vut Moav*—lit. "I (God) will return (with) the captivity of Moav" (Jeremiah 48:47) *sh'vut B'nei 'amon*—"the captivity of the Children of Amon."[143]

COMMENT: Rashi's comment raises numerous questions:

1) Since Rashi is dealing with the word *v'shav*—"He will return" only, he should have cited in his caption *only* the word *v'shav* and remarked "It should have been written *heyshiv* (He will *cause* to return), our Rabbis learnt

---

[141]The verb *v'shav*—"He will return," in the "Kal" form, not being "causative," implies that He Himself will return from captivity!

[142]*Sifrei* on Numbers 35:34; *Megillah* 29a.

[143]In the First Printing the reading is *v'shavti et sh'vut b'nai Amon*, but there is no such verse in the Bible, only: *v'shavti sh'vut Moav*, as in our text of Rashi. In *Sifrei*, *Mas'ei* 161 we read: "And when they return, the *Shechinah* will be with them, for it is stated: "The Lord your God will return with your captivity, etc.'"

from this, etc." Why does he copy also the words: "The Lord your God your captivity"?

2) Why does he delete in his comment the words "the Lord your God," not writing: "He should have written *the Lord your God* will cause to return, etc."?

3) Commenting on the words "from the midst of a thorn-bush" Rashi writes: "Not a different tree, because of: 'I am with him in his misery?' " (Rashi to Exod. 3:2, cf. Psalms 91:15). If so, why does Rashi write that we learn this (that the *Shechinah* is with Israel in their misery in exile) from *here*. Besides, "I (God) am with him in his misery" is an explicit verse in Psalm 91:15, so why did the Rabbis have to *deduce* the idea from our verse?

4) What is Rashi emphasizing with the wording: "He *caused* 'Redemption' *to be written* of Himself." Why didn't he write simply: "and when they will be redeemed, He will return with them"?

5) Why does Rashi introduce the second explanation with: "It may be said further" rather than the usual: "Another explanation"?

6) Why does he write: "the *day* of the gathering in the exiles is so great and so difficult, etc."? Surely the difficulty is in the *ingathering* of the exiles itself, not in the *day*? Moreover, for God who created heaven and earth and all their hosts, the gathering-in of the exiles is not a *great and difficult* accomplishment?

7) Why does Rashi add: "And also in connection with the gathering of the exiles of other nations, we find the same expression"—what does this add to the explanation?

8) Why was there a need for *two* explanations of the verse?

We may explain as follows:

1-2) Rashi was bothered by two questions here:
   a) It should have written *v'heyshiv*—in a causative form (*hif'il*) and a "transitive" verb, since there is a "direct object" *et sh'vutcha*, i.e., "He will cause your captivity to return"—not as stated in the Kal formation and "intransitive" verb *v'shav*, whose action remains with the doer, i.e., "He Himself will return."
   b) In verse 2 it states: "You will return to the Lord your God, hence it is clear that *v'shav* in this verse refers to "the Lord your God."

Therefore Rashi states: "He should have stated (only): He will return your captivity," and *not* repeat "the Lord your God" (already in verse 2)? Rashi replies: "Our Rabbis learnt from this, etc." Accordingly there *is* a need to write the *intransitive* form, *v'shav*—"He Himself will return" *and* to repeat "the Lord your God."

3) From the verse: "I (God) am with him in his misery" we may learn that God commiserates with the Jewish People, as stated: "In all their troubles, He is troubled" (Isaiah 63:9). (See Ibn Ezra and Radak for the meanings of the "written" and "read" *ketiv, kri* forms.) But that the *Shechinah Itself* dwells, as it were, together with Israel in the misery of their exile can be derived *only* from here."

4) The difficulty Rashi had was: "If God Himself, as it were, was in exile together with Israel, He would be bound by the rule: "A prisoner cannot release himself from prison[144]—how then will He redeem Himself with Israel? Therefore Rashi continues: "And when they will be redeemed, he *caused* "Redemption" *to be written* of Himself," namely: Even *before* they (God and Israel) go into exile, He *causes to be written a condition* that the nations[145] will have no power over Him at the time of Redemption, and there will be no need for Him to redeem Himself—as it were.

5) In the second explanation Rashi wrote: "One may further say" (and not the usual "Another explanation") to point out that this is his own interpretation, not the Rabbis'. Also, because this explanation does not *negate* the first explanation, but adds to it another aspect of the redemption: besides "He caused Redemption to be written of Himself," etc., also: "The day of the ingathering of the exiles is so great, etc."

6) By writing: "The *day* of the ingathering of exiles, etc." Rashi alluded to the controversy between R. Eliezer and R. Joshua regarding the question whether Israel will be redeemed *only* if they repent or even without repentance. In the opinion of Rabbi Joshua, when the time of redemption arrives, they will be redeemed even if they do not repent.[146] Meaning: The actual ingathering of exiles is *not* difficult for God to accomplish, but the "day" of the ingathering, i.e., that when the *day* comes they will be re-

---

[144]*Berachot* 5b; *Nedarim* 7b.
[145]And their guardian angels above.
[146]See the controversy at great length in *Sanhedrin* 97b–98b. Cf. Rambam, *Hilchot Teshuvah*, Chap. 7:8 who ruled that redemption will come only *with* repentance, i.e. at the end they *will* repent.

deemed even *without* repentance, that is a great and difficult thing, for surely the "Attribute of Judgment" will prosecute *against* it!

7) Since Rashi wrote: "The day of ingathering the exiles, etc.," it is not necessarily tied to the ingathering of the Jewish exiles, but a general phenomenon. If so, why does the verse state: "The Lord *your God* will return *your captivity*"? Rashi replies that in regard to Israel there is the matter of "And you will be gathered *one by one*, etc.," i.e., the day of ingathering the exiles is *great* and *difficult*, etc. Also regarding Israel there is the aspect of "the *Lord* your God will return"—He Himself will return together with them. "Also in connection with the gathering of the exiles of other nations we find this expression"—i.e., that God *Himself* will return them: "I will return the captivity of Moav."

8. The problem with the first explanation is that "the *Shechinah* dwells with Israel in the misery of their exile" applies mainly to the time of *exile*. Why does the Torah write this in reference to their *redemption*? Therefore Rashi offers the second explanation: "It may be further said"—the verse teaches an aspect that relates to the nature of *redemption*.

The difficulty with the second explanation is: The main point alluded to by: "the Lord God will return, etc." is in relation to *Israel*, as stated further "He will bring you together again, etc.," not the other nations—since one cannot say about them that the *Shechinah*, as it were, dwells with *them* in exile! Therefore Rashi cites as the *first* explanation that the main allusion is "the *Shechinah* dwells with *Israel* in their exile." However, there is yet another allusion regarding the nature of the redemption, which is a general aspect relating also to other nations.[147]

---

[147]Cf. further illuminating points in Rashi: *Be'urim le-Ferush Rashi al ha-Torah*, Part II, pp. 411–13.

Vayeilech

31:12 *Ha-anashim, hanashim vehataf—*
"The men, the women, and the small children."

RASHI: The men—to learn; the women—to listen (to the Torah); and the small children—why did they come? (Since they are not capable of learning or even listening?) To give a reward to those who bring them.[148]

COMMENT: Question: If the small children are incapable of learning or listening, why does one get a reward for bringing them?

One can explain this according to the Mishna: "The Holy One, blessed be He, wished to *privilege* Israel,[149] therefore He gave them a lot of Torah and *mitzvot*, etc.,"[150] namely: The Almighty *commanded* to bring the small children, even though they do *not* understand, and if one fulfills the decree of the King (God) one receives a reward.

One may further explain: "To give a reward to those who bring them"—a reward for the parents who privilege their small children with *learning* the words of the Torah, which are thereby *impressed* on the minds and souls of the young—even though they do not as yet understand them. Thus it is related about Rabbi Joshua ben Chanania: "Once the Sages of Israel came in to visit R. Dosa ben Horkinas. When he saw Rabbi Joshua he said "I remember his mother bringing his crib to the synagogue, *in order that his ears should cling to the words of Torah.*"[151]

---

[148]*Chagigah* 3a. Cf. also Tosafot there s.v. *nashim lishmo'a*—"The Yerushalmi states that this exegesis opposes Ben Azzai's view (in *Sotah* 20) that a person is *obligated* to teach his daughter Torah." Therefore they came only "to listen," but not to study.
[149]Cf. *Mishnayot Mevuarot* by P. Kehati at *Makkot*, Chap. 3, *Mishna* 16.
[150]*Makkot* 3:16; cf. Maimonides' commentary to this Mishna.
[151]Yerushalmi; *Yevamot*, end of chapter 1. Cf. Rashi on *Avot* 2:8: "Joshua ben Chanania—happy is the one who gave birth to him"—"because he was fluent in all learning ... But I heard, because his mother caused him to become wise, for all the days that she was pregnant with him, she would *visit every day all the study halls of the city* and say to them: "I beg you, pray that this fetus may become wise; therefore:

295

Happy is she who bore him." The above can be further supported by the Chasidic aphorism: "Chasidism (Chasidic lore) is heard by the soul." Cf. the booklet "Hayom yom" for 24 Adar I, which the "middle" second Lubavitcher Rebbe said to R. Hillel Paritcher. This also applies to Torah in general, as per the evidence of R. Dosa ben Horkinas.

Ha'azinu

32:17 *Lo elohah*—"Non-gods."

RASHI: As the Targum renders: They sacrifice to devils/demons "in which there is no use," for if there had been some use in them (as e.g., the sun, moon, stars), the provocation to anger (*kinah*) would not be double, i.e., 1) the act of idol-worship itself, 2) that they are worshipped even though they are useless.

Chadashim mikarov ba-u—"New ones, who came but lately."

RASHI: Even the nations were not used to them. If a gentile saw them, he would say: "This is a Jewish idol."

Lo se'arum avoteichem—"Whom your fathers did not dread."

RASHI: Whom your fathers did not fear; (lit. it means) their hair (*se'ar*) did not stand up because of them—it is the nature of a person's hair to stand up out of fear. So it (*se'arum*) is explained in *Sifrei*. One can also explain *se'arum* as a similar expression to: "And *se'irim* will dance there" (Isaiah 13:21); *se'irim* are demons,[152] namely: Your fathers never made these demons (satyrs).[153]

COMMENT: The problem here is it first states that the demons are "non-gods," but immediately afterwards the verse calls them "gods" (they know not)? Therefore Rashi comments: "As the Targum renders—in which there is no use"—they have no ability or power. However, this implies that if there

---

[152]Satyrs, cf. Rashi on Levit. 17:7.
[153]*Sifrei* 318; *Yalkut* 945; cf. Exod. 7:9 and *Chizkuni* thereto: *tzroch* is an expression of ability and power.

was some use (= ability) in them, there would be no provocation? But verse 16 states: "They provoked "incensed" (*yakniuhu*) Him with strange things"— without distinguishing between those that have a use and those that have no use? Therefore Rashi explains: "Had there been some use in them, the provocation to anger would not be *double*, etc."

Thus we read in the *Sifrei*: "Had they worshipped the sun, the moon, the stars and planets and to (other) things that the world has a *need* of (*tzorech*) or benefit from—the provocation to anger would not have been double. But they worship things that do not benefit the world, but harm them (the inhabitants)." According to the *Sifrei* "non-gods" *Lo elohah* means: there is no *need* or *use* for them in the world.

You may ask: Why is there a need for two explanations of *se'arum*? Answer: According to the *Sifrei* there is a difficulty: Since the verse describes them as "gods they knew not, new ones who came but lately" then surely they did not fear them, because they were *new* and they did not yet have any experience of them—and it goes without saying that they did not *dread* them (*Lo se'arum*)? Therefore Rashi gives as a second explanation *se'arum* is similar to *se'irim*—"demons." According to this interpretation *lo se'arum avoteichem* is an explanation of "New ones, who came lately," i.e., the demons (satyrs) whom they worship are so "new" that even your fathers did not make such demons—they are only from *this* generation.

But according to the second explanation it should have stated *lo s'eerum* (similar to *se'ir*—"demons") or *lo his'eerum*, or *lo si'arum*? Therefore Rashi cites the *Sifrei* that it is an expression of fear.[154] The first explanation, however, is closer to the plain sense, because it does not change the vocalization of the word *se'arum*.

32:46 *Simu levavchem*—
"Take to heart (or: "pay close attention," lit. "set your hearts")."

RASHI: It is necessary that a man's eyes, heart, and ears should all be attentively directed to the words of the Torah, and thus it is stated: "Son of man, see with your eyes, and hear with your ears and set your heart (on all that I shall show you" ... i.e., the plan of the Temple—Ezekiel 40:4). We can infer from this: If in the case of the model of the Temple, which is seen with one's eyes (Ezekiel's), and measured with a rod, it was necessary that a man's (Ezekiel's) eyes, ears, and heart be attentive (to its details)—then

---

[154]Cf. Jeremiah 2:12: "Be appalled O heavens, at this; be *horrified*, utterly dazed!" *sa'aru meod*—i.e., *to tremble out of fear*. Also: Ezekiel 27:37: *u-malcheihem sa'aru sa'ar*— "Their kings shook with trembling."

to understand the words of the Torah, which are like mountains suspended on a hair (i.e., many laws are derived from a single word in the Torah)—all the more so is close attention necessary![155]

COMMENT: Question: Eyes and ears are not mentioned in our verse, only "your hearts"—why does Rashi add eyes and ears?

One may explain as follows: The statement in this verse "Set your hearts ... to be careful to *perform* all the words of this Torah" is the main goal, namely: to awaken the *heart* to the observance of the Torah. How does one arrive at an awakening of the heart? This is explained in Ezekiel: "See with your eyes, and hear with your ears (and *then*) set your heart, etc"—by seeing with the eyes and hearing with one's ears, one arrives at setting (i.e., attention) of the heart.

The above exegesis is an example of the principles: (lit.) "His friend tells about him" (Job 36:33); also: "The words of the Torah are poor in their (own) place, but rich in another place,"[156] namely: "The obscure can learn from the explicit statement,"[157] or: "this one shuts, but the other one opens up."[158] Whatever is obscure in one verse was stated explicitly in Ezekiel. In this manner it is clear that we can derive a logical inference (*kal vachomer*)!

This may be compared to R. Yochanan ben Zakkai's statement regarding his disciple R. Elazar ben Arach's reply to the master's question: "Which is the best way (in life) that a person should cleave to?," to which R. Elazar replied: "A good heart." R. Yochana ben Zakkai responded to this answer: "I agree (approve) with the words of Elazer ben Arach more than with *your* replies (of the other disciples), for in *his* words, all yours are (already) included."[159] Hence the heart is the main part, and all the others—including the eyes and ears are *means* by which to arrive at the goal (the heart).[160]

---

[155]Cf. Mishna *Chagigah* 10a: "The laws of the Sabbath, Festivals, sacrifices, and misappropriation of Temple property (*me'ilot*) are like mountains suspended by a hair, for there are few verses regarding all those, but numerous laws"; *Sifrei* 335.
[156]Yerushalmi, *Rosh Hashana* 3:8 cited by Tosafot *Kareitot* 14a s.v. *ela*.
[157]Rashi on Gen. 7:3.
[158]Rashi Numbers 21:21: "These verses need each other. This one shuts, but this one opens up."
[159]*Avot* 2:10.
[160]See *Yalkut* 947. The Rabbis emphasized greatly the virtue of *all* of the organs of the body participating in the study of the Torah. Cf. the numerous statements to that effect in *Eruvin* 54a.

Vezot Hab-rachah

33:1 *V'zot hab'racha . . . lifnei moto—*
"This is the blessing . . . before he died.

RASHI: Very close to his death, "for if not now—when?"[161]

COMMENT: You may ask: Why *did* Moses wait till "very close to his death" before blessing Israel? If they *were* worthy to be blessed, he should have blessed them long before his death, so that they should benefit from his blessing for as long as possible. If they were *not* worthy of a blessing, God forbid, he should not have blessed them even before his death?

A number of Rashi commentators grappled with this question and suggested a variety of explanations.[162] One commentator writes: "Because at that time (right before his death) a person sees what he couldn't see during his entire lifetime; also his blessings are more likely to be fulfilled at that time."[163]

---

[161] *Sifrei* 342. The First Printing of Rashi has the following addition: "It is the way of the righteous to leave as a will their blessing at the time of their dying, as Isaac said: "that I may bless you before the Lord before I die"" (Gen. 27:6). This is the plain sense. But the Midrash states: "The Angel of Death came to take away his soul, but Moses delayed him and first blessed them—before the Angel of Death." The version of the Alkabats and Zamora printing is clearer, thus: "the Midrash states: The Angel of Death came to take away his soul, but Moses delayed him. He first blessed them *before him*—this is the meaning of "before he died," i.e. *"before the Angel of Death who was putting him to death."* Cf. *Tanchuma Berachah* 3, but there it states: "Moses said to him (to the Angel of Death): Go away, for I wish to praise God—"I shall *not* die, but live and relate the deeds of the Lord" (Psalms 118:17). *Tanchuma* does not mention that Moses delayed the Angel of Death *in order* to bless Israel. But the exegesis: "before he died—before the Angel of Death" does appear in *Tanchuma.*

[162] Cf. e.g., *Be'er Mayim Chaim; Gur Aryeh; Maharik* (cited by C. D. Chavel in his *Peirushei Rashi al ha-Torah*); *Maskil LeDavid.*

[163] *Be'er Mayim Chaim.*

Another writes: "Because if they would bless them during their lifetime, people might think that he blesses him because he needs him, or that he gave one a greater blessing than another."[164] One states the reason is because at the time of death, their souls cleave more.[165] However, this reason is rather weak when applied to Moses[166]—unless we say that Moses did so (blessed them right before his death) to allude to other righteous people that they should do likewise.[167]

All of the above are good reasons, especially the educational consideration of the Maharal. We may add another reason: Moses waited till close to his dying before he blessed the tribes, because throughout his lifetime he observed the nature and development of each tribe, so that he may know what kind of blessing is most appropriate for each tribe, commensurate with its nature and its material and spiritual state. This he could know only "right before his death"—"for if not now when?"[168]

33.2   *Ve-atah*—"And approached (or: came)."

RASHI: To Israel.

Meyriv'vot kodesh—"From the holy myriads."

RASHI: And with Him were a *part* of the myriads of the holy angels, and not all of them, and not (even) most of them; not as is the way of a human being who displays all his riches and glory on the day of his wedding.[169]

---

[164]This reason is also because he needs him more than he needs the other— which does not apply "very close to his death."

[165]"Cleave more," i.e., they cleave more to the *Shechinah* (P. D.) and they see more the future events.

[166]Since "the *Shechinah* always spoke from his throat" (*Zohar, Parshat Pinchas* 232) and regarding Moses it was said: "Happy is he, born of woman, (a human) who is assured that whenever he wished he could speak with the *Shechinah*" (Rashi at Numbers 9:7).

[167]*Maharik*, c.f., *Be'er Mayim Chaim* above.

[168]I.e., after his death he could no longer observe the nature of each tribe.

[169]See *Sifrei* 343.

Eishdat—"A Law of fire."

RASHI: The law (Torah), which had been written before Him long ago in black fire upon white fire. Meaning: He gave to them (*lamo*) the writing of His right hand upon the Tablets.[170] Another explanation of Eishdat: as the Targum renders: "A law given to us from the fire."[171]

COMMENT: Several questions must be answered:

1) What did Rashi accomplish by adding the word "to Israel" after "he approached/came"—what error did he obviate?

2) Why did he add the words: "And with Him were a part of the (holy) angels," which are *not* in the verse?

3) How does the "day of his wedding" come in here?

4) What need is there for two explanations of "*Eishdat*—a Law of fire"?

The explanation is:

1) By adding "To Israel" Rashi accomplished that we should not err in understanding *Meyriv'vot Kodesh* as a name of a place[172] just as: "He came from Sinai and shone from Seir"—rather the meaning is: "He came to Israel."

2) Rashi adds the word *ve'imo*—"And with Him" so that we should not take *Ve-atah Meyriv'vot Kodesh* as *one* unit, meaning: God came to Israel from the midst of myriads of holy (angels), i.e., at first the *Shechinah* dwelt *only* among the myriads of holy angels, but when He came to give the Torah to Israel, He so-to-speak *tore Himself away* from them and came to Israel. This would diminish Israel's honor, for it would mean that God made His *Shechinah* reside in Israel only *temporarily*—during the giving of the Torah and no more! Whereas in truth *Israel* are of primary importance, not the angels—who are only servants to God and Israel, as the Rabbis state: "The *main Shechinah* was among the lower worlds."[173]

---

[170] Cf. Yerushalmi; *Shekalim* 9:1; *Tanchuma Devarim* 5; *Yalkut* 951.
[171] Cf. Exod. 18:18.
[172] Cf., e.g., the new Jewish Publication Society translation: *The Torah*, Philadelphia 1962, p. 389: "And approached from Ribeboth-Kodesh*" and Footnote a) cf. *Meribath-Kadesh* 32:51" evidently taking *Meyriv'vot Kodesh* as a place-name.
[173] I.e., Israel, cf. *Bereshit Rabbah* 19:13.

Rashi adds "miktzat—a part" to stress that the letter *mem* of *mayriv'vot* is the "partitive letter *mem*" and is *not* similar to the letter *mem* in *miSinai, miSeyir, mayhar Paran* where it means: "From Sinai, from Seir, from Mount Paran." Here it means: part of.[174]

He adds the word *malachei*—"The angels," for without it the object to which the word "holy-kodesh" relates as an adjective is missing.[175]

3) Rashi mentions "the day of his wedding" here as a continuation of his explanation above: "He came from Sinai—He went out towards them ... as a bridegroom goes out to greet his bride, etc." Now, just as a groom goes out to greet his bride in the company of his friends—which add to his honor—so too did God, so to speak, go out to greet His bride—Israel—in the company of *part* of His friends, the holy angels.[176]

4) The difficulty in the first explanation is: a) It should have stated *Dat-eysh*—"A Law of fire," meaning: a law written in fire (black fire upon white fire). Whereas now the implication is that *eysh*—"fire" and *dat*—"law" are two things: From His right there was fire *and* a law for them. b) The word *lamo*—"to them" is difficult, since the Torah was *not* given to them (Israel) written "black fire upon white fire"—even if "long ago"—*meaz it was* so written before him!

According to the second explanation it should have stated: *mey-eysh Dat*—"from fire a Law," or *mitoch ha-eysh*—"From the midst of fire."[177] Besides according to the second explanation one cannot write in *one* word *eyshdat* since the fire is *separate* from the law. Now that it is written as one word, it implies that the "fire" is *part* of the "law"—the Torah itself.

As to the symbolism in: "Black fire written upon white fire," one may suggest that "white fire" symbolizes the perfect truth and purity as they are in God's domain—Whose seal is truth.[178] Whereas "black fire" symbolizes limited truth and purity, which human beings can achieve with their limited mental and spiritual capacities. In the Torah there is a mingling of *both* kinds of truth and purity. The Almighty demands of man *only* according to his strength.[179] The reason the Torah was written: "black fire upon white

---

[174]As above 26:1 *mayreishit* where Rashi notes: "but not all of the first fruits." Comp. also: Gen. 4:3, 30:14.

[175]Similar constructions are: Exod. 22:30 *ve-anshei Kodesh*—"Holy people"; Exod. 3:5—*admat kodesh*—"a holy earth."

[176]One may add that the best friends—*shushvinim*—are not only in honor of the groom (God), but also in honor of the bride—Israel.

[177]As stated above 4:12,33,36 *mitoch ha-eysh.*

[178]Cf. *Shabbat* 55a; *Sanhedrin* 64a.

[179]Cf. Exod. *Rabbah* 34:1; *Tanchuma, Tisa* 10; *Pesikta Rabbati* 16:8.

fire" and not the other way, is because it was given to human beings, and *they* can grasp only limited truth and purity (black fire) and live by them, not the absolute truth and purity (white fire) which is the domain of the Almighty.

33:4   Torah—"The Torah."

RASHI: The Torah *which* Moses commanded us is an inheritance to the Congregation of Jacob: we took hold of it and will not abandon it.

COMMENT: You may ask:

1) How does Rashi know that our verse contains only *one* point, and therefore he adds the word "which" to indicate that the phrase "The Torah Moses commanded us" is only an introduction to the words: "(is) an inheritance (to) the Congregation of Jacob"; perhaps it contains *two* statements: 1) Moses commanded us the Torah, 2) An inheritance (to the) Congregation of Jacob?

2) Why does Rashi add: "We took hold of it and will not abandon it"— what does that add to the understanding of the verse?

We many explain:

1) Rashi's difficulty was: Why does it not state "that God commanded us" as in verse 3 "*yisa midabrotecha*," which Rashi explains: "They bear upon them the yoke of Your Torah"? Therefore Rashi explains that "The Torah that Moses commanded us" is an introduction to the following that the Torah is an "inheritance" *morasha* for Israel, for "inheritance" is more applicable to people than the *receiving* of the Torah by Moses and transmitting it to us.

2) In verse 3 it says: "*af choveyv 'amim*," Rashi: "Even when you loved the nations of the world, etc. *Kol kedoshav b'yodecha*—"'All their righteous and pious cleaved to You and did not depart from You, etc.'" *Yisa midabrotecha*—"They gladly accept Your decrees and laws," and these are their words: The Torah which Moses commanded us, etc." In light of *this* interpretation, Rashi explains here: "We took hold of it and will not abandon it"—as he stated above: "they cleaved to You and did not depart from You."

We might stress that the expression: "We *took hold* of it—(*achaznuhah*) and will not abandon it" is especially appropriate to an inheritance, for

Hebrew *achaznuhah* is similar to *achuzah*—"a holding"—(estate) an inheritance. Just as a person is not willing to depart from his forefathers' estate at any price—as we find in the episode of the vineyard of Navot the Yizraeli (I Kings 21:3), so, too, the Torah is to us an "inheritance"—*morasha* and therefore "We took hold of it (as an estate from our forefathers—*achuzah*) and will not abandon it.

33:8   *T'riveyhu vego'*—"You challenged him, etc."

RASHI: As the Targum renders: "You tested him." Another explanation of *t'riveyhu 'al mei merivah*—"You came with a pretext against them." If Moses said: "Hear now, you rebels" (Numbers 20:10), what sin did Aaron and Miriam commit? (Why were they too not allowed to enter the Land of Israel?)[180]

COMMENT: We must understand:

1) Why is there a need for two explanations of "You challenged him, etc.?"

2) According to the second explanation that God came with a pretext against Aaron and Miriam for no fault of their own—God forbid! This is a difficult statement to make, as we have a rule: "The Holy One, blessed be He, does not come with a complaint (pretext) against His creatures"[181]—even against the gentile nations and certainly not against "Aaron, the holy one of the Lord" (Psalms 106:16: "They were jealous of Moses in the camp, and of Aaron, the holy one of the Lord")?

We may explain:

1) The difficulty with the explanation of Onkelos is that it was precisely at Mei Merivah where Moses and Aaron *failed*.[182] If so, how can one say: "and he was found to be *trustworthy*" as Onkelos renders? Besides, it would have been more appropriate to say: *tivchanayhu*—"You tested him, not: You challenged (contended) him"—*t'riveyhu*. The difficulty with the second explanation (You came with a pretext, etc.) is that this relates only to Aaron and Miriam, not to the *entire* tribe of Levi—whereas this verse speaks about the *entire* tribe of Levi; not about Aaron and Miriam?

---

[180] *Sifrei* 349.

[181] *Avodah Zarah* 3a.

[182] See above 32:51 and Numbers 27:14 and Rashi on both verses.

2) This can be explained by the statement of the Rabbis: "The Holy One, blessed be He, is particular with the righteous to the extent of a hair breadth."[183] Therefore, since Aaron and Miriam were present when Moses smote the rock, instead of speaking to it, and did not protest—it is considered as if they sinned—because with righteous people of their caliber God is particular even on a *lack* of action—hence the question: "What *did they do*"—nothing, when they should have protested appropriately!

33:18 *S'mach Zevulun betzeytecha—*
"Rejoice Zevulun in your excursions."

RASHI: Be successful when you go out to do business.

VeYissachar—"And Issachar."

RASHI: Be successful when you sit in your tents to study Torah—to sit (in the Sanhedrin) and intercalate the years,[184] and to fix the day of the New Moon,[185] as it is said: "And of the Children of Issachar, who have understanding of the times ... their heads were two hundred" (I Chronicles 12:33)—the heads of the Sanhedrin occupied themselves with this, and according to *their* fixing of the seasons and intercalation of years.

COMMENT: Why did Rashi have to add: "to sit and intercalate the years and to fix the day of the New Moon, etc."—is the studying of Torah by the tribe of Issachar not sufficient alone? In *this* very verse Rashi wrote: "Zevulun and Issachar made a partnership: Zevulun dwelt at sea-harbors and went out in ships to trade; he made profit and provided food for Issachar who sat (at home or in study halls) and occupied themselves with the Torah. Therefore he mentioned Zevulun before Issachar, because the Torah of Issachar was due to Zevulun"?

Answer: Just so; had the tribe of Issachar *only* "sat and occupied themselves with Torah," without excelling in special fields such as intercalation of years and fixing of the New Moon, which require profound wisdom—

---

[183]I.e., extremely particular, punishing them for the slightest transgression, cf. *Yevamot* 121b.

[184]I.e., to calculate and decide whether to make a leap-year by adding an extra month—Adar II—should the weather conditions of a particular year require such action.

[185]I.e., the beginning of each new month—Moon, by testimony of witnesses who first saw the New Moon.

their studying Torah alone would *not* have justified the partnership. Why not? Because the tribe of Zevulun *also* studied Torah, as Rashi points out in verse 19: "For they will be nourished by the bounty of the sea"—Issachar and Zevulun, "and *they* will have free time to occupy themselves with the Torah" (both Issachar *and* Zevulun).

Issachar's study of Torah did *not* free Zevulun from studying Torah *completely*; rather the *major* occupation of Issachar was studying the Torah. Consequently they became very wise, so much so, that they knew how to intercalate years and fix the order of the New Moons—which are profound wisdom and deep secrets.

34:1 *Meyarvot Moav el Har Nevo*—
"From the plains of Moav to Mount Nevo."

RASHI: There were several levels (lit. "steps" *ma'alot*), from the plain to the summit, but Moses covered them with one step.[186]

Et kol Ha-aretz—"The entire land."

RASHI: He showed him all the land of Israel in its prosperity and the oppressors who would in the future oppress it.[187]

COMMENT: Questions:

1) How is it implied in this verse that "there were several steps"?

2) Why did God show Moses "the oppressors who would in the future oppress Israel," thereby causing him pain right before he died?

Answers:

1) The deduction that there were several steps is from the superfluous words: "from the plains of Moav." It should have only stated: "Moses went up to Mount Nevo," since at the end of *Chukat* it says: "The Children of Israel journeyed and they encamped in the plains of Moav, on the bank of the Jordan, opposite Jericho" (Numbers 22:1). Also in *Mas'ei* at the *end* of all the journeys it says: "They journeyed from the mountains of the passes

---

[186]*Sotah* 13b: "There were twelve steps there, etc." See Maharsha who points out that the twelve steps allude to the twelve tribes.
[187]*Sifrei* 357; *Yalkut* 943.

and encamped in the plain of Moav by the Jordan, at Jericho" (Numbers 33:48). Hence we know that Moses went up from the plains of Moav to Mount Nevo.[188]

It is obvious then, that the Torah wished to emphasize that from the plains of Moav Moses went *straight* up to Mount Nevo. What is the novelty in this? Surely it is that although there were several levels (of mountains from the plains to the summit), yet Moses covered them in *one* step. Why do *we* need to know this? To teach us that Moses' strength did not wane even on the day of his death; his time of dying on account of old age and infirmity had *not* arrived yet. So why *did* he die then. Because that was the decree of the Almighty, and there is no "favoritism" before Him, as it states: "The rich is not given recognition (by God) over the pauper" (Job 34:19 *sho'a* = "the wealthy").[189] Similarly, "The great, mighty and awesome God, Who does not show favor and does not accept a bribe" (Deut. 10:17).

2) We venture to suggest that God showed Moses also the oppressors that would in the future oppress Israel in each generation, in order that Moses should pray for them, for: "The Holy One, blessed be He, desires the prayer of the righteous."[190] Perhaps by his prayers he would succeed in preventing the evil *before* it occurred. By the above explanation: "The entire land" means: God showed Moses the Land (of Israel) in all its situations, in each generation—both in its tranquility and prosperity *and* in its oppression. The vision was more of a spiritual than a physical nature.[191]

34:6 *Mul Bet-Peor*—"Opposite Beth-Peor."

RASHI: His grave was ready there ever since the six days of Creation, to atone for the incident with Peor.[192] This was one of the things that were created on Sabbath Eve "between the twilights" (in the week of Creation).[193]

---

[188]Comp. the statement about Aaron before his death: "Aaron the Priest went up to Mount Hor, etc." (Numbers 33:38) without saying from where he went up, because in the previous verse it is stated: "They encamped at Mount Hor."

[189]Comp. Rashi on Exod. 35:34 and our commentary thereto.

[190]*Yevamot* 64a.

[191]Cf. Ramban: "It could *not* be seen from the top of the mountains, but God showed it to him, by a miracle." See also: *Be'er Mayim Chaim; Lifshuto shel Rashi; Mizrachi; Maskil LeDavid; Mishmeret HaKodesh.*

[192]See Numbers, Chap. 25; *Sotah* 14a.

[193]*Avot* 5:6; *Pesachim* 54a; *Yalkut* 965; *Pirke de Rabbi Eliezer,* Chap. 45.

COMMENT: We must understand:

1) Why was it necessary that the grave be "ready since the six days of Creation," not any later?

2) Why does Rashi add: "And this was one of the things that were created on Sabbath Eve between the twilights"?
The explanation is:

1) The statement "His grave was ready ever since the six days of Creation" is in the category of: "The Holy One, blessed be He, prepares the healing (treatment) *before* the ailment (lit. blow) comes,"[194] just as the ram that was sacrificed instead of Isaac "was prepared for this purpose since the six days of Creation."[195] Since it was not stated anywhere who dug the grave and when, one must say that it was always there, i.e., since the six days of Creation.

2) Rashi adds: "This is one of the things that were created on Sabbath Eve between the twilights" for several reasons:
   a) If the grave was prepared "since the six days of creation," why is it not mentioned as one of the things created during the six days, at the beginning of the Book of Genesis?[196] Rashi answers: The grave was created on Sabbath Eve between the twilights—it is therefore in a special category of Creation, which is not described in the Torah explicitly, but was received by the Rabbis through oral tradition.

3) In order to magnify the miracle, like the other things that were created Friday evening "between the twilights"—all of which were miraculous events that Israel had a great need of at various times, and at times the entire world was in need of some of them.[197]
   Rabbi Menachem "Hameiri" writes: "the ten things enumerated here (*Avot* 5:6)—the very existence, success, and faith of the nation (Israel) depends on them. Were it not for them—this nation could not endure in its perfect faith—which was the purpose of Creation ... the meaning of "between the twilights" is that immediately upon the creation, they *had* to be accepted as a tradition and to be believed that it was so ... also the burial

[194]*Megillah* 13b.
[195]Rashi on Gen. 22:13. The ram was also one of the things that were created on the Sabbath Eve between the twilights (*Avot* 5:6).
[196]My brother R. Shmuel Spalter, may he live and be well, pointed this question out to me, for which my thanks to him.
[197]Such as the rainbow, and perhaps even the demons.

(place) of Moses, the location of his grave being unknown on account of great fear ... "[198]

Rabbi Joseph Ibn Aknin[199] holds: The difference between these ten things that were created "between the twilights" (at the very end of Creation) and other miracles, regarding which a condition was made *at the time of Creation* that they should occur at specific times is: *All* the other miracles were performed through an *agent* at *different* times, whereas these the Almighty Himself created them between the twilights. Why, indeed, between the twilights? Because of their great importance, because the one who *completes* (an act, etc.) is equal to all the rest, as the Rabbis said: "The one who rolls it (the Torah scroll) up, receives a reward that is equal to the reward of all of them" (*Megillah* 32a).

c) Almost all the things that were created on Sabbath eve between the twilights have the common denominator that of being in the category of "God created the remedy before the blow," if one delves into their nature.[200]

34:8   *B'nei Yisrael*—"The Children of Israel."

RASHI: (The word *b'nei*—"being masculine" means:) the males, but about Aaron, because he pursued peace, and made peace between one man and another, and between a woman and her husband, it says: "The whole house of Israel (wept for him)"—men and women.[201]

COMMENT: Why indeed, did Moses not follow Aaron's good example and "pursue peace and make peace between one and man and another, etc."?

This may be explained according to the statement in the Talmud: "In what was your father especially careful? He told him: With the mitzvah of *tzitzit* (fringes)."[202] This is explained in *Tanya* as follows: "This statement refers to extra special carefulness in the performance of *this* mitzvah, over and above the care and attention to the performance of all of the rest of the *mitzvot*. That is why he asked: 'With what was he *more* careful, the

---

[198]Namely, that people should not turn his grave into an idol and worship it [*Bamidbar Rabbah Parshat Balak*; *Sotah* 13a].

[199]*Sefer Musar*, p. 154.

[200]Cf. *Tosafot Yom Tov* to *Avot* 5:6 who writes: "Many opinions were stated about this matter (why "between the twilights" and why just ten things), you can find them in Midrash Shmuel. However, I did not quote any of them, because I do not know which one of them is correct."

[201]*Pirke de Rabbi Eliezer*, Chap. 17; Numbers 20:29.

[202]*Shabbat* 118b.

emphasis is on *more*."[203] This is also the meaning of a "pursuer of peace, etc.," namely: The matter of pursuing peace and making peace between one and another and between a woman and her husband was with Aaron a matter of "*extra special care and diligence, over and above the care and attention he devoted to the rest of the mitzvot.*"[204] This was not the case with Moses: His *special care* and attention was devoted to some other mitzvah.

The special care and attention of Aaron in making peace between people is expressed with great emphasis in *Pirke de R. Eliezer*, Chap. 17: "Moses was accorded loving-kindness only by the men, as it says: The *males* (*b'nei*) of Israel cried over Moses, but Aaron was accorded loving-kindness by both men and women, as stated: 'The *whole* House of Israel cried over Aaron for thirty days.' Why so? Because he was a lover of peace, and a pursuer of peace, and *would pass by in the camp of Israel every day* and make peace between a man and his wife, and one man and another. Therefore the *entire* Jewish People showed him loving-kindness."[205]

Tam venishlam b'rich rachmana desai'an.

FULLY COMPLETED; BLESSED BE THE MERCIFUL ONE, WHO AIDED US IN THE EFFORT.

---

[203] *Tanya*, Part IV—*Igeret HaKodesh*, Chap. 7, p.112.

[204] Cf. *Sefer Hasichot*, 1942, p. 21; *Sefer-Ha-maamarim* 1941, p. 240—both by the Lubavitcher Rebbe R. Joseph Isaac, o.b.m.—where it is explained that the expression: *zahir tefei* means: "which mitzvah illuminated for him" (*zahir* a form of *zohar*— "illumination") in the upper world, more than the other *mitzvot*. See an explanation of this matter in: *Lessons in the Book of Tanya* by R. Joseph Weinberg, Part IV, p. 1339.

[205] The supercommentary on Rashi, *Lifshuto shel Rashi* (Heb.) explains that the Midrash derived from the phrase *Bet Yisrael*—"The House of Israel" used with regard to Aaron which implies males and females (wept for Aaron), whereas in regard to Moses it says: *B'nei Yisrael*—"the males of Israel" (not females). This interpretation is unacceptable: true "the House of Israel" often includes the entire Jewish People- males and females, as in Exod. 40:38; Levit. 10:6; Joshua 21:43 and often; cf. Biblical Concordances, s.v. Bet Yisrael. Similarly the expression *B'nei Yisrael* includes very often both males and females—cf. Concordances, s.v. *B'nei Yisrael*. Hence, the major derivation here is from the word *Kol*—"entire," missing in regard to Moses, but mentioned in the case of Aaron. Therefore the Midrash emphasizes that *here* the word *B'nei* means "sons and not daughters—males but not females."

Subject Index

Aaron, 69, 72–73, 254
  and copper headplate, 90
  death of, 203
  death of sons, 92
  and death with a kiss, 202
  dust smitten by, 70
  and golden calf, 199–200
  and his sons not swerving, 115–
    116
  offspring of, 159
  river smitten by, 70
  unchanging, 171
  weeping at death of, 311–312
Abba, R., bar Kahana, 50
Abraham, 31–32, 40, 79–80, 151,
    153–154, 254
  hospitality of, 35
  inferior to Sarah in prophecy,
    39
  and Jebusites, 265
  moral control over organs, 32–
    33
  and name change, 50
  prayer for Avimelech, 38
Abram, 29, 31
Acha, R., 43
Adam, 75
  and Cain, 132
  created by hands of God, 76
  cursed for his sin, 6
  and daughter, 132
Adam and Eve, 200
  banished from Garden of Eden,
    16, 19
  garments made for, 16
  and the Serpent, 14
  Siamese twins, 13
Adulterers, 165–166
Age at which one becomes
    punishable, 19–20
Agnon, S. Y., 115, 171
Agricultural work, 143
Ahaziah, 203

Akedah, 40
Akiva, R., 71–72, 178–181, 206,
    269
Altar
  created to lengthen man's days,
    82
  overlaid with copper, 90
Amalek, 66, 152, 282–286
  denial of covenant between God
    and Israel, 283
Amon
  captivity of the Children of, 291
Amorites, 241
  guardian angel of the, 242–243
Amos, 153
Angel
  of death, 201
  of destruction, 72
  guardian, 242–243
Angels, 33, 98, 175, 215, 302–304
  created, 5–6
  of destruction, 99
  and free will, 20
  names of, 50
Animal sacrifice, 112
Animals
  blood of hunted, 125–126
Antiochus IV, 17
Anthropomorphism, 125
Asi, R., 128
Atonement, 114, 197–198
Avdimas, R., son of R. Joseph, 137
Avihu, 92
Avimelech, 80–81
Azariah, 136–137

Babel, Tower of, 28
Balak, son of Zipor, 207–208, 210–
    211
  cursing Israel by both names, 210
Barley as offering, 166
Beasts
  sinning of, 22

Bechayey, R., 113
Be'er Mayim Chaim, 83
Be'er Yitzchak, 207
Beer-Sheba, 50
Berditchev, Rabbi of, 115, 171
Bestial act, 166–167
Beth-Peor, 309
Bezalel, son of Uri, 32, 104
  and construction of Tabernacle, 101, 105
  and making of candelabrum, 89–90
Bilam, 207–211
  and the angel, 208–209
  blinded in one eye, 216
  and cursing Israelites, 219
  killed by the sword, 232
  a magician, 211
  a prophet, 231
Bilhah, 101
Bird offering, 112
Birds
  clean, 123
  sinning of, 22
  unclean, 123
Birkat Hanziv, 80
Bloodguilt, 279–280
Book of Good Life, 41
Bread
  of affliction, 270
  unleavened, 270
Bribes, 273–274, 308
Burnt offering, 113

Cain
  marked by God, 17
  marriage to sister, 36–37, 132
Calev, 185
Camels, 49
Canaan
  divided by lottery, 224–225
  land of, given to Jewish People, 141–142
  land of, taken by Israel, 3, 58

quality of, 185–186
spies sent to, 240
Candelabrum
  making of, 89
Chaim, Chafetz, 153–154
Chanania, 135–137, 295
Chance, 284–285
Chanina, R., 97, 261
Chanochite family, 223
Children
  reward for exposing to Torah, 295
Chiram, 254–255
Charity, 280–281
Circumcision, 32–33
Cloud, pillar of, 183, 282, 284
  and stragglers, 282–284
Clouds of Glory, 259–261
Coin of fire, 95
Commandments *See Also Mitzvot*
  613, 97, 245, 257
  and Divine imperative, 80
  do out of love for God, 263
  first one commanded to Israel, 3
  Five, 168–169
  to love one's neighbor as oneself, 38–39
  of Lulav, 245
  none omitted by Israelites, 72
  obeying, 257–258
  payment for manna, 176
  relating to sacrifices, 24
  social, 37
Commandments, Ten, 214, 248–250
  equality of, 81–82
  said by God in one utterance, 81
  tablets both equal, 97, 261–262
  written by finger of God, 261
Conception, 121–122
Conversion of non-Jew, 160, 210
Cooking kid in mother's milk, 269
Copper Snake, 204–206
Corpse
  touching of, 118–120, 197

Creation
  of animals and beasts, 9
  Hebrew language of, 277
  and miracles, 6
  purpose of, 4, 310
  of ram substitute for Isaac, 39
  of Sabbath, 11
  seventh day of, 11
  things prepared for predestined
    purpose during the six days
    of, 39–40, 309–311
Creatures
  allowed for food, 117
Crusades, 27
Curtain of Holiness, 114

Dan, tribe of, 101, 284
David, King, 61, 65, 255, 275
  afraid of day of judgment, 257–
    258
  and census of People, 221
David, Divrei, 177–178
Death with a kiss, 200–202
Demons, 297–298
Desert, generation of, 175–176
Devek Tov, 241
Devils
  sacrifice to, 297–298
Disbelief
  three types of, 284–286
Disciples called children, 252–253
Dispersion
  generation of, 28
  result of sin, 142
Dissension, 195
Divination, 213–215
Divine Name
  pronunciation of, 65
Dosa, R., ben Horkinas, 295

Earth
  containing chemical
    preservatives, 53
  cursed for its sin, 6

  produce of, 15–16
Eating
  prohibitions, 265
Eclipses, 7
Edom, Land of, 203
Egyptians
  arrogance of, 52
  compared with serpents, 75
  evil by nature, 75
Elazar the priest, 199, 224–225
Elazar, R., 5, 27, 50, 201, 261, 299
Eliezer, R., 43, 152–153, 293
Elijah, 25, 151–152
Encampment of Israelites, 161–
    162, 217–218, 220
Enchantment, 213–215
Epic of Gilgamesh, 17
Epiphanes, 17
Er, 19
Esau, 55–56, 65, 199, 203, 209
Eternal life, 16
Eternal matter, 6, 14
Eternal spirit, 6
Ethics of the Fathers, 181–182
Eve, 75
Evil eye, 57
Evil inclination, 21, 153
Evolution, 9
Exile
  after 852 years, 246–247
  time of, 242
  and worshipping idols, 288–289
Exodus from Egypt, 141–142, 190,
    247
  purpose of, 192–193
Ezekiel, 206

Festival of matzot, 184
Festivals
  calculated by new moon, 7
  and phylacteries, 73
  Pilgrimage, 118, 209
Fig tree, 14
First fruits, 287

Flood, the, 167
  generation of, 28, 131
  people who perished in, 19–20
  period of, 24
  prelude to, 18–19
Fountains of the deep, 24–25
Free will, 21, 51, 60, 247, 265,
    274, 288–289
  and angels, 20
  granted only to mankind, 7
Future period See World-to-Come

Gabriel, 59
Gad, 232–233
Galbanum, 95–96
Gamliel, R., 79, 129, 178–181
Gaon of Vilna, 150, 153
Garden of Eden
  Adam and Eve banished from,
    16, 19
Garments, 190–193
Gershon, 161
Gideon, 57–58
God
  attribute of judgment, 21, 294
  attribute of mercy, 21
  determiner of fate of Jewish
    People, 32
  and dominion, 148
  everything belongs to, 196
  face of, 266
  keeper of promises, 18, 258
  knowledge unlike human's, 60
  learn out of love for, 262–263
  love for Israel's virtues, 214,
    254–255
  merciful in judgment, 149
  no fear of, 37, 81
  and punishment for sin, 18
  redeemed Israel from house of
    slavery, 266–267
  and redemption, 291–292

regarding rich and poor
  equally, 101
remembering covenant with
  Jacob, 151
unity of, 251
walking with, 147–148
world belongs to, 164
Golden Calf, 60, 98–99, 103, 172,
  197–199, 219
  and Red cow, 197, 199–201
  and three types of wood, 198
Great Assembly
  Men of the, 27
Gur Aryeh, 177

Haglili, R. Yossie, 71
Hameiri, R. Menachem, 310
Harlot, 165–166
Harvest
  reaping of, 137
Heaven
  gate to, 47
  Jerusalem in, 47
  sacrifices in, 47
  temple in, 47
  voice from, 287–288
Heavenly court, 119–120
Hebrew language, 276–277
Hebrew slave, 86
  wife and children of, 86–87
  with bored ear, 87
Hezekiah, King of Judah, 27, 252–
  253
High Priest
  ox of, 113–114
Hittites, 265
Holy things, 163–164
Horites, 185
Hospitality, 35

Ibn Aknin, R. Joseph, 311
Ibn Ezra, 293

Idolatry, 23, 190, 192
Idol, 18
   worship of, 28, 247, 268, 297
   worshippers, 71–72, 284
Incest, 36–37
Iron, 82–83
Isaac, 40, 43, 65, 151, 153, 209
   ashes of, 152, 154
   and Egypt, 45
Isaac, R., 3, 60
Isaiah, 20, 55
Ishmael, 19, 209
Ishmael, R., 181
Israel, 38–39
Israel, Land of, 45, 55, 308–309
   Aaron and Miriam not allowed
      to enter, 306–307
   Moses not allowed to enter,
      306–307
   property acquired in, 55–56
Israel (nation)
   Children of, 311
   purpose of, 4
Israelites See Jewish People
Issachar, 36, 161, 307–308

Jacob, 38–39, 56, 58, 62, 65, 198–
      199, 209
   death of, 60–61
   dust of, 212
   and humility, 153
   name changed to Israel, 211
   sun setting before its time for
      his sake, 50
Japheth, 19
Jebusites, 265
Jerusalem
   destruction of, 177–178
   pilgrimage to, 210
Jewish
   calendar, 8–9
   festivals, 8

people, 5
people preconceived by God at
   time of creation, 12
Jewish People, 99, 168
   acceptance of the Torah, 305–306
   always alive, 61
   beloved by God, 172
   in the desert, 179, 187–188
   of equal value with the Temple,
      103–104
   and golden calf, 197–199
   and land of Canaan, 129
   enslavement of, 143–144
   held morally responsible for
      one another, 149–150, 188
   more numerous than all
      nations, 255
   Moses and Aaron instructed to
      deal gently with, 69
   Moses intercession between
      people and God, 215
   pronouncing name of God in
      prayers, 65
   pursued by Egyptians, 75–76
   redemption of, 152
   sinners among, 95–96
   task of proclaiming God's
      name, 32, 103, 209
   traits of, 129
   trials in desert, 186–187
   and tribal descent, 223–224
   world created for, 130
   worship one God, 104
Joseph, 52
   and cupbearer, 52
   and natural preservatives, 53
Joseph, R., 128
Joshua, 58, 185
Joshua, R., 152–153, 293
Joshua, R., son of Korcha, 265–266
Joshua, R., ben Levi, 27
Joshua, R., ben Perachya, 127

Jubilee, year of, 86
Judah, Tribe of, 51
    camp of, 161
Judah, R., 19, 30, 250, 283
Judges of Israel, 220–221
Judging, 127–128, 273–274

Kabbalah
    secrets of, 227
Kabbalistic explanation, 113
Kehat, 161
Keturah, 209
Killing
    accidental, 26
    father and offspring on same
        day, 135
    mother and offspring on same
        day, 135
    with premeditation, 26
Kindness
    demonstrated toward Israel, 149
Kingdom of heaven
    yoke of, 266
Kluger, Shlomo, 230
Korban Aharon, 144, 150
Kosher food, 104

Landed property, 140–141
Lands of the Nations, 45
Languages
    seventy of the ancient world, 239
Law of fire, 303–305
Laws
    of Alfasi, 85
    concerning Festivals, 137–138
    of menstruation, 44
    oral, 97
    of sacrifices and Festivals, 10
    of Shimittah, 139–140
    study of, 245–246
Leah, 29
LeDavid, Maskil, 90, 113, 144, 223
Lemech
    and Cain, 18

wives of, 18
Leprosy, plagues of, 123
Levi, Tribe of, 175–176, 306
    named by God, 59
    not counted among the tribes, 59
    and the twenty-four gifts, 60
Levites, 161–162, 168
    assigned to Aaron and his sons,
        172
    gifts due to, 163–164
Light
    goodness of, 5
Lot
    daughters of, 36
Luzatto, S. D., 144

Machpelah, Cave of, 55–56, 265
Maharal, 24, 302
Maharal of Prague, 89
Maharshal, 17, 175
Maimonides, 71, 98–99, 119, 127–
    128
    Principles of Faith, 93
"Make for yourself," 206
Mankind
    bestowed with Divine
        Providence, 76
    centrality of, 22
    created on earth as opposed to
        in heaven, 20
    created for sake of Jewish
        people, 13
    and status regarding animals, 9–
        10, 17–18
    and status regarding plants, 12,
        14
Manna, 11, 176, 186–187
    Israelites ungrateful for, 204
    Serpent speaking evil of, 206
Mara, 187, 249
    sections of the Torah given at,
        189, 250
Martyrdom, 136
Masorites, 160

Meal-offerings, 91, 112, 229
Meat-eating, 126
Mechilta, 79–80, 82, 144
Meir, R., 206
Menorah, 89–90 *See Also*
    Candelabrum
Mental hardship, 143
Merari, 161
Meriva, sin at, 178
Messiah, 58, 93, 120
    ingathering of the exiles, 61,
        291, 294
Messianic times, 20, 145, 153, 241
Micah, 55
Michael, 47
    guardian angel of Jewish
        People, 50, 243
Midian, kings of, 232
Miracles, 6, 43, 52, 58, 81, 106–
        107, 249, 260, 310
    of copper snake, 205
Miriam, 182–184
    death of, 200–202
    leprosy of, 183
Mishael, 136–137
Mitzvot
    of fringes, 192, 311
    of *Pe'ah*, 280–281
    no reward for in this world, 258
    of sanctification of God's name,
        136–137
Mizrachi, 89, 119
Moav
    captivity of, 291, 294
    daughters of, 224
    king of, 207
    Plains of, 139–140, 250, 308–309
Molech, 128
Money lending
    and interest, 141–142
    to Jew, 141
Monotheism, 154
Moon, 8
    goat of the New, 226–227

importance to Jewish people, 9
New, 307–308
sacrifice on the New, 228–229
worship of, 298
Morning offering, 225–226
Moses, 69, 72–73, 116, 200, 254–
        255
    admonishing Children of Israel,
        232–233, 241
    and appeasing the Children of
        Israel, 178–182
    and Bezalel, 104–105
    blessing Israel, 301–302
    complaint to God, 66–67
    and copper snake, 205–206
    death, 201, 309
    and erecting the Tabernacle,
        105–107
    grave ready since six days of
        Creation, 309–311
    grave site, 310–311
    and intimate conversation of
        God, 111
    and killing an Egyptian, 66
    and land of Canaan, 185
    and land of Israel, 106
    and making of candelabrum, 89
    and miracles in Egypt, 89
    and pronunciation of divine
        name, 65
    serving Aaron and Elders of
        Israel, 79
    speaking to God, 112, 179–180,
        215
    speaking to Israel, 140, 179–
        180, 215
    as teacher to Aaron's offspring,
        159–160
    as teacher of Torah, 159–160
    treading on guardian angel of
        the Amorites, 242
    weeping at death of, 311–312
Moshe the Preacher, R., 168, 190–
        192, 197–198, 228

Musaf
  goats, 226
  sacrifices, 228–229

Nachman, R., 60
Nadav, 92
Nakedness, 82
Names
  changing of, 31
  not fixed, 49–50
Nazirite, 167–168
Nebuchadnezzer, 254–255
Nehemiah, R., 180
Neighbor, importance of good,
  162
Nimrod, 255
Noah, 198
  origin of, 19
  period of the sons of, 10
  and the Raven, 25
  and study of the Torah, 23–24

Oholiav, 101
Oil
  beaten, 91
  ground, 92
Old age, 154–155
Onan, 19

Padan-Aram, 55
Passover, 73, 118, 184, 192–193,
  209, 267, 270–271, 288
  connected with forefathers,
  228–229
  during 40 years in desert, 173,
  259
  second, 174
Patriarchs, symbols of, 208–209
Peace
  importance of, 23, 28
Peace offerings, 112–113, 168
  as go-between other offerings
  and the Attributes, 113

number and type of animals for,
  168
Pederasty, 282, 285
Persecution
  by gentiles, 27–28
Pharaoh, 69–70, 255
Plague, number who died in, 220–
  221
Poor
  giving gifts to, 137–138
Prayer, 47
  essence of, 12
  instead of sacrifices, 93
  of Jewish People, 48
  for mercy on behalf of another,
  38–39
Pride, 198
Priests, 168
  gifts due to, 163–164
  spoke in Hebrew, 276
Property
  regarded more than children, 232
Prophecy, 39
  and women, 39
Prophets, 168, 215
  sons of the, 253
Proselyte
  property stolen from, 196
Punishment, 280
  domain of the court, 129
  measure-for-measure, 216
Purim
  Sabbath before, 66

Rachel, 29
Radak, 293
Ram of the Akedah, 39–40, 154,
  310
Ramban, 119
Ran, 33
Ransom, 181
Rashi, 81, 117, 129, 160–161, 173–
  174, 195, 215–216, 220, 225,

248, 253–254, 258, 266, 268–
  269, 275–276, 291–293, 305
Alkabats version of, 175–176,
  249
and *Chullin* 60a, 9
and citing midrashim, 83, 85–
  86, 96–97, 101
and creation of angels, 5–6
defending honor of Israelites, 233
differing from Onkelos, 125, 257
and ethics, 281–282
first printing of, 289
generation of, 27
homiletical interpretation, 3–5,
  69
and judges, 274–275
love for Jewish People, 168, 278
and name on Cain's forehead, 17
opting for Midrash over plain
  sense interpretation, 92
philosophy of, 8, 10, 12, 14–15
plain sense interpretations, 4–5,
  31, 49, 71–72, 136, 180, 255,
  276, 284, 287–289, 298
questioning juxtaposition of
  texts, 200–201
regarding selling out of poverty,
  141
relating laws to Scripture, 77
sources, 210, 231
as teacher of the People, 85,
  92–93, 97, 105, 119, 131, 135,
  139, 159, 269
and teaching about the eating
  of impure animals, 118
and teaching about judging
  colleagues, 127–128
and teaching moral lesson, 112
and teaching regarding corpses,
  118–119, 197
Zamora version of, 175–176,
  249
Rav, 47, 98

Rav Gidal, 47
Rava, 274
Rebecca, 43
Red Sea, 186–187, 191–192
Redemption, 293–294
Refidim, 187, 283
Refuge, Cities of, 26, 248
Resh Lakish, 160, 227
Reuven, 232–233
Rif (Alfasi), 228
Righteous
  birth of, 216–217
  death of atones for sin, 200–202
  deeds of examined in heaven,
    280
  as instruments of God, 33
  prayers of desired by God, 217,
    309
  as protection for their
    generations, 27, 203
  son, 61
Robbery, 23, 28
Rosh Hashanah, 40

Sabbath, 248–250, 268
  desecration of, 189–190, 192
  in the desert, 187–189
  limits for travel on, 76–77
  and phylacteries, 73
Sabbatical year, 139, 268
Sacrifices, 113, 116, 202
  daily, 226
Samuel
  and humility, 153
Samuel bar Nachman, R., 5
Sanhedrin, 161, 174–175, 220
Sanhedrin, heads of, 307
Sara, 29
Sarah, 31–32
  and name change, 50
  taken note of by God, 38
  three blessings of, 44
Satan, 40–41

Satyrs, 297–298
Scholar, 97
School of Hillel, 153
School of Rabbi Ishmael, 279
School of Shamai, 153
Sefer Hazikaron, 189
Serpent, the, 14, 206
   evil by nature, 75
   instigator of Adam and Eve's
      sin, 15
Sexual
   immorality, 23
   prohibitions, 128
Sfat Emet, 171
Shavuot, 118, 209
Shechinah, 35, 44, 58, 61, 98–99,
      133, 291–294
   and dwelling with angels, 303
   presence on earth, 106
   residing in Israel based on
      number of Israelites, 174–176
   residing in the Tabernacle, 103
   residing in Temple, 76, 92, 104
   ten ascensions, 178
   ten descents, 177–178
Shema
   reading the, 277–278
Shimon
   and sale of Joseph, 59
Shimon, R., 75, 178, 180
Shimon, R., ben Azai, 50
Shimon, R., ben Yochai, 27, 98, 278
Shimon, R., ben Zoma, 50
Shir Hashirim, 206
Shofar, 40
Sichon, 242–243
Sign
   blood on the lintel, 73
   eating Paschal lamb, 73
   phylacteries, 73
   of the rainbow, 26–27
Simai, R., 98
Simlai, R., 122, 248

Sin offering, 113, 198, 201, 226–
      227
   communal sacrifice, 198
Sinai, Mount, 79–81, 96–97, 139,
      250, 266
   all of law given at, 139–140
Sinning
   accidentally, 114, 168
   of animals, 130–132
   in monetary matters, 30
   inadvertently by community, 114
   inadvertently by individual, 167
   intentionally, 92, 96
   man causing another's, 131
   with one's body, 30
   of trees, 130–131
Snake, bite of, 204
Sodom, King of, 31
Solomon, King, 202
   prayer, 47
Spirit of folly, 165–166
Stars
   creation of, 8
   importance to Jewish people, 9
Stoning, 285
Sukkot, 118, 209
   and libations for the bulls, 229
   and number of bullocks, 229–
      230
   and number of sheep, 229
Sun, 8–9
   worship, 225–226, 298

Tabernacle, 103
   constructing of, 101
   erecting of, 92, 105–106
Tamar, 51
Tanchuma, R., 105, 117–118
Tanya, 175
Targum Jonathan, 17
Targum Onkelos, 21, 30, 88, 125,
      143, 212–216, 218, 247, 257,
      269, 288–289, 297, 303, 306

Taxes, 288
Teacher called father, 252–253
Tephillin, 245
Temple
  beloved by God, 76
  built by Solomon, 247
  destroyed, 217–218, 226
  destruction of atones for sin, 219
  earthly, 47
  heavenly, 47
  model of, 298
  offering sacrifices in, 137
  spiritual height of, 275–276
  third, 93, 104
  time of the, 229–230
Ten descents, 177
Tent of Meeting, 218–219
Throne of Glory, 4, 80–81
Tiberias, hot springs of, 24–25
Tithes, 164, 287–288
Torah, 168
  and account of Adam and Eve, 16–17
  and account of creation, 3
  attention to, 298–299
  as book of laws and ethical instructions, 4
  as a chore, 285
  considerate of diginity of creatures, 49
  and enumerating daughters, 235
  equal to instruction for life, 122
  equal to law, 122
  five books of the, 168–169
  given as a gift, 96–97
  given in Hebrew, 277
  giving of, 214–215, 303–304
  and gratefulness, 70
  an inheritance, 305–306
  Israel's fate dependent upon keeping, 7

  laboring in, 146, 176–177
  and negative commands, 83
  no chronological order in, 172–173
  perform all the words of, 299
  plaything of the Almighty, 172
  preconceived by God at time of creation, 12
  purpose of, 4
  rewards for laboring in, 146–147
  scholar, 107
  and social commands, 37
  studied by Noah, 23–24
  success in study enjoined, 307
  teacher of, 159
  and teaching conduct of brothers and sisters to each other, 235–236
  and teaching proper conduct, 126
  two kinds of secrets of the, 99
  written on stones in seventy languages, 239–240
Torah Temimah, 61
Tosafot, 61, 71, 99
Tree of Knowledge, 13–15, 75
Tree of Life, 16, 19
Trees
  non-fruit-bearing, 145
  tasting the same as their fruit, 7
Tzitzit, 191–192, 245, 311

Utnapishtim, 17

Vegetarianism, 10

Weights, 281–282
Wife
  choosing of, 43
Wine
  Torah ordained blessing on, 65–66

Women
  equality with men, 13
  three precepts to perform, 44
World
  created for sake of Israel, 8, 10,
    12
  future *See* World-to-Come
  seventy nations of the, 229–230
World-to-Come, 5, 19–20, 76, 98–
    99, 117, 119–120
Writings, 168

Yehoshafat, King, 203

Yochanan, R., 128, 219–220, 278,
    299
Yoke of Heaven, 199
Yom Kippur, 65
Yosef Hallel, 175
Yosi ben Yochanan, 45
Yosi ben Yoezer, 45
Yossi, R., 206

Zevulun, 103–104, 161, 210, 307–
    308
Zhitomir, Rabbi of, 115, 171
Zion, 55

Index of Biblical Verses

GENESIS
1:1, 3–4, 8, 11–12, 129
1:2, 4
1:4, 5
1:5, 5
1:6, 6
1:11, 6
1:12, 6
1:14, 7–8
1:15, 8
1:16, 8–9
1:21, 22
1:22, 167
1:24, 22
1:25, 9
1:26, 9, 17
1:27, 76
1:28, 285
1:29–30, 10
1:31, 10
2:2, 11
2:3, 11, 277
2:5, 12
2:7, 12
2:11, 5
2:18, 13
2:21, 13
3:4, 5
3:5, 13, 75
3:7, 14
3:8, 71, 147
3:14, 15
3:15, 75
3:17, 7
3:18, 15
3:21, 16
3:22, 16, 19
4:14, 17
4:15, 17
4:18, 18
4:19, 18
4:23, 18
4:24, 18

4:26, 18
5, 5, 18–19
5:32, 19
6:2, 192
6:6, 20–21
6:7, 22
6:12, 167
6:13, 23
6:14, 206
7:2, 23
7:12, 25
7:23, 167
8:2, 24
8:7, 25
8:21, 20
9:2, 17
9:3, 10
9:5, 26, 114
9:12, 26
10:1, 19
11:9, 28
12:5, 160
12:8, 29
13:13, 30
13:16, 212
14:23, 30
15:5, 31, 50
17:1, 32
17:5, 31
17:22, 33
18:2, 33
18:3, 35
18:7, 228
18:25, 72
18:27, 254
19:31, 36
19:33, 36
20:11, 37, 81
21:1, 38
21:12, 39
21:13, 39
22:13, 40, 228
23:6, 79

24:10, 43
24:42, 43
24:52, 43
24:67, 44
25:23, 255
26:2, 45
27:22, 65
27:40, 231
28:11, 50
28:13, 33
28:17, 47
29:34, 59
30:40, 228
31:33, 29
32:11, 153
32:16, 49
32:30, 49
32:32, 50
33:3, 208
35:13, 33
36:20, 185
37:19, 59
38:6–10, 19
38:26, 51
39:9, 30
40:14, 52
40:23, 52
41:48, 53
42:24, 59
45:9, 55
46:6, 55
48:16, 57
48:19, 57
49:1, 58
49:7, 59
49:33, 60
50:5, 55

EXODUS
2:4, 182
2:12, 70
3:2, 292
3:12, 142

3:15, 65
3:18–24, 96
5:18, 176
5:22, 66
5:23, 66
6:9, 69
6:13, 69
7:19, 70
8:12, 70
8:14, 18, 22, 27, 116
9:6, 75
9:20, 75
10:26, 75
12, 3
12:1, 3, 184
12:16, 71
12:22, 72
12:27, 184
12:28, 72
12:33, 270
12:39, 184
14:5, 191
14:7, 75
15:1, 248
15:17, 76
15:18, 76
15:23–25, 187, 189
15:25, 249
16:4, 176
16:7, 254
16:29, 76
17:1–7, 187
17:7, 283
17:8, 283
18:12, 79
19, 189
19:3, 111
19:4, 191
19:5, 214
19:8, 112
19:12, 266
19:19, 276
19:20, 79

19:23, 266
20, 248
20:1, 81
20:8, 65
20:16, 215
20:17, 186
20:19, 79–80
20:22–23, 82
20:24, 12–13
21:2, 86
21:3, 86
21:5, 87
21:6, 87
21:13, 26
21:30, 181
22:2, 86
23:19, 269
24:10, 88
24:11, 88
25:2, 268
25:8, 268
25:31, 89
27:2, 90
27:7, 98
27:20, 91
28:38, 90
28:42, 82
29:24, 33, 116
29:40, 91
29:43, 92
30:13, 95
30:34, 95
31:2, 32, 50
31:14, 189
31:18, 96, 169
33:4, 98
33:6, 98
33:20, 266
34:6, 152
34:18, 184
34:26, 269
35:30, 32, 50
35:34, 101

37:17–24, 89
38:21, 103
38:22, 104
38:80, 206
39:33, 105
40:17, 105

LEVITICUS
1:1, 111
1:4, 202
1:13, 112–113
1:17, 112
2:2, 9, 112
3:1, 112
3:2, 202
4:4, 202
4:6, 113
4:7, 113
5:23, 196
8:13, 202
8:36, 115
10:30, 92
11:2, 117
11:8, 118
11:43, 119
12:2, 121
14, 121
14:4, 123, 125, 127
17:13, 125
18:1, 128
18:5, 129
18:15, 137
19:7, 240–241
19:9, 137
19:18, 38
19:19, 212
20:2, 128
20:3, 5, 125
20:15, 130
20:17, 36, 132
21:1, 118
21:12, 45
22:2, 140

22:3, 140
22:5, 140
22:28, 135, 139
22:32, 136
23, 8
23:5, 184
23:6, 184
23:8, 229
23:22, 137
24:21, 71
25:2, 268
25:10, 87
25:25, 140
25:26, 178
25:36, 141
25:38, 141–142
25:39–40, 86
25:40, 143
25:41, 86–87
25:43, 143
25:55, 143
26:4, 145
26:9, 145
26:12, 147
26:17, 125
26:32, 149
26:37, 149
26:42, 151
27:3, 154
27:4, 154
27:7, 154

NUMBERS
1:1, 172
3:1, 159
3:23, 161
3:35, 161
3:38, 161
5:8, 196
5:10, 163
5:12, 165
5:15, 166
5:17, 212

5:22, 165
6:2, 167
6:5, 8, 167
6:9, 167
6:24, 11
7:23, 168
8:3, 171
8:17, 172
8:18, 172
8:19, 154, 172
9:1, 172
9:5, 174
9:7, 174
9:17, 183
10:2, 206
10:36, 174
11:15, 176
11:17, 177
11:21, 178
11:22–24, 178–179, 181
12:2, 202
12:8, 111
12:15, 182
12:16, 183
13:18, 185
14:7, 185
14:22, 186
15:22, 192
15:32, 187
15:40, 192
15:41, 190, 192
16, 40
16:27, 195
18:9, 196
19:2, 198
19:3, 199
19:9, 212
19:22, 197
20:1, 200
20:6–7, 202
20:10, 306
20:23, 203
21:6, 205

21:8, 204
21:9, 205
22:1, 308
22:9, 207
22:10, 207
22:13, 18, 208
22:16, 207
22:22, 209
22:23, 209, 231
22:25, 209
22:26, 208–209
22:28, 209
22:28–30, 40
22:39, 207
23:5–6, 211
23:7, 210
23:9, 212
23:10, 212, 216
23:19, 215
23:20, 214–215
23:21, 214
23:23, 213
24:1, 219
24:2, 217–218
24:3, 216
24:4, 216, 219
24:5, 217
24:6, 219
24:7, 219
24:8, 219
25:5, 220
25:9, 220
26:5, 223
26:44, 223
26:54, 224
26:56, 224–225
28:3, 225
28:4, 225
28:11, 228
28:15, 226
28:19, 228
29:18, 229
29:19, 229

31:7, 232
31:8, 231–232, 235
32:1, 232
32:16, 232
32:17, 232
32:24, 232
33:3, 193
33:48, 309
35:10, 248

DEUTERONOMY
1:5, 239
1:10, 255
1:27, 240
1:28, 240
1:44, 241
2:5, 241
2:16–17, 111
2:31, 242
4:2, 245
4:6, 245
4:24, 285
4:25, 246
4:26, 246
4:27, 247
4:28, 247
4:35, 251
4:41, 248
5:4, 111
5:12, 248
5:27–28, 44
6:4, 251
6:4–9, 266, 278
6:7, 252
6:17, 241
7:7, 253
7:8, 255
7:11, 258
7:12, 257
7:18, 241
8:4, 259
9:10, 261
10:17, 309

11:13, 262
11:13–21, 266
11:22, 285
12:2, 130
12:11, 265
12:17, 265
12:28, 246
13:6, 266
13:17, 268
14:1, 252
14:5, 191
14:21, 269
14:29, 52
15:9, 30
16:1–2, 184
16:3, 270
16:5–6, 184
16:16, 184
16:19, 273
17:8, 275
17:18–20, 51
18:1–8, 163
20:2, 276
20:3, 277
22:8, 279
22:10, 212
24:16, 150
24:19, 280
24:20–21, 281
25:13–15, 281
25:14–15, 281
25:17–19, 66
25:18, 282
25:19, 286
26:12–15, 288
26:16, 287
27:8, 239
28:15, 229
28:64, 288
29:4, 260
30:2, 292
30:3, 291
30:19, 263

30:20, 262
31:12, 295
32:16, 298
32:17, 297
32:20, 206
32:40, 50
32:46, 298
33:1, 301
33:2, 302
33:3, 305
33:4, 305
33:8, 306
33:18, 307
33:19, 103, 210, 308
34:1, 308
34:5, 201
34:6, 309
34:8, 311
38:47, 59

JOSHUA
5:2, 206
10, 58, 81
15:63, 265

JUDGES
5:14, 161
20:16, 114

I SAMUEL
24:16, 253

II SAMUEL
5:6, 265

I KINGS
1:46, 202
6:1, 247
8:27, 268
8:29–30, 47
8:46, 72
8:66, 218
17:6, 25

19:10, 14, 152
21:3, 306

II KINGS
2:3, 252
2:12, 252

ISAIAH
2:2–3, 55
5:1, 275
6:3, 35
13:21, 297
14:14, 254
22:13, 58
24:21, 243
27:12, 291
30:20, 213
36:20, 254
43:21, 4, 32, 103, 193, 210
45:18, 36, 285
48:4, 90
48:13, 76
53:4–5, 203
60:21, 5
62:10, 186
64:1–2, 80
65:20, 19–20
66:12, 220

JEREMIAH
2:2, 184
2:3, 4
10:2, 7
30:10, 61
48:47, 291
50:17, 229

EZEKIEL
1, 33
1:7, 206
8:12, 284
9:9, 284
20:33, 190

28:2, 254
40:4, 298

HOSEA
4:16, 199

ZACHARIAH
MICAH
4:1–2, 55
6:8, 35
7:20, 152

ZEPHANIAH
3:9, 251

ZECHARIAH
14:4, 241
14:9, 251

MALACHI
3:20, 50

PSALMS
2:4, 205
20:8, 65
22:2–3, 255
22:7, 255
24:1, 196
40:5, 52
45:14, 29, 227
49:6, 258
51:19, 96
60:9, 161
68:18, 175
78:20, 179
79:12, 283
89:3, 36
91:15, 292
104:20, 72
106:16, 171, 306
111:16, 3
122:4, 223
127:3–5, 185

132:3, 218
135:13, 65
147:4, 32, 50
147:19, 38

PROVERBS
4:15, 165
6:32, 165
7:25, 165
8:22, 4
9:16–17, 165
12:21, 26
14:28, 210, 255
17:26, 280
19:17, 138
25:21–22, 241
26:27, 128

ESTHER
1:8, 255

JOB
34:19, 101, 309
36:33, 299

ECCLESIASTES
12:13, 50

DANIEL
3:17–18, 136
9:14, 246
10:13, 20–21, 243

NEHEMIAH
10:30, 27

I CHRONICLES
9:23, 218
12:33, 161, 307

II CHRONICLES
2:3, 47

20:37, 203
29:11, 252

Index of Other Passages Cited
Berachot
6a, 175

Betzah
21b, 71

Chagigah
12a, 5

Chullin
84a, 126
90b, 240

Kohelet
4:8, 56
7:2, 202
7:20, 72, 202
12:11, 168

Megillah
32a, 311

Menachot
10a, 47

Moed Katan
28a, 201

Nedarim
32b, 33

Nidah
31a, 122

Orach Chaim
512:3, 71

Pirke de Rabbi Eliezer
38, 56

Sanhedrin
38a, 121
58b, 132
94b, 27
99b, 160
108a, 22
109a, 30

Shabbat
32a, 279
88a, 98–99
127a–b, 128

Shevuot
2b, 114

Sifra
4:4, 129
7:5, 150
8:7, 153
9:4, 144

Sotah
15b, 166
42a, 278

Taanit
5b, 61

Yevamot
29b, 119

Yoma
39a, 119

Zevachim
41b, 114

GEN. RABBAH
34:9, 27
35:12, 27

LEVIT. RABBAH
13:2, 117

About the Author

Rabbi Pinchas Doron was born in Lancut, Poland in 1933. He lived in Israel from 1952–1964 where he was a member of Kibbutz Lavee. Rabbi Doron studied at Teachers' Institute and Hebrew University, where he received his B.A. and M.A. He received his Ph.D. in Hebraic Studies from New York University. He is the author of many titles, including *The War of Truth, Interpretation of Difficult Passages in Rashi, Vols I–IV* (Hebrew), and *The Mystery of Creation*. Rabbi Doron currently lives in Brooklyn.